Ethics

AND THE PRACTICE OF ARCHITECTURE

Ethics

AND THE PRACTICE OF ARCHITECTURE

BARRY WASSERMAN

PATRICK SULLIVAN

GREGORY PALERMO

JOHN WILEY & SONS, INC.

New York • Chichester • Weinheim • Brisbane • Singapore • Toronto

All photographs in this book provided by the authors unless otherwise indicated.

The NCARB *Rules of Conduct* are reprinted with the permission of the National Council of Architectural Registration Boards. Copies of the document are available directly from NCARB.

The AIA *Code of Ethics and Conduct* and *Advisory Opinions* are reproduced with the permission of the American Institute of Architects, 1735 New York Avenue, NW, Washington, D.C. 20006.

This book is printed on acid-free paper. ∞

Library of Congress Cataloging-in-Publication Data:

Wasserman, Barry L.
  Ethics and the practice of architecture / Barry Wasserman, Patrick Sullivan, and Gregory Palermo.
    p. cm.
  Includes index.
  ISBN 0-471-29822-0 (pbk)
    1. Architects—Professional ethics. 2. Architecture—Moral and ethical aspects. I.
Sullivan, Patrick. II. Palermo, Gregory. III. Title.

  NA1995.W38 2000
  174'.972—dc21

                      99-053578

Printed in the United States of America.

10 9 8 7 6 5 4 3 2

CONTENTS

PREFACE... ix

INTRODUCTION.. 1

PART I: AWARENESS **10**

INTRODUCTION TO AWARENESS..................... 11

ENGAGING ETHICS AND ARCHITECTURE 11

THE EVENT THAT IS ARCHITECTURE 15
    Relationships 15
    Special Knowledge 15
    Architectural Processes 16

ETHICAL ISSUES EMBEDDED IN TYPICAL
    ARCHITECTURAL PRACTICES 16

ARRIVING AT ETHICS 20

THE ORGANIZATION AND FOCUS OF PART I:
    AWARENESS 21

SOME BASICS ABOUT ETHICS..................... 22

INITIAL COMMENTS ON THE NATURE OF ETHICS 22

DEFINITIONS 24
    Primary Questions 26
    Philosophical Context 26
    Ethical Reasoning 26
    Texts and Discourse of Ethics 26

ROOTS OF ETHICS 27

THE SPECTRUM OF ETHICS 29
    Meta-ethics 29
    Applied Ethics and Architecture 30

THE ETHICAL NATURE OF ARCHITECTURE.......... 31

ARCHITECTURE'S INHERENTLY ETHICAL NATURE 31

ETHICS AND ARCHITECTURE 32

DEFINITIONS OF ARCHITECTURE 35

ASSERTIONS OF ARCHITECTURE'S ETHICAL NATURE 38

AN ARCHITECTURAL EXAMPLE AND ETHICAL CONTENT 44
    An Architectural Example 44
    Ethical Content 47

A MORE IN-DEPTH LOOK AT ETHICAL CONCEPTS 48

INTRODUCTION 48

FOUR PRINCIPAL ETHICAL THEORIES 48
    1) Action Based Upon Consequences: Teleology
       and Utility 49
    2) Acting from Moral Rules or Principles:
       Deontology 54
    3) Virtue: Excellence 57
    4) Contract Theory 61

OTHER VIEWS ON ETHICS 65
    Religious Morality 66
    Relativism 66
    Ethical Egoism 66
    Feminist Ethics 67
    Continental Philosophy 68

BUSINESSES, PROFESSIONS, AND ETHICAL OBLIGATIONS 70

WHAT IS A PROFESSION? 70
    Duty: Service and Trust 71

THE PROFESSION OF ARCHITECTURE 71

BUSINESSES, PROFESSIONS, AND ETHICAL OBLIGATIONS 74
    Architects and Business Ethics 75
    Architects and Professional Ethics 75

ETHICS AND ARCHITECTURAL PRACTICES 79

THE ARCHITECTURE/ETHICS NEXUS 79

FIVE FRAMING LENSES 80
    1) The Lens of Architecture's Purposefulness and
       Social Benefit 80
    2) The Lens of Material Production 82
    3) The Lens of Aesthetics 85
    4) The Lens of Architecture's Rhetoric
       and Ideologies 87
    5) The Lens of Praxis 90

AN APPLICATION EXAMPLE 92

ETHICAL REASONING 93

OVERVIEW AND PROCESS 93

A CASE EXAMPLE: ENVIRONMENTAL SUSTAINABILITY,
ETHICS, AND POLICIES THAT GUIDE ARCHITECTURE 95
    #1 Definition 96
    #2 Assessment 96
    #3 Speculation and #4 Deliberation 98
    #5 Resolution 102

REFLECTION 102

PART II: UNDERSTANDING **104**

INTRODUCTION 105
    Learning Objectives 105

A CLOSER LOOK AT BEING AN ARCHITECT 106
    A Selected History of the Profession: 1850–1909 106
    The Process (Education/Internship/Licensure) 108
    NCARB: Ethical Standards/State Laws 111
    AIA: *Code of Ethics and Professional Conduct* 113
    Alternative Roles 117
    Professional Characteristics: Leadership 120
    Character/Integrity/Honesty 122
    Community Responsibilities 123
    Professional Development 125

A CLOSER LOOK AT MAKING ARCHITECTURE. 127
    Overview 127
    Design 128
    Architecture Delivery Processes 131
    Construction Delivery Options 133
    Organization Issues 138
    Management Responsibilities 142
    Standard of Care 147
    Risk Management 149
    Employers/Employees 151
    Consultants 155
    The Changing Client 156

**A CLOSER LOOK AT DOING
ARCHITECTURE ETHICALLY** 159
    Overview 159
    Professional Roles, Activities, and Ethical Issues 160
    Architectural Practice Phases; Societal and Professional
      Ethical Considerations 166

PART III: CHOICES **178**

INTRODUCTION TO CHOICES. 179
    Learning Objectives 179

MAKING ETHICAL JUDGMENTS. 180
    Process for Ethical Reasoning 180
    Learning Settings 182
    Learning Exercises 182

CASE STUDIES 184

   Case Studies Organization/Matrix 184

      1: Personal Choices 186
      2: Public Service 188
      3: Cultural Diversity and the Public Architect 190
      4: The Client's House 194
      5: Rezoning 195
      6: The Mayor and the School Board 197
      7: The Neighbor's House 199
      8: The Master-Plan Study 202
      9: Building Codes and City Projects 205
      10: The Elusive Client 208
      11: Employee Rights 210
      12: Two Clients/One Project 212
      13: The Real-Estate-Investment Project 214
      14: Adaptive Reuse/Historic Preservation 216
      15: Life Safety 218
      16: The Fee Proposal 220
      17: The Joint Venture 222
      18: The Cash-Flow Bind 224
      19: The Competition 227
      20: Design Integrity 231
      21: The Client's Project Manager 233
      22: The University Architect 236
      23: Design/Build 240
      24: Building-Material Choices 242
      25: The Building-Code Official 244
      26: The Public-Bid Opening 247
      27: The Private-Bid Opening 249
      28: Construction Observation 250
      29: Post-Occupancy Evaluation 252
      30: Right of Confidentiality and the Public Interest 254

EPILOGUE 258

APPENDIX I: NCARB Rules of Conduct: 1998 259

APPENDIX II: AIA Code of Ethics and Professional
                 Conduct: 1997 269

APPENDIX III: Intern Development Program Competencies
                 and Ethical Considerations 275

APPENDIX IV: Architectural-Practice-Organization, Services
                 Delivery, and Ethical Considerations 285

NOTES TO THE TEXT 293

WORKS CITED IN THE NOTES 305

WORKS RECOMMENDED FOR FURTHER STUDY 309

ADDITIONAL ARCHITECTURAL REFERENCES 313

ADDITIONAL INFORMATION ABOUT
THE PHOTOGRAPHS 317

INDEX 319

PREFACE

This book had its genesis with the receipt of an AIA Educators/Practitioners grant from the AIA Education Committee to develop a course on ethics for use by practitioners in their offices and educators in their classrooms. That original grant was awarded to Barry Wasserman, FAIA, and Patrick Sullivan, FAIA, both on the architecture faculty of California State Polytechnic University, Pomona (Cal Poly Pomona), and Thomas Payette FAIA, president of Payette Associates of Boston. The subsequent course material, "Awareness, Understanding, Choices: Ethics and the Profession in an Ever Changing World," was completed in its basic form in 1989. Its three-tiered iterative learning approach of Awareness, Understanding, and Choices suggested the use of participatory learning processes whenever possible.

As this work was completed, its basic premises were presented in discussions of ethics at the initial AIA/ACSA Summer Practice Institutes in Sante Fe in 1992 by Barry Wasserman and Patrick Sullivan. Subsequently elements of the material were utilized in courses taught at Cal Poly Pomona by Professors Wasserman and Sullivan. Additionally the course premise, outline, and some of the Choices element with initial case studies were presented in workshops at AIA national conventions in Minneapolis (1996), New Orleans (1997), and Dallas (1999), and at the AIA California Council Monterey Design Conference (1998).

Over the ensuing years, it became apparent to Professors Wasserman and Sullivan that there was a need for a comprehensive document on the subject that would expand the material and support more fully the teaching of ethics in school and professional-office settings. Through the AIA/ACSA Summer Practice Institute they had become aware of the courses on ethics developed and taught by Gregory Palermo, FAIA, at the architecture program at Iowa State University and greatly admired them. When John Wiley & Sons approached the professors about writing this book, they immediately called on Gregory Palermo to join with them in the effort. When Palermo enthusiastically committed to the project, our work on this book commenced. It has truly been a collaborative effort and one that benefited each of us.

We could not have completed this book without the encouragement and help of many colleagues and friends.

We are grateful to John Wiley & Sons senior editor Amanda Miller for her enthusiastic support of the project. Without her prodding and encouragement, this book would never have seen the light of day.

We owe a great debt to the AIA Education Committee of 1989, its director Joseph Bilello, AIA and its chair R. Wayne Drummond, FAIA, for its grant support of our initial forays. Joe and Wayne in particular encouraged us to pursue the work in their belief that there is a need for ethics to become an integral part of architectural education.

Each of us has many others to acknowledge.

From Barry Wasserman:

My deepest thanks for the moral encouragement to follow through on the project by Joseph Esherick, FAIA, and Robert Marquis, FAIA. Both were role models for me of practitioners who embodied the meeting of ethics and the practice of architecture, particularly in the context of architects being socially responsible. My thanks to those architects who provided material utilized as some of the bases for the case studies: Luis Colasuonno; Sam Davis, FAIA; Albert M. Dreyfuss, FAIA; Cynthia Easton, AIA; James R. Flathman, AIA; Joseph P. Giattina, Jr., FAIA; Frank Guillot, AIA; John Kaliski, AIA; Ray Kang, AIA; Richard L. Lewis, FAIA; Mortimer M. Marshall, Jr., FAIA; Edward L. Oreman, FAIA; and Frederick M. Yerou, FAIA. My thanks also to Marvin M. Malecha, former dean at Cal Poly Pomona, for supporting a sabbatical to work on the case studies, and to my graduate and undergraduate students at Cal Poly Pomona who field-tested many of the case studies in their classes and whose comments improved them. My gratitude to Bill Wasserman for his photographic contributions. Finally, special

thanks to my wife, Judy Michalowski, whose tolerance, understanding, and support were crucial keys to my seeing this project
through.

From Patrick Sullivan:

It is a difficult task to identify those who helped with the development of the research, draft versions, and final text because most
of my colleagues have been involved with this project. Dean
Hasselin, Professor Paul Neal, and Dean Malecha provided the
academic resources and sabbatical-leave time to research the
issues and develop the theory of the subject. Joe Bilello, through
the American Institute of Architects Education Committee, provided the vehicle to discuss the subject as a defined professional
and academic topic. Professor Wasserman provided the incentive
to pursue and further develop our course "Awareness,
Understanding, Choices" to the status that is presented in this
text. And without Cindy Sullivan, none of this would have been
realized; my special recognition of her extraordinary efforts.

From Gregory Palermo:

My thanks to Sarah Bishop Merrill, Ph.D., for early encouragement and suggestions for this project; to Mary Kane Elizabeth
Zaboglio for review of the interim draft of "Awareness" and for
suggestions on the introduction to the book; to Angeline Smith
Leone for the terrace and garden, and space for reflection; to
Robert T. Segrest, Chair of the Department of Architecture at
Iowa State University, for early encouragement to develop an
ethics seminar, for our discussions about ethics in the curriculum,
and for support by granting administrative leave to pursue
research and writing; and to my ethics-seminar students at Iowa
State University for their questions, which enriched my considerations of ethics and the design professions. Many aspects of architectural ethics, now in much revised form, were explored in
papers prepared for presentation and proceedings publication for
ACSA Regional and National Conferences, and at national meetings of the Association for Practical and Professional Ethics
(APPE). My thanks also to those colleagues at ACSA and APPE
who supported these efforts.

INTRODUCTION

"…the unexamined life is not worth living."
SOCRATES

"We shape our buildings, and afterwards, they shape us."
WINSTON CHURCHILL

Since the fourth century BC, Socrates's challenge to compla-cency, self-satisfaction, and comfort with custom has estab-lished the standards to be met in ethical life. He proposed that we peel away the cloaks of convention and conventional wisdom and look into the heart of issues in order to live life fully, to live well, that is: to live ethically. In modern times, Winston Churchill, speaking to Parliament in 1943 about the reconstruc-tion of the House of Commons, touched upon two of the central essences of architecture: that it is an act of human creation, and that once built, it conditions our existence—architecture is cul-tural mores physically constructed. Socrates's challenge and Churchill's insight ripple through *Ethics and the Practice of Architecture*. For us, the practices of architecture, architects' capabilities to shape the environment, the motives behind our architectural pursuits, and our conduct as professionals are insep-arable—and they are essentially: ethical!

Bringing together the Socratic question and Churchillian observation, this book is about ethics and architecture, or rather architectural ethics. It is less about "ethics *and* architecture" as distinct and separate domains than it is about the ethics that are embedded in architecture and that are special to it: architec-ture/ethics as a unity, a nexus.

During the time that we were working on this book, at one point or another friends, colleagues, professional acquaintances,

1

and students, as they often do, asked each of us about what we were working on. In answering, each of us, in our own way, had a chance to distill our thoughts regarding the central objectives and content of the book while it was in progress. In much the same manner as our answers to those queries, in this introduction we set out the intents, organization, and basic ideas in *Ethics and the Practice of Architecture*.

ORGANIZATION AND USE OF THIS BOOK

The book is written in three parts. Part I: Awareness is an introduction to basic ethical theories and concepts about the overlapping of ethics and architecture. We explore how or in what ways an architectural ethics exists. It is the theory background piece to the book. Part II: Understanding describes the various professional settings, types of architectural practices and building-project processes within which the architect is likely to be confronted with ethical concerns. Part III: Choices is case-study based—we present thirty cases that explore a broad range of ethical dilemmas from practice. Each includes a description of the case scenario, as well as a few questions for consideration. While the cases can be studied by an individual, the expectation is that the cases will be used for team-based activities to identify and address the ethical issues each case raises. This is where one practices applying the knowledge gained in Parts I and II.

We have designed the book to be a reference work for educators and practitioners who are looking for guideposts in the exploration of ethical issues in architecture. For example, in a professional practice course, rather than simply going over the American Institute of Architects (AIA) *Code of Ethics and Professional Conduct*, or how accessibility of the environment to the disabled is an ethical concern, an extended section of the course might be oriented to ethical perspectives of the discipline, and our book would be a key resource. Studio and theory courses may turn to it for background for issues they are addressing. And, for courses that primarily address ethics, if not the required text, we foresee its use as a fundamental part of the course reading materials. We believe this will also be an important office resource book for practitioners—it covers a lot of ground in the types of everyday situations that are faced in the office: Part I provides some ethics background; Part II can be used for in-house education sessions on being alert to ethical situations; and Part III is ready-made for advanced exploration of ethical problems. Then there are continuing-education programs that may be focused on ethical topics: for established professionals, the case-study section will probably be most useful.

ARCHITECTURAL ETHICS

This book is designed to help students of architecture and practitioners better understand the ways in which ethics affects them, or, rather, the ways in which their special knowledge and professional activities bring about ethical obligations.

Being "good" at designing. The departure point for architecture's special ethics is the central activity of architecture: "designing buildings." Leaving aside for the moment *how* an architect goes about designing, consider how an architect knows *what* to design. The work of architecture often begins with a client and the client's expressed desires and ideas about the building or place they need designed. The client would also probably have some land or other site for the project and a budget. These are the initial essential ingredients that help define what is to be designed. As projects are designed, documents are prepared that will enable a contractor to build it. So far, this is an encapsulation of the basic client-architect-contractor relationship in which the architect typically practices architecture.

Being "good at designing buildings" can be thought of as a contingent idea: designing buildings well is dependent upon the degree of satisfaction of the parameters, some of which are touched on above, that define the environmental problem at hand. To be "good at designing buildings," of course, the architect has to *know* about buildings: how they stand up, how systems work, the history of buildings, how to invent them so they have beauty, and so forth. This is the special knowledge that architects *master and profess* to possess and to be proficient at using in their professional activities. Architects have to take into account their client's desires and the planning and technical problems that need to be solved within the finite resources available, *and* must have the knowledge and skills to address the design question being posed to them. Then the architect has to communicate the design to the client so the client understands the design, and to a contractor so he or she can build it.

Being "good" at this is not merely a business or professional skill; it is an *ethical* mandate: one that is called *virtue*. Not like modem religious virtues or chastity, but the ancient Greek concept that to have virtue is to be excellent at the practices, knowledge, and competencies expected of a person with a particular station—in this case, being an architect. It is not only that there is special expertise to acquire, but that the expertise is exercised with tempered judgment. Both the degree of mastery of expertise and the quality of the judgments are part of virtue as it applies to being an architect. We believe that most people would agree that architects ought to be "good at designing buildings" in this sense. Thus, the first idea of what it is to be an architect—to have the capacity to design buildings and to be "good" at it—is actually one form of architectural ethics.

"Good" intentions in architecture. Consider why buildings are built: what the client's hopes, intentions, and motives are. Usually it is so that something will be enhanced, improved, or newly created—e.g., for school, church, community, or office use: buildings that would be bigger to accommodate more people, or renovated to be brought up-to-date, or built new to provide better, more beautiful, more comfortable, and more useful space.

Why we build most often has to do with the desire to *make things better* in the future. This, too, is an ethical standard, for ethics attempts to help us discern what is *good*, or *the right thing to do*. In the case here, to come up with the *right* design for the given situation, one that will be *good* or *beautiful* when judged by some set of standards—standards that in modern American society most often call for functional, well-built, aesthetically pleasing building designs. Although these criteria are not fixed scientifically but rather evolve culturally, particularly the criterion "aesthetically pleasing," they provide an indication of where to turn to base our judgments. Many complex ethical arguments have been written trying to define this mysterious quality "good." Think about it. It is not so easy to define, except by reference to something else as an example. But, *improving life* through the choices we make in a given situation—for architecture, through the design of buildings and landscapes—is one aspect that most people agree is part of the ethical quest for the "good."

Relationships in architectural practices. In our discussion so far, we have mentioned clients and contractors as well as architects. Also of great importance are building users and the general public who will be looking at and affected by the building, and employees of the architect, and consulting engineers who will assist with the design. Which is to say, the architect is involved in a whole array of relationships, directly and indirectly.

How are those relationships to be conducted? For some, such as those with clients and consultants, contracts define various obligations and conduct. Also, there are laws governing professional licensing, the right to practice a profession, and building codes for safety that cover some of these relationships.

However, laws constitute *minimum* standards of performance. It is ethics that provides a richer guide! Trying to decide what *ought to be done*, the *right thing* to do, to determine the best "good" solution, are value-driven quests, ethical quests. How are employers to behave toward employees? How does one treat a consultant? How would an architect resolve a dispute with a contractor? How would the architect assist a community in evaluating alternative designs? How does the architect take into account the impacts a project will have on the natural environment? Beyond technical knowledge and design talent, many of the activities that the architect engages in require judgment, respect, and trust among the community of people participating in and affected by a building project. When such issues come up, they are ethical ones, not cleanly defined in contracts and laws.

Architectural virtues. From the preceding, we can see that there are special architectural ethics—we called them *virtues* earlier—with respect to knowing about *architecture*. These include the fundamentals for designing and the intentions for projects. We can also see that there are other contingent architectural ethics that stem from the relationships and obligations that architects have with a myriad of people in various circumstances, and perhaps even obligations to the natural environment. To some degree, these ethical concerns pertain to all of us in our everyday lives, but they become special architectural ethics when they revolve around the particular activities that are a part of designing and building the landscape we live in.

Architectural ethics beyond designing. About 20% of the architects in the U.S. work in settings other than offices that design buildings. Also, of the 80% who are in architectural-consulting practices, the American Institute of Architects (AIA) reports that only about 60% of their fees are earned for the traditional services associated with schematic design, completing contract documents, and overseeing construction. Combined with the 20% who do not work in firms, there are indications that architects spend 50% of their time on environmental-design activities beyond the traditional scope activities directly related to designing buildings. They have jobs in education, in government, in corporations, in contracting companies, and in not-for-profits like preservation societies, etc. And they provide such services as strategic planning and facilities management.

In those settings, architects have other special ethical duties: for example, code officials have an extra-special duty to be concerned with fire safety and accessibility; facilities directors have a duty to help their corporation make more profit by astute management of facilities, and professors of architecture have a duty to be good teachers. But they may also still have special architectural-ethics demands: they are never "not" architects. That is, as members of a licensed profession, they are responsible for the health, safety, and welfare of the public if they are active in designing within their particular workplace; and they have a duty to be knowledgeable regarding their specialty so that others may rely upon their judgments regarding environmental-design decisions, etc.

One might say that architects are like doctors, lawyers, or the clergy: they are always obliged to exercise their specialized professional knowledge when circumstances call for it, even if they are not "in practice" in the conventional sense. Plus, they incur other ethical obligations that are a part of the place they work.

Buildings and ethics implicit in them. Buildings have ethics in a special way. For instance, a building is not inherently "good" in the sense of a person's being good, in and of him- or herself. Buildings are designed and built in accordance with, and are judged by, the values of the people or communities that commission them; they are usually evaluated as "good" in some way that is contingent upon the culture and place within which they were initially built.

But what if a building is a firetrap by modern standards? Or is not structurally sound enough to withstand earthquakes or people loads (such as the erroneously modified design that resulted in the collapse of a skywalk in a Kansas City hotel, which killed several people)? Or is not accessible to the disabled? Or is excessively wasteful of energy because it is inefficient to heat and cool? What if there is a dispute of over a design, and the client loves it, but the general public does not (for instance, the Vietnam Memorial, which some people demanded be changed to include statues)? Or if many people consider a building to be a blight upon the landscape or to be harmful to the natural environment?

These questions do not pertain to the architect's knowledge or to the conduct of professional relationships, but to the nature of the *environment as built.* They also pertain to physical qualities, such as structural integrity, and to interpreted qualities, such as beauty and meaning. So it may be possible to think of a building as ethical in at least one major way: that of possessing *virtue* in a manner similar to thinking of an architect as possessing certain positive qualities. We explore this and other virtues of buildings in this book later on.

THREE FUNDAMENTAL CONDITIONS OF ARCHITECTURAL ETHICS

Architects and buildings, architectural processes and the relationships among and with the people whom architects engage, have ethical impacts and results — an ethics. And Architecture, then, in its many manifestations is inherently ethical, and that is what we explore and present in this book. To recap our initial thoughts about ethics and architecture, there are three fundamental conditions from which special architectural ethics arise:

1) **The architect,** as a contemporary professional, is expected by the other members of society to master, and to remain up-to-date on, the theoretical and practical complex knowledge and skills regarding planning and designing our habitat — knowledge and skills that constitute the core of the discipline of architecture. This expectation is understood in the commonsense definition of the word "architect," and in the rights to use the title architect and to practice architecture, both of which are nearly universally codified in law in the U.S. and other nations. The architect has an ethical duty to fulfill the responsibilities that follow from that understanding and those rights.

2) **The architectural processes** whereby environmental constructions are brought about — from pre-planning and conceptual design through construction and occupancy — exist within a framework of a myriad of human relationships, of design/construction decisions that need to be made, and of craft and production activities. It is fair to say that architects are expected to creatively exercise their command of the discipline through design processes. Each of the decisions and the work actions becomes an occasion for ethical consideration because the values of the architect, the client, and society-at-large intersect in the practices of making architecture.

3) **Buildings** themselves, and other landscape modifications and interventions both large and small, have an embedded ethics that evolves from their human purposes, the motives and values of the persons and society that design and build them, and the interpretation of them by subsequent generations. The ethics of the constructions we conceive and bring about extend to the use

of natural and manmade resources in their construction and operation, the safety of persons and property, accessibility for those with disabilities, their imepacts on a broad range of people, and the cultural meaning they convey through their aesthetics.

SUMMARY

Architecture — in all of its manifestations from design and decision processes, to theoretical studies, education, and built works — as a discipline, is a collection of practices that is inherently ethical: directed to the well-being of humankind. This is the perspective that we bring to *Ethics and the Practice of Architecture*. By keeping the three fundamental conditions outlined above in mind — rather than focusing on particular architectural practices (which are rapidly changing) and trying to prescribe ethical approaches for each as they exist today (which will soon be out of date) — we present and focus upon the basics in ethical reflection and reasoning that can be applied to diverse architectural circumstances.

Ethics and the Practice of Architecture is intended as an introduction to this ethics/architecture nexus:

1) **We address ethical thought and methods of reasoning, and provide a useful method for discerning ethical dilemmas in architecture.** In Part I: Awareness, we pay particular attention to understanding four basic ethical theories and how they apply to architecture: Ethics based upon the consequences of our actions, morality based upon rules and principles, virtue theory, and the social contract. We also identify five lenses through which to discern the ethical content to architecture: building-program purposes, architecture as material production, aesthetics, architecture's ideologies, and architecture in action: praxis.

2) **We provide a practical guide to the occasions in architectural practices that inherently hold ethical dilemmas.** In Part II: Understanding, it is the nature of the profession, professional responsibilities, and architectural processes that are the starting point for examining ethical obligations. In several charts that correlate architectural practices and ethical obligations and concepts, we explore ethical mandates that emerge from various practice settings, e.g., from private practice to government service, and the phases of architectural production from initial project planning through building occupancy.

3) **We present a case study methodology that is a useful model of how to think through those ethical dilemmas.** In Part III: Choices, we provide case studies, through which to explore resolving ethical dilemmas that arise in the practices of architecture. They are arranged by sub-topics based upon the timeline of architectural projects from pre-design and community planning, to post-occupancy evaluation. The case method, particularly when used by groups and teams, enables a holistic consideration of ethical concerns in situations where multiple issues are usually at stake.

PART I

AWARENESS

INTRODUCTION TO AWARENESS

ENGAGING ETHICS AND ARCHITECTURE

Ethics and the Practice of Architecture is part of the growing body of studies identified as "applied ethics": explorations of the application of ethical moral concepts and reasoning to everyday concerns and choices we are called upon to make regarding everything from telling the truth, to concern for the environment, to how to die. In this book, we bring together theoretical and practical perspectives in the examination of architecture and its ethics. We describe basic ethical theories and outline a method for applying ethical reasoning to the consideration of architectural issues. Within that context, the objectives of Part I: Awareness can be directly stated: a) to introduce the manner in which architecture and ethics intersect; b) the manner in which architecture contains an ethics and special ethical demands; and c) frameworks for assessing and thinking through architectural ethical issues.

To do this, we briefly explore the nature of ethics in Some Basics About Ethics, and the nature of architecture in The Ethical Nature of Architecture. Our pictures of each are not complete, but they set essential definitions in place. The remaining four sections. A Look at Ethical Concepts; Businesses, Professions, and Ethical Obligations; Ethics and Architectural Practices; and Ethical Reasoning, are the centerpiece of Part I: Awareness. Through case-study examples in each section, we illustrate the manner in which ethics and architecture overlap and examine architecture as an inherently ethical pursuit. We end with the delineation of an approach to ethical reasoning as it applies to architecture.

ETHICS—The very word seems to demand being written in capital letters— often seem to loom "out there" as some great,

Source: Visual Resource Collection, Iowa State University

daunting, perhaps even arcane set of theoretical discussions about what is right and wrong, and how to be a good person, to do good deeds, or to accomplish good things in the world. This picture has come into being as philosophers of all points of view have attempted through rigorously argued texts to address how we act in the world, and to define the values and processes we use in deciding what it is we ought to do—particularly in circumstances in which other people are affected by our choices. The greater the effort to define ethical constructs in "pure" terms extracted from everyday realities, for example: trying to define "good" in some absolute way that would hold for all peoples at all times and in all places, the more abstruse and disconnected from everyday life the theoretical discussions of ethics seemed to become. "ETHICS," in this characterization of it as an abstract discipline, seems to not be very helpful with practical applications to such pressing and often-faced questions like: "Is it okay to tell a "white" lie to help a friend?" Or, "Is it okay to protect my personal financial status at the expense of my business colleagues when making a business decision that is legal?"

Architecture—which in a manner similar to ethics begs at least to be capitalized if not written in capitals: "A"rchitecture— is also a discipline of great breadth and complexity with practical applications. Architecture comprises the physical buildings and landscape we have shaped to suit our inhabitation of earth, of course, but it is also a profession, a theoretical study, and includes the processes of both designing and building our habitat. There is also the "beauty" factor: if a building is not aesthetically pleasing or of a certain status of importance, is it "A"rchitecture? While these questions are illumined in ongoing arguments among architecture students, educators, practitioners, and critics, the public says: "Design our school so we like the looks of it!"

While these characterizations of ethics and architecture may be extreme, there is an underlying truth to the condition that both ethics and architecture are expansive, complex disciplines with internally consistent histories, theories, languages, and modes of argument. They address certain engaging questions of major import that we face in our lives: "How do we determine what is right and wrong in order to guide our actions?" and "What should the design of the landscape and buildings that we will inhabit be?" The processes of designing and constructing our habitat, with the presumed intention of improving the quality of life, implicitly require a judgment of the "right" thing to do. It is in this manner that architecture and ethics are joined together, in which there is a special ethics implicit in architecture. This creates the obligation that we, as architectural students and professionals, examine those special ethics.

> **Architecture is about shaping our physical habitat to suit human purposes, and in doing so has the capacity to fulfill spiritual and emotional needs.**

This book's exploration of *Ethics and the Practice of Architecture* takes place in a particular set of circumstances at the turn of the century. Our contemporary global society is characterized by economic and political interactions that have heightened our awareness of cultural diversity and identity. Advances in science, technology, and communication that greatly enhance the quality of our lives also seem to simultaneously destabilize our very personhood: we can be almost anywhere, anytime, with almost any self-created self-image, experiencing virtual worlds. Substantial imbalances exist from nation to nation, and global region to global region with respect to economics, health-care, education, food, and material and natural resources.

Within that context, during the past twenty years, there has been a resurgence of interest in ethics. Ethics provides a basis for considering personal, professional, and communal values with respect to moral questions. Indeed, ethics studies help us determine *if* a situation involves moral questions. Ethical reasoning informs the positions we hold, the choices we make, and the communal or legal policies we may enact as we negotiate the complex dilemmas we face. Ethics applied in everyday life assists in reasoning through, and making decisions about, such moral questions as environmental protection, helping the less fortunate, care for the elderly, euthanasia, genetic engineering, etc. More generally, ethics is concerned with how to go about life, what it means to "live well," to accomplish "good" in the world, and to be "just" or "fair" in one's personal and professional life.

The operative conditions of the contemporary global community and communication media outlined here combine to create a fluidity to the circumstances of life, including the "place-based" world of architecture. It seems to put the traditional role and ethics of architecture as a social construction at risk. Yet, countering that fluidity, the everyday world that we construct, inhabit, and experience is a physical reality. It is anchored in particular places and originates at particular points in time. This designed, built, and inhabited landscape is given form and rendered meaningful. The following three contemporary observations point to the essential character of architecture's enduring presence, and its ethical force:

> The essence of architecture lies not in its *usefulness* — the purely practical solutions it offers to the human need of shelter — but in the way it meets the much profounder spiritual need to *shape our habitat*. In our culture, architecture transcends the mere physical substance of buildings by endowing constructed forms with aesthetic, emotional and symbolic meanings which elevate them to symbols of civilisation.[1]

> A work of architecture is an image, a symbolic expression of the limitations, tensions, hopes and expectations of a community. I also believe that architecture is an ethical discipline before it is an aesthetic one.... This moral dimension is legitimized when architecture is presented ... as something concrete and practical which each individual citizen ... can relate to in a practical way.[2]

> When we build, we have not just a responsibility to ourselves and our clients, but to those who came before and those who will come after.... architecture transcends local issues. Questions of space, light and material, what makes a great building, are separate from client and site. Yet they are realized in a specific way, according to a genius loci.[3]

Collectively these three references open up several lines of thought about the ethical dimensions of architecture. **They are clear statements of architecture's most basic and most clearly understood purposes: that architecture is about shaping our physical habitat to suit human purposes, and in doing so also has the capacity to fulfill spiritual and emotional needs.** In these quotes, there is not only a recognition that architecture embodies the values of society that gives rise to it, but there is also clearly an acknowledged duty toward the future: that aspirations can be realized through works of architecture.

Each of these lines of thought is open to articulation and critique; they demand expansion to be more fully understood. To them can be added the themes of the processes of designing and building, the activities of architecture as a discipline and a profession, and the requisite knowledge and role of the architect, each of which has ethical dimensions.

These themes of personal and professional action, of architecture as object and place, as process and practice, together with its ethical content, are central to our explorations in *Ethics and the Practice of Architecture.* They will be further developed in a series of increasingly critical and probing discussions in Part I: Awareness.

THE EVENT THAT IS ARCHITECTURE

Architecture is a social-political-economic-cultural enterprise. It is not a solitary process; it includes whole communities of people committed to conceiving, designing, and constructing our habitat. It is supported by concepts and practical knowledge of technology, history, theory, cultural heritage, and dreams for the future. The processes of design and construction, and the places constructed both manifest and embody our culture. Designing our habitat is a specially informed process, a practice, or rather, a collection of practices.

Relationships

The practices of architecture include interactions among architects and: clients, building users, contractors, material suppliers, the general public, consultants, partners and staff, and other collaborating designers, such as landscape architects and interior designers. Some of those relationships are formalized through contracts (e.g., those with clients or consultants); others are formalized through governmental regulation or law (regulations regarding public hearings, code enforcement, and professional licensing, for example); and others are contingent or informal extrapolations of the formal ones (relations with building users, material suppliers, construction workers, and the general public).

Special Knowledge

In addition, there is the expectation that architects master and keep current in the core knowledge and skills of the discipline. They have a specific professional duty to possess and exercise competent expertise for the particular architectural projects in which they may be engaged. Does the architect have the building-type expertise to pursue it? The professional expertise from programming to construction administration, from cost estimating to technical specification? Is the capacity to design for functional adequacy, and health and safety, as well as aesthetic quality available? What capabilities with respect to giving form to architectural works have been established? Has a team been assembled that has the full range of requisite competencies for the project?

Architectural Processes

A third area of practices is mastery of architectural processes. How are design processes carried out? What methodologies are used and what ideas inform designing? Who is involved, and how are decisions made? How are teaching and mentoring future architects carried out? What are the procedures by which architects engage the construction process? What are the mechanisms through which research that informs the discipline is pursued? These practices are not linked to particular settings—traditional private offices, academia, or government agencies, for instance—because they encompass practices that pertain to architects and architecture more generally, regardless of setting.

Additional sources of ethical obligations originate in the processes of participation in community affairs with respect to such things as the design of the environment, the provision of *pro bono* services to those in need, and service contribution to the profession itself.

These three fundamental notions:

- Formal and informal engagements and relationships among architects and others;
- The mastery of architectural knowledge and skills, and the competent exercise of professional knowledge and judgment including formgiving; and
- The conduct of architectural and related processes, from research and teaching, to design and construction, to community involvement,

are the principal practices of architecture within which ethical obligations arise.

ETHICAL ISSUES EMBEDDED IN TYPICAL ARCHITECTURAL PRACTICES

Taking a look at typical private architectural practice—the place 80% of licensed architects work—is a good introduction to the range of ethical issues embedded in architecture.[4] In this setting, one may experience a variety of roles from intern to principal. Daily endeavors and decisions are driven by:

- Business choices (marketing, deciding on which projects to undertake, which clients to work with, etc.);
- Design deliberations and critiques (function, aesthetics, concepts); budgets (durability of architecture, value for cost);
- Client and contractor interactions (honoring contracts, fairness, trust and advising clients);
- Contracts (equitable conditions, providing value for service fees, mutual respect, and duties);
- Public presentations (who has the right to know and be advised about projects; who has input to design); and
- Staff development and recognition, etc.

While these are discussed under the guises of business and professional practices, and debates over the classic Vitruvian design trilogy "firmness-commodity-delight," embedded within them are ethical questions. A sampling of these embedded ethical questions:

- What are the motives, values, and intentions of potential clients? Do we concur with their values?
- Who are the people who will be using the places we design? How are they served?
- Who and what are impacted by the project, and in what ways?
- What type of project is it? Is the project's purpose one that we could support?
- Do we honor contracts that we enter into? Are we fair toward contractors and consultants?
- Do we give proper credit to those whose talent and work efforts contribute to the work that is shaped?
- Do discussions of architectural aesthetics during design give rise to consideration of ethics? If so, in what manner?
- Do we advise our clients or simply honor their requests? Are "advising" and "guiding" clients professional "duties," or do architects merely "serve" clients?
- Are architects "professionals"? What is the definition of a "profession," and do members of a profession have special ethical duties?

Many of these questions are anticipated in the AIA's *Code of Ethics and Professional Conduct*, which includes five "Canons" or broad

> **The processes of designing and constructing our habitat, with the presumed intention of improving the quality of life, implicitly require a judgment of the "right" thing to do. It is in this manner that architecture and ethics are joined together.**

principles of conduct: General Obligations, Obligations to the Public, Obligations to the Client, Obligations to the Profession, and Obligations to Colleagues.[5] We explore the *Code of Ethics and Professional Conduct* more fully in Part II: Understanding.

A brief case example may serve to indicate how some of these ethical concerns are embedded in practice:

<table>
<tr><td>

WORK-
ASSIGNMENT
CASE

</td><td>

A colleague of ours, a Jewish woman, requested that she not be assigned to a team that was designing a defense command center for Saudi Arabia. She had resolved in her mind that a military complex was all right to design for Saudi Arabia because Saudi Arabia is an ally of the U.S. and was not endangering Israel (whose sovereignty she felt strongly about). However, as a *woman,* she knew that even in her leadership role as a project architect she would not have been accepted as an equal by the Islamic community sponsoring the project and would not have been allowed to attend meetings, etc. After considering her position on these personal principled issues, and balancing the interests of the firm and the employee, she was assigned by her firm to another project.

</td></tr>
</table>

This case history contains concerns that are ultimately ethical in nature. Specifically in this situation, a number of generic ethical questions emerge:

- **Project type:** How do you feel in general about military and defense complexes (or prisons, or other types of defense and police structures)? Would you design one?
- **Who the client is:** Would you work for a foreign government, even an American ally, if you held personal values that disagreed with its political, social, or religious position?
- **Religious and gender issues:** How do you feel about religious differences? Have you ever felt gender discrimination?
- **Duties to the firm:** What is your obligation within a firm to your colleagues and to the firm itself?

In what ways are these concerns special to architecture?

The concerns raised by the above example lead to similar more broadly based questions and issues regarding public policy and the communal benefits of architectural projects versus personal values. When we continue to examine the dilemma our colleague and the firm faced, a number of more broadly encompassing ethical questions faced in everyday architectural practice come to the fore:

- How does a firm decide which commissions, public or private, to accept? How are ethical aspects of the decision regarded and evaluated?
- Is a project's "type" or "purpose" inherently ethically good or questionable? One might think of socially redeeming projects as being housing for the homeless, temporary homes for disaster victims, or such communal institutions as schools, daycare centers, shelters for abused women and their children, or hospitals.
- How would one determine the ethical dimensions of the project type?
  - By the motives of the client?
  - By the number of people affected?
  - Whether or not the purpose was aspirational and liberating, versus restricting and controlling, in intent?
  - By its expected socially beneficial impact on its client users and the community?
  - By whether or not social conventions (and thus power or majority mores and conventions) are supported?
  - By whether or not ecological concerns are addressed?
  - By whether or not the project (e.g., a school or capitol building) may be designed to serve as a symbol for its use, thus contributing, literally, to "construction" of the culture that gave rise to the project?

Another ethical area alluded to at the end of our example is that of employee relationships in privately owned companies. The partners of the architectural firm in our example case decided that the project type, the client, the contract, and the fees were all in order, and were excited about the project. Given the size of the staff and the concerns "on principle" of the employee mentioned, the firm leadership exempted her from working on the project. This appears to be a very "fair" or "right" thing to have done. But what if many people in the firm objected to the project: some on the basis of the type of building, some because of their disagreements with Islamic belief, others because of gender issues, etc.?

- Being employed in a free market, having sought a position, and having been hired by this particular architectural firm, do employees have "rights" to choose which work they wish to perform based upon their own personal "principles"?
- What sorts of "rights" do employees have?
- What sorts of "duties" toward employees do firm principals have?

We have moved into the classic dilemmas of labor and business ethics, but they are central to the ethics of architectural practice as well.

These questions regarding project purposes, client and personal values, and diverse and multi-cultural perspectives may be uncomfortable questions to pursue in an architectural context. However, by viewing this one case and its aspects of practice, and seeing how many ethical choices are embedded in it, we can begin to arrive at a sense of the omnipresence of ethical choices in architectural practices.

ARRIVING AT ETHICS

One not only must be aware of the embedment of ethics in architecture, one also must develop an awareness of both the range and limits of choice available in dealing with ethical issues. In typical practice situations, which revolve around architectural-design questions, project services, and personal and professional judgments, we discern not only that there is a question of choice, but that the choice may be judged to be strongly ethical in nature. For example:

- Is it ethically *"right"* or *"wrong"* to design a building that is extremely energy inefficient?
- Is the choice of building materials consistent with sustainable design principles? Do you think they ought to be?
- Is it somehow ethically *"good"* or *"bad"* (or at least relatively *more* "good" or "bad" in a given situation) to sacrifice certain functional efficiencies in pursuit of enhanced aesthetic character in a design?
- Are the planning and design of a progressive housing complex mixed with community services that will require the displacement and relocation of families and the demolition of an economically depressed neighborhood *"just and fair"* toward the families that will be displaced?

In considering "right from wrong," "good and bad," and "justness and fairness" with respect to what we "ought to do," we are raising several of the primary questions of ethics.

In considering and choosing our course of action, we may sense that we are personally exercising our professional knowledge skill and judgment well, that is, in a manner of excellence toward positive ends. Excellence of this type — in this case, bringing professional knowledge, judgment, and fairness to bear on everyday environmental concerns in the conduct of architectural practices—is identified by ethicists as *virtue*.

An encompassing condition that affects ethical action is the fact that we are not only within the ethical situation with its primary questions, but also within a cultural milieu that has an impact on our perception of that situation. Living in the Western cultural tradition, in post-Enlightenment, post-Modern times, and being self-consciously aware of the questions raised are the prime instances of that conditioned perception. It is only because we are in this context that we even raise these questions. This encompassing condition is the context from which we inquire: "What should I do, personally and/or professionally as an architect, in this situation?"

The primary questions surrounding ethical choices and the context within which we consider those choices raise some additional basic questions:

- Where do concepts like "good," "the right thing to do," and "virtue or excellence" with respect to architecture arise from?
- Do they have opposites that complete a pair: "evil," "wrong," and "counterfeit or sham," respectively?
- Are they universal, that is, shared by all people? Or are they "relative," that is, relative to a particular time and place, and/or culture and community?
- Are they "real," that is, objectively real, or are they purely "subjective" mental constructs and thus fictive—whether anchored in religion, myth, legend, ritual, local laws, or common practice—even if they seem real?

The field of *meta*-ethics comprises defining and exploring these kinds of questions. They are the "questions beyond the questions" that try to get at the foundations of ethical thought and action.

Without an understanding of primary ethical questions and some understanding of the importance of these *meta*-questions, one will find it difficult to arrive at a firm basis for ethical discussion, choice, decision, and action. Introducing these concerns is the objective of Part I: Awareness.

THE ORGANIZATION AND FOCUS OF PART I: AWARENESS

What are the range of ethical issues faced in architecture? How can they be addressed? Are there processes for considering and

Excellence of this type—in this case, bringing professional knowledge, judgment, and fairness to bear on everyday environmental concerns in the conduct of architectural practices—is identified by ethicists as *virtue*.

making ethical decisions in architecture? Providing approaches to considering and resolving these questions is the intent of *Ethics and the Practice of Architecture*. The various discussions in Part I: Awareness introduce: 1) a basic definition of ethics; 2) the ethical nature of architecture; 3) several main concepts of ethics and ethical theories; 4) the ethics of business and the professions; 5) ethics and the practices of architecture; and 6) ethical reasoning.

The principal topics of ethics, architectural ethics, and ethical reasoning are presented several times in repetitive rounds, each time with increasing depth and complexity. For example, The Main Concepts of Ethics, which uses several architectural examples to illustrate basic ethical theories, builds upon On What Constitutes Ethics. Ethical Reasoning, which explores a single architectural case example from several perspectives, builds upon these two earlier sections. In a second example, a basic definition of architecture and architectural ethics is introduced in The Ethical Nature of Architecture. Building upon this discussion, Businesses, Professions, and Ethical Obligations extends the definition of architecture as a profession and clarifies professional duties. Ethics and Architectural Practices then explores several framing lenses through which the ethics of the architectural profession and architectural work can be examined.

Each iteration of discussion leads to a deepening understanding of architectural ethics. In this way, the discussion of general ethics and architectural ethics reinforce one another. Collectively, the sections provide a basic conceptual background and tools with which to consider ethical questions related to the practices of architects. They set the stage for more detailed analysis in Part II: Understanding and application in Part III: Choices.

SOME BASICS ABOUT ETHICS

INITIAL COMMENTS ON THE NATURE OF ETHICS

In the Introduction to Part I: Awareness, we touched upon the ethical nature of architecture and certain types of ethical questions, but we left the nature of ethics undefined. How do we trace the *intuitively ethical* in architecture back to *ethics* in order to better understand and assess architectural ethical dilemmas?

Ethics is a branch of philosophy that addresses the matters of how we ought to act and how we ought to conduct our lives in a way consistent with virtue and goodness. Around 400 BC, Plato attributes to Socrates two of the more memorable lines that help frame ethics: "…this is no light matter: it is the question, what is the right way to live?"[1] and "I say again that daily to discourse about virtue, and of those other things about which you hear me examining myself and others [what is good, what is justice, etc.], is the greatest good of man, and that the unexamined life is not worth living."[2] The questions that ethics asks, and that give ethics its particular place in human affairs, are pretty direct, and they have been around for a long time in Western thought:

- How is it that I ought to act, to live my life?
- How should I act with regard to others?
- With respect to myself, then, what is it that constitutes "good" behavior?
- Toward what "good" ends should I commit myself?
- With respect to others, what are my duties toward them, toward participating in and organizing a "just" or "fair" or "caring" community or society?

These are classic questions of both Western ethics and twentieth-century Anglo-American ethical studies. Significant critiques have been leveled against their formulation and the literature and reasoning that support their debate, e.g.: by feminists (e.g., partly because almost all ethical theorists have been men, which has led to a public versus private, justice versus nurturing, reasoning versus caring, perspective to ethical debate; and partly because many ethicists have been explicitly dismissive of women, etc.); by advocates of Continental philosophy (which has been critical of the twentieth-century focus on definitions, e.g., attempts at defining fixed perspectives and disassociation of academic ethics from everyday affairs); and by followers of non-Western philosophies (many of which are less anthropocentric than Western ethics). However, all ethical quests, including those of the critiques, are concerned with what manner to live morally. From that shared objective, these questions, broadly and inclusively construed, continue to have validity.

Ethics comprises a study of thought, language, reasoning processes, and judgment that informs the choices people make in their daily lives that affect their own well-being, that of others, and their host planet. Part I: Awareness in *Ethics and the Practice of Architecture* provides a general overview of the topic with a focus on the types of questions faced in ethical dilemmas, the types of ethical theories that are used in considering the central problems of ethics, and the nature of ethical reasoning. While it is not a substitute for more formal ethics studies, the extent of our cover-

Ethics comprises a study of thought, language, reasoning processes, and judgment that informs the choices people make in their daily lives that affect their own well-being, that of others, and our host planet.

age is shaped to provide basic grounding in ethics for those who will be relying principally upon this book for considering ethical concerns in an architectural context. References for further study in ethics are included in the Notes (see pages 293–308).

DEFINITIONS

To build upon our opening comments on ethics, we begin here, as we will later when considering architecture and the architect, with dictionary definitions. While these may be limited definitions with respect to the full richness of the 2,500 years of discourse on ethics in Western thought, dictionary definitions usually distill the essence of the term being defined. Ethics is a distinct discipline:

DICTIONARY DEFINITIONS:

Ethics

A) The *American Heritage Dictionary (AHD)*[3] serves as the starting point in our developing definitions:"l.a. A set of principles of right conduct; l.b. A theory or system of moral values...; 2. The study of the general nature of morals and of the specific moral choices to be made by a person....; 3. The rules or standards governing the conduct of a person or the members of a profession...."

B) The *Webster's New World Dictionary: College Edition (NWD/C)* provides slight variations:"1. the study of standards of conduct and moral judgment; moral philosophy. 2. a treatise on this study...; 3. the system or code of morals of a particular philosopher, religion, group, profession, etc."

C) The venerable *Oxford English Dictionary (OED):* "2.a. The science of morals; the department of study concerned with the principles of human duty. b. a treatise on the subject; 3.a. The moral principles of a particular leader, or school of thought. b. The moral principles by which a person is guided. c. The rules of conduct recognized in certain associations or departments of human life."

D) The unabridged *Random House Dictionary of the English Language (RHD)* is more explicit about the topics of study: "4. *(usually used with a singular v.)* That branch of philosophy dealing with values relating to human conduct, with respect to the rightness and wrongness of certain action and to the goodness and badness of the motives and ends of such actions."

(continued on next page)

E) These definitions from the *Shorter Oxford English Dictionary (SOED)* conclude the introductory dictionary definitions: "I.2. A set of moral principles, *esp.* those of a specific religion, school of thought, etc. … II.3. A treatise on ethics; 4. The science of morals; the branch of knowledge that deals with the principles of human duty or the logic of moral discourse; the whole field of moral science; 5. The moral principles or system of a particular leader or school of thought; the moral principles by which any particular person is guided; the rules of conduct recognized in a particular profession or area of human life."

While each dictionary definition varies somewhat from the others, they share several attributes that may be summarized as follows:

Ethics:

1) Is the study of human conduct and moral values;
2) May refer to a set of values or moral systems;
3) Comprises duties and standards of conduct for individual persons, groups, and professions;
4) Includes writings and treatises on ethics; and
5) Entails critical reasoning with respect to moral considerations.

At this point one may note that *ethics* and *morals* appear to be used almost interchangeably in these definitions. But, *moral* thought is rooted in *mores:* the folkways or social customs of a community of people that become the accepted rules of conduct, including the moral systems, of that community. The *moral* has both a broad construction that may apply to any set of particular beliefs, and is often also used more narrowly and interchangeably with religious values and sexual morality. *Ethics* is rooted in *ethos:* also a collection of basic values, but stemming from the Greek pertaining to character, or disposition, not merely custom. *Ethics* is also defined as the study of moral systems, or the science of morals. For these reasons, we use the term *ethics* here specifically in application to the reasoned consideration of diverse value systems and competing moral claims.

In the following paragraphs, we enlarge upon those starting points.

Primary Questions

Ethics asks certain questions, typically phrased around the concepts of "living well" personally, "doing good" in the world, "doing the right thing" in a situation of difficult choices, and arriving at a "just" decision in a conflict or where there exist competing outcomes. As more generally framed by Socrates, ethics has to do with deciding how to live with respect to self and others. These questions, and others similar to them, are the primary ones that form the framework of our discussion here.

Philosophical Context

Ethics is argued in philosophical terms. First, the field of meta-ethics critically examines the idea of ethics, what ethics is founded upon. The view of the world and knowledge: epistemology—how we come to have knowledge of ourselves, other beings, things in the world, ideas, and values—is central to question of ethics. How we and others come to be in the world and the nature of that *being*—ontological status—has bearing. The nature of, and our use of, language and meaning, the media by which those ethical questions can be discussed, has bearing, too. Explorations in depth of meta-ethics, epistemology, ontology, and semiotics are beyond the scope of this work. We rely here upon the "commonsense" reality of the everyday world. In other words, we acknowledge and accept the existence of physical material constructions, such as buildings and things, ourselves and other human beings as physical presences, other phenomena of the world that we experience daily, and that our ideas and values have a reality as human creations.

Ethical Reasoning

Ethics requires the reasoned examination of the primary questions it asks within the context of understanding ourselves as individuals and members of a community, and of understanding the way we come to know and decide things. The methods of logic, argumentative debate, and problem-solving are used in ethical reasoning. Much of this book uses the methods of ethical reasoning to inquire into ethical questions, and the Ethical Reasoning discussion in Part I examines at least one reasoning path through the many facets of a case example.

Texts and Discourse of Ethics

The questions of ethics, moral reasoning, and the conditions of our status as moral beings are discussed in many texts, ancient and contemporary. Many of the texts have become "required" classics for the study of ethics and philosophy in general, e.g., the early sections of Plato's *Republic*, or Aristotle's *Nicomachean Ethics*, both fourth century BC. Contemporary "classics" in ethics include John Rawls's *A Theory of Justice* and Alasdair MacIntyre's *After Virtue*.[4] Plato discusses the questions of what is good, what comprises duty to self and others, and what is justice in the early parts of *The Republic*. Rawls's classic book, originating in his work in political philosophy, examines how we make fair and just social and political decisions. MacIntyre, building upon roots in, and a critique of, Aristotle's *Ethics*, shapes a contemporary perspective on ethics stemming from virtue and the concept of excellence of conduct. We sketch and summarize the main outline of various ethical perspectives here, explore them more fully later in Part I (see page 48), and reference other works for further study.

ROOTS OF ETHICS

As noted we begin ethical quests when we first ask: What is the right thing to do here? How should I behave? What choices should I make with regard to the dilemma at hand (choices between: "right" and "wrong," or "just and fair" versus "unfair," or "good" and "evil")? What actions should I take with regard to myself and their effects on others? The choices may be ones like whether or not to tell the truth about who accidentally broke a window (lying) or to pilfer a candy bar from a supermarket shelf (stealing), which presumably most people would recognize as "wrong."

Surely, people ought to be truthful, and they ought not steal. But what if the "lie" you are considering would protect a friend from an abusive person who might severely physically punish your friend out of proportion for breaking the window? Or what if you had no money for food in your family and the easily concealed candy bar was for a brother or sister? The broken-window situation includes other ethical issues in addition to "lying": principal among them the idea of punishment, the idea of just deserts (punishment fitting the wrong done), the degree of responsibility for "accidents" compared to deliberate actions, and liability for physical abuse. The candy-bar example also has other ethical implications: Is it "fair" that some people have enough of life's essential goods, such as food, while others are in great need out of no fault of their own? Does it help to measure the amount of harm to the supermarket, which has thousands of candy bars, one of which would barely be missed, compared to the amount of good for the

Applied ethics is the field of study that addresses the application of ethical theory to everyday situations, the practices of architecture included.

brother or sister? Is "lying" or "stealing" always "wrong"? What about all these other issues, such as punishment, fairness, equitable access to life's goods, measuring the degree of benefit or harm? Do these figure into the equation? Are there some times when "lying" or "stealing" may be "right"? How would you decide? Ethical considerations help us sort out these types of concerns and, of course, much more complex life situations.

While early rules of conduct, such as Hammurabi's *Code* of eighteenth-century BC Babylonia, and the discourses of the Greek pre-Socratic philosophers of the fifth century BC, predate Plato's framing of the Socratic dialogues in the early fourth century BC, it is beginning with Socrates and Plato that Western philosophy has been more or less continuously engaged in addressing these sorts of questions. One might call this "ethics proper" or "basic ethics," which has since those beginnings been concerned with the primary questions briefly outlined above. The debates surrounding ethics have generally been considered and framed along four principal themes within which more specific theories are contained.

FOUR ENCOMPASSING ETHICAL THEORIES	1) Doing things that have good results as a result of actions taken (*teleological* theories), which include Utilitarianism (Jeremy Bentham, eighteenth century, and John Stuart Mill, nineteenth century), and other consequentialist theories, such as American Pragmatism (Charles Pierce and William James, late nineteenth and early twentieth centuries), and Machiavellianism (Niccolò Machiavelli, sixteenth century);
	2) Doing things from universal and proper principles and which are duty- and obligation-based (*deontological* theories), among which Immanuel Kant's (eighteenth century) moral theories are the most widely known;
	3) Doing things that promote personal excellence of mind and well-being, thereby promoting the general well-being of a community of people (*virtue* theory), of which Aristotle (fourth century BC) and Stoicism (fl. third century BC onward) are early models, and MacIntyre's and Philippa Foot's work are contemporary models;
	4) Arriving at shared, communal, and minimal limitations on personal liberties so that all may prosper according to their individual interests [*social contract* theory, of which Thomas Hobbes (seventeenth century), John Locke (seventeenth century), Jean-Jacques Rousseau (eighteenth century), Rawls (mentioned earlier), and perhaps Jürgen Habermas (contemporary European philosopher) are exponents].

THE SPECTRUM OF ETHICS

Ethics takes into account the motives, reasons, and methods that inform making ethical choices, and that inform arriving at decisions of how we ought to act toward ourselves and toward others in a community or larger body politic. Various positions hold that "ethics" come to us intuitively or from our human nature, that they exist as *a priori* or God-given forms for us to discover, or that we invent them in order to get along with others while maximizing our own personal ends. There are underlying presumptions and questions within the spectrum of ethical concerns:

- What is the "good" toward which we ought to be moving?
- What principles should we apply in our thinking?
- How do we arrive at justice and fairness in our dealings with others and they toward us?
- What is the relationship of our duties toward ourselves and those close to us and those to the larger communal benefit?

There are some tricky questions about ethics itself, though. The terms, the very words we use to describe the choices in ethics — *right, wrong, just, unjust, good, evil, virtuous, dissolute* — are not statements of fact, but of *value*. If they are not factual, then how can we address the questions of ethics? Are not values subjective and invented according to the experiences we have? If values are not "real" and "factual" like rain or snow, how do we come to know them and how can we use them as the basis for making ethical choices and undertaking ethical actions? Do the language and social customs within which any one of us was raised guide us? Do religious beliefs provide a sufficient guide? Do all of us possess an intuition or innate conscience that will guide us? Is there a psychological emotive quality that drives us to do well or to care for others?

Meta-ethics

Philosophers have expended substantial efforts to explore the fundamental nature of ethics raised by these questions in order to clarify how ethics can be used to inform our actions in everyday life. The questions of where all this comes from: how ethics come into existence, moral values, ethical dilemmas, our status as moral beings, the logic of our activities, their degree of "truth" or "universality," our motives in making ethical choices, etc., are the subjects of meta-ethics: the reflective critical consideration of ethics.

Ethics takes into account the motives, reasons, and methods that inform making ethical choices, and that inform arriving at decisions of how we ought to act toward ourselves and toward others in a community or larger body politic.

In John L. Mackie's terms, a late-twentieth-century philosopher who explored the nature of ethical values, they are the "second order questions upon which the status of ethics is based."[5]

Stemming from G. E. Moore's simple but bedeviling question, posed in 1903, of how we know what "good" is (since it is not an object, is couched in language, and is usually described by relating examples of "good" rather than the "property" "good"),[6] much of twentieth-century philosophical ethics has been engaged in attempting to understand the status (objective, subjective, natural, intuitive, emotive, etc.) of this value term and the others identified above. The matter is not a light one: there is a correlated search to discover the ways *values* logically become the basis for action, for making decisions about what we *ought to do*.

For our purposes here, we accept that we humans are faced with value-driven ethical concerns, and that, while they are slippery and difficult to define, it makes sense to think through ethical questions with reference to those traditional value terms.

It is from these kernels that the contemporary range of ethics discussion springs:

SPECTRUM OF CONTEMPORARY ETHICAL DISCUSSION[7]	<ul><li>Exploration of the major ethical theories (Kantian deontics, virtue theory, contract theory, Utilitarianism, etc.);</li><li>The definition of the value terms of ethics (the good, virtue, right, fair, justice, etc.);</li><li>Meta-ethical exploration of the status of ethics, of the sources of ethical thought, whether or not ethics have some objective quality or are entirely subjective;</li><li>Ethical reasoning and how we arrive at both personal and communal ethical choices;</li><li>The application of ethical theory and reasoning to contemporary issues, such as human genetic engineering, protection of the environment, euthanasia, multicultural respect and accommodation, business and professional activities, etc.;</li><li>The critique of the Western ethical tradition, for example, from Feminist or Continental perspectives.</li></ul>

Applied Ethics and Architecture

At the beginning of this section, ethics is defined not only as theoretical systems of moral thought, but also the study of personal conduct, and the values and standards of groups of people and professions. Applied ethics is the field of study that addresses the application of meta-ethics and ethical theory to everyday situations, the practices of architecture included. Architecture shares space in the applied-ethics spectrum with the professions of medicine, law, and engineering. Our central concern in this book is ethics and how it is related to architecture, architects, and architectural practices. Some instances of how ethics and architecture intersect may seem pretty clear, for example, the ethics of contracts that architects enter into with clients, or the ethics of public safety in design. Other questions may be murky, such as whether or not a design concept for a building is "ethical."

We will return to more in-depth considerations of ethical theories on page 48, and ethics and the professions on page 70. Before we do, we would like to introduce basic ideas pertaining to the ethical nature of architecture itself.

THE ETHICAL NATURE OF ARCHITECTURE

ARCHITECTURE'S INHERENTLY ETHICAL NATURE

Architecture, in its many manifestations, is as much an ethical discipline as a design discipline. A *sine qua non* of architecture is its human purpose—the design and construction of our habitat. As observed by Immanuel Kant: "...the beauty of a house or a building (be it church, palace, arsenal, or summer house), presupposes a concept of the purpose which determines what the thing is to be, and consequently a concept of its perfection."[1] Kant is clear in defining architecture's perfection as inclusive of the degree to which it serves human purposes.

The shaping of particular buildings, in particular places with qualities suiting human purposes, is driven by communal and individual needs and desires: protection from the elements, shelter and support for various specific uses, the satisfaction of the human spirit through architecture's symbolizing capacity, and the satisfaction of our aesthetic sensibilities. One might postulate that we do not undertake habitat construction without some beneficial objective in mind: to protect; to make a home, a factory, a school, or a place of worship; to make an electric generation plant; or to make a memorial. The satisfaction of human intentions and the expected beneficial results—"satisfaction of intentions" and "beneficial results" being "good" for us individually and communally—move architecture into the ethical realm.

This last thought raises the question: Is there an "architectural ethics": ethical architects, ethical architecture, ethical practices? We would argue that architectural practices: designing for utility; working with clients in agency (acting as their representative) or counseling/advising relationships; designing for safety; satisfying communal aspirations for architecture through its function, quality, and character; and working on the virtues of the discipline, which include formal aesthetic and material qualities and their effects, make architecture inherently ethical, and that there is an architectural ethics. There are also ethics that stem from other aspects of the practices of architecture, for instance, business and labor practices that share a business ethics framework, but that are given particular qualities in the architectural context.

The premises regarding architecture's inherently ethical content may be briefly summarized:

REASONING TO
ARCHITECTURE'S
ETHICAL CONTENT

1) Ethics is generally concerned with what we ought to do; how we ought to live; issues of good and evil, right and wrong, the just and the inequitable; and the beneficial ends of life in general.

2) Consideration of these questions has led to an ethics literature regarding human reasoning, choices, and action about the ways of conducting ourselves and choosing among options for action (with respect to personal virtue, politics, and other matters pertaining to beneficial ends).

3) Architecture is concerned with the future state of the environment to suit human purposes: the considerations of what we ought to make, how we should make it, and the places made.

4) Designing what "ought to be" in terms of our habitat and building it explicitly frames a way of life, of experiencing life, of improving life.

5) Architecture — dealing with those aspects of the totality of human well-being and positive ends that can be addressed through the design of the environment — is thus inherently ethical.

The terms of the ethical in architecture are embedded in the more encompassing ground of ethics generally.

ETHICS AND ARCHITECTURE

Ethics asks: In what manner shall I live? What is good? What is excellence/virtue (areté)?[2] What is right action? What is just?

Architecture may ask: What is "good" architecture? What constitutes virtue in architecture and in the practices of architecture? What manner of living is implied in the forms of particular architectural solutions? Do the acts of designing and building our habitat intrinsically embrace the questions that ethics asks? Is there an ethical connection between the "goodness" and "virtues" of architecture and the greater "social good"?

These are among the central considerations of the discipline of architecture, architectural education, and architecture's diverse practices. Answering these questions involves architecture's intents, purposes, and effects, as well as what architecture is and may be. Architecture is an intervention into an existing environmental context in order to shape spaces and places that serve human purposes. Architecture is about *buildings*, of course. Not only is it about what is actually built, but about how it is built and how it looks. It is also about getting to buildings—the *process* of designing and building buildings, the practicing of architecture. And it is about the *future*: we build today what we think will serve our selves, our children, and their children and beyond. Architecture is a reflection upon and a proposal of how things ought to be in the world. It gives tangible form to society's values and is not limited to the image of a place.

Whether people are planning dwellings or schools, libraries, offices, markets, or factories, buildings are proposed to bring some type of order or benefit to society. They form the physical manifestation of social order. They also then define what is "improper" or "out of order". Some buildings are literally meant to control, as prisons do. Others provide places for healing, like hospitals, or symbolize our government, like capitol buildings. Other buildings are conceived to destroy, such as the gas chambers of Nazi Germany and the slaughterhouses of the meat industry. Still other buildings memorialize our heroes and help forge the mythos of our nation and ennoble our culture.

None of these enterprises is "neutral," though. Buildings are physical, built, material, cultural artifacts that are an expression of cultural values. We create them, inhabit them, and are shaped by them. As put succinctly by Winston Churchill in 1943 when proposing that the war-destroyed House of Commons be rebuilt in its original English Gothic mode with a rectangular form and opposing benches to preserve the parliamentary process: "We shape our buildings, and afterwards, they shape us." Churchill first expressed these thoughts nearly twenty years earlier at the Architectural Association in London: "There is no doubt whatever about the influence of architecture and structures upon human character and action. We make our buildings and afterwards they

We would argue that architectural practices —designing for utility; working with clients; satisfying communal aspirations; and working on the virtues of the discipline—make architecture inherently ethical, and that there is an architectural ethics.

make us. They regulate the course of our lives." In making his proposal for rebuilding, Churchill compared the rectangle with facing benches and the space between them favorably to the more common semicircle for legislative assemblies. He contends the architectural form of the Commons demands a choice and requires a public conviction and declaration about the values being supported—a selection of one side over another with which to be associated and seated. One cannot blur one's political position as on an arc. Churchill remarks on this with characteristic wit: "It is easy for an individual to move through those insensible gradations from Left to Right [on an arc], but the act of crossing the Floor is one which requires serious consideration. I am well informed on this matter, for I have accomplished that difficult process, not only once but twice!"[3] Taken together, Churchill's comments capsulize an essential understanding of architecture as being formed by us and forming our experience, as a reciprocation between form and intention, place and action.

Taken together, Churchill's comments capsulize an essential understanding of architecture as being formed by us and forming our experience, as a reciprocation between form and intention, place and action.

Architectural concerns are central concerns of human dignity and being in the world: the *way* of being, the *good* way of being—the same motivating force as ethics' questions. Architecture possesses this quality whether it is conceived in a self-aware, self-conscious society and culture like that of contemporary America, or whether it is "non-self-conscious," ingrained as a stable or subtly changing enduring practice, as is often the case in traditional indigenous societies. Architecture possesses this character even if it is deliberately conceived to be *"anti"*—against—the prevailing conventional architectural fashion, or to be an attempt at pure artistic expression. In those guises, it critiques society and its constructions and attempts to contribute to human flourishing through contrast or the impact of art form. Thus, architecture holds an ethical role. Architecture in all of its manifestations is humanly intentional. It is this intentionality that is its ethical force.

The intentions behind the decision to build, to change our habitat, which give rise to architecture, are speculations on the manner of life we ought to live, which is the primary ethical question. The ethical nature of architecture appears to emerge foremost from this role as a cultural process and product: the designing and building of human habitat, the concretization of social values, of a supposedly improved or enhanced environment, and through that, a "better" existence. Depending upon one's position, those values may be judged imperial and repressive to some, redeeming for others, or benign or extravagant with respect to natural resources, but they are definitely ethical. They raise the ethical concerns of the nature of dwelling, the way of being, the way we ought to give form to the places we dwell, and what that form ought to be. Reflection in architecture, evaluation of what has been built, consideration of theory, and design speculation are all centered around the quality of our constructed environment, its underlying ideas, and its impact on the quality of our lives. Architecture's creative and constructive processes, the built environment that results from them, and architectural reflection are all intrinsically ethical, whether or not the architectural method and presentation explicitly utilize ethical discourse.

In the remainder of this discussion we turn first to definitions of architecture; then move to definitions and assertions of architecture's ethical content and grounding. Later, we will build on this by examining Five Lenses that may be used to examine architectural ethics: 1) purposefulness; 2) material fabrication; 3) aesthetics; 4) architecture's ideologies; and 5) practices in action (see page 80).

DEFINITIONS OF ARCHITECTURE

Architecture, as we define it for our purposes, is: the art and science of design and construction of buildings and landscapes for human inhabitation. In this interpretation, reason and art, process and place, and human intention are included. Architecture is more than buildings. Our habitat is brought about collectively, not solely through the actions of architects, although architects, who are skilled in the art and science of designing buildings and landscapes, are often major participants in development of the built environment in contemporary society.

As with the definition of ethics, we begin here with dictionary definitions. Architecture is defined and commonly understood to be:

A) *OED:* "1. The art or science of building or constructing edifices of any kind for human use.... But *Architecture* is sometimes regarded solely as a fine art and then has [a] narrower meaning ...; 2. The action or process of building."

B) *AHD:* "1. The art and science of designing and erecting buildings. 2. Buildings and other large structures."

C) *NWD/C:* "1. the science, art, or profession of designing and constructing buildings. 2. a building, or buildings collectively."

D) *RHD:* "1. the profession of designing buildings, open areas, communities, and other artificial constructions and environments, usually with regard to some aesthetic effect...; 3. the action or process of building; construction; 4. the result or product of architectural work, as a building."

DICTIONARY DEFINITIONS:

Architecture

These dictionary definitions are clearly not the whole of it, but they have a compelling accuracy at their core. Habitat construction is an intentional act we undertake: art and craft and human intents are brought together regarding the places we inhabit.

> **Architecture:**
>
> 1) Is the particular places we shape in the landscape for our inhabitation;
> 2) Is about their consideration, design, and fabrication; and
> 3) Is a professional practice.

Expanding on the dictionary definition, we see architecture as addressing the forms and images of human habitat, the processes of its invention, its constructive technology, and its material fabrication. It includes the consideration of the history of the forms of places and their inhabitation, as well as speculation about and utopic propositions of what the forms and nature of being singly and collectively could be. Architecture has internal conventions of representation, judgment, and composition. Our Western architectural psyche deals with Vitruvius's shadow in one way or another—honoring or critiquing "durability-utility-beauty," his theory and practice split, and what to know about and how to educate ourselves to become architects—all of which are taken up in his *Ten Books on Architecture* (first century BC). Architecture is the professing and practicing of knowledge and skill about such things.

Architecture's human dimension; its communal nature; its aspiration to mark ritual myth, cosmos, capital, or power; its protection against the elements; and its intention to make changes in the world for continued, presumably "enhanced," "improved," and/or "better," inhabitation make architecture an intrinsically *ethical* enterprise.

Architecture has to do with the design and construction of places for human affairs and human inhabitation. We do not have to discover the first instances of humankind erecting a shelter for protection in the natural wild landscape in order to comprehend architecture's import for well-being[4] because we are *in medias res*, we "dwell" within the constructed landscape. It shapes us, and our perceptions, as surely as we shape it.[5]

Contemporary architecture is a social-*design* enterprise. Reason and creative invention are applied to environmental problems. It is enmeshed in social-economic-political-cultural circumstances. So, too, are the environments studied in architectural history, anthropology, and archaeology, whether remnants of cultures that wrote of themselves or those that were "pre-historical." Architecture is inescapably cultural, changing "as culture changes;"[6] it is community giving itself physical form. Insofar as architecture is rooted in the social and cultural, it is the physical manifestation of the prevailing mores of the time in which it is/was built, bearing a testimony to its era. Architecture's human dimension; its communal nature; its aspiration to mark ritual, myth, cosmos, capital, or power; its protection against the elements; and its intention to make changes in the world for continued, presumably "enhanced," "improved," and/or "better," inhabitation make architecture an intrinsically *ethical* enterprise.

The following is a brief example of how our understanding of the world, the physical one and the one of human relationships, is shaped by this iterative notion of "shaping" and "being shaped by" our habitat. Compare the agrarian landscape of the Central Plains to that of urban Chicago:

The Central Plains

From northern Indiana to eastern Nebraska, the horizon is below one's shoulders, the sky a full hemisphere above. One looks through the landscape across fields and between shelterbelts. The Jeffersonian grid is palpable and visible. Multigenerational farmsteads are still visible in this age of corporate farming. One can discern one's personal place and one's family's place within it. It is a built-agrarian ethos.

Chicago

In comparison the streets and avenues of the near north side of Chicago are bordered with three- to six-story buildings. The area's crowded pavements and storefronts, the above-grade transit rumbling overhead every fifteen minutes, the sky not a dome but a slice, the space of alleyways in lieu of fields, the knowledge that within an arc of twenty miles live four million people in a continuation of this physical structure, combine to give the experience of

(continued on next page)

(continued from previous page)

Chicago its own pulse. The Jeffersonian grid, interrupted by a few diagonals (the historic paths and railway lines that used to connect separate but now merged communities) on the plain, is palpable and present here, too. One can discern one's place within it and one's family's place within it. It is a constructed-urban-industrial-commercial-marketplace ethos.

Each landscape is a complete world with a physical structure that arises from, and in turn shapes, the culture of which it is an exemplar. One obtains a good sense of the distinctiveness of place and its formation of ourselves, issues examined by Norberg-Schulz in his reading and extension of Heidegger,[7] and the construction of ethos, an issue that Karsten Harries considers architecture's ethical function.[8]

ASSERTIONS OF ARCHITECTURE'S ETHICAL NATURE

Without explicit references to ethics, there is a persistent declaration by architects of architecture's ethical nature: primarily through identifying or asserting the benefits that arise from architecture to society. Vitruvius (first century BC) appeals to Augustus on the ethical grounds of making the Roman state's powers and justice visible through the architecture of its institutions throughout the provinces of the empire. Alberti (fifteenth century) links architecture's benefits to society through its capacity to shape the places of leisure, dwelling, work, and commerce of the city-state. Ruskin (nineteenth century) speaks of architecture as an art, and its contribution to human well-being and flourishing through its value as art. Modernism (twentieth century) speaks to architecture's capacity to shape a new non-class-based society through its use of the constructional and environmental technology of its time, and the clean forms of its designs, which are free of bourgeois decorative and symbolic trappings.

The selections in the following paragraphs are relatively brief parts of larger bodies of work that address the more traditionally understood content of architecture: design, aesthetics, function, skills and methods, etc. Despite their brevity, they illustrate how deeply the ethical lies within the architectural.

Architecture *asserts* its role in being/providing "a good" for society through building: the art and craft, theory and practice, and design and fabrication of the environment we inhabit. This assertion of the beneficial goodness of architecture has a long history in Western architectural thought, stemming at least back to Vitruvius. Vitruvius, in his Preface to Book I of the *Ten Books On Architecture*, addresses Augustus:

> But when I saw that you were giving your attention not only to the welfare of society in general and to the establishment of public order, but also to the providing of public buildings intended for utilitarian purposes, so that not only should the State have been enriched with provinces by your means, but that the greatness of its power might likewise be attended with distinguished authority in its public buildings, I thought that I ought to take the first opportunity to lay before you my writings on this theme.[9]

Vitruvius undergirds Caesar's concern for the welfare of society and public order with architecture, through which the goodness power and authority of the State is made manifest. He proposes an ethical architecture, at least in terms of the dominant ethos of his time.

Fifteen hundred years later, Alberti takes up this same theme: the well-being of society through architecture. In his Prologue to *On The Art of Building in Ten Books*, he says:

> Some have said that it was fire and water which were initially responsible for bringing men together into communities, but we, considering how useful, even indispensable, a roof and walls are for men, are convinced that it was they that drew and kept men together. We are indebted to the architect not only for providing that safe and welcome refuge from the heat of the sun and the frosts of winter (that of itself is no small benefit), but also for his many other innovations, useful both to individuals and the public, which time and time again have so happily satisfied daily needs.[10]

After listing various contributions, he begins his summation,

> To conclude, let it be said that the security, dignity, and honor of the republic depend greatly upon the architect: it is he who is responsible for our delight, entertainment, and health while at leisure, and our profit and advantage while at work, and in short, that we live in a dignified manner, free from any danger.[11]

Alberti links individual, communal, and societal well-being to the architect's works.

The first reference in English to the "fine art" of architecture cited by the *OED* is from John Ruskin's *The Seven Lamps of Architecture*:

> Architecture is the art which so disposes and adorns the edifices raised by man... that the sight of them contributes to his mental health, power and pleasure.

These writings address architecture's ethical potential. Assertions of the beneficial impacts of architecture are ingrained in its discourse.

This is a clear expression of architecture's "benefits" to humanity, its contribution to human flourishing, which perhaps could only be interpreted as ethical at its core. This is rooted in the Greek concept of *eudaimonia*. *Eudaimonia*, often loosely translated as "happiness" and unfortunately often equated with "pleasure," carries with it significant demands for the improvement of the mind in many areas of thought, experience, and reflection in order to be a fully realized person, to flourish as a moral being. Knowledge and experience of art and beauty are a part of both well-being and moral being.

Writing in 1965, Christian Norberg-Schulz notes:

> Any closer scrutiny of the last hundred years, however, shows that the new architecture is not a result of the wish for *l'Art pour l'Art*, but has sprung from the strivings of idealistic individuals to make man's environment *better*.[12]

Norberg-Schulz's observation stands in a continuous line of thought that begins with Vitruvius and proceeds through the Modern movement and its post-Modern critique. That line of thought is: that architecture is beneficial to society, and that it can be a vehicle for critical examination and resolution of societal concerns. The arguments on behalf of architecture's social contribution, its power to address society's aspirations for itself, and its potential to affect social conditions with beneficial result continue to the present.

Alberto Pérez-Gómez, Thomas A. Dutton, and Lian Hurst Mann present 1990's perspectives on the theme of architecture's ethical role. In his introduction to *Architecture Ethics and Technology*, Pérez-Gómez observes:

> ...I would argue that the common good has always been a primary concern in architecture.... Because of their irrepressible desire to disclose a symbolic order, architects have traditionally sought to provide individual existence with a built world that reflects the purpose of social institutions and of life in general.... Far from being merely an aesthetic or technical concern, architecture seeks to set human action within an "appropriate" frame, fulfilling this reconciliatory role despite man's tendency to control and dominate fellow human beings and the environment.[13]

In their introductory essay to *Reconstructing Architecture*, Dutton and Mann remark:

> Given that architecture — practice and discourse — is always social, the central questions we address in this book are these: What constitutes "the social project" of architecture in the current historical context? What critical discourses and social practices advance such a project? Can architecture be reconstituted in terms of a new social project?... The social project adopted by the modern movement in architecture pledged generations of architects to the betterment of society. As a particular form of modernity's program of social progress, this social project had a distinct character: it broke with architecture's traditional service to the status quo and committed architectural practice to the emancipation of humankind.... Within the array of responses to the crises of modernity, and to the undisputed failures within modernism in architecture in particular, reside [post-Modern and critical] practices that specifically seek to change the political status quo of power relations in daily life.[14] (Material in brackets is added for clarification.)

In *Building Community*, the Carnegie Foundation study of the status of architectural education and practice commissioned by American architectural organizations (1996), similar perspectives are presented by the non-architect researchers and authors of this report, Ernest Boyer and Lee Mitgang:

> The nobility of architecture has always rested on the idea that it is *a social art* — whose purposes include yet transcend, the building of buildings. Architects, in short, are engaged in designing the physical features and social spaces of our daily lives, which can shape how productive, healthy, and happy we are both individually and collectively.... We found, in short, a powerful wellspring of social idealism among architecture students, practitioners and educators.... we propose four specific priorities

where the efforts of the profession might be creatively chan-
neled to enrich the mission: building to beautify; *building for
human needs; building for urban spaces; and preserving the planet.*[15]
(Original authors' italics.)

Another recent manifestation of ethical intent through design
comes from the Congress for the New Urbanism, a group composed of architects, planners, landscape architects, urban designers, and other urbanists who propose, among other concepts, a
neo-traditional approach to community planning based upon
American small-town spatial patterns, mixed uses, medium density, and pedestrian-circulation patterns in balance with those of
automobiles and public transit. Its *Charter* states, "We recognize
that physical solutions by themselves will not solve social and
economic problems, but neither can economic vitality, community stability, and environmental health be sustained without a
coherent and supportive framework."[16] The *Charter* goes on to
discuss design standards for the city, neighborhoods, blocks,
streets, and buildings — all within the province of architecture
and related environmental-design disciplines — shaping them to
be that "coherent and supportive framework." The Congress for
the New Urbanism is explicit in its conception of the social benefits of certain design approaches.

The preceding writings address architecture's ethical potential. Assertions of the beneficial impacts of architecture are
ingrained in its discourse. Architecture students, interns, and
practitioners are acculturated into this domain — architecture's
essentially ethical premises.

Specific working methods, styles of invented form and image,
links between form and aesthetics and inhabitation meaning and
memory, and the technological and material realization of architecture are not identified in these ethical premises. These internal
disciplinary concerns are the means by which architecture
attempts to address its ethical premises.

The ethical content of architecture is professed from within
architectural discourse in other ways. Vitruvius provides us with
three design imperatives of what architecture *ought to provide:
durability, convenience, and beauty*. Palladio requires that the three
need to be coterminously present in architecture, both private
and public: "That work cannot be called perfect, which should be
useful and not durable, nor durable and not useful, or having both
of these should be without beauty."[17] These go beyond design
imperatives to ethical imperatives. Architectural work that is
lacking in these properties cannot contain virtue,[18] (from the
Greek *areté*, which embodies the concept of excellence of being),

or goodness (from the Greek *agathos*, which defines goodness in terms of how well a person, practice, or thing fulfills the objects of its expected content and roles: a military general must be "general like"; a building must possess the best attributes of "building-ness"). Considered this way, architecture lacking these qualities, lacking these virtues, is not merely faulty design, but an unethical practice.

Today there are many other calls for an ethical architecture:

- "The public architecture of a democracy *ought* to be accessible to the disabled."
- "Architecture *ought* to be designed in a manner consistent with sustainable environmental practices."
- "Context *ought* to inform architecture."
- "We *ought* to save the revered architecture of our past, to reuse it, to reinvigorate it."
- "Architecture has a revealing function with respect to the societal *status quo*, and *ought* to critique it."

These *oughts* are presented, for example, in building codes, preservation-society mission statements, pronouncements of the avant-garde, and the Americans with Disabilities Act, as ethical duties. Other designers and institutional entities are involved with defining and meeting these duties, e.g., code officials, interior designers, consulting engineers, and landscape architects, but architects retain a central role and obligation because of their comprehensive impact on environmental possibilities and order through design.

Architecture's ethics, rarely discussed by name, are most often presented within other guises: architectural discourse on aesthetics or design ideology; or social criticism and reform; or politics and architectural choices and forms. However, there is a body of commentary regarding the ethical implications of architectural processes and production that is intuitively sensed but not explicitly defined and discussed in the terminology and reasoning of ethics.

For example, of 126 articles in the most recent six volumes (v47–v52, 9/93–6/99) in the *Journal of Architectural Education* (*JAE*), while none included ethics, ethical, moral, or good, etc., in its title, and while none were cross-referenced in the *Avery Index* under several permutations of "ethics," and only one included the word *duty* in its title, more than 25% of the articles addressed themes that have ethical underpinnings: multiculturalism and gender; the form, accessibility, and openness of public space; architecture and cultural identity; and architecture and economic power and consumption.

> Architecture's ethics, rarely discussed by name, are most often presented within other guises: architectural discourse on aesthetics or design ideology; or social criticism and reform; or politics and architectural choices and forms.

Of fifty-five Association of Collegiate Schools of Architecture (ACSA) conferences during the period 9/93–6/98, none of which uses "ethics" in its title, among the many with ethical themes were: Building Community; Building As A Political Act; Politics Practice And Education; Political Change And Physical Change; and Sustainability. Recent books that have chapters on architectural ethics, such as *Reflections on Architectural Practices in the Nineties* (1996), and books that substantially focus on ethical issues, like *Reconstructing Architecture: Critical Discourses and Social Practices* (1996), are not entered in bibliographic references as related to architectural ethics.[19] Dana Cuff's *Architecture: The Story of Practice* (1991), arguably the most referenced professional practice text in architecture schools, contains just two index references to ethics. At one location, a single sentence indicates: "In 1909 a code of ethics was adopted," by the profession; the other quotes a 1977 paper that indicates that the ethics of individual architects have been taken over by the ethics of architectural firms, and architectural professional ethics had become more like general business ethics.[20]

Ethical frameworks and underlying ethics concepts have to be teased out of the *JAE* articles and ACSA themes, and searched for under-cover of other topics, in order to be given form. In doing so, it can be seen that architecture is indeed an inherently ethical act.

AN ARCHITECTURAL EXAMPLE AND ETHICAL CONTENT

Architecture and architectural practices are interwoven with ethical content. We say this rather than saying that architecture and its practices include ethical obligations because it is difficult to separate architectural practices from the ethical content that is intrinsic to them. Project purposes, client objectives, the degree to which a design proposal meets the various expectations people have for a project, the relationships among those participating in the project, and the qualities of architectural concepts including their aesthetics are all ethical concerns. The following example presents some additional aspects of the ethical content of architectural practices.

An Architectural Example

At some point, an architect may be sitting at a table at a client meeting, trying to work through an environmental-design problem: a change in the landscape, a building, "the project." To be called an "architect" entails a plain and simple presumption: that the person so-named or granted the title and authority is specially informed with respect to the impact and requirements of design of the environment and architecture. This, in turn, entails a duty on the part of the architect toward the other participants in the design-and-construction enterprise to, in fact, be so informed. The following are two types of project situations for which the architect may be an advisor and provide services:

The project may be a school — in which case it is a public community institution that will be built with public money, and largely used and inhabited by third-party persons outside the group at the table. It will be a place where a community will be socially constructed through the socializing activity "education," and where a community will literally be constructed physically in the institution/image/place "the school." The meeting referenced above begins a process during which the project leadership group will be expected to serve the foremost interests of the community. It may also lead to some type of participatory communal process during design and even during construction if capital funds are limited.	A PUBLIC SCHOOL

Alternately, the project may be a for-profit private commercial development. Roads and infrastructure may need to be extended for the project (largely, if not completely, subsidized by public investment) to twenty-five acres of previously undeveloped land. The financial return for the public will be increased future business and property taxes that will pay off the initial public investment and then lead to "profit," for not only the developers, but also the public coffers. A zoning change may be required but, in order to avoid unnecessary public controversy, it is proposed among the team members at the meeting that the zone-change requirement should not be disclosed in the case of this development until more of the project is firmed up. The envisioned project is intended to become a suburban-neighborhood commercial center to which people will drive. It will need to be designed in an accessible, captivating way for third parties: shop owners, entrepreneurs, and customers. This, too, is community construction and image-making. It is a place of community social construction through its creation of merchandising jobs, the manufacturing of items to be sold, and the furthering of economic exchange in a free-market economy.	A PRIVATE COMMERCIAL DEVELOPMENT

These projects raise a number of ethical questions:

- Is a school a more "socially responsible" project in its program objectives than a commercial development?
- Is it "environmentally responsible" to leave a perfectly good underutilized infrastructure behind to expand at the fringes of cities?
- What sorts of issues are raised with respect to ecological change and sustainable community-building practices by the two projects?
- Should public facilities, such as the school, be accessible to all persons as a matter of right? Should commercial private developments also be accessible?
- In the flow of images and icons of culture, media, and packaging, is each of these two building projects a sign or symbol for something else? If so, what would that be?
- In a world of discriminating judgments, what would constitute a "good" school design or a "good" commercial-development design? How would you judge it?
- As the architect, what values would you apply in designing and judging the design? How would you represent it to the community?
- Does the general public have a right to know about possible pending zoning changes and infrastructure expansion before the commercial project is firmed up? Why?

A few other architectural project examples that deal with social values and their inherent ethical considerations are: providing housing for a specific group (elderly, homeless, AIDS victims, etc.) as a commodity/community service; serving the authority of the state through the design of defense facilities; serving community protection and supporting concepts of punishment and rehabilitation through the design of justice facilities; assisting with tradition building through designing memorials and monuments; and contributing to technological advancement through the design of high-technology facilities, such as genetic-research laboratories or computer-science centers.

Almost every architectural enterprise raises some type of ethical issues. **Ethical concerns are intrinsic to the processes of considering who the clients and users of a project are, how well clients and users are served, how public and private interests are balanced and responded to, how the combination of liberal democracy and capitalism (or other political/economic systems) affect the project, who participates in design activities and decisions, the benefits to the** community, the development of designs and their forms, and the construction process.

Ethical Content

This review of ethical content inherent in project types and practice circumstances is meant not to judge the merits of the ventures listed here or the choices that need to be made, but to reveal the depth of the ethical underpinnings of architecture. Participation in the enterprise of architecture is fraught with ethical choices, including the intent underlying giving form. By making decisions and taking specific personal and professional actions, through which the difficult choices in the processes of design and construction are confronted and resolved, we recognize how ethics is implicitly embedded in architectural practices. It is now possible to see why and how the disciplinary apparatuses and language of architecture and ethics have become as distinctive and complex as they are; why each has attempted to understand its own nature at both the theoretical and the practical levels; and why we need to think of all design decisions with respect to the built environment as ethical decisions.

All four of the key ethical theories mentioned earlier on page 28 are brought into play in the presentation and discussion of the case:

1) The balancing of the *relative merits benefits and costs* associated with how well a project serves community purposes stem from *consequentialist* Utility theory.

2) Duties that professionals are *obliged to perform on principle* because of their expertise and obligations to public welfare stem from the concepts of *deontics*.

3) *Meeting the standards* of the profession or those generally understood to hold for "good" buildings stem from *virtue ethics*.

4) The *agreement* to fund either public or private projects with public money with the objective of meeting both individual and communal concerns flows from *social-contract* ideas.

ARCHITECTURE'S ETHICAL CONTENT AND SUPPORTING THEORIES

The virtue of a building in the ethical sense has to do, to some degree, with how well in its conception and construction it meets or exceeds the specific expectations for it, or how well it meets the abstract ideal criteria, such as those of the Vitruvian triad. The expectations may be limited to those of the owner, architect, and contractor (as might be the case in a private residence), or they may include the general community (as in the case with the design of a new public building, or a private residence that has a strong contrasting visual impact in an established neighborhood).

The virtue of an architect in that same sense has to do with the architect's keeping current in the expected knowledge and skills with respect to practicing architecture, or, on a minimal level, the fulfillment of the obligations of the licensing law. Even without contracts or projects, an architect, by virtue of the competency and skills possessed and the state-issued license, has special ethical responsibilities with respect to, e.g., offering advice regarding design construction and public safety, or participating on community boards and committees that call for exercising professional knowledge and judgment.

With the completion of this introduction to architecture's ethical nature, we now take a more in-depth look at ethical concepts and their constructs so we can develop a better understanding of the underpinnings of ethical choices.

A MORE IN-DEPTH LOOK AT ETHICAL CONCEPTS

INTRODUCTION

When one first begins to consider the field of ethics, it becomes apparent that a multiplicity of perspectives exist that seem to be irreconcilable, and to some degree they are. One is then prompted to ask: if there are so many perspectives, isn't this all academic, rather than applicable to real-life questions? But the various perspectives include two things: concern for Socrates's initial question of how we ought to go about life, and reasoned approaches to the consideration of how to think through this question. What emerges is a sense that important supports for ethical action can be drawn upon from several different theories, which seem to be more or less appropriate in varying circumstances. This is not to say that values and choices are up for grabs willy-nilly, but that aspects of several theories may help us reason through the various complex questions we face.

FOUR PRINCIPAL ETHICAL THEORIES

Whatever one's view of everyday reality or philosophical reflections upon it, sooner or later we are faced with choices that we recognize as *ethical:* choices regarding the primary questions of what is good, right, and just. We noted on page 28 that there are perhaps four broadly encompassing principal ethical theories to which other perspectives refer or within which they are subsumed. The four major approaches to ethical reasoning that we re-present here in greater depth are:

1) Consequences from actions and the evaluation of resultant benefits through utility theory *(teleology);*
2) Actions based upon moral rules or principles of duty *(deontology);*
3) The manner in which we do things and the quality of the things that are made *(virtue);*
4) Agreements about how to co-exist, to pursue common and personal goods, with the least amount of restriction *(contract).*

In the discussion of them, we hope to show how they are relevant not only to everyday life, but also to the central focus of our work here: architectural practices. Architectural examples are used to explain the ethical concepts. Our overview is very condensed and limited. Further study is recommended for a more complete understanding of the concepts we discuss. Useful introductions to key ethical concepts and thinkers who have addressed ethics are identified in the notes.[1]

1) ACTION BASED UPON CONSEQUENCES: TELEOLOGY AND UTILITY

Teleological ethics deals with ends, and the means or actions undertaken to obtain them—ends, or net positive consequences, being the moral objects of the good, happiness, and human flourishing, etc. Utilitarianism and its approach to identifying and calculating the maximized benefit for the greatest number of persons affected in a given situation as the basis for moral action constitutes the prime example of a teleological ethics. Utility theory is the underlying premise to the cost/benefit standards often applied in urban planning and public policy. Working toward "happiness" as a desired end is traced to Greek thought. For a corrupt mode of good ends justifying almost any means to accomplish them, there is Niccolò Machiavelli. Utility theory, which bases ethical decisions on the net benefits stemming from a course of action arises in the work of Jeremy Bentham and John Stuart Mill.

Imagine a society in which the elders, observing the beneficial good lives they experience—ample amounts of food and

> Aspects of several theories may help us reason through the various complex ethical questions we face.

clothing for everyone, orderliness in public affairs, security with respect to outside threats, and such enlightening and enjoyable leisure pursuits as the theater and sport — trace the foundations for their good lives to good health, good education, and a productive work ethic. The elders have discovered that healthy people, well informed about practical and inventive knowledge and energized by diligent work habits, lead productive lives that, in turn, lead to this good collective life.[2] The loss of their good lives as a result of decadence and the failure to keep up the good practices would be, in fact, disastrous.

Weighing the benefits of their good life versus the costs of the work effort required to protect their life quality, the elders decree that all parenting *ought to* inculcate good habits of health, including eating nutritious diets and holding daily regimens of exercise; *ought to* foster learning and acquisition of knowledge and skills, and *ought to* demand the development of positive work habits. This good state of affairs is rooted in the Greek concept of *eudaimonia*. The happiness of *eudaimonia* is not that of joy or giddiness; it relates to a sense of overall human well-being and accomplishment. Good ends and the good practices necessary to achieve them are linked in this teleological ethics.

Contrasting with this Greek ideal, in *The Prince* (1517), Niccolò Machiavelli clearly articulates the concept of the ends (the good ends of a stable, orderly society) justifying the means (even lying or ruthlessness toward enemies, for instance). The adjective "corrupt" is used here because patently "evil" actions of one scope are utilized to justify reaching a positive end of some other scope. For example, his Chapter 8 is titled: "Of those who have attained the position of Prince by Villainy." Machiavelli's is a dark path to goodness!

The modern conception of Utilitarianism was first fully developed by Jeremy Bentham in *Introduction to the Principles of Morals and Legislation* (1789). His work was critiqued and modified by John Stuart Mill in *Utilitarianism* (1863). The two treatises combined with earlier Greek ethical theories pertaining to the pursuit of human happiness or flourishing as the desired consequences of human activity, *eudaimonia*, have formed one of the cornerstones of contemporary ethical reasoning and debate. Utility theory is implicitly used whenever we devise some method to calculate and maximize the benefits versus the risks and costs of a course of action — the greatest amount of good individually and collectively as formulated by Bentham in Chapter 1 of his Introduction — in order to guide our ethical choices.

Building upon this concept, Bentham and Mill proposed that it was, in fact, the objective of individuals and society not only to arrive at good ends, but to *maximize* such well-being. Who would make a case for pain over happiness, or evil over goodness? This well-being is called "happiness" or "the good" toward which we strive. Thus, a course of action could be evaluated in terms of who is benefited and how much, compared to who is not benefited and how much. Bentham proposed a calculus for measuring "good." Mill refined types of goodness and lacks of goodness, and added demands for fair consideration of women and for general goodwill as the basis for Utilitarianism. Many debates surround Utilitarianism and its critical flaws; one is that it could be used to justify slavery on the basis that a few slaves could make life easier for the many. However, often extreme cases are used, and the root sense that good objects should be pursued with good intentions has stayed with us as suasive argument for Utility theory. *Act* Utilitarians focus on the aggregate actions undertaken to arrive at good consequences. *Rule* Utilitarians additionally require a few rules, such as treating all persons as equals, or providing all persons personal security, etc.

How does *Utility theory* come to bear on architecture?

The following scenario may help in understanding Utility theory and its relationship to architecture:

An architect has been selected to design a new school. The district has outgrown its existing high-school facility — not only because of the growing number of students, but also because of the changing education standards that now require computers and better science laboratories, as well as equivalent sports facilities for both boys and girls. The facility is located in an older area of the city that is becoming more remote from a greater ratio of the present-day students. The feeling is nearly unanimous in the community that a new school needs to be built. The members of the community have purchased a site upon which to build it, and have even pre-approved a tax levy to pay for it. The common belief is that a new school would be a great benefit to the children and the community itself. A new superintendent of schools has been hired and, before forging ahead with the new school, has asked the architect to double-check the option of renovating the existing school. This benefit, whether a new building is constructed or the existing one is renovated and expanded, is an ethical one — a long term positive end affecting the whole community.	**SCHOOL DISTRICT CASE: UTILITY THEORY**

(continued on next page)

Awareness **51**

(continued from preceding page)

The architect evaluates the existing school and its site as requested, and makes a judgment that renovating and expanding the
existing school is a viable option — at about 75% of the cost of a
new facility. The architect proposes both schemes to the school
board. The degree to which each option meets the long-term
desires of the community, the capacities of the schemes for
growth, the capacity of each to satisfy new pedagogical demands,
etc., is identified. Construction and equipment costs for the two
schemes, including the already expended money for the new site,
are evaluated. In other words, in his/her professional role the architect completes a benefits/cost analysis (a Utilitarian-ethics-based
analysis) on behalf of the community with respect to the alternative architectural designs. The quality and aesthetic character of
design, the durability of the facility, the contribution to the existing
neighborhood, and the enhancements to community image are all
embraced in the work.

If you were the architect, which course of action would you recommend, and why? What standards would the community use to
make the choice? Is it initial cost? Is it long-term-operations cost?
Is a new school "better" at fostering a progressive image regarding education? What is the "benefit value" of a progressive
image? Is there a cost associated with demolishing the old school
and discarding it? What if the old school could be converted to an
elderly-care center after the new school opened at another location? There is a potency in Utility theory for addressing communal actions precisely because it helps us keep track of, and sort,
ethical options and their risks and benefits, including those
embedded in architectural proposals.

Decision outcomes would be affected substantially if, for
instance, rather than having the unanimity noted in the original
case, the community was split between older persons on fixed
incomes who want to minimize costs and new families with growing incomes who believe they have the capacity to bear increased
school taxes. The vote to fund a school and to buy the land might
have been deferred until the alternative concepts were presented.
There may even be an option to do nothing with the facility and
to bus some of the students to nearby districts for certain activities. The architect in these types of project situations usually
remains in the picture, proposing design alternatives and making
presentations at public meetings. Is Utility theory still helpful in

making architectural recommendations in this case where conflicting desires exist among community decision-makers?

Utility theory is used to evaluate many environmental-design projects and programs. For example, Utility theory strategies may be applied to:

- Historic-preservation options (whether to save or demolish, or to apply demanding renovation standards to historic properties);
- Increases and decreases in land value as the result of architectural projects (for instance, would land values go up or down if a halfway house for paroles was built in a certain neighborhood?);
- Evaluation of the degree of safety in structures and fire suppression (to establish safety-factor multipliers or impose fire-resistsant standards on building construction);
- Assessment of the costs and benefits with respect to public subsidies to private architectural projects, such as stadiums or commercial developments (evaluating the long-term benefit to a community compared to the costs and disruption caused by the relocation of some existing homes or businesses, or which asks that the government exercise its power of eminent domain to acquire property for the greater good, or to provide direct monetary support, etc.).

Utility theory also gains its ethical force in architecture from the historic position that function and human purpose are among the foundational attributes of architecture. Literally, "utility" is a standard for judging architecture.

2) ACTING FROM MORAL RULES OR PRINCIPLES: DEONTOLOGY

Have you ever heard someone say: "Well, you know, we did "X" because it was the right thing to do."? Or, "You really should't lie, cheat, and steal because they're wrong."? When we invoke such concepts as "right" and "wrong" in an absolute sense and require that action be carried out in terms of the invoked duty, as we often do, we are appealing to abstract moral rules or principles to guide behavior. However we arrive at our own guiding principles—through reason, religion, or intuition, for example—in this deontic ethical model, moral rules or principles are conceived to be universal and necessarily apply to all situations. We will use a Biblical example to explain the idea, then move to Immanuel Kant's formulation of the categorical imperative, and then on to a contemporary architectural example.

The fifth of the Ten Commandments of the Old Testament is "Thou Shalt Not Kill." While this is a received God-given rule for those who believe in the Judeo-Christian God and who believe that life is sacred, religious and secular societies the world over have adopted a similar principle as a guide to everyday life. Sometimes the prohibition is literal and complete: Thou shalt not kill another human being—period. Others interpret the meaning with various caveats: with the exception of punishing people for heinous crimes (the concept of the death penalty being a "just desert" (an appropriate punishment) in such cases being the justification for modifying the strict prohibition against killing); or with the exception of killing enemies who are attempting to kill you (killing in self-defense is usually seen as an exception to the general rule against killing); or with the exception of letting the dying die, etc. This particular principle and its various interpretations are being aggressively contested legislatively and legally in the U.S. today on at least three highly volatile fronts: capital punishment, abortion, and euthanasia.

We are not going to enter into those particular debates. They serve to illustrate that acting according to principles has direct application in everyday life. The source of the principles and motives for invoking them are powerful reasons supporting moral action. The key is, how do we go about considering ethical duties based upon rules or principles?

Immanuel Kant attempted to formulate arguments regarding the underlying order of acting in a moral manner according to reasoned principles. In his *Grounding for the Metaphysics of Morals* of 1785,[3] Kant proposed two principal formulations of moral imperatives: 1) categorical imperatives that are obligatory duties binding upon all persons; and 2) hypothetical imperatives that are voluntary choices regarding ethical conduct of prudence and skill, and of necessary or contingent meritorious duties to self and others. He provided instructive examples and tests of each. In the ensuing 200 years, philosophers and ethicists have critiqued and attempted to disprove, modify, or support Kant's thought. It remains today one of the most clearly articulated positions of ethical action based upon moral principles.

Two of Kant's formulations of the *categorical imperative* will serve us here. In one he proposed that we should "Act in such a way that you treat humanity, whether in your own person or in the person of another, always at the same time as an end and never simply as a means."[4] By this he means that all humans are equal; that no human has the right to utilize another human to forward his own ends, or to transgress the freedom of another. For example, slavery treats some humans as inferior and as chattel possessions, not as fully equal persons. Therefore, slavery is unethical—period. A second formulation is to "Act only according to that maxim whereby you can at the same time will that it should become a universal law."[5] In other words, actions that are logically inconsistent and that undermine their own premises are unethical. Kant supplies us with four examples to test his ethical imperatives: the suicide, the lying promise, the neglect of the cultivation of personal gifts, and benevolence toward others from duty.

We are not going to review all of the arguments, but will use a familiar concept: the "white" lie. Often, we consider fabricating a white lie in order to protect someone else. This is an ethical dilemma often faced in the medical profession when a choice needs to be made about whether or not to tell the truth about a terminal illness to a patient. The rationale that creates the dilemma is that the patient may go into a depression or may die even more swiftly, etc. However, presuming the patient has his or her faculties, this disavows the patient full independent standing as an *end*, and denies the patient the right of self-determination and choice with how to live the remainder of life. It also presumes that the patient will not find great relief or even joy in the truth regarding his or her condition. Moreover, if we all told white lies, even with good intentions, pretty soon no one would be able to trust the representations made by others on matters of import, undercutting the premise for telling a protective lie. Without that trust, social discourse would fail. The "white" lie fails with regard to both formulations of the categorical imperative as defined by Kant. For many of those who have debated the topic, lying or concealment even for protective purposes presents a difficult moral case in both private and public matters.[6]

> When we invoke such concepts as "right" and "wrong" in an absolute sense and require that action be carried out in terms of the invoked duty, as we often do, we are appealing to abstract moral rules or principles to guide behavior—*deontics*.

As with teleological Utility theory, we are now faced with the question, "How do the standards of *ethical duties* like these that are *based upon principle* apply to architecture?"

Another scenario may be of use in understanding deontic theory:

You have been selected to design the headquarters for a publicly owned electric-utility company. You have designed a building that the client representatives, none of whom is an architect or engineer, like very much and are prepared to fund and build. Your fee, outlined in approved AIA documents, is based upon a percentage of the construction costs. The building exterior could have been built with a number of different enclosure systems that would not have affected the building appearance or performance, but you specified the most expensive system. Because the client had the funds, you did not disclose that alternative building-exterior systems that would have looked and performed similarly would reduce the building cost (and your fee) by 10%.

Was it ethical, based upon principle, to conceal the lower-cost alternative? What is the reason for your answer? Did the client's ability to afford the project affect your decision? Do you think there is a moral imperative regarding disclosure of a conflict of interest? Do you think you are called upon to exhibit a higher standard of cost control than usual since your fees fluctuate with construction costs? Would your answer change if the company were a private business corporation like Exxon Oil rather than a public utility? What if the client were a not-for-profit community organization that was building a hospice or affordable housing for the poor? Does the status of the client figure into the ethical choice about disclosure of costs and lower-cost alternatives? Does the status of the architect as a professional who possesses specialized knowledge figure into this? Whatever your positions, why do you think so?

Architects are professionals, and they may be governed by ethical duties that are stricter than those of ordinary businesses. Clients are presumed to not have sufficient expertise to know certain things about design and construction (otherwise they would be architects), and the architect is supposed to act for the client's benefit and interests. (These issues will be discussed more completely on page 71.) Disclosure of conflicts of interest—even if clients have the resources to cover costs—is one of the most important ethical duties for professionals and is built into most architectural-licensing laws. This concept of acting from professional duty is an example of deontologically based ethical action in architecture.

3) VIRTUE: EXCELLENCE

Architecture is filled with judgments. We see a building and call it "good," or we refer to an architect and say that he or she is a "good" architect. When asked to justify our judgments, we are not necessarily factually exacting, but we refer to the qualities of a good building: it serves its function well; it is beautiful by some standard; it seems to weather well; it looks like what a—e.g., "church" or some other type of building—is supposed to; it has stood the test of time; it has great spaces and is well detailed; and/or it is well sited, etc. Of the architect, we say that he or she is talented, has a firm grasp of construction technology, is astute in dealing with clients, is a leader in the community on environmental issues, or has a profound mastery of history and theory and brings them to bear in his or her work, etc.

The criteria that we are invoking and extolling in making such judgments are the virtues of that particular building and by extension, buildings more generally. And similarly, the virtues of that particular architect and by extension, architects generally. Each judgment is based upon an expectation of certain qualities being met. The consideration of the excellence of the new building or architect slightly redefines the virtues of a good architect and good architecture. Things (buildings) and persons (architects), as well as processes (the practices of architecture) have the capacity to possess virtues of excellence. We again return to

Things (buildings) and persons (architects), as well as processes (the practices of architecture) have the capacity to possess virtues of excellence in the ethical sense.

Greece, this time to Aristotle.[7] Aristotle's *Nicomachean Ethics* is wide ranging and covers personal virtues, as well as the virtues of various practices, including those of science and *techné:* craft/art production.

Virtue theory, like Utility theory, is an ethics based upon actions—in this case, working toward personal excellence and excellence in the mastery of practices *per se*, rather than basing the value of an action upon its contributions to a future communal beneficial end. Virtue ethics is rooted in the Greek ethics of *eudaimonia*, in this sense incorporating personal excellence and well-being. This is the second use of *eudaimonism*. In Utility theory, it is used in the sense that happiness is the good that is the desired end of actions undertaken for the common total good. Virtue theory is another type of teleological theory, which addresses personal actions that *de facto* lead to good ends. We separate it from Utility theory as a teleology because it pertains to the excellence of things, persons, and practices in themselves. There is an implicit understanding here that a community of persons each exhibiting positive virtue will give rise to a "good" community; and the converse, that a good community will have articulated the roles, qualities, and expectations of persons, things, and practices by which we could judge their excellence. The process, then, is iterative, with each round of action and evaluation leading to a refinement of the definition of excellence.

When thinking of virtues from a modern perspective, we often think about those pertaining to religious morality, which come to us from St. Thomas Aquinas's building upon Aristotle—combining the Christian virtues of charity, hope, chastity, etc., and the cardinal virtues of classic Greece: temperance, fortitude, courage, and prudence. However, rather than being an example of religious duty, Aristotle conceives the virtues of personal behavior as a mean between excesses and insufficiencies of emotions and actions. Thus, he characterizes courage as a mean state between fear and foolhardy confidence; wit, the mean state between buffoonery and boorishness; high-minded honor, the mean state between vanity and little-mindedness.[8] The conditions surrounding ethical action include volition and free will to act voluntarily as opposed to out of coercion; to be responsible for knowing what should be known and not ignorant of it; to act from motives of good intent as opposed to acting out of passion, desire, wishing, or opinion; and to act with deliberation to achieving excellence.[9] The last twenty-five years have seen a resurgence of interest in the ethics of virtue theory.[10]

The concept of personal virtues is almost directly transferable to the concept of virtue as it applies to the architect that we introduced earlier. Architects, by definition, are expected to master knowledge of architecture, design, and building. They must possess certain skills to exercise that knowledge. Thus, to be a good architect, one possessing virtue, is not merely to possess certain knowledge to meet the factual definition, but to be an exemplar of a possessor and professor of that knowledge. The contemporary legal requirements for continued professional education after university graduation and state licensure may be seen as the demand for assuring the virtue of maintaining currency of knowledge in the discipline. It is an ethical demand rooted in the concepts of personal and professional virtue with regard to expectations of architects in a changing, fast-paced society. One's approach to working at architecture, to improving oneself as an architect, is not only a work ethic; it is an ethical act of virtue of this kind.

Beyond personal and professional virtues, Aristotle and, in recent times, MacIntyre, provide insight into the virtues of things (e.g., buildings) and practices (e.g., of architecture and construction). Both Aristotle and MacIntyre use architecture as their model. In Book VI, 1139b38-1140a24, Aristotle addresses methods of work and discusses *techné:* translated as *craft* (by Irwin), also translated as *art* (by Weldon in Navia). This is a mode of knowledge: using reason to produce intentional things is craft/art knowledge. The two translations are set side by side with Irwin on the left and Weldon on the right to illustrate both the slippage and the consistency of the craft/art-production concept:

Aristotle on Craft/Art Production

Now building, e.g., is a craft, and is essentially a certain state involving reasoned concern with production; there is no craft that is not a state involving reason concerned with production, and no such state that is not a production.... Every craft is concerned with coming to be; and in the exercise of the craft is the study of how something that admits of being and not being, becomes something whose origin is in the producer.... A craft... is a state involving true reason concerned with production.	But as architecture, e.g., is an art, and as it may be defined to be a rationally productive state of mind, and there is no art which is not a rationally productive state of mind, nor any such state of mind which is not an art.... All art has to do with creation, i.e., it has to contrive and consider how to create some one or other of things whose existence is contingent rather than necessary, and whose original sources lies in the producer.... Art then... is a certain productive state of mind under the guidance of true reason.

Buildings (architecture) are things or objects of *craft/art* that are brought into existence by *producers*, those who design and create them (architects and craftspersons). They serve human purposes and are inventions of the mind. They come into being as the result of craft supported by reason. The virtue of an architecture, or of building then, lies both in the virtue of the productive process from which it was created (a thoughtless method or action may yield an object, but it does not yield architecture), and the nature of the thing so made to the degree that it fulfills expectations.

Building on this, MacIntyre traces concepts of virtue from the Heroic Age of Greece, through Aristotle and the Stoics, to Aquinas and Medieval ethics, to Benjamin Franklin and Nietzsche. He characterizes virtue as stemming from practices (which we address below), the narrative order of a single human life (a unity within which virtuous character can be perceived), and moral tradition (individual actions taking place in a context of continuing moral tradition or ethos: one learns about drawing and studies architectural history within the enduring tradition of becoming an architect). Virtue is an active work in process in a context. As MacIntyre puts it regarding practices, again using architecture as a model:

> By a "practice" I am going to mean any coherent and complex form of socially established cooperative human activity [creating inhabitable places] through which goods internal to that form of activity [the built environment] are realized in the course of trying to achieve those standards of excellence which are appropriate to, and partially definitive, of that activity [e.g., Vitruvius's standards of utility, durability, and delight, or those of Modernism], with the result that human powers to achieve excellence, and human conceptions of the ends and goods involved are systematically extended.... Bricklaying is not a practice; architecture is.[11] (Material in brackets is added to illustrate architectural examples of each concept leading to his conclusion.)

We began this discussion with two common-sense everyday observations that we often hear in architecture: "That is a *good* building" and "He/She is a *good* architect." Both statements are value judgments regarding the virtue of each as an exemplar of excellent buildings or architects. Neither the building nor the architect could have become so without the virtue of excellent productive practices: the building having become so by the reasoned production practices that gave rise to it, and the architect intentionally, deliberately making himself or herself so by the virtues of practices. *Architecture* and *architects* then, as portrayed in this view, possess the ethical dimensions of virtue. They possess degrees of excellence that can be perceived and judged given the social and professional contexts within which qualitative expectations of them are defined, and because they are the results of teleological practices applied to working toward achieving those qualities.

The ethical merits of architectural practices in this view can be judged on *virtue*, rather than on the basis of utility and the measurement of benefit, or on the basis of obligations and duty from principle. For a building to function well or to be beautiful, or for an architect to be skilled at design, to honor contracts, and to know about construction, the judgment about "goodness" (virtue), is made with respect to the excellence of those practices or qualities and the conditions that pertain to the meritorious pursuit of those practices—the application of reason, volition, and mastery of pertinent knowledge, motivated toward mastery or excellence.

Frank O. Gehry, AIA Gold Medal Winner, 1999 (*Source:* American Architectural Foundation)

4) CONTRACT THEORY

The practices of architecture are filled with relationships between architects and their clients, contractors, manufacturers, and the general public, etc. Some of those relationships are structured through contracts, such as the relationship between the client and the architect. Sometimes the terms of one contract affect the relationship with third parties—e.g., the client/architect agreement addresses responsibilities that affect the contractor. But for many other persons or groups, even though their lives may be substantially affected by an architectural project, there is no written rule or contract. Many of these relationships are affected by financial impacts (e.g., the cost of public improvements that may be borne by taxpayers; a change in property values raises taxes as a result of a new project in the vicinity); others by significant changes to life quality (e.g., relocation of homes to make way for a project; busier but perhaps less safe streets as a result of increased commercial activity; better educational facilities as the result of building a new school). Are any of these relationships and impacts ethical ones? If so, how do we address them?

The fourth principal ethical tradition we present may be of help in these types of architectural situations. It is rooted in individualism, libertarianism, and agreement—the social contract among equals. The underlying principle is the autonomy of individual persons (or groups of persons), their entitlement to certain rights (such as personal security), and their entitlement to pursue their desires, so long as they do not impinge on the rights, pursuits, and desires of others. The communal or political collective establishes sufficient agreement about limitations on certain actions (theft, murder, etc.), and access to certain goods (e.g., food, clothing, education, and work opportunity by which to obtain them) and arrives at sufficient laws or governmental structure to ensure communal stability in order to permit pursuit of the broadest array of the personal ends of the members of the community. The source of moral import lies in fairness and justice. The roots of modern contract theory are in Hobbes, were extended by Rousseau (both of whom primarily addressed the idea of the political state, laws, and methods of governing) and were most recently reinvigorated by John Rawls.[12]

Hobbes, for example, believed that human nature is ego-driven and results in a "war of all against all" as each person acts to obtain the goods of life. He postulated the need for a contract to establish a government strong enough to control this natural state of affairs in order to secure order so that private interests could be pursued (a "morality of mutual advantage"[13]). Rousseau postulated the picture of a more benign human nature that is corrupted by the necessity for living in communal societies that give rise to inequalities. He postulated a social contract based upon democratic principles of voice and voting, etc. Rawls's twentieth-century contribution is in bringing utilitarian and deontic conceptions of the societal good into a contract-decision framework that mediates conflicting status positions and desires. This shifts the focus from power and balance to justice and moral agreement (rooted in a Kantian perspective: "morality as impartiality"[14]).

Much of ethical thought has been concerned with how things *are* (descriptive) and how they morally *ought to be* (normative). For approaching moral questions, various conceptual models have been created to help clarify understanding and resolve the issues at hand. Rawls's *Original Position* is one of these models. As things *are*, decisions regarding the distribution of goods, access to resources, access to the opportunity to acquire social goods, etc., are heavily influenced by the characteristics of stakeholders regarding their accumulated wealth, education, social status, power, health, race, gender, and ethnicity, the dearness of those who may be affected by decisions (spouses, children, friends, or someone halfway around the world), etc. Rawls proposed that in order for ethical decisions to be made regarding the goods that society possesses or seeks, the stakeholders needed to have a different set of characteristics: each would be autonomous and free to act according to conscience; each would be well informed about the situation and able to make proposals; and each would be willing to abide the decision the stakeholders reached. To assure equitable decision-making, they would also be under a "Veil of Ignorance" with respect to their particular advantages and disadvantages or power standing in the community of stakeholders. In that situation, since any one of the stakeholders had an equal chance of being either the most or least advantaged, two principal theorems would come into play in decisions:

1. Each person is to have an equal right to the most extensive total system of equal basic liberties compatible with a system of liberty for all.

2a. Social and economic inequalities are to be arranged so that they are to the greatest benefit of the least advantaged; and 2b. are attached to offices and positions open to all under conditions of fair equality of opportunity.

His proposal combines utilitarian concepts of societal goods, Kantian concepts of autonomy and neutrality, and the social-contract concept of democratically reaching decisions. Since Rawls proposed the concepts of the *Original Position* and the *Veil of Ignorance*, they have been under continuous critique, in a manner similar to the debates surrounding Kant's proposals, or for that matter, almost any particular ethical theory. One difficulty is the impossibility of actually reaching the state of the *Original Position* and the *Veil of Ignorance*. Another is that the *Original Position* and the decision framework it requires seemingly cannot be generalized to large, complex groups that do not agree on basic social values and methods of democratic choice. Nonetheless, contract theory in general (which is the basis for the U.S. Constitution) and Rawls' work in particular have provided a viable alternative to Utilitarianism, deontology, and Virtue theory for reaching just decisions in moral societies.

We present a case here to illustrate how this may work in architecture:[15]

The fourth principal ethical tradition we present is rooted in individualism, libertarianism, and agreement—the social contract among equals.

You are the architect for a private redevelopment project in a city of 190,000 people. It will receive a property-tax abatement and a second public subsidy in the form of inexpensive land that the city will condemn, acquire, and sell to your client at one-quarter of its market value. The details of the design and the public subsidy were developed by the project team and city officials. This seems to be a win/win project: it will mean new jobs; it will revitalize a "rundown" part of the downtown; after ten years, the tax abatement will stop and the city will be repaid for its investment; and the design itself, which has already won "Unbuilt Architecture" and "Urban Design" awards, provides a major facelift for the city. The only problem is that 300 residents and twenty small businesses will have to be bought out and/or relocated — in this case, dispersed to other neighborhoods in the city that are not as close to central services or public transportation. There is money for all of this, and it is legal.

The residents and small businesses have formed an alliance with other neighborhood organizations to oppose the project. Public hearings have been scheduled, and you have been retained to present the scheme at the meetings. A confrontation appears to be brewing, and you will be on the front line.

Are there ethical issues at stake here? In the U.S., is dwelling or having a business in a neighborhood of your choosing a right? Should the rights of the few regarding property and dwelling be weighed against the work and economic opportunities for the many? Do the individual citizens of the neighborhood have the same ethical standing, if not the same power, as the elected city officials who believe the project is in the best interests of the community and have decided to back it?

It is easy to see why Utilitarianism has such force in these types of situations: you just dispassionately add up the numbers of people (300 versus 189,700), identify the costs (of which all the economic ones will be repaid; and the relocated people will have homes and businesses even if they are not the same as the ones they have now), and the total benefits (jobs, increased personal income, more taxes), and be done with it: go ahead with the project. Does Rawls's approach, which also takes into account the status of equality and rights of *all* including the least advantaged, present us with other options?

What would you do? What is your position about the rights of the 300 residents and the twenty businesses? Would you propose starting over with a participatory design process instead of the administrative "closed-door" one pursued up to now? Would you propose modifying the design to accommodate housing and small businesses? Are (or could) architecture and the practices of design process be an avenue for ethical decision-making, reaching agreement in the community, in this situation? Given the outline of the *Veil of Ignorance*, do you think the voice of the few, even if respected, would be suasive? Do you think that unanimity can be reached on such projects as these? How are the rights of the minority protected?

As with several of the other cases, we seem to have moved from architecture to social and public ethical questions that are much larger than the architectural project. And that is exactly the point: architecture is a complex practice that is intrinsically ethical. To design and construct an architectural project is never a neutral event; it requires choices. Buildings are large undertakings: they require public and private financing, natural resources are expended in their construction and in their operation, and by virtue of their being and the practices from which they arise, are communal in their impact. With all of its goodwill, hope and aspirations, and failings, the physical construction of culture embodied in architecture is an ethical enterprise, one that often requires communal agreement. And it requires architects to be ethical beings.

OTHER VIEWS ON ETHICS

The four principal ethical theories that have been presented in depth are those that substantively define classical ethics and to which other ethical perspectives refer for resolution of ethical dilemmas, or within which they are subsumed. A few of these other ethical perspectives merit a brief mention. Among them are:

Religious Morality

This perspective bases morality upon rules given by or received from God, and which are, therefore, immutable. The rules originating in religious morality, regardless of the religion, are often quite positive guides to action and constitute coherent ethical systems. However, the appeal to God based on faith, while valuable to believers, does not lend itself to critical, reasoned reflection and debate with those who do not hold the same religious views. When the believers of alternative religious views and religions come into conflict over an issue, what means do they have for resolving the dispute?

Relativism

Relativism is an ethical perspective that holds that each individual and differing cultures and groups have differing, *equally valid* values that are consistent in their time and place. They are valid for the individuals and community of persons centered around them. Relativism has great appeal in the late twentieth century given the closeness of the global village because it is explicit in engendering respect for difference. However, there are times one system may be in conflict with other persons' values and/or communal systems. The difficulty with relativism is that certain societies may hold certain practices, such as genocide of minorities or enslavement, as valid social customs, while other societies do not. Relativism leaves us at a stalemate with respect to discourse regarding two such systems if they come into conflict, and it precludes external judgment of practices as immoral.[16]

Ethical Egoism

Ethical egoism is a perspective that proposes that humans not only do, but should, act to maximize their self-interest: "I believe this is right for me, so this is what I am going to do." The difficulty with self-interest as the basis for ethical conduct is that it clearly and easily leads to practices that harm others: "I want what you have, therefore, I take it because I am stronger." To not take it is to deny acting according to self-interest; to do so harms others. It may be held that such aggression will be kept in check because rational beings would see that such actions would put their own well-being at risk from a stronger person or group of persons combined against them, and the net result, in fact, would be a civil society with a minimum of restraint on personal pursuit — essentially a Hobbesian contract society. However, an ethics based upon the constraints of avoidance and fear seems unsatisfactory, just as Hobbes's resolution to the problem in his proposal for absolute monarchy does.

Appeals to Religion, Relativism, and Egoism can be shown to lead to non-debatable, polarized circumstances: me versus thee, us versus you, our customs versus your customs. Once persons or communities that hold differing values come into unavoidable contention over an issue, in order to avert physical conflict, war, or submission and subjugation to the more powerful, they must appeal to some system to resolve their conflicting moral objectives. Whether it is discourse and agreements, democratic voting, or utility and convenience, they appeal to an ethical foundation for moral resolution outside their own system. That is why we have first discussed the four main ethical theories through which such contentions are usually resolved.

Two other views we wish to touch upon must be discussed because of their critiques of the main Western ethical tradition (See Part I: Awareness on page 23):

Feminist Ethics

The feminist critique of classical ethics stems from perhaps three standards in particular: a) that ethical formulations have been constructed by men and, therefore, focus on the issues men value in public life regarding politics, property, and justice, etc.; b) that women have been systematically considered less than full ethical participants in those ethics; and c) there are no ethics systems that address the substantive issues of caring, nurturing, and interpersonal relationships, which are a dominant arena of ethical action for women. For instance, the ethics of caring, which is one example among several contemporary feminist alternatives to the public political ethics tradition, is one in which a person's ethical actions are guided by a nurturing and emotive model that stresses relationships over "rules," "principles," or "judgment".

Feminist authors are divided among themselves regarding the primacy of these perspectives, but are united in their conviction that an effective alternative or, minimally, an effective enlargement, of conventional ethics is required. The editors' introduction to *Ethics: A Feminist Reader*, begins:

> Our choice of title for this book expresses an intention to concern ourselves, as feminists, with the whole field of ethical theory. It may therefore be as well to begin by explaining why we announce the book as a *feminist reader on ethics* rather that as a *reader on feminist ethics.* . . .
>
> The general conception of "ethics," or moral philosophy, which has guided our work as editors has been the classical one: ethics

is the theory of the good life (both for individuals and for societies), and it involves the study of value...the normative question of what it is right or appropriate to value....

But to study ethics without paying particular attention to feminism is to be disadvantaged from the outset.[17]

The editors of *Explorations in Feminist Ethics* are more explicit in characterizing the activism and revisionism feminist ethics:

In sum, feminist ethics as currently discussed display the following basic characteristics: they are grounded in a feminist perspective; they seek to challenge, some would say the "masculinist," moral assumptions; they frequently seek to reinterpret moral agency, altruism, and other relevant concepts from a feminist perspective.[18]

Architecture, no less than ethics, is a discipline dominated by men. The terms of history and the march of historical buildings and icons of thought have been designed, built, and scripted almost exclusively by men. Even today, only 10% of the AIA membership is made up of women, while women constitute 30% of architecture students nationally. In the past twenty-five years there has been an expansion of the ratio of women in both the academy and the traditional practice of architecture. This has been accompanied by a feminist critique of the values and methods of architecture, and of the lack of standing of women in the profession. The legitimization of women in practice; corrections to architectural history to include the work of women that has been overlooked if not suppressed; presenting differing collaborative-design models; searching for sources of form in architecture in other models than the Vitruvian one; and inquiry into the gendered structuring of place are parts of that critique. This critique has not developed a substitute alternative definition of architecture; it has broadened the traditional one of buildings and places we design and inhabit, to be more inclusive of the perspectives noted here.[19]

Continental Philosophy

Continental philosophy, while not a unitary philosophical position, shares German and French philosophical and literary roots, and has been critical of the twentieth-century Anglo-American philosophical tradition and its focus on defining normative ethical standards, its analytic meta-ethical debates, and its search for "true" ethical ideals and foundations rather than engagement with social and political action and cultural production.

Continental philosophers of varying perspectives build upon a critique of Kant and the foundations of the Enlightenment's appeal to reason and scientific positive truths to undergird the search for "social truths," in a line through Hegel, Marx, Nietzsche, Freud, Saussure, Heidegger, and Sartre (among others), to Foucault, Derrida, and Lacan (among others). Continental philosophy has looked to linguistics and language, sociological studies, phenomenology and psychoanalytic perspectives to explore: how personal and social reality and meaning are constructed; how such constructed realities are similar or varied from person to person and group to group; and how they form the basis for being in the world and for the assessment of ethical choice. The ethical arguments have not raged around Utilitarianism or deontics and normative definitions of ethical obligations and social contracts, but rather direct teleology—the construction of ethics and culture, by individuals and collectives, through critical thought, discourse, and action—while at the same time debating the provisional contingent character of all such processes and their underlying structures. Architecture, as a social physical construction, as well as other representational media of film, literature, and simulation, figure in this cultural construction.[20]

Despite the arguable validity of their critiques of classical ethics and Anglo-American analytic ethical theory, proponents of both Feminism and Continental thought still face the question: "How do I decide what to do here in this moral dilemma?" To reason through the issues, they may appeal to virtue, to social discourse, or even deontic principles (e.g., all persons have equal standing, freedom, and autonomy, and no person should be subjugated to another, including holders of minority opinion or those who may be minorities on some other basis, such as religious, gender preference, or racial difference). They ultimately rely upon reasoned consideration and the comparison of ethical possibilities.

One thing the diverse philosophical positions agree upon: there are "ethical" things to be done. How to arrive at the "ethical" choice gives rise to this collection of perspectives. The litany of competing and supplanting "ism's" in both ethical and architectural traditions is quite extensive, and is difficult to assess—except by examining the *joint*—the nexus of architecture and ethics, through the action of architectural practices—using that examination as a key to unraveling and revealing the larger encompassing spheres of the two disciplines. This we do below and on page 71.

BUSINESSES, PROFESSIONS, AND ETHICAL OBLIGATIONS

WHAT IS A PROFESSION?

Professions are particular types of occupations.[1] The concepts of *profession* and *professional* have come to be used to identify almost any occupation (his profession is window cleaner), any task performed with diligence and excellence (he does his job like a professional), or an endeavor performed for compensation (she is a professional—as opposed to an amateur—ice skater). We utilize a stricter interpretation. Fundamental criteria for determining contemporary professions that are broadly shared by scholars of the professions include:

<table>
<tr><td>CRITERIA FOR DEFINING PROFESSIONS</td><td>

Professions exhibit a combination of all of these, not just one or two or a few:

1) University-level education in a special area of knowledge that is central to the profession being discussed;

2) Internship and supervised entry-level performance in order to master application of that knowledge in practice;

3) Knowledge and practices that require the unique exercise of learned judgment for each new situation (rather than applied technical knowledge);

4) Establishment of disciplinary identity and uniqueness of the professional group through the establishment of professional organizations, journals, systems of education, and standards for licensing;

5) Autonomy, earned by the profession and recognized and granted by society through state licensing, in defining and mastering the knowledge and practice of the profession, resulting in self-policing with regard to the standards of practice and ethical conduct;

6) Having the knowledge and expertise necessary for the well-being of persons in society.

</td></tr>
</table>

Contemporary professions thus defined are far more limited in number: medicine, law, and usually engineering and architecture. The ministry, the university professoriate, and the military, which have traditionally held professional status at various times in history, are also sometimes included in this more tightly defined group.

Duty: Service and Trust

Two cornerstones of professional standing are the duty to provide *public service* and to merit *trustworthiness*. These are based upon three prime conditions:

- The complexity of the knowledge and expertise that professionals hold;
- The complex practices that are requisite for research and knowledge application;
- The expectation of provision by the profession of necessary services and access to them by society and individuals who do not hold that knowledge.

Many studies of the professions discuss these basic conditions. The duty of service pertains to providing professional services, such as emergency-room medical care, to those who may not be able to afford them, but who need the services. Trustworthiness pertains to the professional obligation to respect the privacy rights and to advance the needs of the client. While *caveat emptor*—"Let the buyer beware"—may apply in normal business transactions, the professional has a duty in trust to fully inform the client and/or the public in professional matters that they do not have knowledge of.

There also are critiques of the claims to unique expertise and the concept of public service and trust, many of them based upon economic conflict-of-interest arguments that arise in the tension between compensation for the professional and the need for access to services by those with limited resources.[2] Despite the debate, the concepts of public service and trust become the foundation for the special ethics of professions compared to those of businesses.

> **Two cornerstones of professional standing are the duty to provide *public service* and to merit *trustworthiness*.**

THE PROFESSION OF ARCHITECTURE

Using the terms outlined above, we can examine architecture as a profession and the architect as a professional. As with our search for the distilled definitions of *ethics* and *architecture*, we turn to the dictionary for *architect*. We do not presume to fully treat the topic. The *architect* is the subject of a whole literature in itself. As in the cases of *ethics* and *architecture*, this introductory definition approach is used as a departure point:[3]

A) *Architect* shares with *architecture* roots in the Greek: *arkhitekton, arkhi-* chief, principal, first in authority *(OED)* + *tekton,* which is variously translated as *builder (AHD), worker (NWD/C), workman, carpenter (WNC), craftsman (OED),* and in the compound form *chief artificer (WNC), master builder* (several sources).

B) *AHD:* "One who designs and supervises the construction of buildings and other large structures."

C) *SOED:* "1. A designer of buildings, who prepares plans, and superintends construction."

D) *WNC:* "One who designs buildings and superintends their construction."

E) *OED:* "1. Master builder. *spec.* A skilled professor of the art of building, whose business it is to prepare the plans of edifices, and exercise a general superintendence over the course of their erection.

Art, craft, technology, technique, and construction are brought together from the various translations of the Greek root of the word in combination with the modern English definitions. An architect is a person with mastery of the art and science of architecture and who oversees the erection of buildings. There is an explicit shift from being the master *builder* (a secondary meaning in modern times) to being a master *designer* and *overseer* of works. The shift from the Vitruvian planner/conceptualizer, to early Medieval master builder, to Gothic era architect/designer is succinctly explored in Spiro Kostof's essay: "The Architect in the Middle Ages, East and West." He notes that while the social standing of the architect may have changed, "What changed was not fundamental to the traditional task of the architect, the *conception* and *supervision* of buildings."[4] (Emphasis added.) What remains central is expected mastery of the content of architecture. Without this, one is simply not an architect.

Vitruvius, Alberti, and Palladio, in their previously mentioned treatises, directly addressed the architect's requisite skills and knowledge. They articulated the core knowledge that architects should hold with respect to: conditions of site and climate, building-construction materials and methods, sound structural capacity and the ability of materials to weather, aesthetic quality, history and precedent, legalities regarding land and construction, safety, the ability to plan commodious buildings, and knowledge of geometry, model building, and drawing to represent their designs to their clients.

The core knowledge of architecture is complex. The path to becoming an architect usually includes a rigorous university curriculum in professional studies, internship under the guidance of a practicing professional, and a state-administered examination. In addition, an expectation of artistic/aesthetic creativity is part of the profession of architecture. The National Architectural Accrediting Board (NAAB) criteria for architectural-education programs and the National Council of Architectural Registration Boards (NCARB) exam sections reinforce the traditional knowledge base, expertise, and creativity of the architect. Today, in order for a person to legally claim the title architect or to practice architecture, these skills and knowledge are built into architectural professional education, internship, and the licensing laws of the U.S. and other nations. These issues will be more fully explored in A Closer Look at Being an Architect in Part II on page 108.

Because architects and their consultants provide architecture's specialized knowledge skills and practices to clients and the public, the actions they take affect the safety of society through the design of buildings for practical functionality, fire safety, and structural integrity. Architects are licensed under the auspices of U.S. law in the name of public health, safety, and welfare. Further, because of their expertise, architects serve as their client's representative in the construction process, protecting their client's fiduciary interests. Depending upon the particular project, architects duties to the users of the buildings they design and to the general public range from designing for accessibility and suitability for the intended purposes, to fiscal responsibility with respect to construction costs.

In modern society, it could be stated that there is an expectation, a right, to decent housing and to buildings and places accommodating society's activities and needs for well-being through the design of medical clinics, day-care and educational facilities, hospices, etc. These types of buildings and facilities are primarily designed by architects. There may also be an expectation and responsibility for architects to offer their expertise on behalf of the public through public service and community leadership with regard to environmental issues.

In contemporary society, architecture as a profession demands that the architect exhibit mastery of this knowledge and capabilities, and exhibit thoughtful, creative exercise of judgment in their application. Given both commonly understood and professionally sanctioned definitions and expectations with respect to architecture, one cannot possess the virtues of, and cannot be, an architect without that mastery.

BUSINESSES, PROFESSIONS, AND ETHICAL OBLIGATIONS

Business and professions are related, but they are not the same thing. Businesses—from toy, automobile, and computer-manufacturing companies, to public-utility companies, to corner markets and dry cleaners, to insurance, banking, and financial investment brokerages—manufacture, package, ship, and sell goods and services to meet the material and economic needs of society for a price or fee. That income pays salaries, purchases and transforms resources, and generates profit that creates wealth and economic return to investors.

Professions provide special types of services: those without which the quality of our lives and our well-being would be diminished or even at risk. In the view of many, professions have more demanding ethical obligations than ordinary businesses.

There are ethical issues with regard to: honoring contracts, not misrepresenting facts or concealing conflicts of interest, responsibilities with respect to not polluting the environment, providing full disclosure to human subjects in research projects, earning income for investors, contributing to community charities, etc. There are also ethical issues with respect to the relationships, duties, and responsibilities among shareholders, partners, employees, and the purchasing public with respect to business operations and representations. Product liability, labor relations, and volunteerism are commonly known and understood areas of legal and voluntary conditions of business operations and performance. Examples of the topics general business ethics addresses are summarized below.

- Contracts (duties, rights, exchange value, etc.);

- The interactions and relationships among employers and employees, their rights and duties toward each other (labor law, etc.);

- Whether or not corporate entities owe duties to the public common benefit (think of the motives and reasoning behind large corporate donations, which lower shareholder profit, to the theater, to the arts, to PBS, to sports teams, to local United Way community fund drives);

- Confidentiality issues, such as those surrounding product development, responsibility for environmental degradation, the use of human or animal subjects for product testing, and the public-health effects of products;

- The conflicts between investor profit and just and fair worker treatment (for instance, using foreign-sweatshop labor to reduce costs);

- Product safety and general public welfare.

Architects and Business Ethics

The *practices of architecture*, to the degree that they are also business practices, incorporate all of these areas of ethical obligations and choice. Architects, whether they practice in privately owned firms; in government; in institutions like universities, corporations, and hospitals; or in construction and engineering firms, are participants in *general business activities*. To that degree, they share the same concerns as other business entities regarding employee relations, responsibility to shareholders or partners or regents, the impact of their decisions on the environment, the general public good, etc.

Architects and Professional Ethics

Professions, while sharing these characteristics of commerce, also provide special types of services: those without which the quality of our lives and our well-being would be diminished or even at risk, such as emergency medical care, legal defense, and structurally sound and fire-safe buildings. In the view of many, professions have more demanding ethical obligations than ordinary businesses. (The works by Kultgren, Larson, and Koehn, identified in Note 1 of this section, are good references for this issue.)

Whether they view professions in a positive or negative critical light, experts in the study of professions rely upon a minimum of three distilled keys from the six presented earlier to differentiate professions from other business enterprises:

<table>
<tr><td>

KEYS THAT
DISTINGUISH
PROFESSIONS

</td><td>

1) Specialized expertise exercised with judgment in unique situations;

2) Autonomy of the professional group;

3) Commitment to public service and trust — a public duty.

</td></tr>
</table>

In these aspects, the nature of a profession is different from business, the primary object of which is to create wealth as a result of making products or providing services. Beyond their expertise and autonomy, there is an additional defining characteristic: that the expertise must be essential to human well-being, essential enough that it is, or ought to be, made available to all persons, regardless of their ability to pay. Medicine, through honoring its Hippocratic oath, and American law, through the public-defender system, come close to this definition. Architecture and engineering come closest to this in their duty to provide safe and secure environments.

Elements of special professional ethical duties that stem from professional roles include:

<table>
<tr><td>

SPECIAL
PROFESSIONAL
ETHICAL DUTIES

</td><td>

- *Privity:* the entitlement to privileged communications between clients and professionals that are not revealed to others (e.g., privilege is granted to the ministry and to psychiatrists; architects may have privileged communications with their clients with respect to confidential projects);

- *Fiduciary* agency: acting as a trustee for clients with respect to their financial interests (e.g., lawyers, while not being financial planners, often act as trustees for estates; and architects, during the construction phase, serve as trustees of the client's resources in authorizing payments to contractors);

- The *preservation of client interests* compared to the interests of others;

(continued on next page)

</td></tr>
</table>

(continued from preceding page)

- Client-professional *relationships built upon trust* and integrity over and above the contractual relationship;

- *Agency* to act on behalf of clients in certain situations for which the clients have insufficient expertise to act on their own behalf (e.g., during the general progress of design, architects may represent their client's interest to government-code officials and at public hearings, and are expected to know the regulations governing construction in the area of the project);

- The duty to provide *pro bono* services to those in need, regardless of their ability to pay (e.g., emergency medical aid to the indigent; public defense for the poor).

There exists, however, a root of doubt about architecture's exclusivity and autonomy claims regarding special knowledge and expertise with respect to the designed environment (including expertise regarding design quality and aesthetics) and, thus, doubts to claims of trustworthiness, that goes at least back to Aristotle:

> There are some arts whose products are not judged solely, or best, by the artists themselves, namely those arts whose products are recognized even by those who do not possess the art; for example, the knowledge of the house is not limited to the builder [architect] only; the user of the house will be a better judge than the builder.[5]

Architects have pursued the professionalization of their practices, and have legislatively implemented the *forms* of the professional ethos: with university-based education, internship, state examination, protection of the practice and title "architect," professional organizations, etc. Whether it is indeed a profession of unique capabilities, of service, and of duty to those in need, remains debatable in the eyes of some.[6] The facts are that many enduring, inspiring buildings and landscapes of the past have been built without professional architects and that today many others (who are not architects) have the knowledge and skills to design and build. Those facts, when coupled with unpopular design directions and a few notable instances of building failures (e.g., the glass falling out of the Prudential Tower in Boston; the collapse of a skywalk in Kansas City), tend to undercut architecture's claims to be a uniquely qualified profession, and thus worthy of the highest level of trustworthiness.[7]

Nonetheless while these fine points of contention exist regarding the exact degree of professional autonomy, the degree of uniqueness of the architect's professional expertise, and the degree of service duty and trustworthiness as they affect architecture's professional standing, architecture is generally included among the professions, and architects are considered professionals. Architects, because of the outcomes of their services—buildings and landscapes that can be considered essential to contemporary daily life—may be dangerous to life and limb if improperly designed, have additional broad duties to protect society in the safety and risk-management aspects of their designs. For this reason, their actions in many instances are governed by building codes that have broader application than any one building and that have cumulatively been improved based upon building construction (and failure) experiences. Additionally the codes of conduct built into licensing laws and the AIA *Code of Ethics and Professional Conduct* are particularly sensitive to conflicts of interest that arise because of the architect's duties to specify construction products and construction technologies, and to control budgets on the one hand, and their responsibilities to serve as fiduciaries and to provide safe, durable environments for their clients on the other.

In this section, we have examined the grounds upon which architecture's status as a profession is validated. Architects have actively pursued and taken on the ethos of a profession. In doing so, they have incurred the general professional ethical responsibilities of public service and trust—which often have to do with trust issues, such as those of privity and fiduciary performance, and public well-being with respect to environmental security, safety, and health, a limited subset of design characteristics. These safety, business, and conflict-of-interest concerns are largely the areas of ethics that were identified in the *Progressive Architecture* survey published in 1988.[8] But what more unique ethics are special to architecture's professional practices? How can we identify them? On pages 31–32 we discussed the ethical nature of architecture in more comprehensive terms than those discussed here. We build upon that discussion in the following and more expansively throughout Part II: Understanding.

Architects have actively pursued and taken on the ethos of a profession. In doing so, they have incurred the general professional ethical responsibilities of public service and trust.

ETHICS AND ARCHITECTURAL PRACTICES

THE ARCHITECTURE/ETHICS NEXUS

We have spent considerable time examining the threads in architectural thought regarding architecture's ethical nature because those threads reveal the durability and depth of perspective from within the discipline of architecture's social and ethical content. And yet, this *ethical content* is rarely given grounding in *ethics*. There is a need to examine the intersection of architecture's ethical nature (see pages 31–48), the primary ethical theories (see pages 48–69), and professional ethical obligations (see pages 70–78). In this Section, we provide a theoretical and practical framework for critical examination of the architecture/ethics nexus.

> In this section we provide a theoretical and practical framework for critical examination of the architecture/ethics nexus.

Given the questions ethics asks and the ethical assertions made from within architecture, how are the two linked? Architecture is a subject of history and sociology, of economics and power, and of aesthetics. Without ethical content, however, or by only asserting its ethics from within, architecture seems doomed to speak to itself, disconnected from any cultural rootedness. Without that rootedness, architecture is capricious art on one hand or iconographic commodity on another—both of which are the manners through which it is perceived and treated by some in contemporary society at large and some social critics.[1]

Manifestoes of architecture assert the ethical intentions of architecture in various forms. How do we get past the intuitive to a reasoned consideration of the ethical issues? There have been a few attempts: David Watkin, in *Morality and Architecture*, explores design image and construction as moral enterprise as seen through Pugin and Pevsner; Karsten Harries critiques aesthetic legitimation for architecture's ethics in *The Ethical Function of Architecture*, instead linking architecture to a manifestation of culture, a construction of ethos; Philip Bess presents an Aristotelian and communitarian view; William McDonough, an ecological view.[2] Yet what remains elusive is the manner in which these and other propositions regarding architecture's *goodness* are ethically grounded. This is where we will begin—searching for a means to access ethical frameworks for architecture.

With discourses and traditions so dissimilar, one may wonder how the two disciplines intersect, and in what ways architecture not only asserts its ethics from within, but also how it may be perceived and understood as an ethical practice. Proposed here, in brief outline, are Five Lenses with which to examine the ethical/architectural conflation.

FIVE LENSES OF INQUIRY	1) Architecture's Purposefulness and Social Benefit
	2) Material Production
	3) Aesthetics
	4) Architecture's Ideologies and Rhetoric
	5) Praxis; Ethics that Emerge in Architectural Practices

FIVE FRAMING LENSES

1) THE LENS OF ARCHITECTURE'S PURPOSEFULNESS AND SOCIAL BENEFIT

The first Lens that we examine is the purposefulness of architecture, i.e., its social purpose in support of beneficial programs to improve life, and its social purpose as a cultural communal construction. Architecture is grounded in human intention and purpose. It is, therefore, subject, as are other human affairs, to judgment with respect to its intentions: who and what purposes are served by those intentions, and how well those intentions are met. These are not only practical or functional judgments, but also ethical ones. For example, some intentions and purposes may be perceived to be beneficial or good (providing a day-care center) or harmful or evil (creating a genocide machine). Intentions, motives, and purposes of architectural undertakings may serve the political, social, and economic interests of democracies, despots, dictators, or military juntas; they may serve the interests of powerful individuals both for and against the public interest; and they may displace or marginalize the weak or the discriminated against (ghettos still exist). Ethical judgment may need to be reached in evaluating architectural project intentions and purposes. Beyond intent and purpose, judgment of how well intentions and purposes are met through architecture is a measure of relative merit or goodness of the built result—"goodness," in this sense, being the ethical virtue of the work.

We are in the world we have inherited, we value it, we imbue it with meaning; it shapes our perspective, as we shape it for ourselves. Architects are one of the participating agents in that shaping, the ones who propose form and images, bringing to bear their specialized knowledge and skills of history, technology, construction, and aesthetics. However, rarely are they very often participants in the critical stage when, individually or collectively, persons or communities decide to intervene and change their world, whether it is to build a church, a school, a new home, a new factory, or a new laboratory.

As we identify these projects, we *type* the world. Just as we could create a chart of architectural challenges from memorials, which have a pure symbolic, memory-constructing aspiration, to nuclear power plants and transplant surgical theaters, which are driven by technological imperatives and functional perfection for safety, we could chart architectural social contribution: from architecture as art; to institutions of communal aspiration (schools, day-care centers, churches, and temples), service and care (hospices, housing for the poor, housing for the homeless, hospitals), civic institutions, places of commerce and labor; to

places of control, such as prisons; and to machinery of war (defensive and offensive machinery conceived quite differently depending on one's "side"). We can characterize methods of designing and decision-making as ranging from self-help, sweat-equity, and participatory models to autocratic ones where persons in power make decisions.

The key is that architects are enmeshed in the making of the environment and are responsible for the critical and ethical consideration of project purposes, social benefits and decision processes. Some hold that architecture's focus on autonomy of its forms and processes, in lieu of focusing on its social engagement of processes, human purposes, and forms, has diminished its ethical role and its value to society.[3] At this point in time, within the general operation of habitat construction, architects can choose with whom and on what to work. Such particular choices are ethical choices.

2) THE LENS OF MATERIAL PRODUCTION

Architecture is a material production. Stating that architecture is material production does not deny the critical power of architectural thought and speculation. It is only that such speculation in drawing, text, modeling, film, and other media, and virtual-reality simulation is *architectural* — of architecture — and a stimulation to imagination and action, but it is not architecture in the sense commonly understood and as defined here: the designed and built inhabitable landscape. That landscape tends to be large-scale and demands many resources for its accomplishment. Once built, even ephemeral portable architecture, such as teepees or yurts, has a physical and enduring presence, even if only for a short period of time at any one location.

Material production uses resources upon which all persons and global ecologies are dependent. Those resources may be used well or wastefully; more than one society has made itself extinct due to desertification of its locale. This aspect of material production leads to a consideration of the matter of construction materials themselves. Construction materials have certain characteristics and qualities. Knowing about materials and how to utilize them for various construction purposes in order to realize a design vision is another aspect of the special knowledge architects are expected to master. It constitutes a *virtue* ethics pertaining to material production.

As with so much else in the modern architectural curriculum, precursors to materials, assemblies, and construction methods courses are found in Vitruvius, Alberti, and Palladio. Vitruvius addresses basic building materials and methods in Book II (stone,

> Architecture is grounded in human intention and purpose. It is, therefore, subject, as are other human affairs, to judgment with respect to its intentions: who and what purposes are served by those intentions, and how well those intentions are met. These are not only practical or utilitarian judgments, but also ethical ones.

brick, timber, mortar, and wall construction), and finish materials in Book VII (stucco, frescoes, and pigments). Vitruvius in the introduction to Book II states:

> I thought it best to postpone this [discussion of proportion and symmetry] until after I had treated the practical merits of the materials out of which, when they are brought together, buildings are constructed with due regard to the *proper* kind of material for each part, and until I had shown of what natural elements those materials are composed.

He continues reflection on the content of Book II in Chapter I:

> ...but in this [book] I shall discuss the use of the building materials which nature provides. For this book does not show of what architecture is composed, but treats of the origin of the building art, how it was fostered, and how it made *progress*, step by step, until it reached its present *perfection*.[4] (Emphasis added.)

Alberti covers similar ground in his Book II, which addresses materials, and Book III, which provides a guide to construction methods and assemblies. Alberti also indicates the reason he dedicates Book III to construction:

> The construction of a building does not entail just setting stone on stone, and aggregate on aggregate, ... for, because the parts are different, so too the materials and methods of construction vary quite radically.... We must now inquire what is *appropriate* in each case.[5] (Emphasis added.)

In his Book I, Palladio not only discusses building materials and methods, expanding them to cover metals, but also includes his own illustrations, the Alberti treatise having first been illustrated by publishers about seventy-five years after his death. He, too, explains his intent:

> ...in the first [book] shall be treated of the preparation of the materials, and when prepared, how, and in what manner, they *ought to be* put to use, from the foundation up to the roof: where those precepts shall be, that are universal, and *ought to be* observed in all edifices, as well private and publick.[6] (Emphasis added.)

The terms of material construction: "proper," "progress," "perfection," "appropriate," and "ought to be" are value terms that define the quality of excellence, or *virtue*.

Beyond the matter of building materials and methods, constructions may be built safely to endure winds and rain, and earthquakes, and gravity, or they may be constructed poorly endangering our lives or ruining our possessions. The *Code of Hammurabi* (eighteenth century BC), is an even earlier example of duty incurred in building. The legal and *moral* obligations with regard to construction contracts, building safety, and construction quality are addressed in Sections 228–233 of the *Code*. Section 274 concerns itself with the compensation to be paid to a builder. The following three regulations provide a good indication of the depth of professional obligations the architect/builders incurred in Babylon thirty-eight centuries ago:

> 229: If a builder has built a house for a man and his work is not strong, and if the house he has built falls in and kills the householder, that builder shall be slain.

> 232: If goods have been destroyed, he [the builder] shall replace all that has been destroyed; and because the house that he built was not made strong and it has fallen in, he shall restore the fallen house out of his own personal property.

> 233: If a builder has built a house for a man, and his work is not done properly, and if a wall shifts; then that builder shall make that wall good with his own silver.[7]

In this *Code*, the obligations to build well, and to build safely, go beyond legal minima. The ethical concept invoked for failure of professional duty with respect to material production is that of "just deserts"—punishment fitting the wrongdoing.

These examples indicate the historical depth and richness of thought regarding material production that underlies contemporary construction. An ethical duty is incurred either individually or collectively when designing and constructing buildings and infrastructure with respect to resource utilization and sustainable patterns of settlement and construction, and with respect to personal health and physical safety. In the centuries since these treatises and the *Code* were published, design and construction have been separated, with the architect almost exclusively focusing on design. But the architect remains responsible for the structural integrity of building designs and for designing and selecting the construction assemblies through which buildings are realized. Thus, contemporary architects, no less than the builders in Mesopotamia, are bound to mastering this material production aspect of their craft, not only as a skill, but as an ethical mandate.

> Knowing about materials and how to utilize them for various construction purposes in order to realize a design vision is another aspect of the special knowledge architects are expected to master. It constitutes a *virtue* ethics, pertaining to material production.

3) THE LENS OF AESTHETICS

The third Lens is that of aesthetics: architecture's relationship to art, its being an art, and its relationship to the philosophy of art and aesthetics, the beautiful and the sublime, and human flourishing. This may be the most debated issue of ethics in architecture because for many it is the self-aware "art"fulness of architecture, the desire to make "beautiful" buildings, that differentiates "architecture" from "mere building." In its role of giving form, beauty, image and meaning to societal expectations, aspirations, or needs, we look to discern architecture's aesthetic embodiment of ethical force.

Architecture, being a material production, results in things, artifacts. One might say that by their very existence and inhabitation, by their duration, even if brief, that buildings' practical intents have been met. What differentiates buildings, as what differentiates other artifactual productions, then, is not the level of service but their aesthetic character, their beauty—aesthetics being: supportive of and/or essential to human well-being; valued in itself; and/or as a discrete presentation of reality or being, valued for its capacity for revelation and representation (depending upon the philosophical or cultural position that is taken).

Source: Brooks Cavin, III

In all cases, aesthetics and beauty matter: either as art production *per se*, or as a beneficial contribution to human happiness or flourishing. Thus, a building's aesthetic embodiment is a part of its virtue, its ethical value. In terms of the first three Lenses presented here, a building's ethical content is interdependent upon social intents, material production, and aesthetic goodness —a restatement of Vitruvius in the terms of ethics. The architect is responsible *ethically* for knowledge of the theoretical and historical sources of form, beauty and appearance, and for possessing the skills and creativity to generate them. The brief exploration of the sources and judgment of beauty, as well as the role of the artist or of aesthetics, etc., that follows, is included in this book to help demonstrate the position that aesthetic embodiment is intrinsic to ethical evaluation of architecture.

Since the Enlightenment, art has had autonomy as its order. That is, the artist's role is an autonomous one in society in that the artist may help define or critique culture in his or her work, and may reveal the essence of conditions of life in a manner distinct from reason and empiricism, but does not owe a duty (for practical or utilitarian purposes) to culture or to others beyond his or her ethic. The Enlightenment perspective of art and its "disinterested" contemplation superseded earlier notions of art's relationship to nature, to the divine, and to society and its role of revealing the true nature of things, and its re-presenting the order of reality in ways that other modes — reason and science — could not. In the Enlightenment view, architecture, being enmeshed in human purposes for inhabitation and aspiration, is a lesser art than the pure fine arts, and cannot exist as art for art's sake. When architecture asserts itself as such, beyond its role as artistic production it has no compelling moral force. That is, it is no longer architecture, which by definition has a conceptual purpose, but art object, which has aesthetic "purposiveness without purpose" as its inherent object.[8] Architecture's virtue as an artistic production is, thus, in suspension between Vitruvius, who posits the aesthetic content of beauty as the differentiating characteristic of architecture above mere building, and the post-Enlightenment perspective that perceives limitations of architecture's role as an art because of its links to utility and material craft.

> In all cases, aesthetics and beauty matter: either as art production *per se,* or as a beneficial contribution to human happiness or flourishing. Thus, a building's aesthetic embodiment is a part of its virtue, its ethical value.

These themes have been taken up in articles by L. Krukowski, who attempts to build a bridge between art, morality, and aesthetics; David Bell, who critiques the conception of the disinterested autonomous artist and connoisseurship as well as the ethical force of architectural forms *per se,* and posits an inter-activist mode of construction and form giving[9]; D. Watkin, who, as mentioned, attacks nineteenth and twentieth-century theoreticians and historians who attach fixed truth and moral agency to architecture of various aesthetic styles and forms; and K. Harries, who argues against aesthetics as the foundation for architecture's ethical function.[10] Architecture today, as throughout history, has an aesthetic component, which, however hotly debated, we hold to be essentially an ethical consideration.

4) THE LENS OF ARCHITECTURE'S RHETORIC AND IDEOLOGIES

The fourth Lens of ethical consideration is that from within architecture's rhetoric and ideologies. We will use a few examples of design-driven ideologies to illustrate this perspective.

As early as Horatio Greenough in the 1840s, observers in America were calling for a "true American architecture," one that would cast off Europe's formal iconic precedents and that would emerge from American climate, functional necessities (the settlement of America, its commerce, and the construction of its institutions), and expression.[11] These themes are later taken up and find manifestation through Louis Sullivan and Frank Lloyd Wright, whose work bridging the nineteenth and twentieth centuries stands in contradistinction to the impact of the 1893 Chicago Exposition, which was still looking to the European Beaux Arts for formal sources.

The Modern Movement's intentions in the first half of the twentieth century were profoundly ethical: to make an architecture of the modern era, to utilize technology of its time, to discard the historical styles and academic architecture, and to address social projects, such as workers' housing. When combined, these strategies were to sweep aside capitalist bourgeois class restrictions and to make a more egalitarian society, using architecture as a vehicle to give it form and expression. Whatever its naiveté viewed in hindsight, this was an ethical stance. Even though after the Museum of Modern Art exhibition of 1931 the aesthetic of modernism was usurped as an object of connoisseurship and adopted by the modern corporation (exactly opposite its original objectives), many of its intentions continue to have ethical merit.[12]

Another ideology with ethical force is that of sustainable design, designing in resource-conserving ways, and with materials and methods that slow the degradation of resources, so that

Source: Visual Resource Collection, Iowa State University

future generations will have a world to inhabit. This is now a growing force in the direction contemporary architecture has taken.

In the Greenough, Wright, Sullivan, Modern Movement, and environmental-sustainability ideologies interlocking intentions, social-political-economic-cultural threads and formal strategies to support them are proposed as the premises for a "true architecture": architecture with an explicit intent to make the world better through design—an ethical architecture. Other conceptual positions, relying upon the relationship of architecture to power, social elites, and controlling mores, and upon architecture's potency to construct order (while simultaneously excluding "others") frame additional aspects of the ethical in architecture that are linked to rhetoric and ideology.[13]

In addition to ethics that arise from *design* ideologies, there are ethics that may arise from *process* ideologies—such as the philosophy that architecture is a "problem-solving process," or that public architecture ought to be the result of "public participatory-design processes," each of which implies methods and means that have an ethical import. Other examples were presented in Businesses, Professions, and Ethical Obligations, as part of the discussion of the professionalization of architecture (see pages 75–78).

Design and process rhetoric and ideologies, which speak to architecture's purposes, aesthetics, and methodologies, define the discipline. Understanding these definitions and acting from them comprise another basic framework for considering architecture's ethics.

5) THE LENS OF PRAXIS

> *Praxis:* "1a. Action, practice; *spec.* the practice of a technical subject or art, as opp. to or arising out of the theory of it; ... 2. an example or a collection of examples used for practice in a subject..." *(SOED)*

The fifth Lens is that of ethics in the action of architectural practices. This lens is keyed to praxis: architecture as a practice or a collection of practices, an art. The practitioner is obliged to master the discipline: its history and theory, its technological foundations, its order of beauty and formal conception, the order of designing and speculation that is part of architecture, its impact on human well-being, processes of community involvement and contribution, and its representational and symbolizing capacity. Practicing architecture is to be based upon that mastery. To do otherwise is to not practice architecture well; to practice without virtue. Virtue is used here in the sense that MacIntyre has recaptured from Aristotle: that of the virtuous praxis of a discipline that defines its content, quality, and ends, and that therefore can judge its excellence. This applies to both the actions of practice and the resultant works of practice.

Architecture is enmeshed in a world of the processes of reflection, conception, design, and construction; of clients, contractors, and individual craftspeople; of those people who use and experience the environments being designed; of contracts, licenses, and safety codes; of the larger general public who may be affected by resource-allocation decisions and the final form of

Source: Jim Burns

architectural solutions; of diverse ethnic, religious, racial, and international cultures; and of financiers, manufacturers, and materials and furnishing suppliers.

Many seemingly everyday events in architectural practices are ethical in their import. Some of these were noted in the Introduction to Part I: Awareness: business and marketing choices (deciding on what projects to undertake, with whom to work, the values of each, etc.); design deliberations and critiques (function, aesthetics, concepts); budgets (durability of architecture, value for expenditure); client and contractor interactions (honoring contracts, fairness, trust, and advising); contracts (equitable conditions, value for service, mutual respect, and duties); public presentations (who has the right to know and be advised about projects); and staff development and recognition. Embedded within these events are ethical questions. Duties to self, the client, the general public, and to the discipline itself can clearly be traced. They are ethical and demand an ethics. It is in the particular questions, in particular circumstances, that architecture's ethics are shaped. When we pull the threads on one of these everyday concerns, what unravels are the deepest questions and premises of the discipline. The ethics that emerge in architectural practices are explored in much greater detail in Part II.

> Many seemingly everyday events in architectural practices are ethical in their import. Duties to self, the client, the general public, and to the discipline itself can clearly be traced. They are ethical and demand an ethics.

AN APPLICATION EXAMPLE

Having developed these Five Framing Lenses for exploring the ethical content of architecture, we can apply various ethical schema to their valuation. Aspects of the first Lens are briefly explored here in terms of the Four Principal Ethical Theories.

The Lens of Purposefulness may at first seem to lend itself to Utility theory, even if the competing purposes are perceived as positive, e.g., a new high school, a street relocation, or a day-care center. Project intents may be evaluated with respect to conflicting beneficial choices, only one of which can be funded. For instance, with limited resources, should a community build a new high school for teenagers or a new day-care center for families with children under four years of age? What is the total long-term benefit to the community? Consequentialist ethics would ask: "How do we measure the near and long-term benefits and/or detriments to the community? Should we choose the one with the highest benefit and lowest negative cost? How would we determine and measure those costs and benefits?" For example, are the criteria social or economic, or both?

A deontic approach may also be taken to evaluate the choice between projects with beneficial public purposes. For instance, justice facilities promote public safety and schools promote education. In principle, which would be the better type of project purpose to pursue at a particular time if resources were limited: the one that promotes education or the one that promotes safety? Is one building type inherently *better* than the other? How would you make the determination?

Virtue theory may even be invoked in the high-school and day-care situation. For instance, the virtue case for the day-care may be made like this: a day-care center for small children enables other family members to work outside the home, to better support themselves than they could without the day care, plus their children would experience cooperative growth and learning environments at an early age, which, in turn, would enable the children to be better at learning and social engagements when they are older. Building a day-care center, in these terms, reinforces community values and practices of self-sufficiency and personal development—which are the virtues of living well. A similar virtue-based assessment could be made for the high school. In this particular case, while Virtue theory helps clarify the merits and virtues within each proposal, it does not help very well with choosing between them.

Another major ethical theory, Contract theory, could be used to examine architectural purposefulness and may be helpful in considering a variety of good options. In the case of choosing among a school, a day care, or a local jail, each of which has some positive contribution to make to the community, each of which has virtues associated with it, and each of which in principle contributes to social construction—rather than relying upon abstract conceptions of how to measure and calculate benefits and costs, or attempting to establish on principle which is the one to build, community discussion and agreement may be the basis for a decision.

In a similar fashion to that described above for Purposefulness, several ethical approaches can be used to explore the ethical parameters of dilemmas that the use of each of the other Framing Lenses has helped discern. Because any one of the Lenses and any one of the ethical theories varies in its capacity to discern and explore differing ethical dilemmas, the Five Framing Lenses and the Four Principal Ethical Theories should be used in tandem to both assess and resolve architectural/ethical dilemmas. Examining issues in this manner can enrich and enhance the ethical practice of architecture.

To explore ethical reasoning as it applies to architectural questions in Ethical Reasoning (see next page), we describe a process that engages concepts regarding architecture and ethics outlined up to now, and use it in a test case.

ETHICAL REASONING

Practicing the profession of architecture is fraught with ethical choices, including those of inventing form. As we have illustrated, almost every architectural enterprise will raise many ethical issues intrinsically to the process of considering: who the clients and users of a project are; what actions to take in the course of a project; the development of building designs and their forms; who participates in design activities and decision-making; the welfare of the larger public community; and the construction process. It is through making the difficult choices in the process of designing and fabricating our environment that the ethics embedded in architectural action is revealed.

OVERVIEW AND PROCESS

Up to now, we have discussed in a general manner ethical concepts, and ethical theories, and have used a few illustrative architectural cases to focus our discussions. For detailed consideration of ethical dilemmas in architecture, the principal concerns here, we need a method for inquiring into ethical questions. The centerpiece for discussing ethical reasoning and thought is another architectural case. It anchors the ethical quest in architectural terms. The objective in the review of the case is to present a general model of how to go about assessing an ethical dilemma. The Five Framing Lenses and the Four Principal Ethical Theories will be used in assessing an architectural ethical problem. In practice, there will often be several people involved in resolving an ethical problem. Ideally, each participant would possess an informed perspective for addressing the ethical questions at hand. Before moving to the case example, we introduce a model process for considering ethical questions.

This model of applied ethical reasoning includes several steps that are helpful in tracing through ethical problems:

> It is through making the difficult choices in the process of designing and fabricating our environment that the ethics embedded in architectural action is revealed.

1) Definition: The first step is defining the dilemma at hand: a) What are the facts that fully describe the situation and its current context? b) Do we have an accurate understanding of the prior conditions that led to the situation? c) Are there specific cause-and-effect events that created the situation?

2) Assessment: The second is discerning the ethical content of the situation, the ethical dilemmas before us. What seem to be the issues in question that make it an ethical dilemma? a) Use the Five Framing Lenses to explore which architectural ethical perspectives are in question. b) Use the Four Principal Ethical Theories to probe the ethical issues.

3) Speculation: The third is developing a set of proposals regarding possible routes of action and identifying possible outcomes that may result from those actions.

4) Deliberation: Having established the facts of a situation, discerned the ethical questions, and suggested some alternative actions that may be taken, the fourth step is further assessment of the problem within various ethical frameworks: utility, deontics, contract, virtue, etc. This deliberation may take into account the diverse interests of the participants in the situation, the underlying principles of a course of action, and its effects on the directly involved participants as well as others who may be indirectly affected, in the present and into the future.

5) Resolution: Fifth is reasoning through the competing possible courses of action, ultimately making a judgment about which course of action to pursue.

There is an important caveat to ethical deliberations and decision-making, which in architecture always involve a number of people or groups. It pertains to the participants considering and involved in the situation: their standing as autonomous persons with free will, acting without coercion; their entitlement to security, safety, and well-being physically and psychologically (perhaps economically, etc.), as a result of an outcome to the situation; their entitlement to being heard on the issues; their mastery of or access to the knowledge required to make an informed judgment to resolve the issue; and their commitment to participating in and acceding to some ethical resolution after reasoned discussion. Participants may be making personal choices, choices on behalf of others (such as children or the indigent), or choices that may affect a larger community.[1]

There is also another caveat: ethical dilemmas are complex; rarely is there an easily identified, singular, "correct" resolution or "answer" to the stated problem. Thinking beyond the straight-line "definition of the issue to solution" is usually required. Each resolution proposal is dependent upon the analysis of the case, the participants in the deliberations, the processes for resolution, and the values being brought to bear. Several iterations of any one or all of the five steps outlined above may be required. Several steps may be going on simultaneously. The value in ethical inquiry is the rigor that it demands of us in considering and deciding upon alternative courses of action that have moral implications in particular situations, even if there do not appear to be any "true" or "correct" answers.

A CASE EXAMPLE: ENVIRONMENTAL SUSTAINABILITY, ETHICS, AND POLICIES THAT GUIDE ARCHITECTURE

Architectural ethical concerns often involve at least three levels of consideration by the architect: those of the values, vision, and objectives of a communal group or society-at-large; personal values and conviction about important environmental issues and their effects on society that inform one's actions as a citizen; and professional values and convictions that inform professional action. To pursue our discussion of ethical reasoning, we will utilize a summary of a debate over sustainable versus nonsustainable design approaches that has an impact on the pattern of human settlement, infrastructure development, lifestyles, and the design of individual buildings: environmental sustainability, and, inevitably, architectural practices.

> Ethical dilemmas are complex; rarely is there an easily identified, singular, "correct" resolution or "answer" to the stated problem. Thinking beyond the straight-line "definition of the issue to solution" is usually required.

Source: Brooks Cavin, III

When designing buildings and the landscape, architects face two general possibilities with respect to the utilization of global resources. The first position is that of sustainable design. It maintains that the resources used in the construction of and the operations (heating, cooling, waste, maintenance, recycling) of buildings and settlements ought to be as resource-neutral as possible, thereby ensuring that our successors inherit a clean, viable earth. The second position holds that sustainable design practices are simply one design ideology among many, that the earth has an amazing capacity to heal, and that humankind has the technological capacity and the will to correct global depletion in order to sustain viability.

#1: Definition

The preceding is a four-sentence statement of an apparently intractable design dilemma. While many facts at first appear to be missing, e.g., the extent of usable resources on the earth, the number of people, the rates at which we humans are using critical resources, all of which make the dilemma very fuzzy, is the problem framed sufficiently to enable discussion? This restatement is brief, but it seems to adequately describe the central circumstance:

1) There is one earth;
2) We humans rely upon the earth's and sun's resources to create and sustain our habitat and lifestyles;
3) Given the objective of maintaining a certain quality of life into the future, should we be expansive or conserving with respect to using those resources?

#2: Assessment

Look at this case with an architectural eye. Which of the Five Framing Lenses apply? We will briefly consider each Lens. Building Purposefulness does not seem to be central here. Essentially, to support contemporary life in almost all societies, modification of the landscape takes place to create farmland; to build dwellings, communities, and cities; to enable transportation across it, etc. Nor does this seem to be a question of aesthetics; aesthetic character and the image of buildings and cities are relatively fluid with respect to the patterns of settlement or the energy conservation of buildings. It is not particularly an exploration of architectural Praxis—except for those working relationships where discussion, persuasion, and agreement one way or another upon using sustainability concepts in a design is called for. Material production and architecture's ideologies seem to be the central issues. If architecture is built not only for the near term, but also for the longer-term time horizon (which is an ideological position in itself), what conceptual design approaches (ideologies), what approach to the selection of building materials, and what methods of construction (material production) should be pursued? While settlement and building-design proposals eventually involve practice processes, aesthetics, and determination of individual building uses, the questions of material production and ideology seem to be the foremost architectural/ethical concerns here.

This outline of an aspect of the contemporary environmental-sustainability-design debate focusing on architecture's material production and ideology is essentially ethical in nature. The first ethical position argues from the facts that we have only one earth, that there is no guarantee that we have the capacity to design ahead of global desertification or the ability to correct unintended environmental disasters in order to ensure future inhabitability. Therefore, it is *imperative* and *right* that we design buildings and settlements in a resource-conserving manner. To do otherwise is *wrong*. The second ethical position argues from those same facts that we have time; that ingenuity will outstrip any detrimental activities as it has in the past, that to sacrifice current reasonable cost-effective solutions, to expend an extraordinary share of wealth, or to demand a change in urbanization and building-design strategies, for instance, on speculation about future disasters is *wrong*. This position maintains that we need to take a balanced approach, to *optimize benefits*.

The first position is that of *deontology*, ethics proceeding from a principle-based position. It is the idea that certain actions are both right and good in principle, and that others are wrong and suspect. Continued life and inhabitation of the earth is a primary concern for humanity. Therefore, designing buildings in a nonsustainable manner, which may lead to fouling our host planet, to the desertification of the earth and our extinction is wrong, *per se*, even if we think we may have the skill to mitigate damage that may result from such design approaches. The second position is that of *Consequentialism* and *teleology*, ethics that proceed from the consideration of the amount of goodness of an outcome as a result of our actions evaluated against the risks or costs of those actions. It takes into account that we socially construct the concepts of what is

> Architectural ethical concerns often involve at least three levels of consideration by the architect: those of the values, vision, and objectives of a communal group; personal values and conviction; and professional values and convictions.

right and wrong; that circumstances vary; and that we need to calculate the net good that results from a particular action with
respect to its costs for a reasonably forecastable timeframe. In this
case, an argument can be made that Utilitarianism is the most
clearly articulated ethics of this position.

At this point in our sustainability example, at least four fundamental issues that ethical reasoning has helped identify have
emerged:

- One is that the primary question raised here is: *What is
  right, the correct thing to do* in this value driven situation of
  choice? How shall I act, and why?
- The second is the assumption that the results of certain
  activities are *good* in and of themselves — in this case,
  preservation of the earth for the future generations. This
  raises the meta-ethical questions of: What is *good?* How do
  we define *good* or *good enough* with respect to environmental
  preservation?
- The third is the commonly held ethical position that our
  choices should be made from a position of reasoned, unerr-
  ing principles, from a knowledge of those principles and
  their proposed universality — deontological ethics.
- Finally, there is a call for reasonable evaluation and calculation of consequences; a choice that holds that the selection of
  a correct course of action is dependent upon the sum result
  of good benefit in a particular situation (Utility ethics).

#3: Speculation and #4: Deliberation

Having uncovered these four issues, we return to our example,
this time suggesting proposals for possible courses of action and
identifying the ethical issues surrounding them:

SUSTAINABLE-
DESIGN-POLICY
PROPOSALS AND
EFFECTS

Among the proposed options open to us is a change in public
design policy to make all building projects sustainable. Such policies might impose energy-use budgets, require life-cycle cost
analyses, demand the recycling and reuse of building materials, or
require that all designs incorporate passive environmental-mitiga-
tion design concepts.

(continued on next page)

(continued from previous page)

Another action that could be taken to enhance sustainable building design might be to control the types of natural resources that may be used. For example, the UN, in order to preserve the global atmosphere, may protect rain forests from any further logging or deforestation because they are a primary agent of atmospheric cleansing.

However, as a result of an environmental preservation and design policy that would no longer allow the use of exotic woods in buildings and furniture, the possibility would then exist that industries in certain nations, (e.g., exotic-wood tree harvesters and the milling and construction product industries that support them), will decline, there will be a loss of jobs, and some people will suffer. Certain nations' whole economies may be at risk in the short term while they develop other industries. The U.S., with less than 5% of the world's population, utilizing 30% of the natural resources consumed globally every year, would be only marginally affected. But what is the U.S. responsibility to those affected?

Environmental-design policies such as those considered above have a broad impact beyond the concerns of the immediately affected community. How are the interests of certain nations of the global community to be weighed against those of other nations and the general population of earth? Which economies, whose livelihoods, whose opportunities for life quality are at risk? For what period to time? Are there forms of assistance, such as job training, for those people who may be negatively affected by an environmental policy decision?

The policy proposals outlined above in our case raise additional ethical questions. In a globally interconnected economy, with certain nations commanding substantial shares of wealth and power, and others seemingly supporting that wealth and/or being less powerful, who makes the choices and decisions regarding equity of opportunity? What happens when one nation's opportunities for resource use and economic development endangers the rest of the world community? What becomes a *right* decision?

Before we summarize another group of ethical issues, consider the following extension of the sustainable-design position:

SUSTAINABLE DESIGN, DESIGN IDEOLOGY, AND CEREMONIAL ARCHITECTURE

> Does the proposed general position that resources ought to be conserved and energy expenditure minimized lead to a totalizing design position that emphasizes reconstruction of our existing places over spreading new construction out to fringe lands to accommodate growth? Does it negate ceremonial and memorial architecture, monuments, or civic and institutional architecture that serve social aspirations other than the Utilitarian? Are there options?
>
> On the one hand we may hold that, "We need the civic and the ceremonial; places of great social import need to be created as part of society's collective aspiration, even if they do not maximize sustainable design practices."
>
> Or we may hold that, "We need to first design for sustainable practice; ceremonial architecture conforms to that starting point."

At this point, four more key issues of ethics have been introduced:

- The first involves the question of what constitutes a *just* decision: What is *just* and *fair* with respect to the impacts the choices being made will have on the people, nations, and ecologies being affected?
- The second is the condition of what constitutes an acceptably *good life*. Is life in a developed country, with its wealth, access to health care, standard of living, and quality of construction, the standard of a *good life?* If it is, shouldn't resources be made available for all peoples of the earth to achieve that same standard? How can this be achieved without bankrupting our host planet?
- The third issue is the recognition that two *good* objectives, one of conservation, and the other of satisfying collective symbolic aspiration through habitat-making, may be in conflict.
- A fourth issue, implicitly brought into this case, concerns *how* decisions regarding conflicting outcomes, even if both are beneficial, would be made. Voting? Negotiation? How is *agreement* reached?

#5: Resolution

We may now be in a position to consider a decision resolution.

The issues embedded in this environmental-design case constitute some of the major questions that ethics addresses:

<table>
<tr>
<td>

1) What is the environmental *good* toward which designers ought to strive?

2) When making choices, how do we ascertain what is *right?*

3) When considering choices, how do we determine a *just decision* in the context of legitimate, differing, contending perspectives?

4) What *process or method* should we use in making an ethical choice in a dilemma that involves many people and many interests?

</td>
<td>

ETHICAL ISSUES EMBEDDED IN THE CASE

</td>
</tr>
</table>

This case may seem a bit removed from everyday architectural practice realities, and reaching a sustainable-design-policy decision may seem to be unattainable. But is it? For example, public policy laws such as the U.S. Clean Air Act, those that established the Environmental Protection Agency, and those that called for hazardous-waste mitigation and the elimination of such toxic and hazardous building products as lead in paint or friable asbestos, which was once widely used in flooring, roofing, building siding, building insulation, and ceiling products, have been enacted and enforced.

Buildings are major users of energy in the U.S. and elsewhere, and most of the energy used is nonrenewable. Current building-design practice in Germany and Switzerland goes beyond controlling building-material toxicity and interior air quality. Very strict energy-usage parameters have been put into law by the general will of the people. Building-design energy-reduction strategies are the combined results of settlement policies, environmentally responsive building design, reduction in embedded energy in building materials, and improved energy efficiency of building operating components. Western Europeans, whose living standards and health care, for instance, often exceed those of Americans, use about half of the energy per person per year as Americans do. Energy utilization and resource consumption in building design is but one of the many choices to be made in architecture that have far-reaching ethical effects.

To recap the consideration of our case example:

RECAP: THINKING
THROUGH THE
ARCHITECTURE/
SUSTAINABLE-
DESIGN ETHICAL
DILEMMA

1) Do you think that enough of the facts that describe the situation and its current context were identified? Are there specific cause-and-effect events that are involved in this case? What would you add to make the case more complete?

2) What are the architectural/ethical dilemmas here? Have they been reasonably well identified from both the ethical and architectural perspective?

3) While a full set of proposals has not been developed, a few have. Are they logical? Are the implications reasonably well defined?

4) Given the facts established, the ethical questions discerned, and the alternative actions proposed, what ethical theories would you apply in considering the case?

5) What proposals would you make with respect to a process for resolving the issues? Who would be involved?

The ethical questions identified in this case have endured in Western philosophy to varying degrees for 2,500 years with continuous debate. And the Western tradition is not the only one that has attempted resolution of these concerns. So far, there are no definitive answers, but in today's world, a review of contemporary ethics literature shows that this particular debate about environmental sustainability and the ethical issues it raises have assumed center stage.

REFLECTION

If there are no fixed answers, no discoverable "truths," to this situation and the myriad of other ones that envelop architecture, then why frame a book around ethics and architecture? Or around this classical tradition of ethical reflection and reasoning?

Ethics shares a similarity with architecture. There are few certainties in architecture beyond gravity and weathering, and perhaps no predictive or generative truths. Yet there exists a reasoned discourse about design, design results, and design thinking by virtue of paradigms regarding architecture that provide a basis for that discourse. Historically, globally, and currently, architects engage in that discourse. In an analogous manner, without provable, irrefutable truths, ethics provides a framework for discourse, understanding, and decision-making regarding issues central to ethical conduct. We hold the point of view that ethics are embedded in architecture, and that the discourses of both disciplines need to be engaged by architects. This is the perspective we bring to *Ethics and the Practice of Architecture*.

At this point, utilizing architectural situations with ethical dilemmas, we have discussed ethics and major ethical theories. We have also proposed general models for assessing which aspects of architectural concerns in any one situation may have an ethical import (the Five Framing Lenses), and for reasoning through ethical dilemmas (the Four Principal Ethical Theories). We now turn to look more specifically at ethics and architectural practices in Part II: Understanding.

We hold the point of view that ethics are embedded in architecture, and that the discourses of both disciplines need to be engaged by architects.

PART II
UNDERSTANDING

INTRODUCTION TO UNDERSTANDING

LEARNING OBJECTIVES

The public, as witnessed by numerous opinion polls, recognizes the architect's commitment to ethics and ethical behavior. These "prestige" polls rank Supreme Court justices, medical doctors, university professors, and architects high in ethical standards.[1] This confidence reinforces the responsibility for architects to fully understand that ethical considerations influence the practice of architecture.

Part II: Understanding focuses in more discrete and explicit detail on the profession of architecture. This section describes how ethical considerations are a part of all levels of decision-making by architects regardless of their role in the profession. It builds on the ethical discourse of Part I: Awareness and its description of the nexus of ethics and architecture.

We begin Part II with a closer look at what it means to be an architect. We do this by viewing a selected history of the profession, the process required today to become an architect, and the ethical standards and responsibility that are required of architects regardless of the myriad roles they may play as members of the profession. Next, we take a closer look at the aspects of making architecture, including design, delivery, and management processes and responsibilities. We then examine in detail the range of decisions that go along with both being an architect and making architecture, and pose a series of questions to focus the application of ethical considerations. Your ability to understand these ethical aspects of the making and doing of architecture builds on the Five Framing Lenses, the Four Principal Ethical Theories, and the Ethical Reasoning processes described in Part I: Awareness.

Part II: Understanding is thus used to reinforce your understanding of the link between ethics and architecture and its effect on architectural practices. It provides the learning threshold for Part III: Choices, which deals with the application of what you have learned from Awareness and Understanding to the comprehensive practices of architecture as exemplified by representatives case studies.

A CLOSER LOOK AT BEING AN ARCHITECT

A SELECTED HISTORY OF THE PROFESSION: 1850–1909

A history of architectural practice from 1850 to 1909 parallels other similar professions and mirrors the events of world history. America was evolving as a nation and relied primarily on European education methods, traditions, and historical precedent. The clergy, medicine, engineering, and law were recognized as professions. Architecture was evolving from a craft to a profession during the nineteenth century. Ethics was not yet defined in professional terms with responsibilities and consequences regarding architectural practice. The years between 1850 and 1909 were a very significant development period for the architectural profession. The period realized the beginning of professional societies, the founding of architectural schools, and the formulation of a code of ethics.

The profession, as we know it in America today, is based on the European educational system of the 1800s. The American architectural practice of the late eighteenth and early nineteenth century was typically lead by a European educated male from a wealthy family.[1] A tour of Europe, followed by a college education, was available only to the affluent because of the expense and social norm. It was almost exclusively a male experience until 1901 when Julia Morgan, the first woman to study at the Ecole des Beaux Arts, entered the traditional educational curriculum. The "educated" architect directed offices; craftsmen and apprentices learned the trade of architecture in the master's studio. However, the architectural profession through the middle of the nineteenth century was disorganized, heterogeneous, and unregulated. Architecture as an occupation operated without standards or regulations.

After the Civil War, American cities and the building industry underwent dramatic, unprecedented change. Immigration, the development of efficient transportation systems, new building products and urban growth presented the opportunity to increase the professional's role in the building of a new society. Large-scale transportation and public-works projects created the need for specialized engineering disciplines. To protect the public interest, the state and city authorities promoted the rise of professionalism through the requirement for guarantees of competence and technical expertise. The city of New York, for example, in 1867 adopted the first minimum housing standards in the U.S. The standards were not codes, but they established a guide for architects that set "rules" for performance.[2]

Education provided the opportunity for the individual that began to change the occupation of architecture. As stated, the European tradition included courses of study at the École des Beaux-Arts, an atelier system in which a group of students in a studio environment completed competitions under the direction of a master who critiqued the students' work.[3] The master was typically an established architect. Social camaraderie, long charrettes, and memorable traditions characterized the atelier atmosphere. One important aspect of the atelier was the group loyalty to each member.

Richard Morris Hunt, the first American architect to study at the École des Beaux-Arts in Paris from 1845 to 1853, founded his practice and established an atelier in New York after his graduation in 1855.[4] Other notable architects who also attended the Beaux-Arts during this period — H. H. Richardson, Charles McKim, John Galen Howard, Louis Sullivan, and Bernard Maybeck — were important architects after 1850. They influenced the development of an American architectural-education system by creating an office structure that stressed apprenticeship, education, and professionalism.

Hunt was instrumental in the founding of the American Institute of Architects (AIA) in 1857 and was influential in the country's first school of architecture, which was headed by his student, William Rogers Barton, at MIT in 1865. Eleven schools were in operation in 1900.[5] By 1912, the Association of Collegiate Schools of Architecture, which exists today, coordinated national academic programs. In 1897, Illinois became the first state to require licensure for architects.

To complete the beginning steps for the professionalization of architecture, in 1909, the first code of ethics was adopted by the AIA.

The social and economic conditions that influenced the professional development of architecture in American between 1850 and 1909 created a system of the beliefs and ideals based on the arts. The strongest influence from the Beaux Arts and atelier expe-

1883 AIA Convention (*Source:* American Institute of Architecture)

rience was architecture's alliance with the arts, the profession's dis-association from crafts, and the respect of a group practice created by a master.[6] Also, the school of architecture established a significant center for the profession. Education influenced professional unity because of the centralized, controlled structure of the institutions that further distanced the architect from the earlier systems of crafts-based training. The new educational experience stressed art, intellect, and theory versus the apprenticeship training in skills and construction techniques.

To complete the beginning steps for the professionalization of architecture, in 1909, the first code of ethics was adopted by the AIA.[7]

THE PROCESS (EDUCATION/INTERNSHIP/LICENSURE)

To be recognized as an architect, an individual usually earns a professional status through a rigorous series of accomplishments, versus an honorary or appointed position. An architect-in-training typically completes more than four years of college education, and serves a defined, regulated apprenticeship where one experiences a variety of work assignments. In addition, testing and licensing procedures are established by an impartial regulatory agency. Each state administers the exam and oversees the actions of individual professionals as well as office organizations.

The architect may then join and agree to the conditions of a professional society, such as the AIA, which has an established code of ethics. The recognized code must have obvious, stringent enforcement policies.

When these conditions are satisfied, the professional does, in fact, know more about architecture professionalism than the lay public and invites more than the usual degree of trust with regard to their area of specialized knowledge.[8] In effect, the professional must, therefore, assume more than the layperson's degree of responsibility. This has established the basis not only for professional ethical standards, but also for the architect's accountability and exposure to liability.

The link between formal education and architectural practice traditionally has been an internship, today's atelier. Time and experiences in one or more offices are structured to provide the intern with a wide variety of practice situations.[9] Usually the young architect works directly with a senior member of the firm, the mentor. Internship, when well structured, involves opportunities for graduates to acquire firsthand exposure to real-life complexities of practice and, in effect, to learn how to apply the knowledge, skills, and abilities acquired in school. The present architectural code of ethics is very clear on the responsibility of the professional with regard to the intern. Canon V of the 1997 Code of Ethics and Professional Conduct, Obligations to Colleagues, clearly states that "members should respect the rights and acknowledge the professional aspirations and contributions of their colleagues."

However, in the recent past the internship program lacked formal organization and a defined curriculum. The individual state registration boards determined the length and nature of the internship required for licensure, usually three years of practical training in the employ of a registered architect. Yet the definition of acceptable nature and experience varied considerably among member boards.[10]

The National Council of Architectural Registration Boards (NCARB), in 1973, undertook a thorough study of internship goals, requirements, and intended outcomes.[11] Four collateral organizations of the profession, the AIA, the Association of Collegiate School of Architecture (ACSA), the National Architectural Accreditation Board (NAAB), and the NCARB, concluded that internship requirements:

- Were unstructured,
- Lacked definition, and
- Had no clear path for successful accomplishment.[12]

> When these conditions are satisfied, the professional does, in fact, know more about architecture professionalism than the lay public and invites more than the usual degree of trust with regard to their area of specialized knowledge.

The profession in the 1960s had promoted a "log-book" concept for recording training experiences, which was unsuccessful. The process did not have a format, a list of required or recommended universal activities that the intern should experience and/or master. Areas of design exposure, construction, document preparation, cost-estimating, client presentations, field administration, and contractor negotiations were areas of practice deemed important, but no single part or alternate parts to pre-registration experience was defined by the local boards.

Again, through the committee method the NCARB and the AIA in the mid-1970s developed the requirements for an Intern Development Program (IDP). The goal of the program was to develop a definition, a process, and a program that would give the IDP an equal status in the profession, similar to education and the examination.

As a result of the program reorganization, a national committee, with all sponsors represented (AIA, ACSA, NAAB, NCARB and the American Institute of Architecture Students, AIAS), oversees the policies and procedures, as well as IDP development requirements. Peer support of the program has grown, and the number of interns in the program has also increased. The records of the completed intern's compliance with the state's practical-training requirements are maintained by the NCARB and are beneficial when the candidate passes the exam and applies for reciprocity in additional states. Also, many states now require IDP participation and documentation as a requirement for practical training. More important, the profession recognizes the individual's and office's ethical responsibility to provide opportunities for exposure to specific areas of practice identified by the IDP.

The IDP currently identifies critical training areas of architectural practice, which require intern experience. Further, the IDP determines the time to be dedicated to each training area and defines the type of activity or exposure the intern should acquire in each area.

The completion of a series of professional exams is the final step in the process of architectural licensure. Individual sections in the exam test a candidate's level of knowledge on a variety of technical topics: structures, mechanical systems, site-design criteria, theoretical topics, design, and site planning. The exam is not about design ability, talent, or an individual's architectural aptitude. It is about an individual's architectural competence and the ability to protect the public. Life-safety protection requires knowledge of building codes, technical knowledge of construction conventions, and fire safety. In addition, a qualified candidate must also understand accessibility standards and energy requirements.

The examination is at present computer-based. Candidates can sit for the test at a scheduled appointment versus the twice-a-year cycle that was a tradition of the "paper test."

Licensure, which is required for designation as an architect, requires passing the exam and satisfying any mandated education and internship requirements.

A study of the profession by Schluntz and Gebert indicated that just over half of those who have been out of school for five years are licensed.[13] After ten years, more than three-fourths of the surveyed architectural graduates are licensed.

Should professional standing affect one's ethics? Does the intern architect have an ethical obligation to the community, to the client, and to fellow workers?

Licensure attests to the individual's competence in the range of knowledge necessary to practice architecture. An important value of registration is the ability to practice independently. A licensed architect can provide the required document certification; an unlicensed architect cannot. Licensure is, thus, an important milestone in one's professional career. Under most state laws, only licensed architects can provide architectural services for major buildings.

NCARB: ETHICAL STANDARDS/STATE LAWS

The NCARB grants a certificate to qualified architects through an administrative procedure called certification. After one's initial license is granted, the NCARB certificate facilitates registration in other states. The architectural-licensure process is considered a responsibility reserved for individual states. To be registered in other jurisdictions, the architect has to reapply for registration. The NCARB acts as a professional oversight organization, maintaining member records and facilitating professional mobility between states and territories. Throughout the history of the NCARB, the organization's primary mission has been the improvement of state laws, rules, and regulations regarding the practice of architecture in U.S. jurisdictions. To enable interstate mobility and access to practice in multiple jurisdictions, the NCARB monitors laws regulating architectural practice to ensure the uniformity of the statutes.[14] The NCARB is primarily concerned with the standards, rules, and procedures as they apply to domestic applicants for licensing that leads to NCARB Certification.

Founded at the St. Louis AIA convention in 1919, the original purpose of the NCARB was to facilitate the exchange of information on examining, licensing, and regulating architects; to foster uniformity in licensing and practice laws; to facilitate reciprocal licensing; to discuss the merits of various examining methods, including the scope and content of examinations; and to strive to improve the general educational standards of the architectural profession.[15] The goals have been modified only twice since 1920. Today the NCARB works as council to member boards to safeguard the health, safety, and welfare of the public and to assist member boards to carry out their duties. The organization develops and recommends standards to be required of applicants for architectural registration; develops and recommends standards regulating the practice of architecture; provides a certification process and architect registration requirements to member boards; and represents the interests of member boards before public and private agencies.

The NCARB functions as a quasi-public organization because, based on the Constitution of the U.S., the authority to guard the health, safety, and welfare of the citizen(s) is reserved to the individual state.[16] Regulation, therefore, of the architectural profession and licensing practitioners is not accomplished nationally but is a function of the individual state or U.S. territory.

In 1902, only three states had laws regulating the practice of architecture: Illinois, the first, in 1897; California, 1901; and New Jersey, 1902. By 1920, seventeen more states had adopted laws regulating the practice of architecture and licensing individuals as architects.[17]

Since 1980, the NCARB's development of a model licensing law and model regulations has stressed most crucial issues involved in the changing environment of professional regulation. This model law deals with such topics as definitions, qualifications, discipline, prohibitions, and enforcement procedures (all ethical issues).

The model licensing law is formulated as legislative guidelines. As discussed, state law contains unique language, organization, and ancillary provisions, which result in exact statutory language. The guidelines, therefore, establish provisions adopted by member state boards in the form of model regulations. Local boards have the power, by statute, to issue regulations to further explain and define the board's statutory authority. The regulations may not contradict the state statute.

Statutory changes are difficult to achieve because of the political process in each individual jurisdiction. Regulations, on the other hand, may be adopted by a board after notice and hearings. The division between the contents of the statute and a regulation is directly related to public policy and should be created by the legislature.

The need to establish defined rules of conduct was intensified by the challenge to the AIA *Code of Ethics* in the landmark Mardirosian suit against the AIA (see page 115) and the investigations by the U.S. Justice Department. Many state boards were using the AIA *Code of Ethics* as the basis for their rules of conduct.

The NCARB's methods to study the background for a standard of professional conduct included a study of related profession's ethical codes, interviews with consumer-affairs advocates, and related research inquiries. The resulting NCARB *Rules of Conduct* were developed as:

- A hard-edged basis for policing and disciplining architects;
- Rules related to the protection of the public and not the advancement of the interests of the profession;
- An understanding that the architect is in a leadership position and that the architect's responsibility is to both the client and, at the same time, a supervising duty to the public;
- Areas of behavior for which an architect risks being disciplined by the state registration's board.

In summary, the NCARB *Rules of Conduct* emphasize five areas of professional activities: competence, conflict of interest, full disclosure, compliance with the law, and professional conduct.

AIA *Code of Ethics and Professional Conduct*

In contrast to the NCARB, a quasi-public organization, the AIA is an affiliate group of licensed architects; other member designations, such as associate, are possible, but to use the AIA credential, one must pass the registration exam. The AIA was founded in New York in 1857.[18] The professional organization originally formed two major committees, Design and Judiciary. The Design Committee, of course, was the primary focus of the institute and established the philosophical direction for the membership. The Judiciary Committee formulated and enforced policies and procedures for the organization. Rules, standards, and professional tenets had to be developed; more important, these regulations had to be monitored and enforced. Discipline, however unpleasant, was the responsibility of the Judiciary Committee.

Founding principles of the AIA focused on professional practice issues and ethical, decision-making conduct. The principal of "caveat emptor," or let the buyer beware, was not held sufficient to protect the buyer of professional services. Therefore, the AIA, the Royal Institute of British Architects (RIBA), and other professional organizations began to establish professional codes of ethics that guaranteed consistency for the client and consistency between professionals.

Since the original organizational meetings of the AIA, very little has changed in the professional's ethical approach to practice. A review of the minutes of meetings between 1857 and 1909 reveals basic practice fundamentals that exist today.[19] The early meetings are memorialized by handwritten minutes that emphasize:

- Professional activities;
- New members (collegial fraternity);
- Business practices;
- Technology;
- Case-study presentations.

The summary of these meetings resulted in discussion and camaraderie. It is very interesting to note, because it is a very contemporary subject, that the assumed inadequacies of fees were central to most discussions.

Other than design matters, early records and minutes of the institute's proceedings indicate that the highest incidence of disciplinary actions involved violations of the profession's ethical requirements.[20] Supplanting, or promoting work from a client who already had a contract with another architect, was the most prevalent offense on which the ethics committee acted. Members guilty of violations were removed from the AIA. The impact of these consequences then, as well as today, might be debated pro and con. Competition aside, the strength of the membership's conviction and commitment to the approved ethical standards is, however, the important concept to recognize.

Although a *Code of Ethics* was not officially established until 1909, ethical concepts and issues remained substantially the same between 1857 and the late 1960s. Major challenges did not occur until after 1968, and then the entire approach to architectural professional ethics was altered.

Founding principles of the AIA focused on professional practice issues and ethical, decision-making conduct.

A literature review of the *Reader's Guide to Periodical Literature*, between 1900 and the present, reveals that no reference was made to "ethics," "professional ethics," "architectural integrity," or "architect's professional ethics" before 1969.[21] It is offered for further clarification that the *Architectural Record* is the only professional periodical listed in the *Reader's Guide*. References relating to ethical topics are prevalent in business and other professional journals. The noticeable lack of interest or exposure by the architectural profession is significant.

The first reference to "architect's ethics" in the *Reader's Guide* refers to complaints brought by State University of New York (SUNY)–Buffalo students, who, in 1969, were protesting competition procedures and practices—an important issue, however, it pales by comparison to upcoming events.[22] During the late 1960s, antitrust actions had been instigated by government agencies that in effect wanted to eliminate the system of fees or fee schedules the profession suggested. The General Service Administration (GSA), the Corps of Engineers, and other government representatives that were responsible for the procurement of professional services did not like the fixed-fee schedules suggested by architectural, and more important, engineering societies.[23]

In the early 1970s, the Justice Department scrutinized the ethical standards of numerous professions and faulted many, including the architectural profession. Complaints were focused on restraint of trade practices suggested by the ethics code, i.e., noncompetitive bidding requirements. Briefly summarized, it was asserted that the AIA's ethical prohibition against members engaging in competitive bidding for architectural services was a restraint of trade and, therefore, a violation of the Sherman Antitrust Act. The issues were real. The AIA had created a suggested-fee schedule, prohibited members from discounting fees, established strict guidelines to advertising, and prohibited competitive bidding through the mandatory code for its members. This type of assertion was unsuccessfully challenged by the National Society of Professional Engineers (NSPE).[24] In 1978 the Supreme Court voted unanimously that any organization's rule against participation in competitive bidding was a violation of the Antitrust Act.

A second court action, a suit brought in 1975 against the AIA by Arain Mardirosian, an architect whose membership had been suspended because of an alleged violation of the supplanting rule, successfully challenged a second key provision of the *Code of Ethics*.[25] Supplanting, the intentional solicitation of a client who has engaged another architect for the same assignment, was considered unethical by the original *Code of Ethics* rules.

The Supreme Court and Mardirosian decisions had a major impact on the substantial changes to the AIA *Code of Ethics* that were made from 1969 to 1985. Ethical aspects to the following practices were significantly modified:

- Architectural-competition procedures (1969).
- Political-contribution policies (1970).
- Recommended-fee schedules (1971).
- The Architect as Developer (1974).
- Design-build roles (1978).
- Reuse of documents (1985).

Before 1970, the authors of the *Code* reflected a sincere desire to preserve the dignity and professionalism of the practice of architecture. Other professions, including medicine and the law, also had similar rules of conduct. Architects stressed professional behavior versus a business-like approach to the delivery of services, not products, to the client. Emphasis has always been stressed regarding the common good, community responsibilities, and service to the public. The changes after 1969 in the *Code of Ethics* were a response to non-architects and potential clients' review of the architect's professional mandates. The *Code* appeared to clients to be a set of rules that were established to protect the architect in the competitive business world.

During the 1970s, however, the U. S. Department of Justice inquiries and investigations of professional standards resulted in changes to many professions, including those of engineering, medicine, accounting, and the law. These changes were based on the resolution of the Justice Department's concern with anti-trust issues, such as restraint of trade.

Because of the sustained legal activity, the mandatory *Code of Ethics* was withdrawn in 1980 and replaced with a Statement of Voluntary Ethical Principles. The history and tradition of the professional has, however, always been based on self-regulating principles and individual esteem. No one was comfortable with a voluntary code. The membership of the AIA again created a mandatory *Code of Ethics*, which was approved in 1987. The *Code* reflected contemporary issues that affect the architectural profession as viewed from the perspective of a third-party business client. The code is reviewed and updated by AIA legal council and an appointed regulatory board, the AIA National Judicial Council. The most recent update, 1997, applies to all professional activities of all members. The *Code* is arranged in three tiers:[26]

- Canons are broad principles of conduct. The *Code*'s five canons are general statements that address obligations to the discipline, obligations to the public, obligations to the client, obligations to the professional, and obligations to colleagues.

- Ethical Standards (E.S.) are more specific goals toward which members should aspire in professional performance and behavior.
- Rules of Conduct (Rule) are mandatory; violation of a rule is grounds for disciplinary action by the institute. Rules of Conduct, in some instances, implement more than one Canon or Ethical Standard.

ALTERNATIVE ROLES

Not all graduating students and those who have passed the licensing exam choose to practice architecture in a traditional manner. An architectural education is an excellent foundation for numerous careers—advertising, development, construction, property management, teaching, and research. A recent AIA census of the profession determined that 18% of the people designated as architects are not working in the traditional office.[27] Another reference, Bob Douglass, Ph.D., reports in his research study that in 1992 nearly 50% of the architects in the U.S. were working outside the profession.[28] The importance of the discrepancy between the two reports is noted, but the fact that a significant number of architects practice in alternative professions is the important focus of this discussion.

In his Ph.D. dissertation study, Douglass studied two groups of graduate architects in nontraditional careers. The two separate groups were identified through interviews, questionnaires, and scientific findings as "seekers and solvers."[29] The seekers can be characterized as reflective, intuitive, and aesthetically oriented. The solvers were more task- and result-oriented.

The solvers typically were employed in a construction field. Job descriptions included construction financing, real-estate developers, construction managers, general contractors, and design builders. The solvers' nontraditional group members, who had stayed the closest to the traditional practice, had the most to say about the profession, and were the most bitter.[30]

Seekers proved to be the most diverse. Their professionals included artists, writers, and inventors. Many were not associated with architecture, building, or the construction industry. Still, they expressed the most allegiance to the profession—"I am an architect."[31]

Actual occupations held by people with architectural backgrounds are shown in the following chart.

ARCHITECTURAL CAREER OPTIONS
ACTUAL OCCUPATIONS OF PEOPLE WITH ARCHITECTURAL
BACKGROUNDS[32]

Architectural Critic	Environmental Planner
Architectural Photographer	Furniture Designer
Architectural Programmer	Graphic Designer
Architectural Renderer	Illustrator
Building Inspector	Industrial Designer
Building Pathologist	Interior Designer
CAD Coordinator	Landscape Architect
Campus Planner	Lawyer
Carpenter	Market Researcher
Cartographer	Model Maker
City Planner	Museum Curator
City or State Architect	Printmaker
Civil Engineer	Professor
Computer Presentation Designer	Property Assessor
Computer-Systems Analyst	Publisher
Construction Inspector	Real-Estate Agent
Construction Manager	Real-Estate Project Manager
Contractor	Researcher
Corporate Consultant	Set Designer
Design/Build Team Manager	Structural Engineer
Developer	Technical Writer
Document Designer	TV/Film Producer

Robert Gutman also elaborates on architects in nontraditional roles.[33] Interestingly, his analysis indicates that industry and manufacturing corporations, in an attempt to improve efficiency and profit, have incorporated architectural service groups internally. Corporations recognize that architects can affect the cost of constructing and maintaining facilities. The demand for efficiencies is also an important goal of the institutions of government, education, the church, developers, and city, state, and federal code officials.[34]

What is the architect's professional role, ethically, in the "efficiency" environment? How does one respond to ethical dilemmas? For example, is the construction budget a result of proven user needs, community requirements, or a political allocation? What role does the corporate architect play in advancing the architectural profession and improving social conscience?

The natural evolution of the "efficiency" scenario results in larger institutions and corporations including architects as a part of their staff. Gutman emphasizes that since World War II there has been a significant growth of "corporate" architects. Between 1960 and 1980, the percentage of architects employed outside private architectural or engineering firms increased from 16% to 34%.[35] In 1982, according to the AIA rosters, 2,300 AIA members were working for federal, state, and municipal governments and more than 500 architects were in industry versus 38,000, the total AIA membership.[36]

Surveys by the editors of *Building Design and Construction* magazine indicate that half of the developers of multi-family housing use in-house designers for all or most of their projects. These developers rely on in-house designers more than developers of any other building type, with the exception of motel and hotel owners.[37]

Other businesses that employ the largest number of in-house architects are not in the building business. Firms that process construction-financing and real-estate-investment transactions require the expertise of educated architects. Banks and insurance companies use architectural staff members to analyze investment, mortgage, and loan decisions.[38]

Also, clients hire architects on retainer to provide general consulting services and special planning assignments, such as the development of the committee criteria when selecting other architectural and engineering professionals. Assignments may vary from maintenance evaluation to design consultation. For many years, the Dean at the Harvard Graduate School of Design was a design critic for IBM projects. Universities, museums, and commercial organizations employ a campus architect, a position that is usually very prestigious and is seen as a valuable reference.

Robert Gutman raises an interesting ethical dilemma regarding architects practicing in nontraditional roles. Because architects are chosen by clients to represent them in negotiations, staff or consultant architects are in a position to minimize the bureaucratic "red tape" during the endless deliberations that create the design and building process. This ability of staff or in-house architects to recommend that the client hire other architects is an example of what Gutman refers to as the economist's definition of supplier-induced demand.[39] It is regarded as a unique capacity of professionals and has been traditional in medicine where physicians, as a matter of course, refer patients to other "specialists" and recommend the scope of services the patient should receive. However, the architectural professional, when considering professional services, must be aware that the client is not personally hiring the recommended architect; in fact, the in-house staff architect is delegating his or her authority to influence the design process.

It appears that the corporate or institution architect must also be aware of ethical situations. The dilemma of supplier-induced demand raises an ethical issue regarding services that are being supplied past the point that a well-informed consumer would choose.[40] Architects can convincingly argue that clients and the public need more services; just look at the lack of well designed environmental conditions. However, when analyzed from the client's point of view, the extent and scope of services that the architect recommends may seem excessive.

To confront this dilemma, expanded professional services, the individual architect and the profession must gain the public's trust. Ethical people exhibit "right" behavior and develop a positive reputation for honesty and design excellence. However, this is a continuous process that must be continually reinforced. To better inform owners, clients, and the general public regarding expanded services, for example, several documents published by the AIA can be used to define and detail the areas of services recommended. It is intended that disclosure, not mystique, will add to the professional's credibility.

If required, new tasks can also be written to define each party's roles and responsibility in the special process. The client then can use the scope of work to review the architect's work. Trust is affirmed because the client is aware of the architect's accomplishments as verified by the work plan. The professional has provided a "blueprint" of recommended services and has completed the tasks according to a defined schedule. The client then understands the scope and value of the architect's expanded services.

PROFESSIONAL CHARACTERISTICS: LEADERSHIP

Whether practicing in a role outside the traditional definition of an architect or as a sole practitioner, professional architects must understand their role in the community and responsibility to society.

Architectural leaders must consistently demonstrate a commitment to integrity and honesty to define one's personal character, a mutual respect for all humanity and the common good.

Any profession, and many businesses, are essentially institutions where results are not necessarily evaluated solely in economic terms. A profession operates according to the values of its leading practitioners. Deciding what values are "good" and "right" is the first responsibility of leadership.

Leaders or managers are guided by ethical values, including honesty, candor, authenticity, and fidelity. A reputation cannot be assumed but must be earned; trust must be continually reinforced. A leader must exhibit an understanding of a larger vision; social responsibility, community values, social utility, and contributions to the group with safeguards for the well-being of individuals. Specifically, the AIA *Code of Ethics and Professional Conduct* defines five obligations dealing with professional conduct that architects as leaders must recognize. In addition, there are the intangible attributes to leadership, such as vision, enthusiasm, and creativity.

One must look to the leader for the behavior that is expected of the larger social organization: the corporation, office, university, etc. The "corporation," however, is only a construct of the mind and the law; it is juristic, not real. It is difficult to assign responsibilities to "corporations." It is possible, however, to define individual ethics with standards of behavior and morals that are expected of leaders of large institutions, values that represent societal attitudes.

Leaders or managers are also guided by the responsibilities of their task to distribute to the system's members benefits that are commensurate with each member's contributions, Canon V of the *AIA Code of Ethics and Professional Conduct*.

Basic leadership qualities require enthusiasm and attention to the people you work with on a day-to-day routine. Communication is one of the most important attributes a leader must consistently maintain. Several leadership principles should be daily experiences.[41]

Expand the Vision

Develop and revise firm goals that can be easily defined. Make sure that everyone in the firm is aware of and has participated in the definition of the vision. Actions based on the goals, therefore, are easy to implement. Also, it is possible to refocus office strategies when business situations change. How do ethics pertain to office actions? Is it fair to only include management members of the firm? What about the interns?

Identify Success

Recognize accomplishments. Use firm accomplishments or acknowledge the efforts of individuals. Emphasize the team efforts required to plan and construct a project. Is it a good idea to list team members on the credits in a magazine article? What about the company brochure? What about recognition of other team members in the brochures?

Humanize the Office

Architectural firms have two major assets, the people in the firm and the reputation of the firm created by the firm's leadership and employees. Success begins with the employees. How is the work environment designed? What about the personnel environment? What ethical considerations are important when recruiting new employees? What about when references are requested?

Creativity Is Architecture

Leadership generates the firm's attitude and success. New ideas must be encouraged and rewarded. Each project presents unique opportunities. How best to recognize those opportunities and design options is a team effort that enables all in the office to share the vision and contribute to the final effort. Is it ethical for the firm to take all the design credit for awards? It is ethical for the project manager to take credit for the building when applying for a new job? People are part of the creative process. Mentoring is an important part of the successful transition of firm leadership.

Risks Are Necessary

Management must encourage creativity; risks are necessary. Risks can be managed and mitigated. For example, exploring design concepts is expected during the planning process. Changing the floor plans during the design-development phase is usually inefficient and can lead to dissension on the consultant team. Is each project treated individually or is the office's body of work holistically managed? When considering obligations to the owner, doesn't the architect ethically "owe" a building design that is on budget?[42]

Ethical considerations and actions are a key element in the definition of leadership. Other personal attributes are required of a leader: character, integrity, and honesty.

CHARACTER/INTEGRITY/HONESTY

In a recent newspaper article, Jack Stark, the retiring president of Claremont McKenna College, remarked that "we have terrific students, but all of the evidence you see out of the freshman surveys is that they tend to be more self-centered, want to make more money and get better jobs."[43] He continued, "That's fine, but it needs to be balanced with a sense of integrity, a commitment to humanity, the community and the nation. A sense of achievement should not be beating the other fellow. It is putting forth your best effort." [44]

Does the educational system spend time on character building? Today, more and more university curriculums are offering expanded ethics courses. As a leader, the architect has an obligation to society to recognize personal values related to community service, volunteerism, a strict honor code ("I will not lie"), honesty, and a respect for the *Code of Ethics*.

The professional must also recognize societal changes. Cultural values determine the norms and values of specific situations. In addition, the professional must maintain high standards of personal conduct. Architectural leaders must consistently demonstrate a commitment to integrity and honesty to define one's personal character, a mutual respect for all humanity and the common good.

Finally, one of the positive findings of the Carnegie report indicates that 40% of the students surveyed stated that their motivation for entering the school of architecture was not money, but improving communities and the built environment.[45] This attribute presents a teaching challenge as well. The need to elevate the professional, so that the study and design of social problems are a priority, requires a real commitment to social responsibility and community. The Carnegie report continues, "The larger purpose of architects is not necessarily to become a practitioner and just build, but to become part of the community that enriches society."[46]

As demonstrated, ethical considerations and actions are a key element in the definition of leadership.

COMMUNITY RESPONSIBILITIES

To be effective and responsible, both the individual architect and the profession must expand the limits of the practice to include the community and societal interests. Greater than the personal trust is the larger public trust that presupposes that the purpose of the profession itself will not be subordinated to personal ends. This requires that beyond the professional's character, beyond the virtues of integrity, honesty, fairness, caring, and respect for others, there is a set of values and concerns that lead to a commitment to community—social responsibility in the broadest sense.

Representative of the ethical underpinnings of acting in a socially responsible manner is a concern for the common good, a respect for human dignity, a commitment to the cause of social justice, and a responsiveness to the effects of one's interventions in the natural environment. With this is mind, one must recognize that today the practice of architecture operates in a complex arena. This arena requires that we have an ethical responsibility not only to one client but to six clients as we engage in our activities:

- The fiduciary client to whom we are legally bound;
- The project users who often have little say in the actual decisions affecting their daily lives;
- The public that interfaces with and whose quality of life is, hence, affected by the works;
- The planet whose very ability to regenerate and sustain us is affected by our interventions in its natural cycles;
- The profession whose power to act is affected by the respect for our cumulative actions; we ourselves who must live with the responsibility to do not less than that of which we are capable.

This awareness is the foundation of our need, means, and direction for engagement in our communities. Three methods for this involvement are to participate, advocate, and regulate.

To participate, one might engage in the political process, either through the pursuit of political office or through appointment. Whether acting as a member of the state legislature, city council, school board, or planning commission, one has the opportunity to offer one's expertise and judgment on issues vital to one's community's well-being. As Vaclav Havel said, "Let us teach ourselves and others that politics can be not only the art of the possible, especially if 'the possible' includes the art of speculation, calculation, intrigue, secret deals and pragmatic maneuvering, but that it can also be the art of the impossible, namely, the art of improving ourselves and the world."[47]

Other means of one's participation include volunteer service to groups devoted to dealing with issues that we deal with in our professional lives: health care, shelter, and environmental protection. There is a tradition in other professions, such as law and medicine, to offer *pro-bono* service as a normal part of one's professional life.

To advocate, one might engage in the active promotion of efforts reflecting the profession's underlying value system. Examples are the active promotion of the AIA to promote livable communities and local efforts to deal with better living conditions.

To regulate, one might engage in the activity of setting up the boundaries that affect the architect's ability to produce significant work. At every turn, we operate within the constraints of a regulatory structure whose purpose is to protect the public health, safety, and welfare. Whether it pertains to sustainable design standards, land use, handicapped accessibility, building materials, building construction, public health, or transportation, we should bring to bear our knowledge and expertise to the regulatory arena and be major players.

Representative of the ethical underpinnings of acting in a socially responsible manner is a concern for the common good, a respect for human dignity, a commitment to the cause of social justice, and a responsiveness to the effects of one's interventions in the natural environment.

It is, of course, imperative that in all these pursuits we always act for the public good and not for what might be deemed our own self-interest. In ensuing sections of this book, some of the ethical aspects of these responsibilities are described.

PROFESSIONAL DEVELOPMENT

The importance of maintaining professional competency, especially in evolving technological service-based professions, such as architecture, communications, and electronics, is a straightforward concept that seems to be imperative when dealing with life-safety issues and ethical considerations to maintain the public trust. At present, the NCARB does not require continuing-education development as a requirement for certificate renewal.

In 1992, the AIA voted to require that members fulfill periodic continuing education as a condition of institute membership while not requiring continuing education for license maintenance.

During the period between 1976 and 1992, the NCARB developed a national program for registration development. The NCARB developed a monograph program called the Architect Development Verification Program (ADVP).[48] The program required that architects seek and verify that new knowledge was acquired during a specific period on a relevant subject. The NCARB established testing procedures and maintains member records. The monographs are designed to deal with contemporary, wide-ranging issues. Most topics are related to new and evolving aspects of architectural technology, technical systems, and regulations.

Basically, the NCARB and AIA approaches to continuing-education requirements are the same. While neither affiliation has specified in detail the study topics or defined testing vehicles, the organizations have defined performance characteristics for each. AIA members must document and report education activities to the institute. Licensed architects report continuing-education activities to states that require ongoing certification. Individuals may choose programs that meet personal needs; however, one-third of the topics should address health, safety, and public welfare.

Both approaches stress the need to verify to the public that architects continue to learn during their careers and that the topics studied are contemporary.

Currently, both the NCARB and the AIA are providing education in ethics, recognizing its importance and, as mentioned, the NCARB has prepared an ADVP series. At its conventions and in its leadership-training initiatives, the AIA stresses ethical considerations regarding professional-practice topics and personal responsibilities.

Research sponsored by the AIA regarding continuing education provides insight with regard to how and why architects learn:

- Architects are active learners already involved in maintaining diverse competencies through a variety of learning methods;
- Architects learn most when they participate in learning activities that address their professional needs;
- Architects typically increase knowledge about practice through self-planned learning projects that involve a combination of learning resources, including both forward and self-directed activities.

Professionals, architects included, academically and intuitively explore different techniques to develop new knowledge, maintain professional competency, and, in general, inquire. Architects continually scan their professional environment for information concerning practice and their specific areas of expertise. The AIA has created member-based Professional Interest Areas (PIAs), which are focus groups designed for specific areas of practice. Related literature sources include journals, product handouts, code supplements, and sales information, which are available for specific areas of knowledge.

Many project types require specific study to determine the background of unique design requirements. The Americans with Disabilities Act (ADA), 1990, is an excellent example of very specific building requirements that are subject to special uses in predetermined locations.

Before and since the development of a defined continuing-education process, architects have participated in programs developed by others. Seminars, conferences, presentations, lectures, and informal discussions have always been an education vehicle for professionals.

A combination of formal and informal resources leads to a lifelong learning process.[49] With regard to ethics, the learning process is best illustrated with case studies taken from professional situations and existing professional findings. Part III: Choices of this text is an excellent example of specific situational topics organized to evoke individual responses to ethical situations (see page 185). Also, the AIA publishes *Code of Ethics and Professional Conduct Decisions*. Individual findings are published that describe questions brought to the AIA's National Judical Council.[50] Discussion and conclusions are usually based on the institute's Code of Ethics.

A CLOSER LOOK AT MAKING ARCHITECTURE

OVERVIEW

In the preceding section we discussed how to be an architect and noted many of the ethical standards and responsibilities associated with the profession. Here, we review the making of architecture. The acts involved encompass three major issue areas: design and construction, practice management, and client relations.

Design and construction raises issues about producing quality designs; about architect's values, asserting what we believe; and about how we can assure that the buildings we design are safe, healthy, and functional. Design is also about how these buildings can be built efficiently within budgets using appropriate delivery systems in a responsible way. These acts all have essential ethical elements that must be considered.

Practice management requires that we understand the implications of our firm organization, and that we understand and clearly express the values of the firm. Architects as good managers must operate our organizations to effectively perform the commissions we successfully seek and the act of making outstanding architecture. Enlightened management requires goal setting, having a recognized mission, and creating personnel and work environments that are humane and supportive. Acting as responsible professionals requires a constant awareness of the expected standard of care. Sustainable practice requires awareness of and care in risk management for both our clients and the profession. These acts, too, all have essential ethical elements.

Client relations require an understanding of the changing client in today's social, cultural, and economic environment. It requires that as architects, we have an understanding of our responsibility for honesty, candor, and open communication. Architects also must have an understanding of the different client-management structures. We must, in effect, be able to become partners with our clients in the process of making excellent architecture. Ethical considerations pervade these processes.

DESIGN

Design is a creative act based on cultural background, education, and researched information. It almost always involves numerous participants, who include clients and members of related professions, disciplines, and trades, such as engineering consultants, regulatory-agencies staff members, construction managers, contractors, and bankers. Design should also include the community, people in and outside the building, and everyone else associated with the life of the structure.

During the design process, ethical considerations are germane to all requisite interchange and interaction. How can the architect respond to all these demands? Is the challenge "doable"? Who is the architect's client?

Traditionally, the profession assigned the "doing" of architecture, the design, to the sole responsibility of the architect, the designer. The activity, "doing," however, is impossible to isolate especially in an ethical context. Design is a collaborative effort.

All with vested interests take part in the process. The designer is really charged with measuring all of the input to create a coordinated design product, usually a building. But with all the alternative professions available to graduates, the design product might also be a stage set or a graphic display.

The design process really begins before the commission is awarded. Marketing, lead generation, and prospecting are important design tasks. As outlined by the AIA documents, these work assignments require definite ethical considerations.[1] During the pre-design phase, the firm's values should be visible and honestly represented. For example, the firm's previous commissions, accomplishments, and personnel responsibility must be properly identified, accurately defined, and clearly presented.

The designer's responsibility is to effectively mesh all of the diverse pieces of the project-design criteria into a "highest and best design." Design of a project requires a mix of the theoretical (e.g., spirit, beauty, and place-making); of the pragmatic (e.g., structure, mechanical systems, roof details, and door schedule); and of the functional (e.g., user satisfaction, comfort, and efficiency). This combination of the theoretical, pragmatic, and functional requires judgments of related priorities for which there are ethical considerations.

Design requires responding to other important issues as well. To what degree should the design reflect societal concerns? To what degree should it reflect sustainable design strategies? Have the client's interests been clearly understood and to what degree should they be served? What happens when the architect feels that client's direction is wrong? What happens when the client's

The design process, then, is one that clearly requires ethical considerations.

budget does not match the client's program? What happens when the client's budget does not match the architect's agenda?

One thing is certain: the profession should continue to focus on producing quality architecture. At the same time, the architect will confront changing ideologies, difficult design schedules, and, as presented by Dana Cuff, countless voices, perpetual discovery, and surprise endings.[2]

The design process, then, is one that clearly requires ethical considerations. This is more thoroughly explored in Section III (see page 185).

ARCHITECTURE DELIVERY PROCESSES

Very important to the discussion of making architecture is the quality of the design and delivery process. It affects the role of the architect and the architect's professional and ethical obligations. Without high-level design skills and ongoing coordination, any process merely becomes an assembly line for products "glued" together with technology. Form, proportion, and delight are imperative aspects of architecture and the delivery process. Without the aesthetic component, the completed project lacks the integrity demanded by the public aspects of a structure in today's society.

As stated, design is a collaborative effort, and the management of the effort is a challenge. Each designer, each office usually has a methodology that is structured to produce good design. The successful delivery process depends on strong personal relationships. The best people, brought together in a positive, collaborative environment with clear responsibilities, bring about the best results.

Ethical considerations become extremely important. Does the design team understand the client/architect contract? Mutual obligations? Project goals? During the design process, is there sensitivity to the project's relationship with the community, its values, and with the people who will use the buildings? Team members must work as a professional unit and, therefore, develop respect for each member through interpersonal relationships that reflect a high level of integrity, candor, and positive communication.

> **Team members must work as a professional unit and, therefore, develop respect for each member through interpersonal relationships that reflect a high level of integrity, candor, and positive communication.**

The architectural delivery process for a building project is a complex assemblage of conceptual, design, technical, and physical parts. The sections of the typical project are not discrete. The parts are usually subdivided, overlapped, and regrouped, but they cannot be eliminated. Also, if one of the parts is substandard, usually the entire project suffers. Each one of these parts has ethical aspects.[3]

Preliminary Design/Pre-design

The idea phase, pre-design, of any project must initially identify all the clients, owners, project users, and community representatives. This phase includes conceptual ideas, architectural programming, and design options for the site and building.

Project Initiation: The identification of project needs, goals and requirements (strategic planning) is developed, usually in report format. What effects will the new project pose to the environment? What about energy, the efficient use of materials, and appropriate land use?

Project Definition: Defining project requirements, contractual obligations, activities, spatial requirements, codes and standards, and cost models (architectural programming) is one of the first steps in the process. What is the state-of-the-art example for this building type? What if cost projections conflict with the client program? What are the client's obligations?

Site Analysis: An analysis of potential project locations are developed to determine physical requirements, limitations, and possibilities. What effects does the new project have on the neighbors? What is the architect's obligation to understand community values?

Master Plan: When appropriate, a master plan is produced that presents the assemblage of the initial findings and technical requirements for the entire project, versus a phase-by-phase development. The final plan anticipates off-site utility needs, circulation, parking, and construction requirements with identified, detailed cost estimates. Does the master plan include a community-presentation opportunity? Have the political bodies been given an opportunity to review the project?

Preliminary Design/Schematic Design and Design Development

These phases produce a best option for the project, which is usually presented in a uniform, defined format. Drawings, written descriptive materials, models, renderings, and computer space simulations are prepared for client review.

Schematic Design: With the selection of the best project option for development, physical-design elements such as plan organization, site orientation, and three-dimensional design are prepared. Preliminary engineering systems design is also completed. Have the consultants been part of the previous steps in the design team process? Have the review agencies been given an opportunity for input before the design is "fixed"? Has the community been solicited for appropriate opinions?

Design Development: The "next-step" development of a project, which defines the functional and aesthetic aspects as well as the appropriate building systems, is prepared using the approved schematic design drawings. Is first-time cost the overriding design parameter or have life-cycle-design methods been used to determine the best "systems" approach?

Construction Documents/Bidding

Documents, which include specifications and technical drawings, are developed and must satisfy codes and material-supplier competition. The construction documents should also include technical requirements, such as general conditions of the specifications to define competitive-bid procedures.

Construction Documents: "Blueprints" are technical architectural and coordinated-engineering drawings with written specifications that establish in detail what is to be built and establish a contractual basis for construction pricing. How have the completed documents satisfied all life-safety issues? Have the requirements for workmanship and proprietary issues been clearly defined?

Bidding: This process invites qualified contractors and subcontractors to submit bids for the labor and materials required to construct the project. Have the construction documents clearly defined all requested "products" and "or equal" provisions? Can the architect's drawings and specifications be used to fairly evaluate requested material substitutions?

Administration/Construction

The building of a project requires the cooperation and coordination of multiple players. To be effective, the architect must be comfortable with the complex process and the ethical aspects of construction.

Construction: Several activities are required during the physical building process. The bidding (procurement), negotiation, purchasing, and award of primary contractors and subcontractors initiate the project. Submittals of fabrication drawings, shop drawings, are reviewed for conformance with original design intentions before the fabrication delivery and assembly of the building components begins. Finally, the construction of the building requires numerous sub-trades and various skilled tradesmen. Interpersonal communication skills, as well as candor and truthfulness, are very important. The architect is required to exhibit unbiased judgment and leadership qualities when dealing with the client, contractor, and subcontractors.

CONSTRUCTION DELIVERY OPTIONS

When the production of the contract documents is complete, numerous contemporary construction variations are available to solve unique project-delivery situations. The historical design-bid-build process is no longer the only method used to plan and construct buildings. Schedule is one of the important client criteria when a new project is implemented — "time is money." Large complex, projects also require stringent management and oversight supervision. Some delivery options redefine the traditional and legal roles of the "cast of players."

New project requirements necessitate new architectural responses. Ethically, the architect must restructure several relationships that have been taken for granted for generations. For instance, who is the true client when the architect answers to the construction manager? How does the designer deal with design alterations by the construction manager, especially those that affect the public or occupant health, safety, and welfare?

> **Ethically, the architect must restructure several relationships that have been taken for granted for generations.**

The choice of a construction-delivery technique is based on several project parameters, such as schedule deadlines, budget limitations, experience of the client's management team, the designer's role, the involvement of regulatory agencies, and any limitations on the procurement process. The selected process affects the project-financing technique, professional consultants, and, ultimately, the total cost.[4] In addition to the normal process (design-bid-build), the client may consider design-build, fast-track, design-design/build (bridging), and owner-build. Contractual arrangements for the construction of a project may include a guaranteed maximum price (GMP), cost-plus, target price, and/or lump sum.[5] No longer is low bid the most important factor.

Several delivery approaches can be compared.[6]

Traditional Construction Process (Design-Bid-Build)

Traditional construction process (design-bid-build) provides guaranteed construction prices and defined plans and specifications that can be reviewed by contractual-law precedent. Review by the client/owner is simplified, and tradition and experience have defined the role of each of the team members. Coordination of all disciplines by the contractor is also expected, which conceptually eliminates construction problems. Because the profession has refined this process with numerous contracts and case law, the technique is understood and explainable to new members of the office and clients, versus the accelerated techniques that follow. Ethical considerations include the nature of obligations to the client, particularly regarding potential conflicts of interest over design quality, material and system designation, and contractor-suggested changes. Candor and truthfulness are required at all times.

Design-Build

Design-build was a technique used to construct a series of similar building types, such as "tilt-up" concrete warehouse structures or "tract" housing projects. The process is now used for large hospitals, court buildings, and large hotels. The design-build technique establishes construction costs at a very early project phase, sometimes at the end of schematic design. The contractor usually retains the architect/engineer (A/E) team. The architect, then, responds directly to the contractor, not the client. Or is the client the contractor? Who is the client? Because the price has been established as a lump sum or GMP, the contractor greatly influences decisions regarding the initial design approach, material selection, equipment, finishes, and light fixtures.

Effective design requires an excellent working relationship, trust, and candor between the designer and contractor. How important is it that the contractor has the same values as the architect? How are client expectations defined? How does the architect respond to the contractor? To the client?

Fast-Track Construction

Fast-track construction overlaps design and construction tasks to accelerate the building process. This technique has been used for large building projects, such as high-rise office buildings, commercial ocean ports, and large-scale airports. Site work and foundations are under construction before the buildings are fully designed. Experienced professionals are required because the coordination of several bid packages for building components is necessary. Components include the foundation package, the structural shell, the exterior building skin, mechanical equipment, and interior finishes. Cost control is more difficult because the numerous bid packages may or may not meet initial cost estimates. Also, management of the fast-track process is a challenge. Because of the multiple-bid packages, more than one general contractor may be required to construct major building components, and it follows that numerous subcontractors will require prime contracts.

The leaders of the process must be forthright and clear with all communications. They should be impartial and employ competent consultants. Conflict-of-interest issues for the architect, such as the relationship of the firm's design-quality standards and the accelerated construction process, must be continually tested.

Design/Design-Build (Bridging)

Design/design-build (bridging) is a hybrid of the design build and the traditional process. One architect representing the client prepares the design documents, schematic drawings, and design-development drawings. The project's design, layout, three-dimensional qualities, materials, and engineering systems—"bridging documents"—are prepared and specified by the architectural/engineering client team. Details are not prepared, and the specifications are developed as a performance document. Specific products, material selections, and equipment details are not called out.

After a competitive-bid process based on the bridging documents, the construction documents are the responsibility of the contractor who usually employs an A/E firm as a subcontractor. The contractor's architect becomes the architect-of-record and seals the drawings.

This construction technique is designed to guarantee a GMP at the end of the design-development phase, to eliminate field disputes, and to reduce change-order claims. Because the contractor prepares the construction documents in concert with subcontractors, no conflicts should arise during the construction of the project.

Without the continued design review of the original architect, it is difficult to realize any design continuity in this process. Several ethical conflicts are also possible. For example, is the second architect responsible to the client or contractor? In effect, who's the client when the A/E works for the contractor? How does the architect deal with client expectations and performance expectations when the architect is responsible to the contractor?

Owner-Build

Owner-build is not a new construction-management technique; however, public agencies have recently begun assuming more responsibilities traditionally assigned to general contractors. Because of in-house expertise (licensed contractors, engineers, and architects), cities, counties, and school districts lead the construction team. The consulting architect's and engineer's role may or may not change. However, as the owner's representative, the architect's role is usually to administrate the construction process and advise the owner/client. Dilemmas can occur. For example, what is the architect's ethical responsibility when the project manager for the school district changes in the field the materials specified, approved, and bid without the specific knowledge of the school board, the client?

This construction technique was originally designed to eliminate the general contractor's profit and reduce overhead expenses. However, the bureaucracy requires a series of check-off decisions that usually require a longer approval process. More time is then required to get started and get finished. What is the architect's public responsibility? Does this process produce actual savings, or does the process just produce perceived savings? How is the public trust in the architect maintained? Mutual obligations, professionalism, and conflict-of-interest considerations create possible dilemmas.

One of the results of nontraditional construction processes developed to replace the general contractor's oversight and coordination duties is the role of a construction manager (CM). The CM works for the client and, therefore, enjoys the confidence of the owner, a direct consultant role similar to that of an architect. As with construction-delivery processes described earlier, the architect's responsibilities can begin to blur. During a construction dispute, does the architect share the confidence and agenda of the CM (also the owner's representative), or must the architect supersede the CMs authority and report directly to the client? This dilemma creates a difficult working relationship.

The CM can expand the client's expertise and staff for a specific project and for the limited planning-and-construction schedule. The clients can, in effect, employ the special expertise they require for a defined fee, limited overhead, and no long-term employment commitment. Since CMs have focused on the changes in project-delivery systems, they have expanded their services to include pre-project development, architect selection, project management, cost control, drawing review, value engineering, and bid evaluation, as well as construction services described earlier.

For the architect, several ethical issues are presented. For example, should the architect evaluate and protect the client's best interest regarding professional services? Is the CM a professional? Who is held to a high standard of care?

In summary, variations in project- and service-delivery techniques will continue to respond to new project challenges. Decisions will still require ethical considerations. Some of the key issue areas include:

- Understood relationship between the owner, architect, and contractor;
- Defined project goals and clear selection criteria;
- Contract oversight and project-delivery coordination.

Also, ethical aspects of the complex construction techniques will require vigilant and constant consideration. Because of the numerous individuals involved in the process, interpersonal communications must always be concise. Trust will be immediately destroyed if meeting minutes contradict established verbal approvals or mitigated compromises to identified problems. Personal integrity must form professionalism and "right" rules of conduct. All participants must be aware of the public welfare and understand the mutual obligations established among the client, designer, and builder.

Organization Issues

To remain current, especially with the aforementioned delivery options, contemporary architects cannot practice in an isolated professional environment. Reliance on experience, talented consultants, and associated team members are critical to the success of the project.

How will the office of the next millennium develop the resources to satisfy the demands of an involved public, a sophisticated client, and a multifaceted construction process? A traditional office structure may or may not be the most beneficial way to approach design services.

The changing scope of work, project sizes, and different building types may require a different professional organization to produce construction documents for future projects. As discussed earlier, methods of both design and construction delivery create demands on the architectural-office organization, which requires techniques to support efficient, effective, quality design.

The organization of a new office or the reorganization of an existing office must consider several issues. The type of ownership structure (sole proprietorship, partnership, or corporation); the new firm's mission, goals, personnel-management philosophy, and fiscal policies; and a defined design philosophy must be compatible with the firm's staff and new project-development expectations.

The management structure can be hierarchical, collaborative, and/or divided into separate studios. The management approach should fit the "culture of the firm." Management techniques and policies in architectural organizations affect employee satisfaction, decision-making, design quality, internal budgets, and firm image.

Ethically, leaders and managers of good firms must exhibit positive, professional actions and "right" behavior. Trust and candor are important personal traits. Choices must be debated openly.

Consider the following case study.

THE NEW FIRM

During the spring of 1999, Bill Smith, Harvey Peterson, and Gloria Silva decided that the time had arrived for them to take the necessary steps to start their own architectural firm. After all, they had graduated five years ago, had worked for various firms, and belonged to various community groups that they felt provided a basis for future commissions. Harvey had known Gloria since high school, their families were friends, and they both had gone to school with Bill. All three had worked in different offices and had a variety of different project types in their portfolios. At lunch on a Friday in March, they made it official. SPS was in business! They respected each other's talents and abilities and were enthused about the opportunity to work together.

The following Sunday afternoon, they met to discuss the goals and organizational structure of the new venture. All three had positions in firms, yet Harvey's firm was anticipating a slow business period during the next six months. Each member of the new firm had thought about becoming a principal in his or her own firm one day and had definite ideas about the structure of the firm as well as the projects that he or she wanted to design. The excitement of the group was obvious, and each of the three discussed plans for the future with great enthusiasm.

Bill Smith had been active in local service clubs and knew a number of business leaders in the surrounding communities. He felt that the direction of SPS would best serve the community if the firm became active in city-redevelopment efforts and *pro-bono*

(continued on next page)

(continued from previous page)

projects for various service clubs. To discuss a number of upcoming projects with his friends, Bill felt that he needed marketing materials. At the minimum, the firm would require an office brochure, graphically appropriate business cards, stationery, and some funds for breakfast, lunch, and dinner meetings. In addition, Bill felt that the firm should pay for his membership to other professional organizations. No one disputed his ideas, yet Gloria inquired about his budget. What was the anticipated payback, and when would the firm get started on the design of the new projects? Gloria's background was in design. She had won all the competitions in school, worked for a published New York architect, interned in Rome, and "understudied" for a leading Los Angeles architect. She was ready to express her own talent while working with new clients. She had an impressive design portfolio to use when seeking commissions for the firm. Gloria felt that she could best serve future clients as the leader of the firm, a sole proprietor, or 51% owner of the corporation. SPS would then qualify as a woman-owned minority architectural firm.

Harvey was quite good at organizing projects and liked to coordinate the consultant's work with the architect's contract documents. He also enjoyed organizing the affairs of the office and was willing to act as the office manager. In that position, he wanted to establish project handbooks and procedures. He especially wanted to explore design-build possibilities with contractors he had met and respected.

Bill Smith had recently attended AIA seminars regarding strategic planning and felt that the final firm-ownership arrangement, the next step for SPS, was to meet in a retreat environment for a weekend to develop a business plan for the firm and the firm's mission statement. Immediate and long-range goals could be discussed, objectives (methods to achieve the goals) could be delegated to firm principals, and evaluation techniques (written action plans with recorded "feedback" reports) had to be prepared and reviewed monthly during the first months of the new firm. Bill suggested a facilitator who could lead the discussion and organize the weekend activities. Harvey also mentioned the need for an attorney who was sympathetic to an architect's personality and an accountant who could organize the firm's books. Gloria asked about an agenda for all the ideas discussed that Sunday afternoon. Some clear questions had emerged, all with ethical considerations.

New smaller firms are usually organized as a proprietorship or partnership. Decisions about their organization raise ethical considerations:

- Should the firm be organized as an equal partnership regarding authority, responsibility, and compensation? (To be organized as a Minority/Women Owned Business Enterprise (M/WBE) requires that Gloria's ownership equal 51 percent.)
- Is it ethical to establish a women-owned firm if the organization is really an equal partnership?
- How will the new principals represent the work they have completed for their present employers? How will the new principals solicit work from their employers' clients?
- Should the form of ownership require personal, fiscal responsibility for all financial obligations?
- If the firm provides *pro-bono* services, who should participate and how should the firm pay for overhead expenses?

> Ethically, leaders and managers of good firms must exhibit positive, professional actions and "right" behavior. Trust and candor are important personal traits.

Briefly, the principal features of each general form of ownership are described.

Proprietorships

A proprietorship, sometimes referred to as a **sole proprietorship,** is the simplest form of practice. The business is the responsibility of one person. No other members of the business have any legal arrangement. The individual and the firm are one.

How can the sole proprietorship provide for the future of longtime members of the firm? Should this be a consideration, or should associates expect to retire when the boss retires? Why should employees remain loyal to a leader who is going to abandon them?

Partnerships

A partnership requires two or more practitioners to provide architectural services. The business entity is not separate or distinct from the partners. In a partnership, each individual (partner) is liable for all of the business and professional debts of the entire partnership, and each partner's assets may be available for claims.

It is preferable to establish a partnership with a specific written document. Items, which should be understood by each partner and written in the agreement, take into account each partner's position in the firm regarding income, loss exposure, and individual partner contributions.

Ethical considerations of a partnership business organization include considerations of truth, honesty, candor, and mutual respect.

How can the partnership influence young architects in the firm? Should junior partners be exposed to equal equity risks? How can original partners retire without financially bankrupting the business? All these questions have ethical aspects.

Corporations

Corporations are separate legal entities with independence under the law. The corporation is a complicated business structure when compared to a proprietorship or partnership. There are legal requirements for boards of directors, income-tax preparation, corporate minutes, and state-by-state reporting regulations. The corporation does create its own entity, perpetual life, which transcends the individual leadership. For example, Flewelling and Moody, a California architectural firm, celebrated the firm's seventieth year in 1998. Skidmore, Owings, and Merrill (SOM) was founded in the 1930s. The breadth of experience and the background of a mature firm establish the public trust (which has been discussed at length in this text).

The corporation exists as a legal independent entity. It can hold and convey property and sue or be sued in its corporate name. Management is centralized in the board of directors, usually independent overseers. The corporation can transfer interests and limit shareholders' liability.

How does the corporation respond to professional and ethical responsibilities? Since the board of directors can be faceless, how does the community engage the architectural corporation? Who is responsible to the client, the board, the president, and/or the project manager? How do employees interact with the board of directors?

MANAGEMENT RESPONSIBILITIES

Whatever form of office structure is selected, proprietorship, partnership, or corporation, architectural offices require an understanding of basic management techniques and the realization of present-day, multiple layers of responsibilities created by larger projects and complex clients. It is very clear to the 1999 AIA Gold Medal recipient Frank Gehry, FAIA, who stressed the rigors of practice—the equal need for excellent management skills, excellent design skills, and the benefits of the computer—in his acceptance speech during the national AIA convention.[9]

Enlightened and responsible management deals with decision-making within an ethical framework. To provide an animated illustration, the following description of events relates the ethical aspects of a management philosophy that provided the basis for policy direction at a major corporation for thirty years. While the manufacturing process and product-promotion-sales issues are not exactly the same as those affecting the management direction for an architectural-services firm, the principles discussed (i.e., honesty, candor, and employer-employee relations) provide lessons for any creative enterprise. The case involves Johns-Manville (J-M), a leading supplier of architectural products, and a prestigious design competition for an important architectural commission sponsored to create a new J-M corporate image.

The events really have two faces. A sympathetic architectural patron supportive of design excellence was seeking an award-winning project to enhance the corporation's image (face one). The corporation's culture, however, was based on a profit-driven management style that overlooked human conditions and based employee relations on actuarial statistics without regard for quality of life or human suffering (face two). The architectural solution had little to do with the management ethics of the large corporation. Since the early 1940s, J-M management had overlooked the company's dangerous employee workplace environment, which was unknown to the general public.

Did the competing architects have knowledge of J-M management priorities? Probably not! If so, should the firms have pursued the following competition?

> **Enlightened and responsible management deals with decision-making within an ethical framework.**

A MANAGEMENT CASE

The pages of a major architectural publication illustrated the results of this national competition to define and construct a national headquarters outside Denver, Colorado, for a major construction materials corporation, Johns-Manville.[10] The company had initiated a major competition to select a design firm to create a new corporate image. The project site, located in the foothills outside Denver, Colorado, was a 10,000-acre Ken-Caryl Ranch that required a design sympathetic to Johns-Manville's desire to preserve the natural environment, create human-scaled spaces, and have room to properly grow. The ranch is a natural sanctuary for wildlife and big game. Several nationally recognized firms were invited and participated.

The winning submission by The Architects Collaborative (TAC) was a shining, metallic-clad, low-profile office complex that cut through the rugged landscape. Two offset triangular sections created large

(continued on next page)

(continued from previous page)

floor areas separated by a light court. The elegant single shape used every site attribute: excellent views of downtown Denver, a strong sense of arrival, image, and sheltered parking on terraced levels behind the structure.[11] Also, as emphasized by John Sheehy, TAC's project architect, "the fast-track building technique required an immediate technical response. The original concept was unaltered. Very few design changes were possible because of the compressed construction schedule."[12] The building won several architectural awards after completion in 1977. It was a well conceived and managed project by all involved.

© Nick Wheeler

In stark contrast, by 1986 Manville (Johns-Manville's reorganized corporate name) was in the process of issuing 80% of its equity to a trust representing people who had sued or planned to sue the company for liability in connection with one of its principal former products, asbestos.[13] During the 1930s and 1940s, information was available to Johns-Manville's medical department, as well as to company executives, implicating asbestos inhalation as a cause of asbestosis, a debilitating lung disease, and lung cancer and mesothelioma, a fatal lung disease. Manville managers suppressed the research. Also, as a matter of policy, they decided to conceal the information from affected employees. For years, the executives and medical staff concealed critical, life-threatening information from consumers and Manville employees.[14]

What was the motivation for the concealment: money, competition, or disbelief? In court testimony, a company lawyer reported that company officials decided that it was more cost-effective to pay for employee death benefits than to provide safer workplace conditions.

A New Jersey court found that Manville had made a conscious, cold-blooded business decision to take no protective or remedial action, in flagrant disregard of the rights of others.[15]

How can this behavior be explained? Gellerman writes in the *Harvard Business Review* that the people involved were ordinary men and women. They found themselves in a dilemma, and they solved it in a way that seemed to be the least troublesome, deciding not to disclose information that could hurt their product. The consequences of what they chose to do—both to thousands of innocent people and ultimately to the corporation—probably never occurred to them.

What lessons can be learned from this case? Why do managers make poor ethical decisions? The Manville case illustrates the line between acceptable and unacceptable managerial behavior. Executives were expected to pursue their company's best interest but not overstep bounds of responsibility to employees and the public. However, management decisions should not be measured in terms of profit only. As professionals, responsible behavior is expected.[16]

The managers of Manville may have believed that they were acting in the company's best interests, or that what they were doing would never be found out, or even that it wasn't really wrong. In the end, whatever their rationalization for the asbestos cover-up, their conduct bankrupted the company and prompted unknown human angst.

The architectural business is not unlike the Manville corporate mission; architectural managers must also respond to the needs of the client. Sometimes it is difficult to determine the proper balance of client ownership, social responsibility, and employee/employer dedication. In retrospect, a study always indicates what should have been! But architects don't manage in retrospect.

In today's challenging practice, the architect daily faces decisions regarding clean air, sustainable environments, use of nonrenewable resources, land density, and healthy building-material content—issues that demand responsible resolutions.

It is the primary responsibility of the professional to protect the life and safety of the public.

The Manville case delineates four rationalizations that can lead architectural managers to inappropriate decisions:[17]

- A belief that the activity is within reasonable ethical and legal limits—that it is not "really" illegal or immoral;
- A belief that the activity is in the individual's or the architectural firm's best interests—that the individual would somehow be expected to undertake the activity;
- A belief that the activity is "safe" because it will never be found out or publicized—the classic crime-and-punishment issue of discovery.
- A belief that because the activity helps the company, the executive leadership will, therefore, condone it and even protect the person who engages in it.

Reasonable Ethical Limits

The idea that an action is not really wrong is not unique. The issue is complex and involves an interruption between executive goals and the manager's actions to achieve the leadership's aims. For example, architectural project managers in ill-defined, ambiguous situations will sometimes conclude that whatever hasn't been labeled specifically wrong must be acceptable, especially if rewards for results are defined. Architects usually do not ask subordinates to do things that both know are ethically wrong. But leaders sometimes leave things unsaid deliberately, thereby distancing themselves from the manager's tactical decision. Good managers do not avoid difficult decisions!

The Firm's Best Interest

Setting aside personal ethical standards in favor of a larger sense that the interests of the firm are more important is the result of a very parochial view of business politics and right behavior. The best interest of the individual or the firm is an extremely difficult, complex definition, especially when the belief leads to unethical conduct. Usually a view that "winning" is all that is important leads to decisions that establish "no rules." Short-term success, when rewarded at the expense of long-term stability, is also a by-product of win-at-all-costs. For example, project hours can be reduced and profits increased when the contract documents are incomplete, yet are advertised for bid before the consultant and architectural drawings are thoroughly coordinated. Bid prices may not be greatly affected. But when substantial construction problems surface, change orders illustrate the competence of the initial, short-term decisions. Is this unethical behavior? Because the behavior affects the client's cost and the welfare of all members of the firm, it certainly merits ethical consideration.

Crime and Punishment

The third belief that risk is manageable because one can get away with it is a very difficult dilemma because it is usually true. A great deal of proscribed behavior escapes detection.

Conscience alone does not deter everyone.

Wrongdoing must be easier to detect. If today's discovery process, in which a plaintiff's attorneys can comb through a company's records to look for incriminating evidence, had been possible when J-M concealed the company's background on asbestosis, there probably would have been no cover-up. The corporation would have chosen a different business course, not protection by bankruptcy courts, and jobs and lives would be different today.

It has been demonstrated that the most effective deterrent to unethical behavior is not to increase the severity of punishment for those caught, but to heighten the perceived probability of being caught in the first place.[18] For example, an inspector's frequent or infrequent visits to a building site changes the entire construction operation. The job is clean, hard hats are worn, and usually all daily logs are current. Architectural managers, therefore, should identify misconduct and exemplify appropriate behavior. Since the main deterrent to illegal or unethical behavior is the perceived probability of detection, a professional should make an example of those who are detected and convicted. A number of state licensing boards publish disciplinary notices of people found in violation of architectural statutes. And today more boards are adopting codes of conduct that deal with ethical issues and guide appropriate disciplinary actions.

The Firm Wins

Professionals sometimes hold beliefs that the firm or institution will condone actions that are taken in its interest. How do we condone loyalty that has gone beyond reasonable limits? What are the consequences for the project manager who directs staff to assign their time to a "winning" project budget while covering further losses on an over-budget project? What kind of management lessons do firm interns learn from this technique? Firm leadership must demonstrate a moral, ethical force in the firm. Leadership is responsible for determining the line between loyalty to the client, the firm, and society and to the self-interests of the individual and individual architectural firm as a business entity.[19] Architectural firms have the right to expect loyalty from employees against competition and detractors, but not loyalty for actions that are against the law, common morality, or societal good.

Most extreme examples of misconduct are due, in hindsight, to managerial failures. One way to avoid oversights is to establish control mechanisms in the operations of the firm, or "inspecting the inspectors." It is the responsibility of the firm's leadership to establish a clear and pragmatic direction, a professional culture that emphasizes a clear ethical foundation as the basis for a good practice.

STANDARD OF CARE

As professionals, architects must manage and operate their business, conduct private affairs, and communicate with the public in a more responsible manner than that expected of most "business people." Education, training, and a license to practice architecture demand a higher standard of conduct and care. The architect is expected to protect the public. The definition of the standard of care is based on English law and requires that the professional exhibit a degree of care, skill, and diligence equivalent to what one would expect from a similar professional. Simply put, it is those actions another architect would exercise in a similar situation.[20]

Legally, the standard of care cannot be determined in advance, only after the fact and usually by the courts. However, the architect cannot wait for after-the-fact judgment. Changing client demands, a litigious societal attitude, and the repetitious aspects of the computer have added to the complexity of architectural practice.

As a professional, the architect is held to a high level of expectation. That is, the architect is expected to develop a considered, responsible, and positive course of professional conduct. It also is expected that professionals will knowingly accept those risks and only those risks for which they are competent and with which they are comfortable.[21] The management of potential risks requires the systematic application of knowledge and understanding rather than the application of rules and rote answers.

Satisfying each client's unique need is a personal, professional duty for which the architect has been educated and trained. In fact, the architect accepts this obligation when their license is issued.[22]

Society recognizes that the architect has unique capabilities and special knowledge. The architect is trusted to use those special skills to benefit society in general and the client in particular. On the other hand, society also recognizes that the architect cannot guarantee an outcome; infallibility is not required.[23]

To maintain one's professional status, therefore, it is important to be current with up-to-date professional knowledge. It follows, then, that continuing education is a professional responsibility.[24] For example, the knowledge and application of codes and standards is mandated; however, a basic understanding of the law also requires an ongoing awareness of societal attitudes and norms.

In addition, when refining one's understanding of the law, the professional should consider three basic categories of obligations:

Contractual, which includes terms, special conditions, schedules, and project requirements such as budgets.

Regulatory law, which includes building codes, license requirements, zoning law, ordinances, ADA requirements, and specific review agency oversight, such as the local fire marshal's standards.

> The definition of the standard of care is based on English law and requires that the professional exhibit a degree of care, skill, and diligence equivalent to what one would expect from a similar professional.

Standard of care, which includes professional and social responsibilities whose norms are established, maintained, and promulgated by fellow architects and society.

Criminal actions or felonies, such as fraud, price-fixing, and bribery, can be easily illustrated and defined. Civil actions, such as those actions brought by individuals seeking redress in the form of money, may not be as easy to understand. Nuisance suits usually require third-party review and sometimes jury deliberation to determine fault and monetary consequences. Civil law has established societal rules so that we can accurately predict the consequences of our actions.[25]

It is important to understand the ethical aspects of the standard of care. Just as the principles of "defensive driving" require that you anticipate other drivers' actions and behavior, architects should place themselves in the "driver's seat" in every practice situation. Undertake only those responsibilities for which one is qualified.

> **It is important to understand the ethical aspects of the standard of care.**

In summary, society relies on the architect to exercise prudence and to act with a reasonable level of judgment and skill.

RISK MANAGEMENT

In addition to being held as a professional to a high public review standard, the architect must also identify those areas of professional and societal interest that may result in risk.[26] It is the primary responsibility of the professional to protect the life and safety of the public. The architect is educated, trained, and tested to provide these services to the client and to associated clients, the community.

Of equal importance is the identification of potential risk to the client. When the architect begins a project, the client must understand the scope of the work, the schedule, and possible project roadblocks. Extended agency reviews, unsure construction markets, material shortages, zoning restrictions, and a controversial project type may disrupt the client's deadlines and fiscal solvency.

Finally, the professional must assume internal risks within the firm. Ongoing workload and payroll burden must be considered when assuming new projects. "Insurance" must cover the client as well as the staff. The firm leadership has a responsibility to understand all levels of risk and to inform those involved with the project at all levels.

Risk is the possibility of loss and/or injury. Loss can usually be defined in financial terms: lack of rent, lack of income, expense for delays. The architectural-development-team's participant most at risk is the client. The architect's ethical responsibility as the client's representative is to be aware of and inform the client of: [27]

Exposure

The client is exposed to the possibility of loss or injury during the building process; the need for insurance, builder's bonds, acceptable delay consequences, and potential product substitutions must be clear to all parties.

Capabilities

The architect requires the additional professional services of the structural, mechanical, and electrical engineer, as well as of the civil engineer, landscape architect, and interior designer.

Responsibilities

As a licensed professional, the architect must exhibit a high level of responsible expectations, a standard of care.

Power

The architect's performance will be affected by the decision-making authority for project decisions, especially during construction administration with regard to such issues as workmanship, product substitutions, schedule delays, and progress payments.

The process of risk management is usually decided during contract negotiations before all the project's facts and circumstances are known, especially if the project is still theoretical in status.

When a project begins, basic tenets should be established; these are contract principles held in common by all members of the design team, owner's representatives, and related consultants.[28] Next establish pre-design tasks, and create a checklist procedure for each duty and personnel assignments necessary for a building project's success. Finally, review the related tasks with regard to the following considerations: [29]

1. What, if any, inherent exposure exists?
2. Who is most capable of handling the exposure?
3. Who is responsible for the exposure?
4. Who has the power to make sure that the responsibility is carried out?

The assignment of the duties should be based on minimizing risks for all involved. It is expected that each party will perform according to written and verbal communications; candor, and honesty are the acceptable norm. In all decisions, the public interest must be observed and protected.

Full disclosure is important. Architects are retained for their professional skill and judgment. Experience and talent need to be demonstrated; reality and boundaries should be established early. Perfection, however, is unrealistic.

Architectural offices should understand the possibility of disputes, but also should establish methods to deal with problems. Don't sign contracts that cannot be enforced, or that provide requirements or guarantees that cannot be met. Insurance, including errors and omissions coverage, should be considered a professional obligation. Quality-control procedures should be continually updated. Third-party plan checks, outside cost estimators, value engineering, peer-review meetings, and responsive, positive management attitude can provide an important firm culture to support individual staff efforts. Disputes can be identified before issues become problems. Upper-level management should become involved at the beginning of a potential problem. Action must be taken with all project representatives present to define alternative strategies and implement a corrective action. For example, at the initiation of a project, schematic cost estimates that exceed the project budget require immediate attention, not hopeful resignation that the project will be altered during design development.

> **It is the primary responsibility of the professional to protect the life and safety of the public.**

Managing risk, whether for the public, the client, or the architect, requires an understanding of what can go wrong, as well as several approaches to inherent problems created by the design process.[30]

Ethical considerations clearly support positive risk-management practices.

EMPLOYERS/EMPLOYEES

The architectural office must respond to changing assignments and responsibilities. Each member of the team in the master's studio or large conglomerate will have to fulfill specific and different professional roles during the course of a project. Different professional situations will create different and sometimes conflicting ethical situations. How does the mentor relate to the new college graduate? How is the architectural consultant team

identified? Who responds to client problems? Also, when one assumes a nontraditional role in the architectural process, where are the individual's responsibilities defined?

Offices are formed and structured to produce excellent solutions to architectural challenges. It follows that offices are composed of varied individuals who carry out specific assignments based on project requirements. Most design offices design a management structure that identifies roles for each professional; however, because the architectural "business" is extremely diverse, it requires employers and employees to respond to numerous roles, sometimes each day. Ethical aspects of this diversity require the awareness of the office's and the individuals' commitment to right behavior. Understanding the AIA *Code of Ethics and Professional Conduct*, for example, should be an office/team effort. Business decisions can be discussed with regard to the ethical considerations. Both employer and employee are part of the process.

Understanding the AIA *Code of Ethics and Professional Conduct*, for example, should be an office/team effort.

It is the definition of the role, or more precisely the definition of the responsibility attached to the role (ethics), that may lead to conflicts and interpersonal struggle. For example, who is given credit for the design of the project? If the office is truly a "team" or operates as a "studio," then the entire responsible group should be singled out for design excellence.

In a small office, architects are able to follow a commission from the proposal stage to construction completion. During this two- to three-year process, the architect must wear a variety of "hats," each reflecting a difficult role. The interview "hat" produces the best possible public appearance: an architect who is knowledgeable, informative, and cooperative. The design "hat" produces a problem-solver, an imaginative creator. The technical hat produces an organized, astute person with technical skills. The construction-administration hat produces a congenial person, detailed and thorough. Maybe this is why the profession attracts so many varied personalities; one has to be flexible to be part of the profession.

Each role entails different ethical considerations. The public-appearance mode requires candor and accuracy, with proper identification of the firm's strengths, as well as respect for the firm's inadequacies, such as a shortage of personnel, inappropriate experience in a building type, and lack of research-grounded building histories. The design mode requires a commitment to creativity, problem-solving, and state-of-the-art systems. A positive relationship with the client ensures that the design is understood and that the client has been kept an active participant in the process. The technical mode requires a commitment to professional continuing education. People responsible for the detailing of buildings must be aware of construction-industry norms and new techniques. Ethically, the office must provide training opportunities for staff to remain current or slightly ahead of the information curve. What is the appropriate way to indicate building details? What should be specified to maximize public, client, and user welfare?

Each role entails different ethical considerations.

Finally, during construction the architect must partner with the builders. Conflicts and requests for information must be addressed in a timely, objective manner to keep the project going. The contractor shares many of the architect's ethical obligations. A forthright relationship requires that all sides avoid conflicts of interest and respect the final goal of the project, which is an excellent building project for the client.

The multiple-role description is a key to understanding the architectural office's employer/employee relationships and responsibilities. In fact, the role responsibilities are usually established by ownership, rank, and experience. It is very difficult for the young intern to reinvent the architectural design style of the office if the principal is a strong designer. Tradition is difficult to set aside, especially in smaller offices. Sociologist Judith Blau stresses in her extensive study of architectural firms that a professional ethos, or guiding moral principles, tends to construct the behavior of the designer and employees, in effect by assigning the status of "master value" to design.[31] The architect is trained to assume responsibility for design to the extent that one's identity is justified by the credit. But design is a small part of the process and sometimes, therefore, establishes a social rift between the designer and usually all others. The ethical dilemma presented by assigning more importance to one role than another is obvious in the conduct of a professional practice. Stifled designers and unappreciated technical staff have no future and usually leave the firm. It must be the ethical practice of the leadership to recognize the professional consequences of implied office philosophy versus the day-to-day actual operations of the practice.

Dana Cuff's work emphasizes that the architectural profession has established the culture of today's office practice.[32] The intended relationship of employer/employee has been established by the historical precedent of architectural practice—the studio, the team, everyone sharing roles. In reality, the profession's historic link to the fine arts, which established the atelier, or studio, approach to practice, doesn't fit the demands of today's service-delivery methods.[33]

For an office to provide complex services and to effectively operate as a team, the employer/employee environment must operate at several organizational levels that include staff, consultants, and the community. The office should provide a healthy and decent workplace for all staff. The humanistic level is still important to the individual in every category mentioned. Personnel policy and procedures should be fair and provide an equitable balance for all members of an office. Individuals should be recognized as the most important element of the architectural service-delivery system. Mentoring, an ethical mandate,[34] is extremely important. Employees also have obligations to the firm.[35] New employees of the office must understand traditions and the professional philosophy of the firm. Members of the firm must also share in the culture of the firm. Enthusiasm, commitment, and a positive work ethic should be important personal attributes of all office members. All of these elements have an ethical foundation.

Members of the firm must also share in the culture of the firm. Enthusiasm, commitment, and a positive work ethic should be important personal attributes of all office members.

Because of identified large-project demands, many offices have to be larger and provide expanded services. In these cases, employer/employee relations must recognize that the larger office size must respond to more complex organizational issues. Some policies may require additional attention and ethical considerations. When larger projects are commissioned, office team members must respect the firm's organizational structure. A personal commitment to open communication and candor is an important aspect of project development and scheduling. Team members require recognition for specific as well as group accomplishments.

CONSULTANTS

The complexity of the design-and-build process is a daunting experience. The detailing of millions of connections in a house-framing plan and the application of planning approvals for an environmental-impact report are typical assignments the architect routinely coordinates.

Numerous contemporary responsibilities have created a need for focused consultant input. New seismic findings and technical data require stringent structural analysis. Life-cycle considerations and potential costs require efficient buildings that are easy to service and repair. Environmental considerations require land-use solutions that complement the natural habitat. Building materials must also be selected that respond to a locale's climate and sustainable requirements. One person cannot assume responsibility for these complex technical requirements. Consultants must complement the designer's responsibilities during the conceptual layout of the project and the final material detailing of the contract documents.

It is important to recognize the ethical considerations of the consultant-selection process.

It is important to recognize the ethical considerations of the consultant-selection process. The architect is really recommending the consultant team; this is, in fact, an endorsement. Has the firm previously worked with the consultant? Does the consultant have a successful track record? Have the consultants worked on similar types of projects? Can you support representations of your consultant team?

The team of people that includes the multiple disciplines necessary to produce the documents for any architectural project must understand the contemporary requirements of interpersonal relationships.[37] The team members also must understand general ethical considerations of business and society. Any strong, successful team recognizes and follows the fundamental team-relationship foundations of cooperation, understanding, trust, and confidence. Blau's study of firms indicates that the more participatory the office, the more effective it is in terms of business, design quality, and success with consultants.[38] An open relationship with all team members promotes a well-coordinated project. Individually, the consultants cannot produce technically proficient, complete solutions to building-design problems.

As the leader, the architect is responsible for bringing together all parts of the production sequence. Constant communication is important. Clear, unambiguous, and consistent decisions are required.

In the leadership role, the architect must emphasize collaboration between the consultants. The overlapping responsibilities must be outlined and reviewed at each step in the process. The complexities of a normal project have to be reduced to identify components that can be tracked as the production of the drawings and technical specifications progresses. Usually the project's complexity leads to the consultant and architect having integrated responsibilities. Who's responsible for what and why? What areas of the process require identification and close coordination? Mutual obligations must be clearly defined. The leader or architect must delegate responsibility without losing sight of his or her professional, legal, and ethical accountability.

As is usually expected, the success of the effort depends on the firm's commitment to project organization, proper scheduling, and appropriate review processes.

Above all, good interpersonal communication and a mutual understanding of the consultant team's accountability are the components of successful relationships and responsible projects.

THE CHANGING CLIENT

Historically, the patron selected the artist (architect) to create family treasures, cathedrals, and inspiring structures.[39] Today, most clients are more complex, more economically diverse, and directed by a wider range of objectives. The architectural firm has to go through the selection/interview process to be awarded new commissions. The "merchant prince" has become a client with several departments, advisors, and competing political agendas. In addition, the client may be attracted not only to an architect, but also to an interior designer, contractor, engineer, construction manager, and/or in-house corporate architects. The client may be the community, a multinational corporation, a public or private institution, or a single family seeking a contemporary residence. The ethical dilemmas presented by each unique situation require an understanding of the identity of the client. What values are important, and whose values are being considered? Who is the direct client, and how do their needs mesh with those of the larger community? Who defines quality? Who produces quality, and who pays for quality?

The contract process has also significantly changed. Historically, contracts developed by the AIA became the standard for client/architect agreements because the courts have recognized them as being fair to both parties. This attitude is changing. Institutions as well as business and commercial clients have developed personalized professional-service contracts that they feel better protect their interests. It is extremely difficult to dictate terms to a "changing client." Architects must be aware of any contract provisions that have an impact on their professional ethical responsibilities.

It is important for architects to understand their responsibilities to their client. Ava Abramovitz summarized the design process of the 1990s in the *Architectural Record:* "The architect makes recommendations. The client makes decisions."[40]

Ethically, the new market demands create dilemmas. How are architects supposed to represent the firm when they have some of but not all of the background required for the requested service? If a firm creates an association with a local firm or a specialized consultant, how should this relationship be represented to the client? Who will be the responsible party? Who will the client call back?

Architects are often unable to communicate with the client because the two parties do not speak the same language nor listen to each other!

At distinguished award presentations of the annual AIA conventions, it is not uncommon to hear a project explained as "a representation of an historical allusion within the contextual linearity of our time." Another award recognized that structure "embodied the syntactical nuances of today's semiology." Architects are really just talking to each other with the mutual exclusion of the public and, especially, the client.[41] Architects should think, write, and converse at the highest intellectual level. They should challenge themselves and their colleagues. However, architects also have an obligation to the profession and to the client to explain in "lay" terms what they do and how they do it.

Listening to the client is one of the most important communication responsibilities of the architect. As Barry LaPatner illustrates:

> My own experience in negotiating contracts on behalf of architects with corporate, developer and government clients are instructive as to how architects can run afoul of the need to listen more clearly to the client. During the course of sorting out the myriad business and legal issues involved in the design for a new high-rise in New York City, a discussion ensued with the owner over why the high-tech nature of the design warranted a higher-than-usual fee. The owner wanted legal assurance that my client, a well-established, award-winning architect, would not over-design the building, and would bring it in on time and on budget.
>
> "I need him to understand," this frustrated real-estate powerhouse said of the architect, "that he cannot keep showing me his design for a stainless steel curtain wall when it is not in the bud-

> **Architects must be aware of any contract provisions that have an impact on their professional ethical responsibilities.**

get. No matter how many times I insist that he take down his façade drawings and show me alternate schemes, he continues to put them back up, every meeting." The architect by my side then proceeded to renew his argument with the developer about the sanctity of his design, ignoring the warning signs that this issue could threaten his status as the project architect. Only when I asked for a recess of the negotiations and explained, in private, what would happen to him if he persisted (forget the higher fee I was trying to secure for him—he would be out of a job) did he reluctantly agree to take down the offending drawings.

Was it ego that made this architect insist he was right? Was it an inability to listen to the signals of the client, or was it an instinctive approach that had worn down many clients in the past and thus become acceptable for every situation?

Regardless of the rationale, such inflexibility has no place in today's dealings with the business world. Rarely will architects or any service professional remain on the job or get a future commission with an "I-know-what's-best" attitude. Architects often convey to the public an impression of being aloof and aristocratic, an image that may hurt architects professionally.[42]

Architects should be committed to design and the production of excellent architecture. But using this attitude to override valid client considerations is not in the architect's nor the profession's best interest. Ego and personal conviction are important to a creative endeavor; however, "excess" can be a problem and an ethical dilemma.

The client is also changing the nature of design services. Traditionally defined services as explained in AIA documents have been expanded by clients to include such new services as maintenance cost estimates, post-occupancy evaluation studies, and building diagnostics.[43] In addition, because of the client's increased desire for design recognition, firms are now being asked to prepare specific designs for building façades: "façade architecture" and/or "imageability."[44] Change is also a positive reflection of the designer's ability.

Excellence in design has been recognized as a corporate asset. New Ford automobiles, the design of the Gillette razor, and Apple computer designs have all been credited with the success of the identified corporation's "bottom line."[45] Clients seek intelligence from those willing to provide information, creativity, and objectivity in the shortest amount of time for the most reasonable fee—not always the lowest. Ava Abramovitz states, "Great architecture is realized when good clients and good architects work together to accomplish the client's goals."[46]

When meeting the "changing client" and considering the larger community responsibility, specific ethical considerations should be emphasized during the initial project marketing, during the contract negotiations, at the beginning of the project, and during the construction/program-administration stages of the design assignment. The client and architect should:

- Understand the local political and community climate.
- Match the architectural services to the client's larger social goals (what's also good for the community).
- Demonstrate prior socially responsible projects with references and illustrations.
- Determine how expanded services can be provided to satisfy expanding client requirements (day care, job sharing, community service, etc.).[47]

Every member of the firm should be aware of the firm's ethical culture, especially when the culture includes community commitments.

A CLOSER LOOK AT DOING ARCHITECTURE ETHICALLY

OVERVIEW

The preceding sections have discussed issues associated with being an architect and making architecture. We now review in more detail the ethical considerations implicit in those activities. Every decision affecting the practice of architecture requires informed thought and has ethical aspects. To better understand the types of ethical decisions that confront the architect, two different scenarios are presented. The first looks at Doing Architecture from the perspective of the diversity of professional roles. The second looks at doing architecture from the perspective of the traditional phases of architectural practice. This latter perspective is further explored in the Appendix where two variations are presented, one dealing with the threshold competencies of the Intern Development Program (IDP) and one dealing with architectural practice organization and services delivery. All are explorations of the Lens of Praxis as described in Part I: Awareness.

These scenarios are presented in formats that focus on their related ethical aspects. A series of questions is posed for each listed activity that raises related issues of ethical consideration. The reader, either individually or as part of a group, should consider possible answers to the questions based on the knowledge they have gained from the earlier parts of this book. One learning approach encourages the reader to go through the exercise and prepare several alternative answers to the questions posed to establish a reflective personal dialogue about the nature and relative impact of ethics on each position taken. Another learning approach invites the reader to participate in group discussions that deal with the questions. Group interactive activities such as role playing and debates will stimulate this discussion. Also, group participants can expose different points of view from outside the reader's own purview, hence enhancing the learning experience.

After studying the ethical framework posed in Section 3, the reader will have a better understanding of ethics and its discrete relationship with the aspects of doing architecture.

PROFESSIONAL ROLES, ACTIVITIES, AND ETHICAL ISSUES

As outlined earlier in this book, the definition of the traditional architect and the activities that architects undertake have been expanded. The practice of architecture is increasingly diverse as it continues to mirror societal needs and norms. The impact of the technology and communication revolutions has also expanded the profession's domain. Diverse opportunities and professional demands require advanced architectural knowledge and expertise. New settings and roles also require the architect's ethical consideration of an expanded set of perspectives.

The following chart categorizes a variety of professional practice positions, the key activities associated with each role, and an ethical issues framework for each role. The charts identify significant questions that relate to each position and its ethical framework.

When reviewing the questions, think about each from different perspectives; first, from that of the architect in the designated role, and second, all those who interface with that professional. Consider the ethical theories and five lenses described in Part I: Awareness. Then, using the learning processes previously described, take a position that represents your ethical stance.

PROFESSIONAL ROLES, ACTIVITIES, AND ETHICAL ISSUES

ARCHITECT'S ROLE	PRINCIPAL ARCHITECTURAL ACTIVITIES							ETHICAL ISSUES FRAMEWORK
	TEACHING	POLICY	ENFORCEMENT	FACILITATION	MANAGEMENT	BUDGET	DESIGN/PRODUCTION	
Private Practice		•		•	•	•	•	See the following charts for "Architectural Phases"
Government/Code Official (Federal, State, City)			•					Health, Safety, Welfare Professional Judgment
Government/ Policy Administrator (GSA, HUD, State, City)		•		•		•		Public Interest Professional Judgment
Government/ Program Manager (Federal, State, City, Schools)				•	•	•		Public Interest Professional Standards
Government/ Project Management (Federal, State, City, Schools)				•	•	•	•	Accountability Professional Standards
Institutional/In-House (University, College, Hospital)		•		•	•	•		Public Trust Institutional Interest
Corporate/In-House		•		•	•	•	•	Public Trust Corporate Well Being
Developer/In-House				•	•	•	•	Professional Standards Community Trust
Contractor/In-House				•	•	•	•	Professional Standards Professional Conduct
Consultant Firm/In-House		•			•	•	•	Professional Standards Professional Conduct
Educator/Researcher (Full and Part Time)	•	•						Professional Conduct Judgment
Volunteer (Vista, Habitat, Community)				•			•	Social Responsibility Trust

ARCHITECT'S ROLE	SIGNIFICANT QUESTIONS FOR ETHICAL CONSIDERATION
Private Practice	Note: See the full list of questions on the charts that follow for "Architectural Practice Phases."
Government/Code Official (Federal, State, City)	When do industry standards and special-interest needs create a conflict of interest? When is a code interpretation rather than strict book adherence valid? When is political direction valid? How does one interpret legislative and regulation intent? Who should be responsible for it? How does one separate fairness from favoritism? What constitutes public health and safety? How does one enforce adopted codes and regulations that have been superseded by later published versions?
Government/Policy Administator (GSA, HUD, State, City)	How does one deal with conflicts between public policy and program needs? When can public-interest goals and special-interest goals coincide? What are the differences between the innovative and the customary? When is each valid? Who defines the policy administrator's responsibilities? To whom are policy administrators accountable? When should the budget direct policy implementation? Who defines public interest?
Government/Program Manager (Federal, State, City, Schools)	How does one deal with conflict between program and community needs? On what terms is confidentiality acceptable? When is full disclosure acceptable? What is the relationship between personal and professional bias? Does either create a conflict of interest? How can one be impartial? Can expediency be justified when compared to standard procedures and processes? On what terms? How should short-term needs be considered versus long-term benefits?

(continued on next page)

(continued from previous page)

Architect's Role	Significant Questions for Ethical Consideration
Government/Project Management (Federal, State, City, Schools)	How can one be objective when settling disputes?
	When does one deal with construction issues that conflict with industry standards? With industry customs? With agency guidelines?
	Can there be conflicts between contract language and fairness?
	How does one deal with conflicts between project expediency and expected project quality?
	When is personal judgment acceptable as professional competency?
	What are the accountability conflicts between the contract, a superior, and the public interest? What are resolution options?
Institutional/In-House	How does one deal with differences in the individual needs of building users, staff, and directors?
	How does one deal with differences between institutional needs and fiscal solvency?
	Is there a difference between public responsibility and institutional responsibility?
	What is a valid basis for evaluating innovative design, technology, and material proposals?
	Is there a responsibility to deal with conflicts between institutional mission and project requirements?
	How does professional judgment relate to management authority?
Corporate/In-House	How does one define the differences between corporate well-being and public interest? Between corporate policies and professional standards? Between corporate economic perspectives and professional judgment?
	What is the corporate architect's responsibility to maintain professional integrity?
	Are there different standards for supporting roles rather than leading roles in corporate management?
	What is the corporate architect's responsibility to exercise unprejudiced and unbiased judgments?
	What are valid situations for confidentiality? For full disclosure?

(continued on next page)

(continued from previous page)

ARCHITECT'S ROLE	SIGNIFICANT QUESTIONS FOR ETHICAL CONSIDERATION
Developer/In-House	Are there special responsibilities that are commensurate with the role as a community builder?
	To what degree and on what basis does one respond to community desires? To values?
	In speculative design, what is the program basis for determining generic-user needs?
	Do short-term investment strategies carry responsibilities for protecting long-term public interest?
	When is client/developer confidentiality valid? When is public candor a responsibility?
	What is the developer's responsibility to produce good projects? By whose standard?
Contractor/In-House	Who has the responsibility for exercising architectural judgments?
	Do professional-conduct standards take priority over the contractor's policies and practices?
	Who is responsible for correction of field construction errors and omissions? Professional errors? Contractor errors?
	Can there be a conflict of interest between professional judgment and the contractor's decisions?
	Can there be a conflict of interest regarding the responsibility to protect public health, life safety, and welfare?
Consultant Firm/In-House	What is the relationship between professional standards and consultant standards? What are consultant standards?
	What is the consultant's responsibility to exercise professional judgment?
	When do consultant-firm priorities, principles, and values take precedence over architectural values?
	Who is responsible for public interest, policies, and actions?
	Who is responsible for resolving design-quality issues?

(continued on next page)

(continued from previous page)

Architect's Role	Significant Questions for Ethical Consideration
Educator/Researcher (Full- and Part-Time)	Does one have a responsibility to be a good teacher? By whose standards?
	Does one have any responsibility to teach objectively?
	How does one deal with faculty-student issues such as reuse of student work, borrowing ideas, fairness, and changing student grades?
	Who should validate research findings? The researcher? A third party? A blind review?
	How does one deal with conflict-of-interest issues regarding sponsored research?
	What are faculty responsibilities regarding student respect and recognition?
	What is the relationship between professional standards and obligations and intellectual deliberations?
	Does professional judgment conflict with personal deliberation?
Volunteer (Vista, Habitat, Community)	What constitutes *pro-bono* work?
	How does one resolve conflicts between professional standards and user desires? User needs?
	Who determines the public good? What if it conflicts with professional judgment?
	Should liability issues affect professional and/or social responsibility?
	Who and what are the determinants of design quality? Of project quality?
	How does one determine a standard of trust?

Architectural Practice Phases: Societal and Professional Ethical Considerations

In a traditional architectural practice, architects are continually involved in activities that relate to their profession, community responsibilities, and business development. When providing architectural services, they are involved in a series of activities ranging from initial contract through final project delivery and occupancy. These phases of practice are delineated in the following charts as encompassing six main areas: General Practice, Contractual, Preliminary Design, Contract Documents/Bidding, Administration/Construction, and Follow-Up/Post Occupancy.

The first chart is organized by phases and outlines the main issues and activities that require ethical consideration. Societal and professional categories are subsets that relate to their prime ethical perspective.

The second set of charts further defines each phase with a series of questions requiring ethical consideration.

Study the question that is posed. Does it raise issues of community responsibility? Does it raise issues of contracts and business practices? Does it raise issues of professional duty and responsibility?

Do any of these issues require ethical considerations? If so, what is the ethical content and import?

Develop potential answers to each of the questions. How would your answers change if you were the client, represented the community, or were a member of the architect's team? Think also about these answers in terms of the ethical theories and the Five Lenses described in Part I: Awareness. Finally, take a position that represents your ethical stance.

ARCHITECTURAL PRACTICE PHASES
ISSUES REQUIRING ETHICAL CONSIDERATIONS

	GENERAL PRACTICE	CONTRACTUAL	PRELIMINARY DESIGN
Societal	Social Responsibility/ Public Policy Issues Community Involvement	Contract Negotiations Client Education Client Understanding Decision Making	Process Issues Involving Community Interaction Who's the Client? Political Issues
Professional	Personal Responsibilities as a Professional Job Seeking/ Marketing Advertising	Contract Negotiations Liability Work Scope/Process Client Responsibilities/ Rights	Architectural Programming Codes and Regulations Design Issues Budget Issues Management Issues

	Contract Documents/ Bidding	Administration/ Construction	Follow-Up/ Post Occupancy
Societal	Approvals Code Issues Specifications	Public Interest Life Safety	Findings/Issues
Professional	Approvals Clear Definition of Required Product or Service Bid Issues Proprietary Issues Document Review Standard of Care Specifications Product Research Cost Analysis	Observation/ Inspection Administration/ Change Orders	Performance Issues Representation Issues Reporting Issues Mitigation Issues

Societal

Social-Responsibility/Public-Policy Issues

What is the architect's role in the resolution of such public-policy issues as: responsible growth management, natural-resource protection, energy conservation, homelessness, affordable housing, historic preservation, health in the workplace, environmental enhancement, pollution control, accessibility, artistic freedom, cultural enhancement, the public good and the disenfranchised, regulatory protection of public health, safety, and welfare?

How do architects support policy resolution without appearing self-serving?

What should be the role of the NCARB, the AIA, and the ADPSR, etc.?

Can architects take a public posture at odds with their clients and preserve the integrity and relationship of all involved?

Is there a difference between personal action and the "firm's" or the "organization's" posture?

Whose responsibility is it to criticize fellow professionals in matters where socially responsible designs are at issue?

When does one reject a commission?

Should architects provide *pro-bono* services?

Community Involvement

Should architects participate in the political process? How?

How and when should architects contribute to consensus building and conflict resolution?

Is participation in design review boards a professional responsibility?

Should architects take a leadership role to resolve public-design controversies?

What types of conflict-of-interest issues can be associated with community service?

Professional

Personal Responsibilities as a Professional

Do professionals accept unique and particular personal responsibilities?

Should one's personal actions reflect one's professional representations?

Do both employers and employees have responsibilities to each other?

Should moonlighting by employees be acceptable? On what terms?

Should the firm be responsible for employee projects completed outside the firm?

Should continuing education be expected? For whom? At whose cost?

Does the office have a responsibility to mentor its junior employees?

Should the "winnings" from a successful competition be equally distributed to the members of the development team?

(continued on next page)

GENERAL PRACTICE	ISSUES/QUESTIONS REQUIRING ETHICAL CONSIDERATION

Professional

Job Seeking/Marketing

How should the firm describe previous experience and the assignment of individual responsibilities?

Should the office or the individual be credited with past success and failure?

Does the credit line for a project move from office to office with the individual?

How should a professional's qualification be presented for a project type one has not dealt with before?

Does the professional try to influence one's references?

Advertising

How does the professional present the background and qualifications of the office or the individual office associate?

When multiple firms participate in a project, does the credit line show specific responsibilities in print advertising, in the firm brochure, in competition entries, and in press releases?

Should press releases for awards that involve multiple firms delineate the particular role each firm performed on the project?

CONTRACTUAL	ISSUES/QUESTIONS REQUIRING ETHICAL CONSIDERATION

Societal

Contract Negotiations

What are responsible criteria for project selection?

Does one "walk away" from a project that one philosophically disagrees with in terms of responsible public policy?

Should architects agree to replication of previous projects?

Is it in the long-term interest of the client, user, and public to not specifically investigate each project's needs before deciding on a solution to a problem?

It is the architect's responsibility to inform the client of his or her personal belief system?

Client Education

Should the architect provide planning seminars for a new client?

How do you provide an unbiased evaluation of similar, completed projects? Your competitor's projects?

Is it the client's obligation to participate in continuing education programs?

Should the client understand the "steps" in the project development process?

(continued on next page)

(continued from previous page)

CONTRACTUAL	ISSUES/QUESTIONS REQUIRING ETHICAL CONSIDERATION

Societal

Client Understanding

Should one inform the client of all potential ramifications of the project?

What are the architect's responsibilities regarding public questions about the project?

What is the architect's responsibility regarding the client's project proposal when it is subject to public controversy?

Decision-Making

Does one have a responsibility to expose any potential conflicts of interest that might affect one's unbiased performance of the contract in terms of public responsibility? In terms of prior associations?

What if the architect has an interest in a project process, policy, or product that could predetermine the project solution?

Professional

Contract Negotiations

What is the architect's responsibility regarding adequate, fair fees that reflect the architect's anticipated workload and provide the capacity to produce a quality project?

Should the architect be responsible for the client understanding all of the contract provisions?

It is acceptable for the architect to commit to a schedule when the firm does not have the capability to meet the client's deadline?

Liability

When should the standard of care be the prevailing basis for project-design decisions?

To what degree should the architect be responsible for life and safety issues?

Does the architect have a responsibility to protect the client by carrying errors-and-omissions insurance?

Should the architect's insurance coverage ever determine the architect's performance?

What should the architect's responsibility be for work performed by consultants selected by the client? Retained by the client?

Work Scope/Process

What should the architect do when the client's project scope and schedule are out of synch with the architect's assessment of the appropriate schedule to accomplish competent work? Quality work? Publicly responsible work?

What issues beyond the project definition should be considered to protect the project quality for both the client and architect?

What extra services are in the client's interest? Why?

What extra services are in the architect's interest? Why?

Are third-party reviews desirable? If so, to whom should the reviewer be responsible?

(continued on next page)

CONTRACTUAL	ISSUES/QUESTIONS REQUIRING ETHICAL CONSIDERATION

Professional

Client Responsibilities/Rights

When is a client's requested change a "right"? When is it not?

Should clients expect that a project design is theirs? Why?

To what extent should the architect be responsible for changes to contract documents required by a permit-issuing agency?

To what extent should it be the responsibility of the client to understand the architectural process?

Define "unforeseen." When should "unforeseen circumstances" legitimately be a client's responsibility?

PRELIMINARY DESIGN	ISSUES/QUESTIONS REQUIRING ETHICAL CONSIDERATION

Societal

Process Issues Involving Community Interaction

Should the designer initiate and participate in an interactive design process (i.e. "Take Part," RUDAT, etc.) to involve the community in the design process?

Could a public process constrain the client's options?

What actions should architects initiate when they realize a conflict between the client's program direction and community interests?

Who's the Client?

How do you satisfy societal needs in comparison to the client's project needs? When and by whose decision should this become an issue?

To what degree does the architect serve the indirect clients (building user, public, planet, profession, self)?

Political Issues

Should the architect design within the parameters of public policy and political directives?

What should the parameters of public bodies be when establishing design policy?

What should the profession's position be about "design directives" ("mission" style, "Cape Cod" style)?

What should the scope of decision making by design review boards be? Should architects have a say in their makeup? Why?

What should the responsibility of the architect to the client with regard to "approvable" design be?

Should the architect be subject to review by nonprofessionals?

How should the architect respond to a client request for minimum legal code compliance (building, fire, ADA, Energy, etc.) when public-policy intent is to go beyond minimums?

(continued on next page)

PRELIMINARY DESIGN	ISSUES/QUESTIONS REQUIRING ETHICAL CONSIDERATION
Professional	**Architectural Programming**

Architectural Programming

Who should be responsible for the architectural program?

What is the responsibility of architects to design to other program decisions when they disagree?

To what extent should architects demand direct program input from actual project users?

Codes and Regulations

What should the architect's responsibilities be with regard to code search, analysis, and application?

What should the architect's responsibility be for consultant code search, analysis, and application?

On what basis should the architect seek code, regulation, and regulatory variances?

Design Issues

To what degree should the architect's values, ideology, and aesthetics determine primacy in the preliminary design process?

What responsibility does the architect have to the client when their design opinions clash?

To what degree should the architect let the project program be the primary design determinant?

How, when, and why should architects involve their consultants in project-design deliberations?

What is the architect's design responsibility with regard to a professional standard of care?

How might an architect respond to a client request to design a "state-of-the-art" project?

Budget Issues

What are the architect's responsibilities beyond specific program requirements regarding standard of care?

Is there a responsibility for the architect to present life-cycle cost analysis to the client as part of the project cost assessment?

Management Issues

Who should be involved in determining internal design budgets? Why?

How should the budget determine the required or necessary design time for a project?

CONTRACT DOCUMENTS/ BIDDING	ISSUES/QUESTIONS REQUIRING ETHICAL CONSIDERATION

Societal

Approvals

Should the architect seek to circumvent public-approval processes (code checks, permit approval, etc.)?

Should the architect participate in a public-approval process that, while legal, may violate public trusts?

Code Issues

To what extent and on what basis should the architect treat codes as minimum standards?

How does the architect deal with a conflict between code requirements and a proposed project solution that does not comply, yet is deemed to be the best aesthetic, functional, and cost-effective solution?

Specifications

Should the architect be required to "know everything" about all the products included in a typical building project?

Should the architect be liable for health problems to project users caused by the project's building materials?

Professional

Approvals

Should the architect seek to expedite public-approval processes (code checks, permit approval, etc.)? If so, by what means?

Should public-building departments assume responsibility for mandated document changes based on their code interpretations?

Do architects have a responsibility to see that their client has a thorough understanding of the project when approving the architect's request to move to the next stage of the contract?

Clear Definition of Required Product or Service

What are the architect's responsibilities regarding the accurate description of a designated product or service?

How does the architect exchange information regarding the success or failure of an approach, product, or service specified?

Bid Issues

Do architects have a different responsibility to their client when establishing the bid criteria?

To what degree should the architect consider the client's and the contractor's interest? Why?

(continued on next page)

(continued from previous page)

CONTRACT DOCUMENTS/ BIDDING	ISSUES/QUESTIONS REQUIRING ETHICAL CONSIDERATION

Professional

Proprietary Issues

What role does the architect play in the selection of materials, products, and construction techniques?

When is it appropriate for the architect to specify proprietary items?

When a client requests a proprietary design from the architect, what is an appropriate response from the architect?

Document Review

Is there a difference between in-house and third-party reviews?

When is each appropriate in the client's interest, the architect's interest, and the public's interest?

Who should be responsible for construction-document review in the architect's office?

Should the approval of contract documents for a building permit by the appropriate legal authority be deemed as adequate document review?

Standard of Care

What impact should the architect have on the establishment of the acceptable standard of care?

How should the architect define differences between the standard of care and the client's program? The contractor's alternative proposals? The code official's design-change requirements? The architect's perception of good practice?

Specifications

What responsibility should the architect bear for the performance of the materials and methods specified?

Should there be a difference in the architect's responsibility when specifying "performance" rather than "prescriptive" requirements?

Product Research

What is the architect's responsibility to stay abreast of new product options? To evaluate these options?

Should an architect accept a client's research? If so, on what basis?

Cost Analysis

What are the architect's options and responsibilities when the initial project-cost assessment of the desired design solution exceeds the client's stated budget?

ADMINISTRATION/ CONSTRUCTION	ISSUES/QUESTIONS REQUIRING ETHICAL CONSIDERATION

Societal

Public Interest

Are there differences between the public interest and the client's interest? What impact should this have on the architect's decision-making process?

When architects observe construction practices that they feel are questionable, what is their responsibility?

Should permit-approval agencies be informed of construction-phase changes?

Is the architect the right party to judge the quality of the contractor's efforts?

Life/Safety

When does the architect discuss the concept of public safety?

Should academic institutions provide continuing education regarding public safety?

Professional

Observation/Inspection

Who should determine the qualifications of the observer? Of the inspector? Of the construction manager?

Does the contractual difference between "observation" and "inspection" change the architects' responsibilities when they become aware of construction deficiencies? Of changes from the contract documents?

Does the architect have any responsibility to take action when a questionable construction technique is observed? What if worker safety is involved?

Administration/Change Orders

Can the architect be impartial when determining the value and validity of a change order that deals with an architect's errors or omissions?

Should the architect be responsible to only the client?

What is the architect's responsibility when the client has retained a construction manager to manage the construction phase?

Societal

Findings/Issues

What is the architects' responsibility to take appropriate action if they find that the project is being operated to the detriment of some or all of its users?

What responsibility does the architect have to assess the project after occupancy for its performance as a "healthy environment"?

What is the architects' responsibility to take appropriate action if they find that the project is being operated to the detriment of the public interest?

What is the architects' responsibility to take appropriate action if they find that the project systems are being utilized to the detriment of environmental quality?

Who is responsible for research and development: the office, the profession, or the industry?

To what degree should the academic community be responsible for research?

How does the architect report discrepancies between planning goals and the finished project?

Professional

Performance Issues

What is the responsibility of architects to do a post-occupancy evaluation of their completed projects? For whose benefits should this be done?

What are the issues associated with the architect performing an uninvited post-occupancy survey?

Should architects revisit their completed projects over time to evaluate performance? Conformance to original program goals? Conformance to original maintenance and operating procedures?

Representation Issues

Who should bear the cost of an architect's post-occupancy evaluation? Should this be determined by the architect's contractual relationship?

When the architect performs a post-occupancy evaluation, whose interests should the architect represent?

(continued on next page)

(continued from previous page)

FOLLOW-UP/ POST OCCUPANCY	ISSUES/QUESTIONS REQUIRING ETHICAL CONSIDERATION

Reporting Issues

What responsibilities do architects have to report observed design, product, and construction deficiencies? To whom?

What is the responsibility of architects to report failures or potential failures associated with their project designs? To whom? Why?

Mitigation Issues

How can the architect initiate the mitigation process?

During the mitigation process, whom does the architect represent?

When the client decides to mitigate post-occupancy problems, what is the architect's responsibility? Is compensation appropriate?

PART III
CHOICES

INTRODUCTION TO CHOICES

LEARNING OBJECTIVES

Ethical considerations should be a fundamental part of the decision-making process in most of what we do as architects. The learning objective of Part III: Choices is, therefore, to give the reader insight into the range and importance of ethical considerations that infuse the decision-making process in which architects are involved, whether in being architects or making architecture.

Part III: Choices provides you with the opportunity to apply what you have learned from Part I: Awareness and Part II: Understanding. This section utilizes case studies as the tool for having you take your discrete knowledge gained of ethical theories, principles, architectural relationships, ethical reasoning, and practice frameworks and to apply it holistically to problem resolution. These case studies, which are based on real professional-practice situations, replicate with their many nuances the interactive complexity of the ethical issues faced in most situations involving the making of architecture and/or being an architect.

Part of your learning challenge is to become more aware of the complexity and interdependence of ethical-issues resolution. Another part is to more fully understand the value of bringing ethical considerations to bear on your decision-making process.

While there may be some "universal" ethical truths as discussed in Part I, the reality is that the ethical stance you take is ultimately a personal one. Your positing of your ethics in these case situations and others like them should reflect the set of values and principles you wish yourself and others to live and practice by.

Many of these case studies raise ethical issues that go beyond the strict boundaries of the case. Do ethical considerations require you to look closely at everyone's point of view? Do they require you to evaluate issues that may exist outside the tight frame you have been looking at and consider wider impacts? Additionally, they raise some fundamental ethical questions. Do ethical considerations help you to make decisions that you can truly justify to yourself and your client, and that, where applicable, serve the public good? Do they open possibilities of dealing effectively and responsibly with those who might disagree with your course of action? Do they serve to provide a foundation for the quality of architecture? These are all questions that you should answer affirmatively as you engage in the ethical practices of architecture.

These case studies afford you the opportunity to develop through application your ethical stance and reasoning processes. No matter the size or scope of the decision to be made, your ethics is a critical determinant of who you are, in what you stand for, in what you do, and in what your professional practices truly represent to your colleagues, your clients, your community, and your conscience.

MAKING ETHICAL JUDGMENTS

PROCESS FOR ETHICAL REASONING

Dealing with the case studies is an exercise in problem-solving. This has been discussed previously in Part I: Awareness. You must go through three stages to deal with the dilemmas that these cases pose: **Assessment, Evaluation,** and **Resolution.**

Assessment

Assessment involves a thorough analysis of the case situation, which should include an inquiry into the ethical questions raised. Part of this analysis should consider the probable point of view of all the participants in the case. The assessment should also include an assessment of both the known facts and the unknown. Finally, the analysis should involve an assessment of the various ethical theories and frameworks described in Part I that could be integral to determining a resolution to the case.

Evaluation

Evaluation involves a determination of possible outcomes to the case situation. This should include an evaluation of the outcomes' impacts on each of the participants, as well as on those indirectly affected by them. The evaluation should also include an analysis of the degree to which ethical issues have an impact on the case-resolution options. This stage of the process then involves the development of alternative case resolutions. It is important to look at the issues from varying points of view rather than trying immediately to come up with your answer, which is really a considered weighting from your point of view of the options you discover through your analysis. In making this decision, you have probably synthesized your position with regard to the various ethical dimensions of the case. Take the time, however, to first outline the various options and to then delineate the impacts on all involved given the scenario you are investigating. Also, prepare a list of values and ethical principles that you are using as a base against which to determine your position. Remember what you learned about this in Part I: Awareness. As a first step toward final synthesis, you will find it useful to go through how you would deal with the case resolution if one of the ethical considerations were given the highest importance. Then you might look at the same case with the assumption that another of the ethical considerations was the primary prerequisite to reaching a position. And since the cases always involve others, you must ask how they would see it from their point of view. In this way you will develop both a series of true alternatives that could be followed, as well as a clearer understanding of the interrelationships between the available options. This, then, creates the setting for a considered final stance regarding how you would handle the situation described, and which now represents a true synthesis of your evaluations.

Resolution

Resolution involves making a decision as to how you would act in this case as an architect presented with the particular case dilemma. You will see that the road to be taken is dependent on both your inherent values and those of others involved, as well as perhaps some universal ones. When making a decision, you will find that you are involved in a negotiating process between competing positions. Sometimes it will be clear that this involves a choice between right and wrong, but it may well involve a choice between right and right or some waystation between. Finally, prepare for yourself a defense of the resolution that you propose. Assess whether in coming to it you have merely rationalized your position or have truly taken a position in which you can be ethically secure.

LEARNING SETTINGS

These case studies can be used in group-discussion sessions or as part of an individual learning process.

If a group-discussion setting is utilized, it is important to limit the group to six to eight individuals in order to allow for meaningful participation by all within a reasonable time frame. One of the benefits of a group process is the opportunity for the sharing, testing, and promulgation of points of view by all participants both during and after the resolution of the case situation. It is important in the group session to have someone act as a facilitator to ensure that all have an opportunity to express themselves. It would be useful to have one person act as a recorder, writing down the direction of the discussion so that the participants can have a record for further study of the differing aspects of how the group members considered the case and developed their resolution.

If an individual learning setting is utilized, you will find it useful to share your case resolution with a colleague, professional or personal, whom you respect. This will provide you with the opportunity to self-evaluate the conviction with which you have arrived at your position as you assess it in the context of the feedback you receive.

LEARNING EXERCISES

Has your study to date in Part I: Awareness and Part II: Understanding enabled you to see where the ethical issues lie embodied in the choices you must make to resolve these cases? Has your study to date enabled you to sort out the ethical issues? Has your study to date enabled you to prioritize the issues for you, thereby guiding you in your answer to the choices you would make when resolving the issues raised? Has your study to date enabled you to defend your position to yourself, your colleagues, and any others who would be affected by them?

The following exercises are designed to help you answer these questions, as well as to be aware of your own ethical values and priorities. The exercises are also designed to give you insight into the ethical dimensions of these cases and related practice situations that can often require interactive decision-making. No solutions are proffered because these will vary with your own perspective. However, unethical or nonethical solutions should become apparent to you. Using these exercises should reinforce for you the importance of thinking and acting ethically as you engage in the practices of architecture.

- After reading the case study and reviewing the discussion, take a position on the solution that you would propose for the given situation and the questions it poses. Utilize the ethical-reasoning process described above.

- Indicate which of the Five Framing Lenses from Part I were involved in your arriving at your solution to the questions posed by the case, and to what degree. Look at whether the solutions you propose would be the same if you tried to solve the problem from the perspective of each of the other parties in the case. If the solutions vary, indicate why in terms of the ethical rationale used. This should provide you with insight into the difference that the ethical theories delineated in Part I can have on problem resolution. This part of the exercise should provide you with insight as to whether you have absorbed all the ethical influences that come to play in real case situations. It should also indicate to you the degree to which you see the impact that the interrelationship of potential ethical positions and the complexity of the case itself have on each other.

- Delineate to what degree ethical considerations are a factor in the resolution you propose for each of the case studies. Compare these with the delineation made by one or more professional colleagues. If there is a difference, evaluate why. Remember, you are not evaluating the validity of the ethical justification for the position you have taken; rather, you are trying to ascertain the relative importance of ethical implications in the total decision-making process and to determine if you have seen this clearly.

- Write your own case study. Field-test it on another architect. Did this person perceive this as a case that involved ethical considerations in its solution? Did this person identify the set of ethical issues that you intended to address? Did this person see the case as one that had the same level of complexity that you had envisioned it would have? The answers to these questions should give you some feedback on your ability to view professional-practice situations in terms of their ethical aspects.

- After sharing your solution to the problem posed by the case study considered, evaluate the degree to which your position is based on your own internalized ethical code versus that of the architectural profession, of outsiders looking on, of other colleagues, and of those with whom you would relate to professionally in future scenarios connected with similar circumstances.

- For group-discussion sessions, develop a consensus position on the case resolution. Compare the consensus position with that which you would take if you were the sole decision-maker. If there is a difference, provide yourself with an analysis as to why.

CASE STUDIES

CASE STUDIES ORGANIZATION/MATRIX

The case studies are organized in a traditional, professional architectural-practice sequence. They are listed in order by practice phase according to the prime phase of practice in which the case described occurs. Many of the cases, however, have aspects that expand and/or relate to phases other than the one under which the case is listed and, thus, involve the integrated aspects of practice. The case studies could also be organized holistically by ethical-issue areas. These are delineated in the responsibility issues. which reflects the main ethical-issue areas that are part of professional practices. The resulting matrix relates the practice-phase case organization to the responsibility-issues case assessment. You can utilize this matrix to find a case to study relative to a particular phase of practice or a particular ethical focus. The matrix additionally demonstrates the multifaceted considerations that you encounter as an architect when dealing with the ethical context for your decision-making.

RESPONSIBILITY ISSUE	Social Purpose	Cultural/Societal Values	Community Values	Design Values	Public Health and Safety	Public Interest	Professional Principles	Professional Conduct	Business Practices	Personal Values	Personal Welfare
PRACTICE PHASE											
Professional and Community Service/ General Practice											
1　Personal Choices	●									●	●
2　Public Service	●								●	●	
3　Cultural Diversity and the Public Architect		●				●		●			
Office Management/Policy											
4　The Client's House			●	●					●	●	
5　Rezoning			●				●		●		
6　The Mayor and the School Board			●					●	●		
7　The Neighbor's House				●			●	●			
8　The Master Plan Study						●	●	●			●
9　Building Codes and City Projects					●		●	●			
10　The Elusive Client							●	●			
11　Employee Rights							●	●			●
Contractual/Programming Phase											
12　Two Clients/One Project				●					●		●
13　The Real Estate investment Project				●			●		●		
14　Adaptive Re-use/Historic Preservation		●	●		●		●				
15　Life Safety	●				●		●				
16　The Fee Proposal								●	●		
17　The Joint Venture								●	●		
18　The Cash Flow Bind								●	●		●
Schematic Design Phase											
19　The Competition							●	●	●		
20　Design Integrity	●			●			●		●	●	
21　The Client's Project Manager				●			●	●			
22　The University Architect			●				●	●			●
Design Development Phase											
23　Design Build				●		●	●	●			
Construction Documents Phase											
24　Building Material Choices					●		●		●		
25　Building Code Official					●		●	●			●
Bid/Contracting Phase											
26　The Public Bid Opening						●		●			
27　The Private Bid Opening							●	●			
Construction Phase											
28　Construction Observation					●			●	●		●
Post Occupancy Phase											
29　Post-Occupancy Evaluation						●		●	●		●
30　Right of Confidentiality and the Public Interest					●	●	●	●			

CASE STUDY 1:
Personal Choices

You and your partners are longtime friends. You were all educated in Quaker schools, were classmates in architecture school, and then during the Vietnam War became pacifists and did alternative service (or went to Canada). Subsequently, each of you returned to school and then worked for different firms but kept in touch with one another. After collaborating on a design competition in which your entry took second place, you decided to form a partnership and go into practice. When you formed the partnership, you all agreed you would not take on any military or war-related work because of these personal commitments.

In the ten years that your partnership has existed, it has earned a good reputation for itself by producing design-award-winning work that has included community facilities, schools, and multiple-family housing. The firm has grown from the original three partners to a professional staff of six, all of whom have been with the partnership for at least three years.

The last year has witnessed an economic recession, and many firms have seen their workload diminish. Employment in the profession is down, and some firms have failed. Now your business, too, is slower, and there is a real possibility that your firm will be unable to continue in its present form unless some projects can be found quickly. At the moment, the firm has nothing in the pipeline, having just missed out on several projects that were either curtailed by the economic conditions or for which its Request For Proposal (RFP) submittal was unsuccessful. The partnership receives a call from some friendly colleagues who head a large firm that is known for its management and production skills and has existed over the years by doing government work. Your firm is offered the opportunity to be a design participant on a series of projects for which the large firm has contracts.

The friendly colleagues have indicated that they wish to upgrade the quality of their firm's design work, that they feel that this arrangement would be the most efficient way to accomplish this expeditiously, and that this collaboration would benefit both firms. The projects they have contracts for are:

- An Air Force-base, i.e., hangars, a control tower, etc., in an adjacent state;
- An elementary school on an Army base in Germany for children of the military;
- A Coast Guard barracks on the East Coast;
- Temporary facilities for U.S. peacekeeping forces in Kosovo;
- Marine guard housing at the U.S. Embassy in Costa Rica;
- A new chapel at a National Guard base nearby

You and your partners meet to decide which assignments, if any, you would take (and why or why not?). This is the first time in many years that you and your partners will be discussing your founding commitment not to engage in military or war-related work. In the ensuing years, the world has changed, personal lives have changed, and economic needs have changed.

Discussion

- Can you develop and justify **your** position regarding each opportunity to yourself, your partners, your staff, your family, and your friendly colleagues?

This is a case in which you are confronted with your moral philosophy at several different levels. You are forced to look at the relative importance of your original pacifist commitment to questions of ethical responsibilities; to the continuation of the firm you have helped build; and to the economic well-being of your colleagues, staff, and family. The issue of what the partnership stands for and what the impact of this decision will have on its future is a consideration. The issue of what kind of work a firm takes on continually involves ethical assessments of options like these. This is a consideration that can surface from the environmental, political, social, and economic stance of your clients, your colleagues, and yourself.

Source: Jim Burns

CASE STUDY 2:
Public Service

You are the principal in a small architectural firm with eight employees. Your firm's office is in a small town. The office has actively supported local community affairs, from sponsoring a Little League team, to supporting the municipal orchestra. You have involved yourself in local politics and actively campaigned for the recently elected mayor.

The mayor has just called to inform you that she would like to appoint you to the town-planning commission. In her opinion, the planning commission has not been very effective in protecting the local quality of life against the pressures of both new commercial and residential developers who, while bringing a promise of economic prosperity to the town, have been unwilling to explore nongeneric designs or to make any extra effort to enhance the local environment on the grounds that they were economically unfeasible. She hopes that you will provide leadership as a design professional and provide a movement toward sensible growth management, and commensurate design sensibility and environmental protection and enhancement. She feels that you should take advantage of this opportunity to provide a public service to your town.

You are aware that the town is in the process of selecting a design/build team to provide a build-to-suit lease-back project for a new town hall and community center on a parcel of land that the town has designated near the center of the town's commercial district. Although it is a public-use project, you believe that it can serve as a demonstration project to the development community that good design is possible within the constraints of for-profit-oriented development.

You have been approached by a reputable contractor you are friendly with and who is based in the town. He has put together a financial team to back his proposal to the town to build and own the project. He has asked you to be his architect and has given every indication that he has done so out of respect for your design work. He has indicated that he is aware that this project, because of its public use and importance, needs special attention, but he has also indicated that he believes that his strength lies in his ability to do "quality work of reasonable scope within tight budgets." In previous conversations with him, you have had friendly discussions and disagreements over his perceptions of the merits of using life-cycle cost approaches to development projects, the increasing difficulty of getting anything done within an environment of increasing regulatory control, and the need to control public expenditures. You like the contractor and trust him as a businessman. In fact, both of you were active supporters of the new mayor during the recent campaign despite some philosophical differences. You believe that he has the best chance of being selected by the town to produce the project.

Your office workload is light at the moment, and receiving this commission could make the difference between a good year and a great year.

You ponder your options. Wouldn't it be possible to accept the appointment to the planning commission and be a part of the development team for this important town project? Couldn't you excuse yourself from any planning-commission hearings that dealt with approvals of the project? The mayor has indicated that she might support this as a way of her obtaining the architect's talents to the fullest.

Discussion

- Does the potential for a conflict of interest exist? Is there any difference between appearances and actuality?
- Where will you have the most impact on the common good for your town, both short-term and long-term?
- What impact might your decision have on the architectural profession?
- What is the proper balance between your responsibility to your practice and its employees and your responsibility to your community?

The issues surrounding your participation in public service are important ones. While they can have an impact on a particular project, as in this case, they are often unrelated to specific projects but rather to overall practice. The question of your professional responsibility to perform *pro-bono* service or work is one of the issues here. Resolving these issues can often place a priority on personal values.

CASE STUDY 3:
Cultural Diversity and the Public Architect

An architect is director of a historic preservation agency with a five-member board. The agency has a mandate to review and approve building-permit applications for alterations and additions to certified historic buildings. The agency is also responsible for approving any construction in official historic districts. The agency determines policy and then the architect, an appointee of the board, manages it and carries it out.

When a permit for alteration to a historic building or construction in a historic district is proposed, the architect first determines compatibility of new work with the historic context. Based upon this review, the architect then approves or disapproves the scope of the proposed work and, when appropriate, suggests alternative approaches to inappropriate proposals. The architect, in performing his or her duties, is required by the city's historic-preservation ordinance to use the *Secretary of the Interior's Guidelines for Rehabilitation* when approving or disapproving work. These guidelines are performance standards that provide a flexible framework for careful renovation. Their goal is to maintain a structure's or district's historic appearance and integrity. The *Guidelines* encourage the reuse and repair of existing character-defining features and materials. At the same time, the *Guidelines* discourage new uses, additions, and construction techniques that alter historic features or obfuscate an understanding of the history that the building, site, and/or district represent.

One day the architect receives a permit application for a small residential remodeling project. Checking the city's register of historic monuments and neighborhoods, the architect confirms that the permit is for alterations to a building within the boundaries of a forty-block historic neighborhood. The architect also discerns that the structure, though not individually listed in the historic register, is like other historic buildings in the neighborhood: a somewhat rundown turn-of-the-century, wood-sided Craftsman bungalow.

The application proposes the replacement of wood siding and shingles with stucco, a material not generally used during this neighborhood's period of construction and significance. The architect knows that the *Guidelines* discourage the substitution of materials that diminish the identity of districts. The architect is also aware that recently, historic-preservation groups in the community have expressed concern to the agency that some newer homeowners and absentee landlords, many of them recent immigrants, have stuccoed their wood bungalows without building permits to save both time and money. The groups have stated that these alterations are threatening the neighborhood's historic integrity. They are upset that the agency hasn't taken any legal action to deal with this.

The architect, evaluating the information at hand, disapproves the permit application and proposes that the owner repair and repaint the existing siding.

Several days later, the architect receives calls from two agency board members, one of whom is the board chairperson, as well as from the new owner of the house (who does not speak English). All are upset that the permit application has not been approved. Through a translator, the owner states that he is trying to make his house beautiful for his grandchildren, to leave them something of value upon his passing. The owner further states that in his native country, stucco is considered to be a permanent and durable material. He does not want to leave his grandchildren a house that requires constant maintenance. He points out that in good faith and accordance with the law, he has applied for a permit to do the work. The board members state they are sympathetic with the owner's concerns and demand that the permit be signed unless the building itself is deemed historic. In their opinion, the integrity of the neighborhood will not be further compromised by this remodeling.

The architect decides to reevaluate the request and considers the following aspects of the case:

1. The individual building is not historic. When the structure is considered individually, there may be no legal reason to disallow the stucco work, even though it is in a historic district.
2. The individual building is in a historic district. Compatible work on a nonhistoric structure reinforces the identity of the neighborhood as a whole. The *Guidelines* encourage this approach, local preservation groups actively support this approach, the agency board has supported this

approach in other parts of the city, and the city ordinance requires use of the *Guidelines.*

3. The owner's perspective is based upon cultural values that differ from those expressed by the preservation groups. The city is on record as supportive of its cultural diversity.
4. Some homes in the historic neighborhood have been remodeled using stucco without receiving permits to do so. This action may now be challenged by the preservation groups.
5. Two board members, one of whom is the board chairperson, have stated a clear position: Sign the permit unless the building is designated as historic.
6. The architect has the authority to make this decision, although it can be appealed to the full agency board. The architect has had the strong support of the agency board for being a particularly effective director.

Discussion

- Does the public architect serve the agency board or the city ordinance requiring use of the *Guidelines?*
- Does the public architect have a responsibility to preserve his effectiveness with the agency board?
- What is the architect's responsibility with regard to those homes previously remodeled without permits, and is this affected by his decision about this permit?
- What is the public architect's responsibility when differing community values clash?

An architect in public service often must deal with situations from a different perspective than that normally encountered in private practice. By the nature of the architects' position, whatever it may be, they are serving the public, a group rife with parochial views of their rights, and the public good, a term ripe for interpretation. Architects in private practice continually deal with architects in public service and must try to understand the perspective they operate from if this relationship is to be a fruitful one for all who have a stake in the process. Architects in public service also have a responsibility to try and understand the perspectives of all those they deal with who have a stake in the process, directly or indirectly. This case deals with classic relationships and conflicts between laws, rights, and ethics.

CASE STUDY 4:
The Client's House

An architectural firm received a commission to design a large new home for a well-known media personality. The site was in the hills of Berkeley, California, overlooking San Francisco Bay and the city. The area had been the devastated by a fire that had burned the entire neighborhood and denuded the area of its signature landscape of lush tree growth.

After the fire there had been an effort to mobilize the affected landowners to work with the city to develop a master plan for the rebuilding that would enable the area's natural environment to regenerate. These efforts had not produced a consensus plan, however, and it was clear that the land owners intended to pursue rebuilding on their lots on an individual basis as soon as practical. The city agreed to process the necessary permits quickly and to let the land owners rebuild to the maximum allowable area on their lots. Many of the destroyed homes had been built years earlier, and the rebuilding would take place under updated building codes.

The architects regarded this commission as an opportunity to demonstrate their design skills and to set the tone for future rebuilding of the area. Their client had received an early insurance settlement and would be one of the first land owners to rebuild. The finished project would be very visible initially both from within the neighborhood and from the nearby arterial streets now that the previously dense tree growth had been burned away.

The client developed a program for the home that required a considerably larger building than the one that had originally occupied the lot. This larger home was now allowable under the city's regulations. The lot was on the uphill side of a street on a natural promontory. There were buildable lots on either side and directly below. All would be affected in terms of privacy and ambiance by the design of this home.

The architects developed a schematic design that they presented to the client for approval. The client was appreciative of their initial effort but told them that he wanted them to go back to their drawing board and revise their design. The client felt that the design, which did not utilize the property width to the minimal setback lines, did not maximize the view. For the same reason, he also wanted the design to maximize the vertical building envelope, which it didn't. The client also felt that, while the vernacular was an interesting one that related to some discussions they had engaged in, the design was a personal statement by the architects, and although engaging and sophisticated, it wasn't particular enough for his taste.

The architects countered the criticism by pointing out the desirability of preserving as much of the site as possible for new trees and landscaping, from both an ecological perspective and from a community-image standpoint. They also indicated that they believed that if they maximized the lot's vertical envelope, this could have a negative impact on the adjoining lots. It would take away some of the view and privacy that all of the residents had before the fire. As for the vernacular of the design, the architects felt that the client saw sophistication as banality, and that the client was unduly striving for a design that would be too flamboyant for the neighborhood when it was fully rebuilt.

The client indicated that he understood the architects' concerns but that he expected them to understand his as well and come up with a positive resolution in a revised design that both he and the architects would be proud of.

The Architects returned to their office to resolve the dilemma between the values of the community , their client, and themselves.

Discussion

- The architects were aware that the community values were the hardest to get a handle on. The community wanted this area to be rebuilt in a way that would preserve its value, re-create its ambiance, and allow each individual maximum freedom in the rebuilding program and design vernacular. In some instances, these goals were in conflict with one another.

- The architects knew that the client had many important contacts and that his positive recommendation could lead to future commissions. But they now realized that the client was primarily concerned with satisfying his individual ego and perceived rights.

- The architects also recognized that their own values were being tested. They wanted to produce a sophisticated signature design that could demonstrate their talent and lead to future commissions both in this area and elsewhere. Whatever was built would be highly visible and become a statement about their design philosophy and creativity. They felt a keen sense of loss for the ecological environment that had been a part of the neighborhood before the fire, and they felt it should be reconstituted as much as possible.

- What options did the architects have, how should they pursue them, and why?

This case deals with the kinds of decisions that can test a firm's ultimate philosophy. It portrays the dichotomy that can develop for architects between their own ambitions, those of their clients, and those of a community. It poses issues that may well affect the economic success of the firm. It deals with issues that may only be visible to the architects both at this stage and upon project completion. Ethical considerations pervade the issues that the architects must resolve and have implications for them that clearly go beyond the confines of the particular. The case raises issues as to whom the architects are ultimately responsible. It also raises the issue as to what the architectural profession is responsible for in the pursuit of design excellence.

CASE STUDY 5:
Rezoning

The architectural firm of Smith and Jones Architects is approached by a developer that has just purchased a large piece of property currently zoned as industrial and located next to a major river adjacent to the downtown of the city. The client explains to the architect that it is his desire to build a large multiple-story office building on this site overlooking the river to take advantage of the view. He states that he wants to maximize every possible square foot of leasable building and provide the minimum amount of parking required by code. He intends to apply for appropriate rezoning based on a design package. The developer states that he has been impressed with the quality of the design work of the architects on other office projects in the city. He asks if the architectural firm is interested in being retained to design the project.

The architects know the site and are excited by the potential it offers to do an exciting design. They are pleased that the developer has approached them out of respect for their creative abilities.

Before committing to this new client, however, the architects decide to discuss the potential project with the members of the local planning department and ask for their reaction to such a project. The planners are aware that the site is one of the few remaining unbuilt pieces of property on the river and is subject to rezoning consideration because of changes in the community's growth patterns. The planners quickly explain to the architects that putting a large office building on the site could result in an overload on an existing two-lane access road. They go on to explain that the nearby residential community, containing both R-1 and R-4 parcels, has already protested a previous project by a previous owner requesting large-scale "big-box" commercial use on the property. Both the planners and the community feel that the land should be developed primarily as residential to be compatible with the adjacent residential parcels. They also go on to explain that a multiple-story project at this location could block the public-view access of the river. The planners conclude by declaring that the planning department staff would oppose a multiple-story office building but is open to considering a reasonably sized residential- or mixed-use project proposal. They cannot commit to the stance that would be taken by the planning commission or the adjacent community.

The planners have made some very good points. After this meeting, the architects tend to agree that the project as desired by the developer really could be deemed as over-building on one of the last remaining unbuilt sites on the river. They also recognize that the community was correct in opposing the earlier "big-box" proposal. They presume that on principle the community will also oppose this rezoning request.

The architects ponder how to respond to the developer's offer to hire them.

Discussion

- Do the architects ignore what they have discovered, accept the commission, and fight for the right of the developer to build his office building as he is proposing?

- Before accepting any commission, do the architects try to convince the developer to propose a different-scaled project on the site, which the architects, in their own minds, feel would be more acceptable for the community but could generate far less return for the developer?

- Do the architects accept the commission and then make an effort to convince the developer to change parameters of the project?

- Do the architects decline a commission and allow the client to go elsewhere and find another architectural firm that will proceed with his wishes?

This case presents a situation in which the decision to be made has an impact on the very philosophy of the firm and, thus, perhaps its very viability. It may well determine the what, the whom, and the where for projects that they have an opportunity to do in the future. It involves some ethical dilemmas posed by the public, private, and personal aspects of the decision to be made.

CASE STUDY 6:
The Mayor and the School Board

The new mayor of a new suburban city strongly recommended that the newly elected school board, whose members were a slate that he had strongly supported, seriously consider ABC Architects for the design of a prototypical junior high school. The school was to be built on a site selected some years earlier when the community was unincorporated and part of the county. The mayor knew several principals of the firm well, and they had supported him in his recent election effort. He indicated to the school board that he had the utmost respect for their design ability and their integrity.

The school board interviewed eight architects for the project, seven of whom had designed one or more schools. ABC Architects had not, and said so in the interview, indicating that the architects' ability to approach the design problem from a fresh perspective should be viewed as an asset. They stressed their problem-solving ability and their design talent. After due deliberation, the school board selected ABC Architects to design the school and entered into a contract for professional services. ABC Architects was excited about this opportunity to demonstrate its ability to perform school design.

Shortly after this, the site for the prototypical school was deemed inappropriate for school use because of some unanticipated environmental problems. The school board then decided to establish a complete site-selection process that would include a master plan for all future anticipated school sites.

The school board then also commissioned ABC Architects to assist in this site-selection master-planning process, which would now designate the new site for the prototypical school. This master-planning process ensued for twelve months. During that time, the mayor made increasing and, from the school board's perspective, illegal attempts to influence the board members in the performance of their regular duties, including their assessment of their superintendent of schools. The dispute between the two quickly became public, and the community was divided over whose side to support.

As this was happening, ABC Architects met regularly with the school superintendent and members of the school board about the master plan's development. During this time frame, ABC Architects had little professional contact with the mayor.

As the dispute grew more intense, it seemed clear that a major confrontation was coming. ABC Architects' recommendations for site options and the subsequent notification to start work on the prototypical school-design contract would probably be subject to the outcome of this confrontation. Just before completion of the master plan, the mayor contacted a principal of ABC Architects and specifically asked for information on school-board procedures, directions given to the architects during the master-plan development, and the superintendent's performance in particular. The principal pondered what his response should be.

Discussion

- Does the nature of the prior relationship between ABC Architects and the mayor bear on how the firm should respond to the mayor's request?
- Did the mayor, as an elected official, have a special right to know whatever ABC Architects knew about the board's business and the superintendent's performance?

- Should ABC Architects take a public position with respect to factual issues within its expertise if that position placed the firm on one side or the other of the dispute?
- Should ABC Architects take a public position with regard to subjective issues if that position placed the firm on one side or the other of the dispute?
- To what degree does having the school board as a client relate to the issue of the public-trust responsibility of ABC Architects?
- Should the potential impact on ABC Architects' contract for the prototypical school have an impact on the firm's decision?

This case requires that the principal consider the broad issue of the impact of this decision on the firm's philosophy, and its perception both externally and internally. At the same time, it involves the principal in some very pragmatic practice issues that pose consideration of both short- and long-term impacts. These issues range from dealing with future work potential, to present office stability. To whom and to what should the firm be responsible? In this situation, ethical considerations abound, and legal ones will not provide any definitive answers.

CASE STUDY 7:
The Neighbor's House

John and Susie Normal want to build a house for themselves and their two children, John Jr. and Candy. John Sr. had an ongoing relationship with the architectural firm Domicile Plus, with which he had been building some small developments, always with an informal but written agreement. The Normals select a site near the end of a cul-de-sac in a new and very exclusive subdivision. Mr. Tract, the developer of the subdivision, will allow architects to design homes in the subdivision with certain restrictions, although he prefers to use his own staff of building designers. At any rate, his company builds all the houses, no matter who designs them.

Domicile Plus architects meet often with the Normals, work out a design satisfactory to all, and prepare a full set of drawings. Mr. Tract builds the house, and the Normals move in and are very pleased. They love the house and show it off to their friends. They are about to live happily ever after, until...

An older couple, the Bellushis, who have several grandchildren, ring the Normals' bell one day. The Bellushis have just purchased the last remaining lot on the cul-de-sac and very much admire the Normals' house and would like to know the name of their architect. The Normals proudly tell them and give Domicile Plus a great reference.

Several months pass, and the Normals get a call from Mr. Tract, the developer and builder. "Hello, John. I am sitting here with some preliminary drawings of a house for your neighbor Mr. Bellushi, which were just delivered from Domicile Plus. They look very much like the ones for your house. Before we proceed, I would like to know if you mind." Well, John Sr. hits the ceiling. "Of course I mind; we have a unique house. We paid a lot. This is our place." "Okay, Okay. I'll make some changes so they won't look the same," claims Mr. Tract.

Construction on the house begins, and as it progresses, under the watchful eye of the Normals, it is apparent to them that this new house is exactly like their own. They call their lawyer, Mr. Tort.

Mr. Tort fires off a lawsuit against the Domicile Plus architects, Mr. Tract, and the Bellushis, thereby stopping construction. His claim is that the Normals paid for a unique dwelling, the ideas that make up the design were in part their own since the architects would not have derived those solutions without discussion and collaboration with the client, and that Mr. Tract and the Bellushis had no right to copy it. Further, he claims that the Normals' property value has been diminished since theirs is no longer a "one-of-a-kind" house.

In their defense, the Domicile Plus architects state that they had not done a full set of drawings for the Bellushis and had never intended to copy the house, only to make it somewhat similar to satisfy their new client. They said, however, that even if had they copied the house, it was their design and they had rights to it. After all, they made the drawings. Admitting that the Normals had input into the design, they further claimed that another architect would likely have solved the problem differently, thereby making this particular design a signature of the Domicile Plus architects and no one else. The architects were upset that Mr. Tract had modified their Bellushi drawings and was building an apparent replica, though sited a bit differently.

When the case got to court, the judge was not happy. He was particularly dismayed that so little effort had been expended to solve it before it got that far. He compelled the parties to return to negotiations.

Mr. Tort and the Normals then hired another architect, Mr. Clean, to suggest various changes to the Bellushis' house that would satisfy the Normals that there were indeed substantive visual differences, and satisfy the Bellushis that the house was still what they wanted. It should be noted here that both houses, while quite well designed and constructed, would look, at least to the lay public, similar to the other houses around it. This was intentional since Mr. Tract, when developing the subdivision, controlled the height, colors, and materials of the designs and insisted on this contextual similarity.

Mr. Clean suggested an architectonic front court with a low fence to change the frame of the house design. He also suggested various subtle changes in the roof line; some changes in the sizes, proportions, and placement of windows along the street; and some variations in the use of the exterior materials.

These design modifications satisfied the Normals and Mr. Tract, but the Bellushis would have none of it. They wanted a replica of the Normals' house. They said that their purchase of the lot from Mr. Tract was based on their understanding that this was possible. They threatened to countersue both Mr. Tract and the Normals. The parties returned to court without a negotiated settlement. The architects involved expected to be called on to explain their actions and pondered their responses.

Discussion

- What was the responsibility of the Domicile Plus architects to their original client?
- What was the responsibility of the Domicile Plus architects to their new client?
- What is the responsibility of Domicile Plus to themselves with regard to their design (their "intellectual property")?
- What is the responsibility of the new architect, Mr. Clean, to all the parties?

This is a case in which the principal architects of Domicile Plus are called on to defend the very principles under which they practice. Were they aware of this when they made the decisions about the second commission? If so, what were the ethical aspects to these principles? It is important to realize that regardless of the project size, your basic principles may be tested so you should be cognizant of them before you are forced to confront them as perceived by others. As for the other architect, Mr. Clean, he, too, has been required to evaluate his principles in agreeing to enter into this situation.

CASE STUDY 8:
The Master Plan Study

A developer retains an architectural firm to produce a master plan for a large parcel of property that he owns. The property in question is within but at the edge of the community's currently designated urban-limits zone. He is a deep-pockets developer. In other words, he can afford to land bank the property for a considerable period of time, as he has indeed done to this point. Now, with new residential development beginning to take place in the vicinity of this parcel, he wants to take advantage of this growth and develop the commercial space to serve it. Because of his previous development efforts elsewhere, he has commitments from a number of retail businesses to take space in his development if he can move quickly. He understands that the community's general plan indicates residential and commercial use for this parcel. The developer instructs the architects to design a total community plan that meets the community goals for this parcel. He indicates to the architects that he sees this as a great community-development opportunity. He gives the architects his program for commercial space and instructs them to meet the general plan's maximum housing densities allowed for his parcel.

The developer has been a developer of traditional suburban development in the past. He states to the architects, however, that he is excited by their previous design for an unrealized but published competition design for a sustainable development incorporating cluster south-oriented housing, narrow vehicular roads, common open-space areas, a pedestrian focus, on-site waste treatment, and the like.

The architects proceed to produce a design that meets the developer's program and reflects sustainable-design principles.

The project as designed is then submitted to the local planning commission for approval. The commissioners express some concern over the amount and location of the commercial-development element of the plan. The developer indicates that this is, however, a critical economic component and necessary if the project is to be feasible. During the discussion the commissioners appear to be willing to accept this because of the redeeming qualities of the residential component. They are anxious to see a project approved that sets a standard for future growth in the area. They express this while noting that recent nearby residential-development proposals show little innovation. The final approval decision is, however, put off for two weeks until the next meeting to allow the commission staff to take one more look at the developer's economic rationale for the commercial proposal, which is designated as the first phase of the development. The commission indicates that a positive staff report at that time will lead to an enthusiastic approval. There is no discussion of any performance requirements for the developer.

After the meeting the developer indicates to the architects how pleased he is with their work. He indicates, however, for the first time that he is really not very interested in pursuing the residential development because he does not see much profit in that endeavor compared to the projected return from the commercial development. He tells them, "Without your residential design, we would never obtain approval for the commercial proposal.... and that's what this is really all about for us. I don't truly need to move ahead with any residential development if we can get this project off the ground quickly. Besides, I'm not actually sure that the market is really ready for what you've designed, although it sure has been an effective selling tool to the commission as I thought it would be when I hired you guys."

The architects are caught on the horns of a dilemma. The developer and the architects are scheduled to return to the planning commission in two weeks to seek the final approval of a master plan that the architects now know may be a misrepresentation of what the developer intends to actually follow through on. What action, if any, should the architects take?

Discussion

- The architects are concerned that if the whole plan is not carried forward, there could be some negative community impacts. They are also concerned that a delay in the progress of the residential development will lead to efforts by this developer or subsequent developers to change the sustainable design to a traditional one that would not reflect the values that they as architects stand for and that they feel are so important to the future of this community. They realize now that their client has no fundamental belief in the design principles that they have utilized.
- The architects realize that the commission has so far exhibited a willingness to approve the proposal without encumbering it with any performance requirements. The architects believe that their design proposal has presented the commission with a standard for future development and as such is serving the public good.
- The architects are aware that their reputation in the community could be damaged if their design efforts are ultimately viewed as part of a deceit by the developer to secure an approval that he otherwise might not have received.
- The architects understand that their client is a major player in the development community and that his continued satisfaction with their work could lead to many other opportunities to work for other developers interested in pursuing their design ideals.

This case raises the issue of the importance of a firm setting some overall policies regarding how to deal with potential conflicts between responsibility to the public and responsibility to one's client. The issues frequently go beyond strict legal, contractual obligations and certainly embrace ethical considerations.

The whole issue of "whistle-blowing" has prompted a debate between public and private parties, with the courts supporting protection of the "whistle blowers." However, the debate is and will remain open regarding who, when one, and why one engages in the act. Part of the answer to these issues, perhaps the critical one, is dependent on ethical considerations. This policy decision is easier to deal with if the potential condition has been discussed before it comes up in one's professional life. This is true for both firms and individual practitioners. This case is a clear indicator of the importance of the need for ethical considerations to be a mainstay of management policies.

Building Codes and City Projects

A city architects-and-engineers department contacted Architect W to provide
architectural services for the remodeling of
the building known as the Annex, which is
connected to City Hall. The work was also
to include some remodeling of the City Hall,
through which the buildings were to be
linked and the interior user spaces to be
merged. A portion of the City Hall, including the mayor's office, had just been remodeled from designs and drawings produced by
the city department.

Architect W, a woman, had successfully performed architectural work for another city agency in the past and expressed interest in this project. The representative of the city department,
Architect M, indicated that his department was making a shift to
do more work with outside firms, with a particular emphasis on
retaining women and minority architects. After interviewing
Architect W, the city department hired her to provide full professional services for the project. For her first task, Architect W sat
with Architect M and developed a detailed scope of her work for
the project based on the project scope and budget established by
the city department before it received approval from the city
council for the project to proceed.

The first step in the project was to measure and document
the existing conditions. Architect W quickly determined that the
Annex alone contained 6,650 square feet of tenant space. The
building had undergone a number of previous remodelings,
which had to be carefully investigated during this process. The
next task was a careful code analysis. This analysis showed that
there was inadequate exiting for the proposed uses. It also showed
a need for fire sprinklers because the building's proposed tenant
spaces would exceed 5,500 square feet, the allowable code exemption for this type of building use and construction.

During the scoping sessions, these possibilities had never
come up. When Architect W indicated that they would have to
be accommodated with an increased building budget and with an

increase in her professional fee, Architect M expressed surprise and consternation. Because this was city property, there was no requirement for the project to undergo review and approval by the city building department. He indicated that the project budget was not easily supplemented and that the building had contained city tenants for a number of years under the existing fire protection and exit conditions. He suggested ignoring the situations since they were not in the approved scope of work.

Architect W was concerned and contacted an older architect mentor in the city for advice. He said " W, haven't you noticed the maze- and trap-like corridors when you take your plans to the fire department for review? Who do you think reviewed those plans? The city has been operating out of code for years!" Architect W then contacted the director of the city building department whom she knew. He said that his hands were tied since the law permitted the city to build for itself outside his review and jurisdiction.

Architect W then stated to Architect M that as architects, they were both responsible for protecting the public health, safety, and welfare. Architect M, now concerned, brought the issue to his superiors in the department, who were not architects. He also directed Architect W to proceed with her work. She refused to finish the documents until the issues were resolved. Architect M's supervisor then called her into the department office and stated that she was not responsible for the fire sprinklers and that they were amending her contract to make this clear. Then he asked, "Can you now proceed?" W indicated there was still the exit problem and was told that he would quickly resolve that and get back to her.

Architect M called Architect W the next day and asked that the documents be completed as per the original program, which contained no new exits, and that they be completed by the original contractual submittal date. When Architect W indicated that this would not be possible because of the time lost in discussing these issues, she was informed that if she couldn't complete them by that date then she was to release herself from her contract and turn over the documents to his department and they would complete them.

Architect M indicated that Architect W was being more difficult to deal with than other architects with whom the department had worked earlier and that this could affect her professional reputation.

Architect W was now at a critical decision point. She was under contract to the city for a project with a predetermined scope, had been told that she would not be responsible for one code issue that had surfaced, had been directed to ignore another one, and had been further directed to finish the work on time or release herself from her contract so that the city could complete the work itself. What should she do?

Discussion

- Should Architect W simply resign from the contract and let the city proceed as it had in the past?
- Should Architect W go public with the dispute?
- Should Architect W proceed with the work as requested? On what terms?
- Should Architect W take any professional action regarding Architect M?
- Should Architect W let her decision be affected by the issues of women and minority opportunities?
- What is the justification for Architect M's position in this case? Is it supportable?

This case raises an issue that can occur at many stages of a project dealing with public clients. What is the responsibility of the architect when faced with legal ground rules for practice that differ from those for the private sector with respect to perceived aspects of public health, safety, and welfare? This issue can surface during the design process, the production process, and/or the construction process. It can pose difficult dilemmas for all architects involved in the situation, regardless of which side of the problem they are on. How to deal with it and its potential ramifications are better dealt with if an ethical foundation for practice has been established by architects, whatever their practice role may be.

CASE STUDY 10:
The Elusive Client

Architects ABC were hired by a developer to renovate a 100-room Single Room Occupancy facility (S.R.O.) to be funded through the housing department in the downtown of a large city. They had been recommended by a contractor who had worked with them before and who was acquainted with the developer. They went through a process of selection after which they were informed that they had been chosen for the job. This project was a needed one in the community, and the architects were enthused about this opportunity to design it.

The architects prepared a full-services contract and submitted it to the developer. The developer then indicated to them that his attorneys were revising the contract a bit but that he wished for work to start immediately. He asked the architects to prepare an interim letter of agreement, which they did. This was promptly signed by both parties. The architects then asked for a retainer before beginning work, and it came to them without any hesitation.

Three months or so into the job, the developer told the architects that he was having differences with his partners. The architects were still operating under the provisions of the letter of agreement because the revised contract, which they had agreed to, had not been signed and returned by them. During this period, the architects had been working amicably with the developer and had never met his partners. The architects had completed their schematic design, and it had been reviewed positively by the city housing department.

Shortly thereafter the architects were asked by their client, the developer, to meet with him to review the most recent progress of the work. The meeting was held in the architects' office, and at the appointed time some people arrived whom the architects had never met before. These individuals indicated that they were the major partners and that they were paying the fees (which at this point were outstanding). They asked that the work be presented to them while they waited for their presumed client, the developer, who would be late.

The developer finally arrived while the meeting was underway, but he was very quiet. The partners, on the other hand, had been and continued to be extremely vocal and demanded changes in the design. They also indicated that they intended to revise the submitted contract to limit the architects' participation in the construction phase to progress-payment-approval only. The partners stated that they wanted to have final control of any material going into the project once it was under construction. The tone of this discussion was such that the architects were concerned that the partners might, in fact, be planning to siphon off funds from the project after it had been finally funded based on an accepted bid price.

At the close of the meeting, the architects stated that they could accept some changes in their contract but could not relinquish all control over how the project was to be built. They further indicated that they needed to think about their continued involvement in the project now that both the scope of their work and the participation of the developer client were apparently changing.

After the partners left the meeting, the architects talked with their original developer client. He told them that while he was a partner, he was not a major one. He had started as a consultant to the other partners, having been brought to the project when its feasibility had seemed hopeless. When he turned the project around, he had become a partner responsible for managing the project. However, now that the project was on track, the major partners were taking it back into their full control. He indicated that he wanted to fight this and asked the architects to support his contention that he had performed well for the major partners and that it would be best for the project if he retained his role.

The architects were now confronted with how or whether they should proceed to see this needed community project through to fruition.

Discussion

- Should the architects perform their services while harboring their suspicions?
- Do the architects have an obligation to inform the city housing department of their suspicions?
- Should the architects continue given the changed role of the developer and, if so, under what terms?
- Do the architects have an obligation to the major partners, as the actual client, to see the project through? Would this

require the partners and the architects to agree to some form of contract modifications?

- Do the architects have an obligation to support the original developer in his internal struggle with his partners?

This case involves professional principles, office policy, and management decisions with regard to contract obligations. How often is work started prior to actual contract signing? How often do the clients' principals change during the course of a project? How often have architects prepared themselves for these conditions and the potential dilemmas they can cause? The preparations for handling these types of situations involve legal considerations in terms of how one has protected oneself contractually and ethical considerations as to how one deals with situations beyond the legal contract framework. This situation, which perhaps could have been prevented from happening, illustrates the need for entering practice equipped to deal with one's own ethical foundation.

CASE STUDY 11:
Employee Rights

Architectural Firm A finds itself with an increase in its workload, which appears to be temporary. A decision is made that additional help is needed, but management does not feel comfortable in making a long-term commitment to "permanent" staff. Concurrently, Firm B is experiencing what appears to be a temporary decline in its workload because of a delay in the start of construction documents for a major project. The partners in Firm B are convinced that the project will proceed, and they are very reluctant to lay off any of their key staff members, who will be needed when the project goes forward. One of the principals in Firm B contacts a friend who is a principal in Firm A to inquire about the possibility of loaning an employee to Firm A for a period of approximately six months.

The qualifications of the Firm B employee and the duration of her availability fit Firm A's projected needs, and the employee agrees to the concept of a loan to Firm A for a period of six months. All concerned are in agreement that the change is temporary and that the employee will return to Firm B at the end of the loan period. The Firm B employee reports to work at Firm A.

Before the expiration of the loan period, however, the temporary employee approaches the principal of Firm A to whom she has been reporting and announces that she would prefer to stay with Firm A, rather than return to Firm B when the loan period is up. The employee states that she finds the work at Firm A more challenging and feels there is more opportunity for growth and experience in project types to which she has not previously been exposed. During the time this employee has been with Firm A, the firm's workload has continued to grow, and it now appears that the addition of "permanent" staff is probably in order. The principal has been impressed with the employee's ability, attitude, and performance, and would like to have her as a member of the "permanent" staff.

The principal calls his friend at Firm B and informs him of the situation. The friend indicates that he is glad that the loan worked out, but that Firm B is in need of the employee as a member of its own staff and expect her to be a productive part of it for at least the time equivalent to the time that it loaned him out.

The principal mulls over what he should do.

Discussion

- Should Firm A offer a "permanent" position to the employee, on the premise that the employee alone has the right to decide where she works?
- Should Firm A advise the employee that it would like to have her join the firm, but indicate it feels a commitment to honoring its agreement with Firm B? Should Firm A, therefore, plan to return her to Firm B and advertise for new staff?
- Does the employee have any responsibilities to Firm B?
- Does Firm B have any obligation to honor the employee's wishes?
- If the employee returns to Firm B and then quits shortly after her return and seeks to be hired by Firm A, what should be the position of Firm A?

In this case, a dilemma for the principal architect occurs between his obligations toward his firm and, thus, his personal welfare, and his obligation to his professional colleagues. The case also poses the issue of what will be the perception of his ethics by his fellow principals, his staff, and his professional colleagues. Is this likely to have any impact on the welfare of his firm? It is but one small facet of the issues surrounding employee and employer rights. There are also some of the same issues to be considered by the employee who may well be put in a similar management situation sometime in her future but who now has particular desires that may well effect her career opportunities. These issues have an ethical dimension whether they are focused on just disengagement, just compensation, just benefits, just credit, or the like.

CASE STUDY 12:
Two Clients/One Project

You are the architect for a neighborhood shopping center. Your client is one for whom you have provided services in the past and whom you expect will be a continuing client with future projects. This client has been willing to see that this development type makes an esthetic contribution to its community. Your contract is for shell and core work only, with the tenant spaces to be developed as tenants are secured. Your contract has a provision for tenant improvement work as an additional service.

Your client signs a lease with a retail tenant who wants to retain you directly to do the interior architecture and tenant improvements for her store. You have done work for this tenant in the past and expect to do more in the future. This client has retained you particularly for your creative design and your previous work for her has won some design awards.

The tenant wants a large identification sign to be placed over the entrance to the store, but this will require approval by the local planning commission. You feel that such a sign could be in conflict with the design of this particular project, but you recognize the marketing importance of this signage. The tenant client directs you to develop the design for the sign and to submit it to the planning commission with a request for approval.

Your shell-and-core-work client objects to the sign on the grounds that it will affect his negotiations with potential tenants for the remaining space in the center. However, he recognizes that the lease does not specifically prohibit such a sign, provided the tenant secures all necessary approvals and permits. Your shell-and-core-work client tells you of his displeasure with the proposal and strongly suggests that if you pursue the approval of the sign, you will probably not receive any more work from him.

Learning of this situation, the tenant client informs you that if you do not pursue this application with due diligence, you will not receive any more work from her. Even though the tenant client probably has much less future work to offer you, she is still an important client and you have agreed to provide full services for her.

You obviously have a strong conflict of interest between satisfying the desires of the shell-and-core-work client, those of the tenant client, and your own regarding design intentions. You also are aware that the outcome of this disagreement could have an economic impact on your practice. You ponder how to resolve this dilemma.

Discussion

- Do you tell the shell-and-core-work client that you are obligated to pursue the application for the tenant client and risk losing this client for future work?
- Do you tell the tenant client that you feel that such a sign would be undesirable from the point of view of the overall project appearance and decline to pursue the application?
- Do you share your dilemma with both clients? If so, on what basis do you pursue a resolution of the situation?
- Do you have any ethical obligations to either client?

This case deals with an unintended conflict between an architect's clients. It also deals with conflicts between an architect's design intentions and a client's desires. Both of these situations have many historic precedents and involve evaluations of whose priorities are the most valid. In the process of dealing with these situations, you must examine the validity of your options in terms of their impact on your basic ethical precepts. This is important because architects must also consider the users, the public, and the environment as clients even though they are outside the contractual spectrum. When issues like those in this case show up in situations where these considerations are a factor, you must have a grasp of what your ethical precepts are as you evaluate your resolution options.

CASE STUDY 13:
The Real Estate Investment Project

Agroup of architects were given an oppor- tunity to design a second building in their city for a client for whom the architects had recently designed a home-office build- ing. This completed building is one of the architects' best projects and had won local design acclaim from the public and the pro- fessional design community. The client had received numerous kudos for its contribution to the cityscape and was exceedingly proud of its new home.

There were several differences between the two projects. The first had been budgeted to be designed as an institutional Class A building, and the program called for the design to create a community asset, a memorable image, and a superb work envi- ronment.

The second commission was for a rental-office building to be treated only as a corporate real-estate investment with a reduced budget, though still a Class A building.

On the first project the architects reported directly to the board of directors, who had a personal interest in all aspects of the project.

On the second project, the finance committee of the board had retained a professional project manager to be fully responsi- ble for overseeing the project. The project manager's responsi- bility was to ensure that the project was designed within a prede- termined feasibility budget, to secure leases, and to see that within the budget the project was satisfactory to the tenants. The architects were to report directly to the project manager for this project.

The site for the first project was two full city blocks, which allowed many options for architectural-configuration bulk and mass. The final project of 600,000 square feet had evolved as a five-floor courtyard structure with myriad variations in its bulk. It not only fit well into its immediate surroundings, but also enhanced them and set a standard for future development in the area.

The site for the second project was a city block containing a multilevel parking structure owned by the client and an empty

20,000-square-foot corner lot, formerly the site of a service station. The clients' program called for a 350,000-square-foot office building and required that the garage was to be retained, with no reduction in total site parking spaces. Air-rights encroachment of the new building over the existing garage was possible if it could be handled within the project budget constraints. The architects' preliminary assessment of the site and the owner's program indicated that the only viable solution would be a high-rise structure. This would call for the client to apply for a zoning variance because the site was just outside the downtown high-rise zone. Inasmuch as the site was directly across the street from a newly constructed twenty-five-floor corporate signature building that has major views across the site, the architects assumed that those tenants and the building owner would oppose any rezoning request.

The first site offered a range of design options that led to a design that provided some major urban-design contributions to the that area of the city. The second site did not provide the same degree of possibilities given the client's stated program, even with a rezoning.

It seemed clear to the architects that the second project did not offer nearly the same opportunities for design excellence that the first project produced. They realized that the completed project would inevitably be compared to their earlier work for the same client, probably without a complete understanding of the difference in the design parameters. However, the architects recognized that this was an opportunity for the firm to design its first high-rise building. The architects pondered whether they should accept the opportunity, reject it, or try to change the parameters they had been offered.

Discussion

- If you as an architect took the job, how would you protect your reputation?
- If you as an architect took the job, what conditions would you insist on?
- Do the architects have a responsibility to indicate to the client their concerns over the program and management options presented to them before entering into any contract?
- If you as an architect took the job and a negative public reaction to the project ensued, how would you deal with your responsibility to your client and your responsibility to your community?

- Do the architects have any responsibility to respect the entitlements that the corporate-office-tower owners thought they had secured through the location of their building on the edge of the existing high-rise zone?

This is a case in which a decision that appears to be a simple business decision has some ethical aspects to it, aspects that can be important factors in how the firm is perceived by both its future clients, its colleagues, and the public. It has been easy for some professionals to accept a commission under difficult conditions with the comment, "If I don't do it, someone else will do it worse." This suggests either a rationalization or a perception that the professionals' abilities will provide their clients with a project that overcomes any obstacles to excellence. Whichever the reality, architects have a responsibility to be sure that they are defining excellence in its highest terms. They must also be clear on those terms and evaluate the impact of this on their ethical stance. This case also deals with issues of fair play in a world where the definition of that concept is in constant flux, depending on the players. This is all the more evidence of the need for architects to continually be in touch with their own ethics.

CASE STUDY 14:
Adaptive Re-Use/Historic Preservation

An architect was employed to do an adaptive reuse restoration of a major public building by a public agency.

The building, a civic auditorium, was historically significant but was not in use because of serious code deficiencies. Exhaustive studies by the city showed that while there was usage need for the building interior in its original form, there was more significant need for it in a revised form that would allow for greatly expanded usage. The city's restoration program provided that the exterior be retained in original form with the work, which changed the use to be confined to the interior. The changes in the interior were to be respectful of the historic fabric of the building while meeting this new program. The agency completed and approved a design that satisfied the program for the revised use, construction documents were completed, and construction bids were received.

A community group that opposed the interior changes as being destructive of the historic significance of the building requested that the agency stop the project by not awarding a construction contract. At a public meeting of the agency, the architect defended the position of the public agency vigorously, based not only on the city's studies, but on his own beliefs that adaptive reuse was a valid strategy for preserving historic buildings. At the same meeting, the community group declared its intention to stop the project via a lawsuit or other legal means. The agency put a temporary hold on the project.

The community group was able to put an advisory public referendum on an upcoming electoral ballot and subsequently its position for a historic restoration only of the building was supported in a close vote. The public agency then canceled the project and the architect's contract.

About one year later, a Request For Proposal (RFP) to architects from the public Agency was sent out to restart the project as an interior and exterior restoration only. A key agency representative encourages the architect to submit a proposal. The agency representative indicates that the agency had been very satisfied with the architect's performance under the original contract and would be pleased to utilize the architect this second time around. He indicates that the agency has the same high regard for the architect's credentials as when he was first selected. The architect knows he has the advantage of having the existing building on CAD and that he has intimate knowledge of all of the code problems. His project architect for the original adaptive-reuse project is available, and the architect's office could use the work.

The architect, however continues to believe that the adoptive reuse originally proposed is the best solution.

The architect considers whether to submit a proposal.

Discussion

- Do you as an architect seek the new design contract for a project with which you have philosophical differences?
- Should you vie for a public project when you are aware that your credibility as a believer in the project may well be suspect by the community?
- How do you evaluate the relative importance of business economics and philosophical commitment?

- If the architect seeks the new design contract, how should he present himself and his qualifications to the agency?

This case raises many questions that architects can face on any project for which they are presenting their qualifications. The need to communicate what you stand for inevitably exposes your ethical convictions and the degree to which they are important. The situation can also require that you have some perception of the ethical perspective of the potential client. The degree to which you are successful in demonstrating your convictions can be as important as the demonstration of your talent. The degree to which you remain true to your convictions in every facet of practice can have a material effect on your success. It is important to evaluate the professional decisions you make in terms of your fundamental-belief system, and that requires that you assess your ethical stance on the issues involved.

CASE STUDY 15:
Life Safety

A nonprofit developer retains an architectural firm to remodel into apartments for low-income senior citizens two rundown, partially vacant and vandalized eighteen-story apartment buildings containing 576 units that are located in an earthquake-prone city. The buildings are currently under the jurisdiction of the city's housing agency, which has been anxiously looking for ways to rehabilitate them. The developer's proposal is the first potentially viable one made to the agency despite months of solicitations.

The apartment buildings, built in 1964 of post-tensioned concrete, were designed by a well-respected architect, engineered by a renowned structural engineer, and built by a reputable builder. They met all of the building codes and seismic requirements in effect at the time of construction. However, they have proven to be a social disaster as a living environment.

The present architects and their structural engineer initiate their contract with a thorough walk-through visual inspection of the buildings. They come away with the conclusion that the buildings fall short of current seismic requirements, particularly in their use of discontinuous shear walls. The architects and the engineer are concerned about the future stability of these buildings in the light of a recently released analysis of building performance during some recent, major, international earthquake events. The professionals note, however, that the buildings do not seem to have suffered serious damage over the years despite several nearby seismic events.

The present building code that the city uses states that if the use (occupancy) remains the same, the buildings do not require a seismic upgrade.

The nonprofit developer has a limited budget and has indicated that it wants to spend all available funds on creating amenities that are visible and that will enhance the livability of the units and the buildings (i.e., remodeling kitchens, adding community rooms and lounges, landscaping, etc.). The developer is convinced that this is the only way the apartment complex will be restored to a socially viable living environment for its new occupants. The developer directs the architects to prepare a project program and a resultant design that reflects this approach, being fully aware both of the architects' concerns and that the city code does not require seismic upgrade.

Now, however, the architects are confronted with a dilemma as to what the priorities of the project program and ensuing design should be. The architects are well aware that there is a demonstrated need in the community for affordable low-income senior housing. They are excited about the opportunity to be a part of a solution to this problem. Before proceeding further, though, they ponder what their next step should be.

Discussion

- Should the architects turn down the design commission unless the nonprofit developer agrees to a total (up to current code) retrofit, even at the expense of some of what the architects recognize are necessary amenities if the project is to be socially viable?
- Should the architects insist that the developer fund a thorough structural investigation to determine the risk to public safety involved by the present building design?
- Should the architects insist that the buildings be brought up to a standard that they would determine would prevent loss of life, at least, though not necessarily loss of property, based on today's seismic knowledge?

- Should the architects proceed with the project on the developer's terms given the present codes' allowances and produce a design that uses the available funds fully to provide the needed amenities? Does the fact that the architects have a contract with the developer carry with it any ethical obligations concerning responding to the client's directions?
- Should the architects make their concerns publicly visible to parties other than their client, the nonprofit developer?

This case concerns a situation in which, during the first phases of a project, the architects are confronted with the reality that the project may differ from what was anticipated when the contract was entered into. In particular the issue is not as much about a project-scope change and any resultant fee impacts as it is about a change that deals with project philosophy and potential outcomes. This case is representative of situations that too often are not anticipated or visible during the contractual process. The architects' legal responsibility will not provide the absolute answers to the situation. Rather, there is placed on the architects a demand to consider their ethical precepts for guidance in arriving at a resolution.

CASE STUDY 16:
The Fee Proposal

XYZ Architects were to be interviewed as a potential firm to design a church by the church building committee. The firm understood that it was one of six firms under consideration.

Before the interview, the architects learned that the church had a contract with an engineering firm to provide consultant services to support the church in its effort to procure the proposed building site. XYZ Architects indicated to the church that it was not interested in being interviewed while another firm was under contract. The attorney for the church informed XYZ Architects that the consulting engineering firm would not be considered for the design of the proposed church.

Once the property had been procured, the engineering consultant would be released.

XYZ Architects then agreed to be interviewed. The architects were interviewed at their office by the chairman of the building committee. During the interview, in response to a question, they made it clear they would not submit a fee before the church implied that XYZ was the selected firm. A few days later, however, the chairman requested XYZ to submit a fee proposal without any assurances beyond the statement it was now on a short list of two firms and under serious consideration. At that time, XYZ submitted a fee proposal.

After not hearing further from the church for approximately thirty days, XYZ Architects called the building-committee chairman to get an update on the status of the final selection process. To the architects' surprise, they were informed that a contract had already been negotiated with another firm. The chairman told them that the decision had been difficult, particularly in the light of the design strengths of the XYZ Architects and their strong client references. XYZ later learned that their fee proposal had been provided during this thirty-day period to the other firm, which then agreed to accomplish the requested services for $15,000 less than XYZ had proposed.

The XYZ Architects pondered whether they had any legal or professional recourse.

Discussion

- Did the owner and/or the firm to whom a contract was awarded act in an ethical manner?
- Did the architects violate their own ethics in submitting their fee proposal when they did?

This case deals with some of the realities of fee proposals and competition. Competition over fees is not forbidden under the current professional codes or the current law. But the nuances here clearly invoke ethical questions and perhaps legal ones. When one submits a proposal, whose property is it? How should it be considered by all of the parties that become involved? Are there inherent answers to these questions, or are they modified by the conditions under which the situation is initiated by each of the parties? Are one's ethical positions established just within the parameters of the published ethical canons? Is what is legal necessarily ethical? The whole arena of fee negotiation is one in which these considerations are particularly fragile.

The AAA Design Group, a local firm, created a joint venture with H20 International to pursue a criminal-justice project for the county in which AAA Design Group is located. The purpose of this joint effort was to provide a method for the AAA Design Group to overcome its lack of experience in the criminal-justice field, and for H20 International to become more competitive by aligning itself with a local firm.

The joint venture was subsequently short-listed and then interviewed for the project. To the interview panel, H20 International displayed exceptional expertise in this field, and the AAA Design Group capitalized on being a well-respected firm that was local and, therefore, close to the project. The panel selected the joint venture over its competitors and recommended it for the commission. A contract was issued to the joint venture by the county, work was begun, and subsequently the programming, schematic-design, and design-development phases were completed. After submission, the county approved each of these phases.

While the joint venture was waiting to receive authorization to proceed with the contract-documents phase, the county project director met with a principal of the AAA Design Group and voiced his satisfaction with the performance of AAA. At the same time, however, he voiced his total displeasure with the performance of H20 International. He went on to ask if the AAA Design Group could complete the project independently since he felt H20 International was difficult to deal with and had already contributed the special expertise that had brought that company to the project in the first place. He indicated that approval to proceed would await an answer to his request.

The principal of the AAA Design Group was relieved to know that he still had the respect of his client, but he was now faced with the unpleasant task of deciding where his most substantial obligations lie. Were they with his client, his own firm, his joint venture partner, or some combination of these entities? He had had a very good working experience with H2O

International during the project-design process to date. From his perspective, H2O had been aggressive, but not incompatible, in dealing with the client when pursuing the resolution of several issues that clearly would affect the final quality of the project. The AAA Design Group and H2O International had, however, decided to put off any discussions of continuing their joint-venture arrangement in the pursuit of further work until this project was under construction. The principal of the AAA Design Group was concerned with the impact his decision would have on the future of the joint venture. He was also concerned about the ffect his determination would have on his prospects for doing future work for the county, which had some major public facilities scheduled for future design and construction.

Discussion

- Should the AAA Design Group take steps to dissolve the joint venture and then proceed to complete the project independently under a new agreement with the county?
- Should the principal inform the county that he has a binding agreement with his joint venture partner and state that if the county is unhappy with the H2O work and does not want it to continue under the present contract, then AAA must withdraw from the project as part of the joint venture's anticipated contract termination, thereby leaving the work to be completed by some other firm?
- Should the principal reorganize the joint venture by assuming complete leadership and eliminating any need for the county to interface with H20 International during completion of the project under the original agreement? If this approach is taken, should it be made with or without informing the county?
- Should the principal try to go around the county project director in resolving this issue?
- What are the principal's obligations to H2O International? What are H2O International's obligations to the AAA Design Group?
- What are the County's obligations to the Joint Venture?

This case raises a series of issues about the difference between legal and ethical obligations in client/architect relationships. Most large projects extend over a period of time and have a complexity that can inevitably create some stresses in this relationship. While the actual contract between the client and the architect may deal with a process for resolution, it often is not capable of dealing with all nuances of the particular situation. The same can be said for interprofessional relationships. Agreements between participants in joint ventures or professional associations do not always consider the stresses that such arrangements may undergo. The same can be said for agreements between architects and their consultants. When resolving all such circumstances, regardless of the project size or scope, professionals need to look at ethical considerations rather than simply legal ones.

CASE STUDY 18:
The Cash Flow Bind

Don is the managing partner of a forty-person office. The partnership of the firm is structured so that the founding principal has 65% of the stock, with the remaining seven associate partners each having equal shares of the remaining 35%. The founding principal has selected the associate partners for their potential to carry on the firms' significant work and sold them their stock in the firm at a jointly agreed fair value. Don is one of the associate partners and receives additional compensation for his role as managing partner. The founding principal receives compensation that is considerably higher than that of the associate partners.

Don was elected to his position by five of the seven associate partners a year ago. At that time the firm was undergoing a management reorganization, with the founding partner announcing that he would be reducing his active participation in the firm, though not necessarily his compensation, in anticipation of his retirement in the next year or so. He indicated that upon retirement he wanted to divest himself of more of the firm's stock to the existing associate partners so that they would have fiscal control of the firm. Don and one other associate partner expressed a desire to assume the role of managing partner at this important time as the firm dealt with the approaching change. At a partners' meeting, each presented his case. The founding principal stated that he wished this to be the decision of the associate partners since it primarily involvd their future. A friendly election then took place, at which time Don was elected.

Subsequently, during the past year there had been further dialogue within the partnership about the role of the managing-partner position. Some felt that this partner should be responsible only for the firm's fiscal management. Others felt that the managing partner should be the one to provide the firm's philosophical leadership, as well as manage its fiscal health. Don was a strong proponent of the larger role.

The office is now quite busy although not currently working to full capacity. Several potential contracts are in the offing, however, and the office has been holding onto its full staff in anticipation of the increased workload that any of these projects will require upon the contract signing and the client's authorization to proceed. Don has indicated to these potential clients that several named "key" staff members will be available to work on their particular project when a project start is authorized since the employees' present workload assignment has been tailored for just such a situation.

Don receives a phone call from one of the firm's regular consultants requesting payment on his last invoice, which is now two months overdue. The consultant states that he assumes that the architectural firm has been paid for the work inasmuch as he knows that the firm has been authorized to proceed onto the next phase of the work for that project, which he is still working on. He says that if he, too, is to proceed, he needs to be paid up-to-date. Don promises that he will look into the matter.

Don then has a meeting with the firms' newly hired in-house accountant, who tells Don that the firm is now in a cash-flow bind. A client with a large outstanding account has just called to say that it would be delaying payment much later than anticipated because of unforeseen circumstances. The firm recently took out a loan from their friendly banker in anticipation of the delayed receipt of some outstanding accounts receivable, but it did not anticipate this situation. In fact, the anticipated receivable that will now be delayed indefinitely was a factor in the success of the firm's loan application, as was the fact that it was guaranteed by the founding principal.

The accountant also tells Don that the firm just received the full payment for services rendered from the client whose project the consultant is working on. The accountant has indicated in the meeting that this entire payment will have to go to meeting both the firm's payroll and the first principal and interest payment for the bank loan, both of which are due shortly, at the end of the month.

The firm's in-house accountant sees only a few options that can provide some fiscal stability and allow for payment to the consultant now. He recommends to Don that the firm: immediately furlough a number of staff members and reduce staff salaries, have the founding principal take an immediate major salary cut, have the associate partners take immediate salary cuts, or develop a workable combination strategy. Whatever action is taken, it will likely have to stay in place until the anticipated new contracts are not only signed but also produce actual receipts from their first billings.

Don feels that the direction he takes on this matter will ultimately be seen as a reflection on his ethical priorities. It is his belief that leadership should depend on a strong ethical underpinning. Don wants his partners to perceive him as a strong leader. Not fulfilling obligations to the consultant, releasing staff members promised to clients for certain projects, perhaps compromising the firm's capabilities by ultimately losing staff members, or reducing needed compensation are all strategies that have ethical aspects.

Don ponders what to do.

Discussion

- What is the firm's responsibility to the consultant firm?
- What is the firm's responsibility to its employees?
- What is the responsibility of the partners to their families?
- What is the responsibility of the founding principal to his associate partners?
- What is the responsibility of the associate partners to the founding principal?
- What is the firm's responsibility to the prospective clients, who have been promised particular staff members for their projects?
- Should Don make a unilateral decision for the firm and inform the partners of what he has done?

This case becomes more complex as one thinks about it. There are risks for Don, his associate partners, and the founding principal. The risks here are embodied in such questions as: Will consultants continue to want to work with the firm? Will potential employees want to come to work for it? Will furloughed employees be willing to come back when asked? Will the founding partner become disillusioned with his planned retirement strategy? Will the associate partners feel that they are carrying an unreasonable burden? Will the managing partner be viewed as less than acceptable as the firm's leader? Will the firm's client base become disillusioned with the firm's integrity? There are no clear answers in these trying circumstances. What may be deemed as sound business practice for the firm in this instance clearly has a strong ethical determinant to it. And Don's decisions will clearly test his ethical underpinnings.

CASE STUDY 19:
The Competition

ABC Architects had a long-standing relationship with a Fortune 500 company and served as the head of a multidisciplinary team that developed its 350-acre parcel as a suburban office park.

Eight years into the project, a public group formed a foundation to build a memorial to the state's veterans, and set about a statewide search for an appropriate site. The Fortune 500 company responded and provided the foundation with a site at no cost with the understanding that the memorial would complement the company's office park.

The foundation then selected a competition advisor and held a one-stage design competition that was open to architects, landscape architects, and artists.

ABC, because of its relationship with the Fortune 500 company, decided to submit a design. The firm was not among the finalists.

However, before the final selection was made public, the competition advisor called ABC Architects to say that the winning entry was produced by an architect who didn't have the time, experience, or staff to complete his design. Neither the competition requirements nor the winning architect had considered this eventuality.

The competition advisor, the foundation, and the Fortune 500 company were worried about this predicament. Would ABC Architects contract with the foundation to work with the winner and help produce his design? The architectural firm agreed to meet with the winner to consider the possibility.

They met, and the following stipulations were discussed. ABC Architects acknowledged its duty to produce the winning design. ABC stated that the design required development and that it would communicate with and make all presentations to the owner. The firm's architects also said they would try to accommodate the winner's views with respect to the design development, but that they would not accept ultimate responsibility without ultimate control. ABC then explained its rigorous in-house design-review process, which would be applied without exception to this project. ABC and the winner agreed to all of these stipulations.

The foundation was advised of and pleased with the outcome: the ABC architects would be the prime architects and the winner, their design consultant. The agreement between ABC and the design consultant would be worked out directly between the two.

Work began. The first design review was held between ABC and the winner. The design was compared with the competition program and the project objectives written by the winner. Some problems were identified; however, no decisions on their resolution were made. The next meeting was set.

Immediately afterward, the winner went to the foundation and complained that his design was being changed. The foundation told him to discuss his concern with ABC but to stop worrying; if the foundation did not agree with the need for changes, it would not approve any. The foundation also told the winner to cease direct contact with them and to work through ABC with whom the foundation had its contract.

The foundation told ABC of its conversation with the winner.

ABC then met with the winner again, reiterated the stipulations, and reminded him that his design had not been changed; it was being studied, but nothing could happen until he cooperated. He then refused but maintained contact with ABC. The project was deadlocked.

Three months later, the ABC architects advised the foundation that it could not make any progress without the cooperation of the winner and resigned the commission. ABC suggested that if the foundation and the winner could not find another architect to produce the winning design, the foundation should consider the second- and third-place winners, both of whom were capable of executing their designs.

Several months later, the foundation contacted ABC. The winner had withdrawn and taken his design with him. The foundation was not satisfied to proceed with either the second or third place winning designs and wanted a new design. Would ABC accept the commission?

ABC did so, and the following article appeared in the local newspaper:

IT'S THEIR MEMORIAL, BUT WAS ARCHITECTURAL CHOICE FAIR?

One year ago the Veterans' Foundation announced the winner of its proposed memorial. The Foundation conducted a juried competition in which Mr. Winner bested 20 entries. Last week the Foundation announced that the designer of its memorial would be Mr. ABC, who entered the competition but was not among the four finalists. Last week's announcement made no mention of Mr. Winner or the competition it publicized a year ago.

What happened to Mr. Winner, and how did an architect who wasn't even a finalist receive the commission?

The Foundation says it made a sensible choice. Winner and other finalists say it's all politics, and the deal stinks. Here's what happened.

The Foundation hopes to build a $4 million memorial next to Fortune 500's office park. The Foundation invited architects to submit designs in a juried competition. Mr. Winner won, and as per competition rules, was paid $5,000 for his submission.

But there was one small hitch. Mr. Winner is a registered architect, but he could not fully execute the contract. He is on the staff of an engineering firm, but entered the competition as an individual; he admittedly lacks the necessary time, equipment and staff to complete a project of this magnitude. And so it was agreed that Mr. Winner would associate with a full-service architectural firm.

It is customary for designers to select their own associates, but Mr. Winner was told his associate would be ABC Architects. It is not a coincidence that ABC is also designing Fortune 500's office park. The memorial is not technically a part of the office park but Fortune 500 donated a 13-acre site for the memorial. The political and aesthetic links between the office park are thus strengthened by having the same architect in charge of both projects.

There may be logic in choosing ABC to carry our Mr. Winner's design, but as a practical matter, Mr. ABC can be prickly. Mr. Winner found himself in an impossible situation. "Mr. ABC wanted to do something with the design that I was uncomfortable with. I was supposed to be the design consultant, but I could not control my own design. There were major, wholesale changes to my design that under no circumstances would I have entertained."

Eventually, Mr. Winner bailed out, taking his design with him. But instead of calling on the second- or third-place finalists, the Foundation gave the whole project to ABC Architects.

The upshot is, one of the most politically well-connected architects in the state, who also happens to be designing the office park, winds up with the commission. In hindsight, the competition looks like a pretentious publicity stunt which cost the participating architects more than $30,000 each. The second-place participant called the choice "a slap in the face of every architect who entered the competition."

The Foundation said they acted within their guidelines. "There was never any intention that these designs would be ranked for contract. There was no requirement that the second- or third-place prize would have any part of the project," said the Competition Advisor.

Such a position flies in the face of fairness. The Foundation was not required to hold a competition. It has the right to hire any architect it chooses. But the fact is, it did have a competition, it did award the commission to the first-place winner and it did hire an architect-of-record with whom the Winner could not get along.

ABC Architects should resign this commission!

The principals of ABC met to discuss the newspaper article and its potential impact on their staff morale, as well as their future business prospects. They pondered any steps they should take and prepared to meet with staff members to explain their position.

Discussion

- Did ABC Architects have a conflict of interest in agreeing to produce the winner's design?
- Did the winner have an obligation to find an architect who could produce his work before submitting his design?
- Did the winner breach ethical standards in "going public?"
- Did ABC Architects breach ethical standards in accepting a commission for a completely new design?
- Do ABC Architect's actions reflect positively, negatively, or not at all on the architectural profession?
- Is the appearance of collusion enough to suggest that, ethically, ABC Architects should resign the commission?

This case deals with circumstances that can arise during the schematic-design phase of a project on which one is associated with another architect. This situation can occur between associations formed not only out of mutual convenience, but also out of mutual friendship. Written agreements do not often deal with unintended circumstances between the parties involved. They also rarely prepare one for the unexpected external consequences of the situation. In these situations, the resulting decisions often benefit from ethical considerations.

CASE STUDY 20:
Design Integrity

You are the senior partner and senior design principal in a firm of fifty. After forty years with the firm, you are preparing to retire. You have taken on one last major project, a university building, and have engaged several of the firm's most promising young designers in the design process as part of the project-design team. It has been your hope that through this direct association, your design philosophy would be thoroughly absorbed and understood by these potential future associates. It is your desire that your design philosophy continue as a legacy to guide the future direction of the firm.

You have decided to institute a process whereby the project team will make a presentation of the project to all of the members of the office at a lunch-time forum at various stages of the design effort. This will give all members of the firm the opportunity to discuss and critique the work to date in terms of its philosophy, quality, and validity. The first such presentation has just taken place with the completion of the schematic design.

You and your design team had presented the project, and the initial comments were laudatory. "The best thing we've done." "An aesthetic tour de force." "Clearly derivative of some of our early work." "Should establish the required memorable image desired by the client." Then a comment came from a new employee, a recent graduate. "I heard Henry Cobb say that buildings must 'be useful.' I don't think this one is by my definition." Another voice expressed concern over the quality of the work environment for some of the building occupants and referred to an article by Joan Goody in which she stated, "Disdain of the user is immoral." Another voice then said that her professor always quoted the philosophy of the artist/architect Hundertwasser: "You are a guest of nature.... Behave." In their view this project design imposed on the natural system and didn't truly represent sustainable design and the basic parts should be reconsidered. "But isn't beauty what we should be focusing on?" was a retort by another in the audience. "We should be focusing on the deeper meaning of the design. This project will be standing 100 years from now," said another. The debate ended only with the need for all to return to their afternoon's work.

This stimulating and robust discussion made it clear to you that there was no unanimity among the younger members of the firm as to what the design philosophy of the firm should be. As you prepare to meet with your design team following the presentation, one particular comment made at the end of the lunch-time forum reverberates through your mind: "It's clearly not yet good enought…even if you have used up your allocated budget!" The comment had been made by a new young associate partner whom you respect.

You know you did not articulate clear answers about the design's intentions in the passionate context of the discussion. You also had to admit to yourself that you had not fully considered some of the issues that the project's most passionate critics raised. Your immediate reaction was that there was some validity to their "global" concerns. While you had a strong commitment to the aesthetic as being representative of your design philosophy, you realized that your philosophy went beyond that and might still be one subject to growth and change.

You have a client presentation scheduled for the following week and you are sure the client, for whom you have worked before, will be pleased with the present design. You know that you have already exceeded the office budget for the schematic phase. What do you tell your design team about what to do next?

Discussion

- Who ultimately do you design for? The contractual client, the project occupants, the public, the planet, the profession, or yourself? How does this affect the fundamental ideological, philosophical, and pragmatic premises of the design? Is there an ethical dimension to these questions?

- What are your obligations to your practice? To your associates? To your staff?

- Your project design can and most probably will be read and interpreted many different ways by those viewing it and experiencing it during its lifetime. What impact should this have now on the design?

- At what point does the design process become subject to office economic constraints?

This case begins to deal with the whole range of issues surrounding the design process. These start with the decision as to the type of project one is willing to work on, the project client that one is willing to work for, the philosophical intentions one brings to work, the question of how primary the design effort is in the whole scheme of the contractual obligations, the question of how to evaluate the relative primacy of who really is the client, the question of how design relates to the expected life of a building with no assurances as to its use during this time frame, the question of the ego satisfaction of the participants in the design process, and the question of the relation of sound business practice to the production of quality. The difficulty comes from not only the need to establish your position on the issues but also the need to decide their relative priority, because this will have a definite impact on the quality of design. Dealing with these issues requires reliance on one's ethical foundation. This case is an illustration of the value of considering the Five Framing Lenses discussed in Part I: Awareness.

CASE STUDY 21:
The Client's Project Manager

Architects ABC enter an invitation-only design competition for the design of a major public-agency office building and research laboratory. The specific goals of the competition as set by the agency board are to secure a bold architectural design that can be viewed as a demonstration project reflective of the agency's policy goals for energy conservation, building strategies, and user-responsible, healthy work environments. A building program and budget have been provided to the design-competition participants.

Architects ABC win the competition, sign a contract with the agency, and are directed to complete their design and then develop construction documents for a public bid process. The agency states publicly that it is proceeding with a project that carries out the winning design, meets the agency's publicly stated goal of setting an example of "responsible design" for the private sector, and meets the agency budget (established before the competition).

The public-agency board delegates full project-delivery responsibility to an in-house project manager, who is to work with a previously retained construction-management Firm that had managed the project through the programming, site-selection, and competition phases.

During the design-development phase, some conflicts arise between the architects, the special consultants retained by the architects as part of the competition team for their environmental design expertise, the owner's project manager, and the construction-management firm.

These conflicts revolve around design options and priorities, which include: Should building-design and mechanical-system strategies minimize indoor-air-pollution hazards, both in terms of problem initiation and problem solution over the life of the building? Should building design utilize sustainable strategies, such as the major use of plant material for shading, cooling, and comfort (physical and psychological), if there is an associated unprogrammed maintenance cost and no building code requirement? Should building design utilize system strategies to maximize system efficiency in terms of program goals viewed as unproved by the project manager (because of his experience/exposure) despite contrary evidence produced by the design team?

Architects ABC and its consultants maintain that the project design is being compromised by the unwillingness of the owner's project manager and the construction-management firm to deviate from their positions on these issues, which are based on their limited prior experience. The owner's project manager cites project costs as a major concern (initially because of bid options and long-term because of his perception of operating costs). The architects show design-development trade-offs and life-cycle cost studies to back up their recommendations and still have the project meet the agency's construction budget.

The owner's project manager threatens to recommend to the agency board that it fire Architects ABC if the firm does not carry out his directives. An impasse is at hand. The architects ponder what they should do.

Discussion

- Should the architects resign their commission? Should the architects attempt to go around the delegated Owner's project manager to lobby the agency board?
- Should the architects surreptitiously ask a third party to intervene, as an adversary, in this case, i.e., a public non-profit organization that is an agency critic in public hearings over their environmental rule-making stand on major (but nonrelated) public-policy issues. Intervention might take place through the third party's expression of interest in the progress of the building design and the cost accountability for the project in light of concerns about the agency's general policy stance. This need not require the third party to reveal its knowledge of the architects' concerns.
- Should the architects continue with the commission, acknowledging that a compromised project can still approach original goals even if it does not reach them?
- Should the architects continue with the project and make decisions without client acknowledgment on any subsequent design choices to be made during construction-document development that the architects feel would affect project integrity and might not meet the project manager's specific approval if made visible to him?
- Do the owner's representatives have an ethical obligation to pursue the architects' recommendations if they are consistent with the client's original stated intentions?

In this case, the architects are confronted with their ethical obligations in the context of their contractual ones. Which are the overriding obligations? Are the architects entitled to compromise their project's integrity in this situation? All of these questions have an ethical dimension because of the very issues that they speak to. Whatever way the architects deal with the situation, they will have had to confront their own personal ethical stance.

CASE STUDY 22:
The University Architect

Linda was recently appointed to the position of University Architect on the campus of a major state university. She serves at the discretion of the university's President but reports directly to the university's Vice President of Administrative Affairs.

Linda accepted the position of University Architect because of the opportunity to direct the development of a new campus master plan. The university's President indicated to her when he offered her the position that he wanted this plan to be the lasting legacy of his administration. He stated that he had spent the past year engaging the campus community in a strategic planning process to redefine its mission. That process was now completed and provided for him a satisfactory future vision for the university. He now wanted a new master plan to provide a framework for the enhanced growth of the university in its stated mission to be an academic leader, an asset to its local community, and a model for learning in the twenty-first century. The President also indicated that he had no preconceived notions about the plan's final form or content, although he did intend to see that it would be economically beneficial to the university. He also said that it was imperative that it be completed expeditiously and within the allocated budget. He was under some pressure from the university board of trustees to meet external fund-raising targets, and he felt that he needed a bold plan as a visual image of the future to aid him in his quest for funds. While directing Linda to work closely with the Vice President of Administrative Affairs, he indicated that he was placing his trust for a successful result directly in her hands.

Under Linda's initial leadership, the university conducted an open-selection process that resulted in the retention of a leading educational architectural firm to develop the master plan. In the course of preparing the university's Request For Proposal (RFP) for the project, it had become apparent to Linda that this was going to be a complicated project because of the nature of the recently completed strategic-planning process that was to serve as its basis. Apparently because of the difficulty of achieving a consensus on priorities, the final document that the process produced had, in her opinion, a quality of generic vagueness to it. She was concerned that it could be interpreted in a number of different ways depending on the reader's particular bias. In particular, the issue of growth was treated vaguely. In addition, the local community had not been involved in the strategic-plan generation even though it could potentially be affected by its physical-planning implications.

As a result, Linda structured the proposed contract for the selected firm to provide for an extended initial-design process that would facilitate the full exploration and reiteration of alternatives. The actual contract negotiations had been conducted under the auspices of the Vice President of Administrative Affairs, whose budget contained the funds for the master plan effort. During the negotiations, Linda realized that the major concern of the Vice President was to secure services that would not exceed the budgeted amount. She had indicated to him that it was imperative that they allow for contingency costs because of the complicated nature of the assigned task. She also had suggested that they could surely seek support from the President should this be necessary since he seemed so committed to a successful project. The Vice President replied that he would cross that bridge if they came to it, and negotiated a tight fixed-fee, time-specific contract with the architects.

As the first stage of the contract, the firm had conducted a number of open meetings with the various constituencies that the new plan would affect. During this process, it became clear to Linda and the architects that there was little consensus about what should be the primary determinant of the master plan. The university's President favored a plan that would provide the largest economic benefits to the university, which had gone from a position of being publicly funded to one of being partially publicly supported. The faculty as a whole was committed to a plan that reflected the inherent philosophy of the university: one of openness, accessibility, and enhanced intellectual capital. A vocal minority of the faculty was fully committed to a master plan that was solidly based on ecological principles on moral grounds, and that to do less for any reason was unworthy of an educational institution in this day and age. The local community was committed to anything that enhanced its economic capital, marketability, and prestige without negatively affecting its perceived quality of life. The community members were, in fact, very wary of any physical growth that would bring more people to the campus.

Linda was impressed with the openness with which the architects had conducted the constituency meetings and the thoroughness with which they had recorded their findings. She authorized the architects to move into the next phase of their contract and prepare a preliminary master plan that took into account the various priorities each of the constituencies expressed.

The architects then prepared a preliminary master plan within the contractual time frame. They had investigated a number of alternatives based on the various priorities addressed during the plan's preparation and included these studies as a part of their submission. Because the original open-meeting process had taken them longer than they had anticipated, they had not taken the time to review the alternatives with Linda before this submission. The master plan was based on the architects' interpretation of the needs and their merits of the constituencies with whom they had met. They were confident that their preliminary plan represented a bit of something for every constituency and submitted it to Linda for review and authorization in order to be able to proceed to the next stage of their contract. This phase entailed a public presentation of their work to date. They were confident that they would be successful in gaining its acceptance.

When reviewing the work, Linda came to several conclusions. First and foremost, she felt that the preliminary plan was not good enough according to her professional and personal standards, although it might in fact be acceptable to many and was competently done. She was disappointed that the plan was not a bold one. In particular, she felt that the architects' approach was weak in dealing with sustainable-design issues. On a pragmatic level, she also felt that the impacts of the campus growth as indicated might not be sustained by the design solution during the Environmental Impact Review (EIR) that the final plan would have to undergo. Finally, she was concerned that the design interpretation by the architects of the constituencies' desires was such that the preliminary plan should probably be reviewed with each group individually before presenting it to the groups as a whole. She was wary of closing off the participatory process in a way that could lead to polarization rather than consensus because of the perceived lack of this being a truly iterative design process. Linda was also aware that the preliminary master plan did not fully incorporate many suggestions the President had made to maximize future revenue sources for the university. She realized that the contract between the university and the architects did not provide for enough time or funding to deal with all of her concerns. She pondered what options she had to deal with the situation.

Discussion

- A revision at this point could subject the university to a charge for extra services under the contract.
- Any time delay or use of contingency funding at this stage could be unacceptable to the Vice President of Administrative Affairs.
- Is Linda an employee solely responsible to administer and facilitate the master-plan preparation? Is she a constituent of the process to the same degree as the mentioned constituents? What role do Linda's personal design attitudes have in this process?
- Should Linda take into account her own future with the university in determining what to do next?
- Given the nature of the criticisms of Linda, what are the architects' responsibilities at this point? Are they determined purely by the contract provisions?

This case involves the responsibility of an architect acting as a client representative. The architect in this situation faces a potential conflict between choosing an option that is safe in that it fits strictly within the contract parameters, and choosing an option that may jeopardize her job but that has a better chance of leading to a valid solution to the problem she has been charged with resolving. For Linda, taking the ethical path may result in personal loss and still not match the project to her aspirations for it. Does she have the option of delaying the resolution of her concerns until later in the project? In other words, does one have an obligation to act on a problem when one perceives it, or can one take the risk of dealing with it further down the road? This is an issue that inevitably forces one to examine one's ethical precepts.

CASE STUDY 23:
Design / Build

Architect ABC was approached by the General Contractor XYZ Company and asked if it was interested in submitting a proposal to a local school district for a 250-student activities and classroom building with a budget of $4.5 million for design and construction. The school district intended to utilize a design/ build process and was interested in seeing what quality of project it could receive from an architect/contractor team. The district had invited six contractors to submit proposals with the understanding that this would be a design competition. The "Request For Proposal" called for an architect to prepare a schematic-design package in association with the General Contractor that conformed with a predetermined performance specification furnished by the school board. Architect ABC indicated that it was very interested in participating. The firm had worked with the contractor previously on a large institutional project it had designed and for which the contractor had been the successful low bidder.

The General Contractor retained Architect ABC to provide the design services necessary to complete the proposal. Architect ABC, therefore, was working for and under the direction of the General Contractor. The schematic-design package was prepared and submitted with the proposal to the school board.

The General Contractor/ABC team was successful and was awarded the design-and-construction contract based upon the merits of the architectural design and the fact that the project as proposed was within the school board's budget.

At this point in time, the project cost negotiated by the school board with the contractor was a fixed price of $4.5 million for the design as submitted. The contractor's profit would be increased if it could find ways to deliver the project for less than the $4.5 million contract price. A potential variable in the process resulting from the nature of a schematic-design package was the degree of conformance to the performance specification of the architectural design to which the General Contractor and Architect ABC were now contractually bound.

The General Contractor then authorized Architect ABC to proceed with contract documents based on the architects' successful design submission and the performance specification that the school district had provided. The architects were now required to reflect the performance specification and the details and materials implied by the schematic-design drawings in the detailed set of drawings that provide what in their professional opinion met the requirements of the school-district contract.

The architects initially prepared the design-development drawings and specifications. After reviewing them, the contractor told the architects to reduce the quality of certain items and to simplify the design. The architects asked the contractor to provide evidence that their design as now developed would put the project over the $4.5 million contract price. After discussions with the General Contractor's estimating staff, the architects were not convinced that the changes requested were necessary and were concerned, in fact, that some of them would cause the design to be weaker than that submitted. Further, the architects were concerned that some change items would not meet the owner's performance specification, and the project would be of a lesser quality than what the architects thought in good faith their schematic design package represented. The contractor disagreed and assured them, "There will be no ensuing difficulties with the school board inasmuch as the building is essentially what was represented by the design." The General Contractor directs Architect ABC to produce the final construction documents based on the changes. The architects ponder what to do in this situation.

Discussion

- Should the architects bring the controversy to the attention of the school district?
- Should the architects retain the services of an independent estimator to evaluate his design-development drawings? If so, who should pay?
- Should the architects resign from the project team? What is the responsibility of the architects to the contractor, who brought them into this project?
- Should the architects do everything in their power to see that the proposed quality of the project is adhered to?

- Do the architects have a right to interpret quality when their schematic-design package does not clearly spell out what constitutes this in the next stage of design resolution?
- How much responsibility for quality rests with the school board for its decision to move ahead with a guaranteed contract price based on a schematic design?

This case presents a classic conflict-of-interest situation. The architects find themselves caught between the need to assess their responsibility to their contractual client (the General Contractor), their actual client (the school board), and themselves in the sense that whatever is built is a direct reflection on their talent and ability. This problem is not uncommon in design/build associations because the issues are not foreseen initially. When foreseen, they are too often dealt with outside the framework of the ethical dilemmas that could result from any party's actions. In this case, is it wrong for the contractor to seek to maximize its profit? Is it wrong for the architects to protect their vision from what they view as unwarranted compromise? Where performance specifications are issued there can be much room for interpretation. Quality is also a word that is subject to many interpretations. It is easier to look back and see how a situation like this could have been avoided than it is to solve it. Once again, the message here is about the efficacy of ethical considerations as a crucial part of architectural practice.

CASE STUDY 24:
Building Material Choices

You are the principal-in-charge of a project for the design of an automobile showroom-and-service complex. The project is located on an urban site near the city core and entails a complete remodeling of and addition to an existing building. The construction documents are at 95% completion, and you are reviewing them for your project manager before their final completion. You are particularly interested in the manner in which your staff carried out your directive to maximize the use of recycled materials for the project's construction. Both you and your client had settled on this initially as a major strategy to make the project environmentally responsible. As you review the drawings and specifications, you note that the design team has been diligent in following your directions. A wide range of materials are being utilized in the project, some of which you perceive as very innovative.

You note that a number of the materials are in exposed conditions and that others, while concealed from view, are exposed to the mechanical-system operation. You are aware from a recent continuing-education seminar that you attended on issues of indoor air pollution that some recycled materials have potential toxicity associated with their use and that their use can lead to health problems for building occupants. You note that the specifications do not require any toxicity certifications or the like.

When you raise the issue of the latter with your project manager, he states that the proposed material usages were based on projects and sources listed in materials the office had acquired from a local recycling organization. He and his staff had pursued no independent research on the materials or their use. You express some concern about two particular material usages based on some anecdotal information that you had heard about at the continuing-education seminar. Your project manager indicates that changing these materials will involve a project-completion delay because of the many places they are used; he also mentions the resultant impact this would have on redesign and document revision. Doing valid independent research on the impact of these materials would also cause a delay because this would call for acquiring the services of an independent consultant.

You know that you are already over your internal project budget for production of the design. You also know that the imminent deadline for the delivery of the completed bid documents to the client is very important to your client because of his interim financing schedule. You are also aware that an unhealthy work environment can expose you to serious liability if conditions jeopardizing the health of building occupants can be demonstrated.

You ponder whether to dismiss these concerns because you have no hard evidence that any real problems will result.

Discussion

- The facility and its occupants are already surrounded daily with the toxicity associated with automobile emissions because of the facility use and its urban location.
- You are aware that there is no certainty that this facility will remain in this building over its lifetime. Automobile agen-

cies in other parts of the city have been shuttered within ten years of their opening, such being the vicissitudes of the automobile industry.

- You doubt that your client will be sympathetic now at this late stage of the design process to any additional fees required to investigate your concerns. Additionally, you are concerned about making the issue visible to your client now since this could bring into question some of your performance and threaten your credibility with your client.
- Your project design, to your knowledge, has met all applicable building codes.
- The anecdotal information has been communicated to you by a reliable source.
- You have wanted this project design, both aesthetically and environmentally, to bring your firm positive public and professional exposure and recognition.

This case involves the issue of risk management in the context of the architect's responsibility to protect the public health, safety, and welfare. It is another instance in which one's legal responsibilities may not coincide with one's ethical obligations. At what point does one overtake the other?

CASE STUDY 25:
The Building Code Official

John is a licensed architect who the mayor appointed a year ago as the chief of the Bureau of Building Inspection in a small city. The bureau is responsible for the issuance of building permits, required field inspections, and permits for occupancy for all construction in the city. The bureau utilizes the Uniform Building Code (UBC) that the city has adopted, as well as the Federal ADA Standards for its review process. Over the years the bureau has also developed interpretations of these codes and standards when it has appeared necessary and when discretion is clearly advisable, and has made these available to the building industry.

When the mayor selected John for the position, he indicated to him that he had a lot of respect for John's high reputation within his profession and for his perceived integrity. He stated that while he was sorry that the previous chief had retired, he was confident that John could "fill his shoes."

During John's first weeks on the job, he conducted his own review of the bureau's performance. He became concerned by what he saw as an inordinate number of code variations granted by his staff when executing their responsibilities. He had been a member of the national UBC-writing team and felt that the code was very valid as written. He was also aware that it, like any other code, was conceived as a minimum acceptable public standard.

Recently, John has come under fire from a number of architects and developers for being too rigid in his code enforcement. As one critic stated, " John goes by the book, regardless of the situation. He is inflexible even when the public welfare and safety are fully protected. In fact, there are times when suggested alternatives to specific code requirements would increase the level of protection but we can't get them approved." Another critic indicated that John has instructed his plan checkers to not use any of the bureau's past code interpretations without his specific approval. This, the critic maintained, has led to innumerable delays in gaining required approvals from the bureau. A number of architects have complained that decisions that they thought had been made during a preliminary plan check with department staff were ignored or refuted during the final plan-checking process. All stated that John had been confrontational when they had met over the issues.

A major developer has gone to the mayor and threatened to withdraw from a number of his proposed construction activities in the city unless the bureau's leadership is either changed or its policies are amended to reflect past practices under its previous director. The controversy has been made public by the local newspaper, which has not only reported on it but raised the issue of community economic well-being versus acceptable life safety.

The mayor calls John to his office for a meeting about the situation. The mayor indicates that he is not sympathetic with a management style that provokes confrontation. He indicates that the city cannot afford to lose the development community's interest in the city. He is concerned that the developers have threatened to move their projects elsewhere. The mayor states that the art of politics is the art of compromise and directs John to find a way of solving the problems he has heard about to everyone's satisfaction. He indicates that to his mind this means "listening to and being sympathetic to the complaining applicants, who are, after all, professionals in their own right." In the absence of this approach, the mayor says that he will replace John with someone who will make this problem go away. However, he makes it clear that he understands that public health and safety are at stake here, and he certainly does not want to put the public at risk. He says, "There are more exceptions than rules to both English and French, yet both have successfully worked for generations. Surely there is more than one way to deal with some of these code issues other than the way some national body has tried to come up with a generic answer." The mayor gives John two weeks to work on the problems and tells him to return at the end of that time and present a report on his proposed resolution.

John ponders his options. He can go along with the mayor's wishes and ease up on his interpretation of the UBC. He can form an impartial committee of professionals to assess the validity of the applicants' complaints. He can return to the past standards of operation of the bureau with the knowledge that he is unaware of any problems that have resulted from them to date. He can tender his resignation to the mayor. He can go to the media and try on his terms to open the whole issue to further scrutiny.

Discussion

- Should any one individual undertake to determine unilaterally the acceptable level of public risk?
- What is the responsibility of an appointed public official when confronted with disagreeable instructions from his supervisor when that person is an elected public official?
- Who actually bears liability for any public-health or -safety problems for projects whose plans have received the city's building-permit approval?
- Does the bureau chief have the option of making decisions in the context of broad public policy and impact if it conflicts with national safety standards?
- Can the bureau chief walk away from a situation such as this? If so, on what terms?
- Is there a conflict of interest on the part of the developers or architects who are complaining on the basis that their professional expertise is being given short shrift?
- Is there any conflict of interest on the bureau chief's part between his previous role as a member of the UBC-writing team and now as a UBC-enforcer?

This case illustrates the difficulties architects in a public office can face when dealing with private-sector professionals or industry colleagues. It can cover even more difficult ground when regulatory responsibilities are part of their job. Do public officials serve a different and/or broader constituency than those who come before them? If so, does this necessarily give their views priority when they deal outside specific legal guidelines? Are the ethical considerations different based on what side of the counter one is on?

CASE STUDY 26:
The Public Bid Opening

A local school board commissioned the ABC Architectural firm to design an addition to an elementary school in Small Town, America. The board's budget for the project was $1.2 million. The architects included one additive alternate and seven deductive alternates in the bid package to give the client the flexibility to adjust the scope of work if necessary once the bids were received.

The bid opening was conducted at the architects' office. This was a public opening, and each of the five contractors was represented as the numbers were read aloud. Listed below are the companies and their bids, including alternates.

BIDDER	BASE BID	ADD. ALT. 1	DED. ALT. 2	DED. ALT. 3	DED. ALT. 4	DED. ALT. 5	DED. ALT. 6	DED. ALT. 7	DED. ALT. 8
A	1,157,702	60,000	10,500	9,000	4,000	10,000	5,000	3,000	3,000
B	1,161,018	62,587	18,000	8,002	3,576	5,592	10,821	2,748	2,460
C	1,146,018	59,550	17,633	4,625	4,236	16,036	4,498	3,000	1,500
D	1,230,621	——	——	——	——	——	——	——	——
E	1,090,000	61,000	12,000	9,000	1,000	14,000	8,000	2,000	1,000

The apparent low bidder, Company E, with a base bid of $1,090,000, was identified once the bids were opened. The bid award was based on the base bid. Even with the additive alternate of $61,000, the low bidder still remained low, and everything appeared to be in order.

The next day Company E called the architects to inform them that its electrical subcontractor had made a serious error in his sub-bid to Company E. According to the general contractor, the subcontractor had omitted the cost for the light fixtures. This cost amounted to approximately $20,000. The general contractor said he would probably have to withdraw his bid if the $20,000 could not be added. The contractor pointed out that even with this addition to the contract, Company E would still be the low bidder. The contractor asked the architects to approve his amended bid or to approve an additive change order for the $20,000 during the course of the contract.

The architects have worked with the general contractor before and views him as being honorable and honest. They have never worked with the second low bidder. The architects ponder what to do.

Discussion

- Should Company E be allowed to adjust its bid upward $20,000 to account for its electrical subcontractor's error?
- Should the architects inform Company E that its bid was valid and cannot be changed or withdrawn at this point?
- Should the architects declare Company E's bid invalid and obligate the owner to accept the second low bidder, Company C, thereby obligating the owner to pay an additional $47,702 to $67,702 more?
- Is it enough to determine the legal responsibilities here, or do ethical considerations complicate the decision-making?
- Does the fact that it is a public project complicate the decision?
- Is there any potential for conflict of interest here?
- Is there any potential for litigation by any of the parties?

In this case, the architects are wearing the hat of the public servant and as such are confronted with trying to determine what is in the public interest. The rule of law and its juncture with the ethical frame can pose a dilemma, yet the ethical frame is clearly a part of the consideration regarding resolution.

CASE STUDY 27:
The Private-Bid Opening

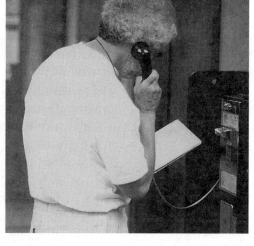

An architectural firm has completed the construction and bid documents for a large commercial project, and the project is being bid on by a selected list of general contractors. The private-bid opening is to be held at 2 P.M. in the architectural firm's office on a previously designated day. Six general-contracting firms have been invited to submit proposals. All six have arrived with their proposals at the firm's office before the 2 P.M. deadline. Some of the contractors' representatives have brought portable phones so they can stay in contact with their offices and make last-minute adjustments to their company's proposals. The architects have also made one of the telephones in a nearby room available.

At 1:55 P.M., the contractors assemble in the architectural firm's conference room. Shortly thereafter, one of the architects announces that it is 2 P.M., asking if anyone disputes the time. No objections are heard, and the bid opening proceeds. As the first bid is being opened, the representative of Contractor C is summoned to the nearby room for a telephone call. This person immediately leaves the room and returns to the conference room a few moments later with no comment.

After all of the bids have been opened and read aloud, it is apparent that Contractor A is the low bidder, Contractor B is second, and Contractor C is third in close bidding. The architect announces that the bids will be presented to the owner and that all of the parties will be advised of the owner's decision. No objections are raised by any of the parties present, and the bid opening terminates at 2:15 P.M.

At approximately 2:20 P.M., the architect receives a telephone call from the senior vice president of General Contractor C. The contractor accuses the architect of having opened the bids before 2 P.M., and indicates that he received a lower framing bid just before the 2 P.M. cutoff. He contacted his representative, who was present at the architects' office, so that he could lower his bid. His representative indicated to him that the bids were already being opened. The contractor also indicates that had he been able to make this adjustment, his firm would have been the lowest bidder. The contractor asks that this matter be brought to the owner's attention for resolution. He believes that he should be declared the lowest bidder or that the project should be rebid.

All the contractors are known to the architect to be reputable and responsible. The architect, in fact, invited them to bid with the owner's approval.

The architect ponders what to do about this request.

Discussion

- Is it the architect's responsibility to secure the lowest possible bid for the owner?
- Is it the architect's responsibility to see that all of the bidders are treated fairly? Equally? Is there a difference?
- Should the architect advise the owner that Contractor C has presented a revised bid that, in fact, makes him the lowest bidder and that this revised bid should be considered?
- Is there a different standard operative here because this is a private-bid opening, rather than a public one?

This case requires the architect to judge his performance as well as that of those who seek his positive consideration. This must be done in the context of the architect's responsibility to his client, both legally and ethically.

CASE STUDY 28:
Construction Observation

A young architect is approached by an acquaintance, a contractor/developer, to design an innovative, terraced, earth-sheltered, passive-solar, nine-unit residential condominium on a tight, sloping urban site. The site is near the homes of both the architect and the developer. Because the developer will also be the contractor, the architect is asked to provide professional services only through the completion of construction documents. The architect agrees to this arrangement.

The limited site information provided by the contractor/developer indicates that a city storm/sanitary sewer is buried along one edge of the property. However, the exact location is not given. The architect includes this limited information on the site plan.

The architect completes a full set of construction documents, which the contractor/developer submits to the city. Based on these documents, which are approved for construction, the contractor/developer receives a building permit for the project.

During initial construction, the architect occasionally visits the site voluntarily and informally after hours. He notices some changes in the footing construction from the work described in his construction documents, but he does not contact the contractor/developer about them. He also notices a few changes in the framed-wall openings from what he had indicated but concludes that the design integrity is not seriously threatened. One evening not long afterward, the contractor/developer calls to talk about the project. He says that he is excited about the way the project is beginning to become a reality now that the building framing is underway.

The contractor/developer indicates that he did have one "small" problem during the initial excavation phase, when he discovered that the sewer actually runs diagonally across the site and would cross under the new building's foundation just beneath the footings. He states that he strengthened and revised the footings as designed where they cross the sewer rather than be involved in re-siting the building. He says that he also found an old manhole that he has bricked up and covered. The excavations were backfilled quickly so that the city building inspector wouldn't see the sewer's true location and stop the work "unnecessarily" inasmuch as the contractor/developer felt he had acted in a safe manner. As a result, the building construction was right on schedule, and he congratulates the architect on the clarity of his construction documents. The contractor/developer concludes by indicating that he just wanted to keep the architect posted as to how things were proceeding and will continue to do so during the rest of the construction phase.

A few days later, an individual informs the architect that he is seriously considering accepting an offer from the contractor/developer to become a partner in the development. He indicates he is very excited about the design and has a lot of respect for the architect's abilities. He further states that he believes that the architect should be involved in providing subsequent construction observation and intends to insist on it as a term of the new partnership. He says that he is a firm believer in the desirability of architects being retained for full services through the completion of projects that they have designed.

The architect ponders how to deal with this news.

Discussion

- What, if anything, should the architect tell this potential investor about the construction history, as he now knows it, of the project? He knows that it is against city policy to allow construction over any of the storm/sanitary sewers.
- What are the obligations of the architect to his original client in this situation?
- What obligation, if any, does the architect have to report to the city building inspector the site-construction changes that he now knows have taken place, deviating from the documents that were the basis of the city's issued building permit?
- Should the architect agree to provide the construction observation services if requested?

This case is one in which the architect is thrust into an unanticipated situation that requires him to make a decision outside the expected framework of practice- and formalized-contract provisions. The decision does, however, directly affect his practice responsibilities and options. This kind of unforeseen situation can occur in many different ways during the stages of practice. Inevitably, there is an ethical dimension to the issues raised.

CASE STUDY 29:
Post-Occupancy Evaluation

Architect XYZ received a commission for the design of a large office building from a state agency that has an ongoing office-construction program. The building program called for an innovative project design that would illustrate the feasibility of designing for reduced-energy usage from that mandated by the state's Energy Code within this typical building's energy budget. The building program also called for the project to be a demonstration of a user-responsive, healthy, productive workspace, particularly for clerical workers, who were the majority of the occupants.

Architect XYZ completed the project on time, within budget, met the users' needs, and received public acclaim. The agency issued publicity materials that proclaimed that this project demonstrated the direction that responsible office-building design should and could take. It was an affirmation of the agency's philosophy and its regulatory mandates.

One year after completion of the building, a partner in Architect XYZ revisits the building to attend a public workshop on some public-policy issues with which the agency is currently dealing.

While attending the all-day session, the partner tours the building and observes several conditions that lead her to suspect that the building is not being operated as intended.

The partner makes several informal inquiries and determines that the building's energy usage is no longer being monitored and that the building systems operations are apparently being determined by the lowest current cost options rather than total energy consumption.

The partner also notes that some operational/design strategies that affect human comfort have been subverted without full user awareness that they exist (i.e., opening windows were locked, daylight sensors were disconnected, task lighting was scattered, and the programmed pattern of open office spaces was subverted).

The partner mentions this to some agency staff members that she encounters during her walk-through, with whom she had worked with during the project's development. They indicate that some of these "changes" were the result of upper-management decisions reflective of overall agency budget cuts and, in some instances, were the response to some users who did not adjust immediately to the new environment.

The partner is aware that the agency has continued to tout the building as a demonstration of its philosophy and accomplishments. Architect XYZ has utilized this project as a prime demonstration of its abilities as it seeks new work. The public-agency client has served as a strong and positive reference for Architect XYZ in these pursuits.

The partner ponders whether she should take any action based on her observations.

Discussion

- Should Architect XYZ "blow the whistle" on the agency with the intent that the building be restored to its designed conditions? If so, how, and in what forum?
- Should Architect XYZ "blow the whistle" on the agency with the intent to stymie future funding for agency projects if it does not demand safeguards requiring compliance to project programs? If so, how, and in what forum?
- Should Architect XYZ "let well enough alone"?
- Should Architect XYZ offer services to the agency to facilitate remedial steps? For a professional fee? For free?
- What are Architect XYZ's ongoing responsibilities to the agency, the building occupants, the public, and the architectural profession?

This case illustrates conditions that can arise from the reality that once architects finish their contract responsibilities for a project, they are not necessarily finished with the project. Architects should be prepared and knowledgeable with respect to this reality. This awareness should be framed in terms of their ethical responsibility, as well as their legal liability for the public-health, -safety, and -welfare aspects of their project over time. Architects clearly have a stake in the way that their buildings fulfill their original intent, particularly with regard to their fullest aspirations for them.

CASE STUDY 30:
Right of Confidentiality and the Public Interest

Architect Jones, whose practice is primarily in forensic architecture, has been retained as a potential expert witness in a lawsuit involving the construction of a major high-rise public building in a city away from his locale. The issue to be resolved deals with the design of the building's window-washing equipment and the liability for some required construction phase change-orders. The change orders in question deal with both changes in the specified equipment and the impact of these changes on the building-construction schedule. More than $1 million is in dispute.

The architectural firm that designed the building is one of the parties named in the lawsuit, which also involves the building contractor, the window-washing-equipment subcontractor, and the public-agency client. The architectural firm has authorized its attorney to retain Architect Jones for expert-witness services on its behalf. The letter of confirmation from the attorney acknowledging Architect Jones's retention states that, although he will be working under the direction of the attorney, he will look solely to the architectural firm for payment of all invoices for his services.

To initiate his services, Architect Jones is directed to review the original contract drawings for the building and a portfolio containing the contested-change orders and correspondence relating to the design of the window-washing equipment. Upon his completion of an initial review of this material, Architect Jones is directed to make a site visit to the building to become better acquainted with the issues involved. He is told that he is free to look at anything he wishes and will be aided in this examination by the building operations staff.

While at the building, Architect Jones takes the time to make a thorough tour of the facility, as well as to look at the installed window-washing equipment. He has seen the building in published form and has admired the design. While not personally acquainted with the architectural firm that designed the building, he has been an admirer of its work over the years. His tour confirms his earlier impressions from the published photographs that the building is a superior piece of design that seems to work well for its tenants and its community. At one point in the tour, he does note some exiting conditions that he finds a bit odd, but he assumes that they nevertheless meet the applicable building codes.

Several days later, Architect Jones is in the attorney's office to discuss his visit and his review of the documents he has been furnished, and to request some additional information that he assumes exists and can be made available to him. While he is in the office, one of the partners comes in and tells Architect Jones that he is conducting a deposition of one of the other litigants' expert witnesses and invites him to sit in as a silent observer. After sitting in on the deposition, Architect Jones decides he needs to revisit the site to reexamine the window-washing equipment in operation.

During his return visit to the building, Architect Jones again encounters the exiting condition he previously noted. This time, he walks through the entire exiting system of which it is a part.

Upon his return from the site visit, Architect Jones communicates two findings to the attorney. First, he indicates that he believes that he can provide a reasonable defense for the architectural firm's actions regarding the issues involving the window-washing equipment. However, he also indicates that he has encountered an exiting condition in the building that he feels should be corrected. He states that although it may be a legal design, he has serious reservations about its ability to protect the public in a time of emergency exiting. Before he can continue with the conversation, the attorney tells Architect Jones that he must not raise the issue until the litigation is over because it may color the architectural firm's case. The attorney indicates that he does not want it to come up in the scheduled deposition of Architect Jones by the attorney for the opposing litigants, which he foresees as being very aggressive. The attorney cites his "client's right of confidentiality," which he states is the overriding consideration in this situation and which is legally defensible.

As a specialist in Forensic Architecture, Architect Jones is well aware of the cited "right" and recognizes it as a condition of his contract with the architectural firm. He also is well aware that any peripheral communication about the exiting issue may well become visible to the other litigants. However, he has always had a personal concern for the viability of building exiting systems because of a family tragedy resulting from the failure of such a system.

Architect Jones ponders what he should do. He is convinced from looking at the contract documents that the exiting condition he questions was on the plans the local building department had approved for construction. He is also of the opinion from the gist of conversations with the attorney that there is a long-standing respectful relationship between the attorney and the architectural firm.

Discussion

- Is there a conflict between the "client's right of confidentiality" and any architect's obligation to protect the public health, safety, and welfare?
- Do architects have a professional obligation to respect the terms of any contractual agreement they enter into?
- Should Architect Jones "let well enough alone" inasmuch as the situation involves his personal opinion only?

This case raises a series of issues. Does an architect have a responsibility to make public any concerns over the public-health and -safety issues of an encountered building? Does this responsibility vary based on whether the building was: the design of the architect, the design of others, encountered during a contractually related visit, encountered on a professional-interest basis, or encountered when the architect was a member of the general public? All of these conditions are a form of post-occupancy evaluation. As for the practice of forensic architecture at any scale, are there any implicit ethical responsibilities that all parties involved should recognize?

EPILOGUE

We began our path through *Ethics and the Practice of Architecture* with the consideration of Socrates's challenge to live ethical lives and Winston Churchill's insight into the essence of architecture as constructed culture. We proposed that thinking of our topic as "architecture *and* ethics" is a flawed conception because our position is that ethics is not added to architecture: architecture is inherently ethical. **We contend that architectural/ethics is a unity based upon the interlocking joint where human aspirations to reshape the landscape for enriched living, the expertise of the architect, the practices of architecture, the events and processes of designing and building our habitat, and the built works intersect.** We explored that concept of the architecture/ethics nexus as we progressed through the book.

Through our exploration, we believe that we have provided insight into, and brought to light, aspects of the ethical nature of architecture: of architects and the profession, of architectural processes, and of buildings themselves. In so doing, our conviction that **architects have a clear responsibility to be ethical** in their practices has been strengthened. We have provided here for you the requisite content and methods in Part I: Awareness, Part II: Understanding, and Part III: Choices to enable you, as an architect, to accept this responsibility.

A colleague, the writer, critic, and community designer Jim Burns, wrote in his notebooks about the design process: "... **the why of the creation drives the *how*... values determine how how responds to *why*.**"

Consideration of **values**—societal, professional, and personal —have always had a critical impact on the accomplishment of the contributions we as architects have made to the world of the past, the present, and the future.

We dedicate this book to the recognition that we have a continuing **ethical responsibility** to future generations to leave a legacy of works and actions that are no less than they **could** or **should** be!

APPENDIX I

NCARB RULES OF CONDUCT: 1998

Rules of Conduct
National Council of Architectural Registration Boards
1735 New York Avenue, NW Suite 700
Washington, DC 20006
(202) 783-6500
www.ncarb.org

This document was revised in July, 1999, and supersedes all previous editions.

INTRODUCTION   259
RULE 1   COMPETENCE   263
RULE 2   CONFLICT OF INTEREST   264
RULE 3   FULL DISCLOSURE   264
RULE 4   COMPLIANCE WITH LAWS   266
RULE 5   PROFESSIONAL CONDUCT   267

INTRODUCTION

These rules of conduct are published by the NCARB as a recommended set of rules for member boards having the authority to promulgate and enforce rules of conduct applicable to their registrants.

Immediately following the 1975 annual meeting, the Board of Directors charged the NCARB Committee on Professional Conduct with drafting a set of rules of conduct for use by member boards. The Committee worked on these rules over an eighteen-month period. Initially, the Committee searched the existing rules of several of its member boards. From this search a preliminary set of rules of conduct covering a multitude of matters was prepared. The preliminary rules were finally revised to a draft set of rules in February, 1976. That draft was submitted to representatives of various governmental agencies and professional organizations in March of 1976. On the basis of informal comment received at that time, the rules were again revised. In November of 1976, another series of hearings with governmental officials was held and further revisions took place.

Thereafter, these rules were distributed broadly with requests for comment, and in February of 1977 the Committee on Professional Conduct, taking into account the comments received, revised and redrafted the rules into their present form. The rules were approved by the member boards at the 1977 annual meeting. At the 1982 NCARB Annual Meeting one amendment to these rules of conduct was approved adding a new Section 5.1 and renumbering subsequent items accordingly.

Certain of the Committee's assumptions are clarified as follows:

- It is the Committee's belief that a set of rules of conduct which will be the basis for policing and disciplining members of the profession should be "hard-edged" rules and should not include those precatory injunctions which are often found in a list of professional obligations. For example, the Committee believes that it is an obligation of all registered architects to assist interns in their development. But the Committee could not conceive of making the failure to perform that obligation the basis for revocation of registration, suspension of registration, or reprimand. Thus, the rules set forth below have all been subjected to the critical test of whether or not an architect violating any one of the rules should be subject to discipline. It is the Committee's judgment that the rules proposed are all rules for which it is appropriate to command compliance and threaten sanctions.

- The Committee views these rules as having as their objective the protection of the public and not the advancement of the interests of the profession of architecture. The Committee believes, however, the profession is advanced by requiring registration holders to act in the public interest. There are, however, various rules of conduct found in many existing state board rules which seem more directed at protecting the profession than advancing the public interest. Such a rule is the prohibition against allowing one architect to supplant another until he or she has adequate proof that the first architect has been properly discharged. Without doubt, such a rule makes the practice more civilized, more orderly, and under some circumstances, exposes a client to less risk. On the other hand, it was frequently pointed out to the Committee that clients may often wish to verify the competence of a retained architect by engaging a second architect, and it hardly seems appropriate for governmental regulation to prevent that from occurring. Similarly, prohibitions against brokers selling architects' services, fee competition, advertising, free sketches, and the like, seem more appropriately included in professional ethical standards than in rules to be enforced by state agencies.

In protecting the public, there are two general areas of concern. First, non-architects dealing with an architect (beginning with the client and including all other members of the construction industry) should be protected against misrepresentation, fraud, and deceit. It has long been recognized as a proper function of government to protect the consumer of services from such wrongful behavior. Second, the users of a project on which the architect has worked must be protected from a building which is unsafe. This kind of protection by a governmental agency has an even longer history.

- The Committee sought to avoid burdening the architect with standards of conduct which were unreasonable to expect. At the same time, the Committee took into account the fact that the public views the architect or in the case of an engineering project, the engineer, as the only registered professional involved in a leadership position in the construction process, and relies on the registered professional to help safeguard the public interest. Rule 3.3, derived from a similar rule found in the Alaska State Board's rules of conduct, recognizes the special responsibility of the registered architect. In this regard, the architect is not unlike the lawyer who, while enjoined to defend vigorously the position of his client, must under certain circumstances abandon his partisan effort on behalf of his client by virtue of his duty as an officer of the court to advance the cause of justice. Similarly, accountants have in recent years been compelled to insist on positions which are not in their client's interest but which are necessary in order to provide the public with full disclosure. So the architect has a fiduciary duty to his client, while at the same time has a supervening duty to the public.

- As has been stated above, these rules are intended to set out those areas of behavior for which an architect risks being disciplined by his state board. The enforcement of these rules is the subject of a paper entitled "Procedural Requirements for Discipline of Architects by State Architectural Registration Boards," prepared and distributed by the Professional Conduct Committee. Enforcement, of course, raises quite special problems. State registration boards are notoriously understaffed and underfunded. Nonetheless, the Committee believes the experience of some of our member boards in using available resources to assist in enforcement will provide guidance to other state boards who have despaired of being able to enforce rules of conduct in the past. The paper on enforcement suggests strategies by which the state boards can police the profession and can effectively enforce these rules. The Committee, however, does not believe that an infraction of each of these rules will yield the same punishment. Obviously, any disciplinary body takes into account a multitude of mitigating circumstances. In addition, a first infraction of some of the rules would, in all likelihood, not result in disciplinary action. For example, very few responsible and honorable architects avoid negligence completely in their careers. On the other hand, the board must have the right to discipline and, if necessary, revoke the registration of an architect with a demonstrated record of incompetence.

- The Committee struggled with the question of the necessary proximity between the act proscribed and the public interest involved. As an example, we can pick out three points on a line all leading to unsafe structures which the public clearly has an interest in preventing. The first point, for purposes of this illustration, is architects bidding against each other on the basis of fee. There is evidence that buildings constructed from the work of architects who have won the job on the basis of a low fee have more problems than buildings generally. As a second point on the line, buildings designed by architects who suffer from substantial physical or mental disabilities contain a much higher risk of defects than buildings generally. As a final point on the line, there is the architect who has been chronically negligent in his past projects and is likely to perform with similar negligence in the future. The Committee was compelled to ask itself whether the odds were sufficiently high in connection with the competitive bidding issue to warrant a registration board attempting to protect the public at that point on the line. A similar question was raised concerning the architect whose competence is physically or mentally impaired. In a sense, disciplining the architect after the defective building had been discovered was the least effective way of protecting the public. This kind of inquiry resulted in the Committee's deleting any reference to competitive bidding in its rules but retaining a rule concerning physical or mental disabilities on the grounds that the protection of the public required that the board have power to step in when it has evidence that such a condition exists and that it is likely to impair the competence of the architect. Similar inquiries were made in connection with many of the other rules set forth in this document.

GUIDELINES

RULE 1 COMPETENCE

1.1 In practicing architecture, an architect shall act with reasonable care and competence, and shall apply the technical knowledge and skill which is ordinarily applied by architects of good standing, practicing in the same locality.

Commentary

Although many of the existing state board rules of conduct fail to mention standards of competence, it is clear that the public expects that incompetence will be disciplined and, where appropriate, will result in revocation of the license. 1.1 sets forth the common law standard which has existed in this country for a hundred years or more in judging the performance of architects. While some few courts have stated that an architect, like the manufacturer of goods, implies warrants that his design is fit for its intended use, this rule specifically rejects the minority standard in favor of the standard applied in the vast majority of jurisdictions that the architect need be careful but need not always be right. In an age of national television, national universities, a national registration exam, and the like, the reference to the skill and knowledge applied in the same locality may be less significant than it was in the past when there was a wide disparity across the face of the United States in the degree of skill and knowledge which an architect was expected to bring to his or her work. Nonetheless, the courts have still recognized this portion of the standard, and it is true that what may be expected of an architect in a complex urban setting may vary from what is expected in a more simple, rural situation.

1.2 In designing a project, an architect shall take into account all applicable state and municipal building laws and regulations. While an architect may rely on the advice of other professionals (e.g., attorneys, engineers, and other qualified persons) as to the intent and meaning of such regulations, once having obtained such advice, an architect shall not knowingly design a project in violation of such laws and regulations.

Commentary

It should be noted that the rule is limited to applicable state and municipal building laws and regulations. Every major project being built in the United States is subject to a multitude of laws in addition to the applicable building laws and regulations. As to these other laws, it may be negligent of the architect to have failed to take them into account, but the rule does not make the architect specifically responsible for such other laws. Even the building laws and regulations are of sufficient complexity that the architect may be required to seek the interpretation of other professionals. The rule permits the architect to rely on the advice of such other professionals.

1.3 An architect shall undertake to perform professional services only when he or she, together with those whom the architect may engage as consultants, are qualified by education, training, and experience in the specific technical areas involved.

Commentary

While an architect is licensed to undertake any project which falls within the definition of the practice of architecture, as a professional, the architect must understand and be limited by the limitations of his or her own capacity and knowledge. Where an architect lacks experience, the rule supposes that he or she will retain consultants who can appropriately supplement his or her own capacity. If an architect undertakes to do a project where he or she lacks knowledge and where he or she does not seek such supplementing consultants, the architect has violated the rule.

1.4 No person shall be permitted to practice architecture if, in the board's judgment, such person's professional competence is substantially impaired by physical or mental disabilities.

Commentary

Here the state registration board is given the opportunity to revoke or suspend a license when the board has suitable evidence that the license holder's professional competence is impaired by physical or mental disabilities. Thus, the board need not wait until a building fails in order to revoke the license of an architect whose addiction to alcohol, for example, makes it impossible for that person to perform professional services with necessary care.

RULE 2 CONFLICT OF INTEREST

2.1 An architect shall not accept compensation for services from more than one party on a project unless the circumstances are fully disclosed to and agreed to (such disclosure and agreement to be in writing) by all interested parties.

Commentary

This rule recognizes that in some circumstances an architect may receive compensation from more than one party involved in a project but that such bifurcated loyalty is unacceptable unless all parties have understood it and accepted it.

2.2 If an architect has any business association or direct or indirect financial interest which is substantial enough to influence his or her judgment in connection with the performance of professional services, the architect shall fully disclose in writing to his or her client or employer the nature of the business association or financial interest, and if the client or employer objects to such association or financial interest, the architect will either terminate such association or interest or offer to give up the commission or employment.

Commentary

Like 2.1, this rule is directed at conflicts of interest. It requires disclosure by the architect of any interest which would affect the architect's performance.

2.3 An architect shall not solicit or accept compensation from material or equipment suppliers in return for specifying or endorsing their products.

Commentary

This rule appears in most of the existing state standards. It is absolute and does not provide for waiver by agreement.

2.4 When acting as the interpreter of building contract documents and the judge of contract performance, an architect shall render decisions impartially, favoring neither party to the contract.

Commentary

This rule applies only when the architect is acting as the interpreter of building contract documents and the judge of contract performance. The rule recognizes that that is not an inevitable role and that there may be circumstances (for example, where the architect has an interest in the owning entity) in which the architect may appropriately decline to act in those two roles. In general, however, the rule governs the customary construction industry relationship where the architect, though paid by the owner and owing the owner his or her loyalty, is nonetheless required, in fulfilling his or her role in the typical construction industry documents, to act with impartiality.

RULE 3 FULL DISCLOSURE

3.1 An architect, making public statements on architectural questions, shall disclose when he or she is being compensated for making such statement or when he or she has an economic interest in the issue.

Commentary

Architects frequently and appropriately make statements on questions affecting the environment in the architect's community. As citizens and as members of a profession acutely concerned with environmental change, they doubtless have an obligation to be heard on such questions. Many architects may, however, be representing the interests of potential developers when making statements on such issues. It is consistent with the probity which the public expects from members of the architectural profession that they not be allowed under the circumstances described in the rule to disguise the fact that they are not speaking on the particular issue as an independent professional but as a professional engaged to act on behalf of a client.

3.2 An architect shall accurately represent to a prospective or existing client or employer his or her qualifications, capabilities, experience and the scope of his or her responsibility in connection with work for which he or she is claiming credit.

Commentary

Many important projects require a team of architects to do the work. Regrettably, there has been some conflict in recent years when individual members of that team have claimed greater credit for the project than was appropriate to their work done. It should be noted that a young architect who develops his or her experience working under a more senior architect has every right to claim credit for the work which he or she did. On the other hand, the public must be protected from believing that the younger architect's role was greater than was the fact.

3.3 If, in the course of his or her work on a project, an architect becomes aware of a decision taken by his or her employer or client, against the architect's advice, which violates applicable state or municipal building laws and regulations and which will, in the architect's judgment, materially affect adversely the safety to the public of the finished project, the architect shall

(i) report the decision to the local building inspector or other public official charged with the enforcement of the applicable state or municipal building laws and regulations,

(ii) refuse to consent to the decision, and

(iii) in circumstances where the architect reasonably believes that other such decisions will be taken notwithstanding his objection, terminate his services with reference to the project unless the architect is able to cause the matter to be resolved by other means.

In the case of a termination in accordance with clause (iii), the architect shall have no liability to his or her client or employer on account of such termination.

Commentary

This rule holds the architect to the same standard of independence which has been applied to lawyers and accountants. In the circumstances described, the architect is compelled to report the matter to a public official even though to do so may substantially harm the architect's client. Note that the circumstances are a violation of building laws which adversely affect the safety to the public of the finished project. While a proposed technical violation of building laws (e.g., a violation which does not affect the public safety) will cause a responsible architect to take action to oppose its implementation, the Committee specifically does not make such a proposed violation trigger the provisions of this rule. The rule specifically intends to exclude safety problems during the course of construction which are traditionally the obligation of the contractor. There is no intent here to create a liability for the architect in this area. Clause (iii) gives the architect the obligation to terminate his or her services if he or she has clearly lost professional control. The standard is that the architect reasonably believes that other such decisions will be taken notwithstanding his or her objection. The rule goes on to provide that the architect shall not be liable for a termination made pursuant to clause (iii). Such an exemption from contract liability is necessary if the architect is to be free to refuse to participate on a project in which such decisions are being made.

3.4 An architect shall not deliberately make a false statement or fail deliberately to disclose accurately and completely a material fact requested in connection with his or her application for registration or renewal or otherwise lawfully requested by the board.

Commentary

The registration board which grants registration or renews registration on the basis of a misrepresentation by the applicant must have the power to revoke that registration.

3.5 An architect shall not assist the application for registration of a person known by the architect to be unqualified in respect to education, training, experience, or character.

3.6 An architect possessing knowledge of a violation of these rules by another architect shall report such knowledge to the board.

Commentary

This rule has its analogue in the Code of Professional Responsibility for lawyers. Its thrust is consistent with the special responsibility which the public expects from architects.

RULE 4 COMPLIANCE WITH LAWS

4.1 An architect shall not, in the conduct of his or her architectural practice, knowingly violate any state or federal criminal law.

Commentary

This rule is concerned with the violation of a state or federal criminal law while in the conduct of the registrant's professional practice. Thus, it does not cover criminal conduct entirely unrelated to the registrant's architectural practice. It is intended, however, that rule 5.4 will cover reprehensible conduct on the part

of the architect not embraced by rule 4.1. At present, there are several ways in which member boards have dealt with this sort of rule. Some have disregarded the requirement that the conduct be related to professional practice and have provided for discipline whenever the architect engages in a crime involving "moral turpitude."

The Committee declined the use of that phrase as its meaning is by no means clear or uniformly understood. Some member boards discipline for felony crimes and not for misdemeanor crimes. While the distinction between the two was once the distinction between serious crimes and technical crimes, that distinction has been blurred in recent years. Accordingly, the Committee specifies crimes in the course of the architect's professional practice, and, under 5.4, gives to the member board discretion to deal with other reprehensible conduct. Note that the rule is concerned only with violations of state or federal criminal law. The Committee specifically decided against the inclusion of violations of the laws of other nations. Not only is it extremely difficult for a member board to obtain suitable evidence of the interpretation of foreign laws, it is not unusual for such laws to be at odds with the laws, or, at least, the policy of the United States of America. For example, the failure to follow the dictates of the "anti-Israel boycott" laws found in most Arab jurisdictions is a crime under the laws of most of those jurisdictions; while the anti-Israel boycott is contrary to the policy of the government of the United States and following its dictates is illegal under the laws of the United States.

4.2 An architect shall neither offer nor make any payment or gift to a government official (whether elected or appointed) with the intent of influencing the official's judgment in connection with a prospective or existing project in which the architect is interested.

Commentary

4.2 tracks a typical bribe statute. It is covered by the general language of 4.1, but it was the Committee's view that 4.2 should be explicitly set out in the rules of conduct. Note that all of the rules under this section look to the conduct of the architect and not to whether or not the architect has actually been convicted under a criminal law. An architect who bribes a public official is subject to discipline by the state registration board, whether or not the architect has been convicted under the state criminal procedure.

4.3   An architect shall comply with the registration laws and regulations governing his or her professional practice in any United States jurisdiction. An architect may be subject to disciplinary action if, based on grounds substantially similar to those which lead to disciplinary action in this jurisdiction, the architect is disciplined in any other United States jurisdiction.

Commentary

Here, again, for the reasons set out under 4.1, the Committee chose to limit this rule to United States jurisdictions.

4.4   An employer engaged in the practice of architecture shall not have been found by a court or an administrative tribunal to have violated any applicable federal or state law protecting the rights of persons working for the employer with respect to fair labor standards or with respect to maintaining a workplace free of discrimination. [States may choose instead to make specific reference to the "Federal Fair Labor Standards Act of 1938, as amended", and "Equal Employment Opportunity Act of 1972, as amended" and to state laws of similar scope.] For purposes of this rule, any registered architect employed by a firm engaged in the practice of architecture who is in charge of the firm's architectural practice, either alone or with other architects, shall be deemed to have violated this rule if the firm has violated this rule.

RULE 5 PROFESSIONAL CONDUCT

5.1   Any office offering architectural services shall have an architect resident and regularly employed in that office.

5.2   An architect shall not sign or seal drawings, specifications, reports or other professional work which was not prepared by or under the responsible control of the architect; except that (i) he or she may sign or seal those portions of the professional work that were prepared by or under the responsible control of persons who are registered under the architecture registration laws of this jurisdiction if the architect has reviewed in whole or in part such portions and has either coordinated their preparation or integrated them into his or her work, and (ii) he or she may sign or seal portions of the professional work that are not required by the architects' registration law to be prepared by or under the responsible control of an architect if the architect has reviewed and adopted in whole or in part such portions and has integrated them into his or her work. "Responsible control" shall be that amount of control over and detailed professional knowledge of the content of technical submissions during their preparation as is ordinarily exercised by architects applying the required professional standard of care. Reviewing, or reviewing and correcting, technical submissions after they have been prepared by others does not constitute the exercise of responsible control because the reviewer has neither control over nor detailed knowledge of the content of such submissions throughout their preparation. Any registered architect signing or sealing technical submissions not prepared by that architect but prepared under the architect's responsible control by persons not regularly employed in the office where the architect is resident, shall maintain and make available to the board upon request for at least five years following such signing and sealing, adequate and complete records demonstrating the nature and extent of the architect's control over and detailed knowledge of such technical submissions throughout their preparation.

Commentary

This provision reflects current practice by which the architect's final construction documents may comprise the work of other architects as well as that of the architect who signs and seals professional submissions. The architect is permitted to apply his or her seal to work over which the architect has both control and detailed professional knowledge, and also to work prepared under the direct supervision of another architect whom he or she employs when the architect has both coordinated and reviewed the work.

5.3 An architect shall neither offer nor make any gifts, other than gifts of nominal value (including, for example, reasonable entertainment and hospitality), with the intent of influencing the judgment of an existing or prospective client in connection with a project in which the architect is interested.

Commentary

This provision refers to "private bribes" (which are ordinarily not criminal in nature) and the unseemly conduct of using gifts to obtain work. Note that the rule realistically excludes reasonable entertainment and hospitality and other gifts of nominal value.

5.4 An architect shall not engage in conduct involving fraud or wanton disregard of the rights of others.

Commentary

Violations of this rule may involve criminal conduct not covered by 4.1, or other reprehensible conduct which the board believes should warrant discipline. A state board must, in any disciplinary matter, be able to point to a specific rule which has been violated. An architect who is continuously involved in nighttime burglaries (no connection to his daytime professional practice) is not covered by 4.1 (crimes committed "in the conduct of his or her architectural practice"). Serious misconduct, even though not related to professional practice, may well be grounds for discipline. Lawyers commenting on the rules had little trouble with the standard set in 5.4; it applies to conduct which would be characterized as wicked, as opposed to minor breaches of the law. While each board must "flesh out" the rule, murder, rape, arson, burglary, extortion, grand larceny, and the like, would be conduct subject to the rule, while disorderly conduct, traffic violations, tax violations, and the like, would not be considered subject to the rule.

5.5 An architect shall not make misleading, deceptive or false statements or claims.

Commentary

An architect who fails to accurately and completely disclose information, even when not related to the practice of architecture, may be subject to disciplinary actions if the board concludes that the failure was serious and material.

APPENDIX II

AIA CODE OF ETHICS AND PROFESSIONAL CONDUCT: 1997

PREAMBLE

Members of The American Institute of Architects are dedicated to the highest standards of professionalism, integrity, and competence. This Code of Ethics and Professional Conduct states guidelines for the conduct of Members in fulfilling those obligations. The **Code** is arranged in three tiers of statements: Canons, Ethical Standards, and Rules of Conduct:

- Canons are broad principles of conduct.
- Ethical Standards (E.S.) are more specific goals toward which Members should aspire in professional performance and behavior.
- Rules of Conduct (**Rule**) are mandatory; violation of a rule is grounds for disciplinary action by the Institute. Rules of Conduct, in some instances, implement more than one Canon or Ethical Standard.

The **Code** applies to the professional activities of all classes of Members, wherever they occur. It addresses responsibilities to the public, which the profession serves and enriches; to the clients and users of architecture and in the building industries, who help to shape the built environment; and to the art and science of architecture, that continuum of knowledge and creation which is the heritage and legacy of the profession.

Commentary is provided for some of the Rules of Conduct. That commentary is meant to clarify or elaborate the intent of the Rule. The commentary is not part of the Code. Enforcement will be determined by application of the Rules of Conduct alone; the commentary will assist those seeking to conform their conduct to the Code and those charged with its enforcement.

STATEMENT IN COMPLIANCE WITH THE 1990 CONSENT DECREE

The following practices are not, in themselves, unethical, unprofessional, or contrary to any policy of The American Institute of Architects or any of its components:

1. submitting, at any time, competitive bids or price quotations, including, in circumstances where price is the sole or principal consideration in the selection of an architect;
2. providing discounts; or
3. providing free services.

Individual architects or architecture firms, acting alone and not on behalf of the Institute or any of its components, are free to decide for themselves whether or not to engage in any of these practices. The Consent Decree permits the Institute, its components, or Members to advocate legislative or other government policies or actions relating to these practices. Finally, architects should continue to consult with state laws or regulations governing the practice of architecture.

CANON I

GENERAL OBLIGATIONS

Members should maintain and advance their knowledge of the art and science of architecture, respect the body of architectural accomplishment, contribute to its growth, thoughtfully consider the social and environmental impact of their professional activities, and exercise learned and uncompromised professional judgment.

E.S. 1.1 Knowledge and Skill: Members should strive to improve their professional knowledge and skill.

Rule 1.101 In practicing architecture, Members shall demonstrate a consistent pattern of reasonable care and competence, and shall apply the technical knowledge and skill which is ordinarily applied by architects of good standing practicing in the same locality.

Commentary: By requiring a "consistent pattern" of adherence to the common law standard of competence, this allows for discipline of a Member who more than infrequently does not achieve that standard. Isolated instances of minor lapses would not provide the basis for discipline.

E.S. 1.2 Standards of Excellence: Members should continually seek to raise the standards of aesthetic excellence, architectural education, research, training, and practice.

E.S. 1.3 Natural and Cultural Heritage: Members should respect and help conserve their natural and cultural heritage while striv-

ing to improve the environment and the quality of life within it.

E.S. 1.4 Human Rights: Members should uphold human rights in all their professional endeavors.

Rule 1.401 Members shall not discriminate in their professional activities on the basis of race, religion, gender, national origin, age, disability, or sexual orientation.

E.S. 1.5 Allied Arts & Industries: Members should promote allied arts and contribute to the knowledge and capability of the building industries as a whole.

CANON II

OBLIGATIONS TO THE PUBLIC

Members should embrace the spirit and letter of the law geverning their professional affairs and should promote and serve the public interest in their personal and professional activities.

E.S. 2.1 Conduct: Members should uphold the law in the conduct of their professional activities.

Rule 2.101 Members shall not, in the conduct of their professional practice, knowingly violate the law.

Commentary: The violation of any law, local, state or federal, occurring in the conduct of a Member's professional practice, is made the basis for discipline by this rule. This includes the federal Copyright Act, which prohibits copying architectural works without the permission of the copyright owner. Allegations of violations of this rule must be based on an independent finding of a violation of the law by a court of competent jurisdiction or an administrative or regulatory body.

Rule 2.102 Members shall neither offer nor make any payment or gift to a public official with the intent of influencing the official's judgment in connection with an existing or prospective project in which the Members are interested.

Commentary: This does not prohibit campaign contributions made in conformity with applicable campaign financing laws.

Rule 2.103 Members serving in a public capacity shall not accept payments or gifts which are intended to influence their judgment.

Rule 2.104 Members shall not engage in conduct involving fraud or wanton disregard of the rights of others.

Commentary: This rule addresses serious misconduct whether or not related to a Member's professional practice. When an alleged violation of this rule is based on a violation of a law, then its proof must be based on an independent finding of a violation of the law by a court of competent jurisdiction or an administrative or regulatory body.

Rule 2.105 If, in the course of their work on a project, the Members become aware of a decision taken by their employer or client which violates any law or regulation and which will, in the Members' judgment, materially affect adversely the safety to the public of the finished project, the Members shall:

(a) advise their employer or client against the decision,

(b) refuse to consent to the decision, and

(c) report the decision to the local building inspector or other public official charged with the enforcement of the applicable laws and regulations, unless the Members are able to cause the matter to be satisfactorily resolved by other means.

Commentary: This rule extends only to violations of the building laws that threaten the public safety. The obligation under this rule applies only to the safety of the finished project, an obligation coextensive with the usual undertaking of an architect.

Rule 2.106 Members shall not counsel or assist a client in conduct that the architect knows, or reasonably should know, is fraudulent or illegal.

E.S. 2.2 Public Interest Services: Members should render public interest professional services and encourage their employees to render such services.

E.S. 2.3 Civic Responsibility: Members should be involved in civic activities as citizens and professionals, and should strive to improve public appreciation and understanding of architecture and the functions and responsibilities of architects.

Rule 2.301 Members making public statements on architectural issues shall disclose when they are being compensated for making such statements or when they have an economic interest in the issue.

CANON III

OBLIGATIONS TO THE CLIENT

Members should serve their clients competently and in a professional manner, and should exercise unprejudiced and unbiased judgment when performing all professional services.

E.S. 3.1 Competence: Members should serve their clients in a timely and competent manner.

Rule 3.101 In performing professional services, Members shall take into account applicable laws and regulations. Members may rely on the advice of other qualified persons as to the intent and meaning of such regulations.

Rule 3.102 Members shall undertake to perform professional services only when they, together with those whom they may engage as consultants, are qualified by education, training, or experience in the specific technical areas involved.

Commentary: This rule is meant to ensure that Members not undertake projects which are beyond their professional capacity. Members venturing into areas which require expertise they do not possess may obtain that expertise by additional education, train-

ing, or through the retention of consultants with the necessary expertise.

Rule 3.103 Members shall not materially alter the scope or objectives of a project without the client's consent.

E.S. 3.2 Conflict of Interest: Members should avoid conflicts of interest in their professional practices and fully disclose all unavoidable conflicts as they arise.

Rule 3.201 A Member shall not render professional services if the Member's professional judgment could be affected by responsibilities to another project or person, or by the Member's own interests, unless all those who rely on the Member's judgment consent after full disclosure.

Commentary: This rule is intended to embrace the full range of situations that may present a Member with a conflict between his interests or responsibilities and the interests of others. Those who are entitled to disclosure may include a client, owner, employee, contractor, or others who rely on or are affected by the Member's professional decisions. A Member who cannot appropriately communicate about a conflict directly with an affected person must take steps to ensure that disclosure is made by other means.

Rule 3.202 When acting by agreement of the parties as the independent interpreter of building contract documents and the judge of contract performance, Members shall render decisions impartially.

Commentary: This rule applies when the Member, though paid by the owner and owing the owner loyalty, is nonetheless required to act with impartiality in fulfilling the architect's professional responsibilities.

E.S. 3.3 Candor and Truthfulness: Members should be candid and truthful in their professional communications and keep their clients reasonably informed about the clients' projects.

Rule 3.301 Members shall not intentionally or recklessly mislead existing or prospective clients about the results that can be achieved through the use of the Members' services, nor shall the Members state that they can achieve

results by means that violate applicable law or this **Code.**

Commentary: This rule is meant to preclude dishonest, reckless, or illegal representations by a Member either in the course of soliciting a client or during performance.

E.S. 3.4 Confidentiality: Members should safeguard the trust placed in them by their clients.

Rule 3.401 Members shall not knowingly disclose information that would adversely affect their client or that they have been asked to maintain in confidence, except as otherwise allowed or required by this **Code** or applicable law.

Commentary: To encourage the full and open exchange of information necessary for a successful professional relationship, Members must recognize and respect the sensitive nature of confidential client communications. Because the law does not recognize an architect-client privilege, however, the rule permits a Member to reveal a confidence when a failure to do so would be unlawful or contrary to another ethical duty imposed by this Code.

CANON IV

OBLIGATIONS TO THE PROFESSION

Members should uphold the integrity and dignity of the profession.

E.S. 4.1 Honesty and Fairness: Members should pursue their professional activities with honesty and fairness.

Rule 4.101 Members having substantial information which leads to a reasonable belief that another Member has committed a violation of this **Code** which raises a serious question as to that Member's honesty, trustworthiness, or fitness as a Member, shall file a complaint with the National Ethics Council.

Commentary: Often, only an architect can recognize that the behavior of another architect poses a serious question as to that other's professional integrity. In those circumstances, the duty to the professional's calling requires that a complaint be filed. In most jurisdictions, a complaint that invokes professional standards is protected from a libel or slander action if the complaint was made in good faith. If in doubt, a Member should seek counsel before reporting on another under this rule.

Rule 4.102 Members shall not sign or seal drawings, specifications, reports, or other professional work for which they do not have responsible control.

Commentary: Responsible control means the degree of knowledge and supervision ordinarily required by the professional standard of care. With respect to the work of licensed consultants, Members may sign or seal such work if they have reviewed it, coordinated its preparation, or intend to be responsible for its adequacy.

Rule 4.103 Members speaking in their professional capacity shall not knowingly make false statements of material fact.

Commentary: This rule applies to statements in all professional contexts, including applications for licensure and AIA membership.

E.S. 4.2 Dignity and Integrity: Members should strive, through their actions, to promote the dignity and integrity of the profession, and to ensure that their representatives and employees conform their conduct to this **Code.**

Rule 4.201 Members shall not make misleading, deceptive, or false statements or claims about their professional qualifications, experience, or performance and shall accurately state the scope and nature of their responsibilities in connection with work for which they are claiming credit.

Commentary: This rule is meant to prevent Members from claiming or implying credit for work which they did not do, misleading others, and denying other participants in a project their proper share of credit.

Rule 4.202 Members shall make reasonable efforts to ensure that those over whom

they have supervisory authority conform their conduct to this **Code.**

*Commentary: What constitutes "reasonable efforts" under this rule is a commonsense matter. As it makes sense to ensure that those over whom the architect exercises supervision be made generally aware of the **Code,** it can also make sense to bring a particular provision to the attention of a particular employee when a situation is present which might give rise to violation.*

CANON V

OBLIGATIONS TO COLLEAGUES

Members should respect the rights and acknowledge the professional aspirations and contributions of their colleagues.

E.S. 5.1 Professional Environment: Members should provide their associates and employees with a suitable working environment, compensate them fairly, and facilitate their professional development.

E.S. 5.2 Professional Recognition: Members should build their professional reputation on the merits of their own service and performance and should recognize and give credit to others for the professional work they have performed.

Rule 5.201 Members shall recognize and respect the professional contributions of their employees, employers, professional colleagues, and business associates.

Rule 5.202 Members leaving a firm shall not, without the permission of their employer or partner, take designs, drawings, data, reports, notes, or other materials relating to the firm's work, whether or not performed by the Member.

Rule 5.203 A Member shall not unreasonably withhold permission from a departing employee or partner to take copies of designs, drawings, data, reports, notes, or other materials relating to work performed by the employee or partner that are not confidential.

Commentary: A Member may impose reasonable conditions, such as the payment of copying costs, on the right of departing persons to take copies of their work.

RULES OF APPLICATION, ENFORCEMENT, AND AMENDMENT

APPLICATION

The **Code of Ethics and Professional Conduct** applies to the professional activities of all members of the AIA.

ENFORCEMENT

The Bylaws of the Institute state procedures for the enforcement of the **Code of Ethics and Professional Conduct.** Such procedures provide that:

1. Enforcement of the **Code** is administered through a National Ethics Council, appointed by the AIA Board of Directors.
2. Formal charges are filed directly with the National Ethics Council by Members, components, or anyone directly aggrieved by the conduct of the Members.
3. Penalties that may be imposed by the National Ethics Council are:
   (a) Admonition
   (b) Censure
   (c) Suspension of membership for a period of time
   (d) Termination of membership
4. Appeals procedures are available.
5. All proceedings are confidential, as shall the imposition of an admonishment; however, all other penalties shall be made public.

AMENDMENT

The **Code of Ethics and Professional Conduct** may be amended by the convention of the Institute under the same procedures as are necessary to amend the Institute's Bylaws. The **Code** may also be amended by the AIA Board of Directors upon a two-thirds vote of the entire Board.

*1997 edition. *This copy of the* Code of Ethics *is current as of March 22, 1997. Contact the General Counsel's Office for further information at 202-626-7391.*

APPENDIX III

INTERN DEVELOPMENT PROGRAM COMPETENCIES AND ETHICAL CONSIDERATIONS

The Intern Development Program (IDP) is an intern-training program of the National Council of Registration Boards (NCARB). It has been developed and is offered in cooperation with the American Institute of Architects (AIA). The IDP consists of training requirements, training-area descriptions, and recommended core competencies.

These training activities provide the intern participant "Awareness and Understanding" and "Skills and Applications" knowledge. The IDP charts and information guiding the participants in the program do not deal with the ethical aspects of the activities. The following charts indicate the sixteen specific IDP training areas and some significant questions for ethical consideration for each of them. This material is the **authors' summary and interpretation of IDP material** derived from *Intern Development Program Guidelines 1998–1999*, as published by the NCARB, July, 1998.

The purpose of this section is to provide interns and their mentors with an understanding of the ethical aspects of architectural practice as they relate to the IDP training approach. The following study guidelines indicate actions to be taken by interns and provide a framework for discussion of these aspects with their mentors.

Study Guidelines

Study the question that is posed. Does it raise issues of community responsibility? Does it raise issues of contract and business practices? Does it raise issues of professional duty and responsibility?

Do any of those issues require ethical considerations? If so, what is the ethical content and import?

Develop potential answers to each of the questions. How would your answers change if you were the client, represented the community, or were a member of the architect's team? Think also about these answers in terms of the ethical theories and the Five Framing Lenses described in Part I: Awareness. Finally, take a position that represents your ethical stance.

INTERN DEVELOPMENT PROGRAM

IDP TRAINING AREA	AWARENESS AND UNDERSTANDING	SKILLS AND APPLICATION	SIGNIFICANT QUESTIONS FOR ETHICAL CONSIDERATION
Programming	Determine the background of the architectural programming. Review completed architectural programs.	Prepare a scope of work. Interview clients. Prepare a code review. Prepare adjacency diagrams.	How do you identify all of those who are affected by the project? Who is the client? How do you evaluate the community impact?
Site-and-Environmental Analysis	Review several project-type master plans. Select service books and articles for review.	Review AIA Document B141. Review scope of work for site-analysis services. Review drawings with civil engineers; locate utilities, topography, and special conditions. Review requirements for sewage-treatment systems.	How do you identify community needs? How do you evaluate public impacts? On what basis do you determine impacts of natural and manmade systems (cultural heritage)?
Schematic Design	Read several architectural contracts with regard to schematic-level requirements. Review previous schematic-design presentations. Review budget versus the actual time required to prepare drawings and presentation materials.	Prepare a contract for the schematic-design phase. Assist with the preparation of schematic drawings for different project types. Attend client meetings. Prepare a schematic report comparing design spaces with program intent.	On what basis do you analyze budget and design-cost implications? How do you establish priorities for dealing with all of the client needs? What societal conflicts has the design created? What neighbor conflicts has the design created? What is the responsibility for investigating valid alternatives?

IDP TRAINING AREA	AWARENESS AND UNDERSTANDING	SKILLS AND APPLICATION	SIGNIFICANT QUESTIONS FOR ETHICAL CONSIDERATION
Engineering-Systems Coordination	Review technical materials and engineering literature for all of the disciplines, including civil, structural, mechanical, electrical, landscape, acoustics, lighting, etc. Locate technical manuals and bulletins related to systems design (and costs). Review existing projects to determine the location of systems and its relationship to architectural details, structural, mechanical, electrical, etc. Locate central points of distribution, chases, "service-entry," room-size requirements, etc.	Assist with the architectural-document preparation for engineering design. Attend concept meetings with engineers. Review and coordinate drawings and written specifications. Relate results of coordination tasks to each discipline and meet to resolve conflicts.	To what degree have the consultants been members of the design team? To what degree is the architect responsible for the consultants' competence? Has the design changed without engineering input? Who is responsible for preparing notes and documentation of all meetings and important correspondence? Who should sign off on them?
Building-Cost Analysis *(The estimation of the probable construction and project cost.)*	Review several cost-estimating publications, such as *Means, Saylor,* and *Dodge.* Review cost-estimating methods: Uniformat, square-foot comparables or building-type cost per square foot, and materials and quantities (unit cost). Develop with the client appropriate project costs for telephone, furniture, fixture, equipment, testing, fees, insurance, etc. Review previous building-type cost estimates versus contractor's bids. Review a completed schedule of values. Review value-engineering principles and techniques. Evaluate life-cycle cost analysis. Review inflation in the construction trades.	Work with appropriate team members to prepare a cost estimate. Determine construction schedules with regard to the placing of materials and architects drawing the process (e.g., painting at the end of the job).	Should there be value engineering? Should life-cycle analysis be performed? What should be done when the budget and the design do not match?

(continued on next page)

IDP TRAINING AREA	AWARENESS AND UNDERSTANDING	SKILLS AND APPLICATION	SIGNIFICANT QUESTIONS FOR ETHICAL CONSIDERATION
Code Research *(The process for evaluating federal, state, and local regulations that relate to the public health, safety, and welfare as applied to a specific project.)*	Review and understand the basic organization and principles of a building code. Be aware of the Uniform Building Code (UBC), the Southern Building Code (SBC), the Building Officials Code of America (BOCA), and related codes or regulations, such as The Americans with Disabilities (ADA), a civil-rights law sometimes adopted as a state or local code or sometimes adopted in part and amended (both code and federal law apply). Review other code references, such as the National Fire Protection Agency (NFPA) regulations.	Prepare a code search for a specific project. Participate in an ADA survey of an existing facility. Compare National Fire Protection Association (NFPA) regulations to the enforced building code in difficult geographical locations (e.g., a jail in California versus a jail in Arizona; a shopping center in Massachusetts versus a shopping center in Texas). Establish an agency-review checklist for a specific project. Prepare a code-review drawing (exiting, fire separation, etc.) for a specific project.	Has the intent of the ADA been followed? Should codes be treated as minimum requirements? What should be done when the adopted code to be followed is not current?
Design Development *(The development of details and material selection, engineering systems and final siting following the schematic-design approval by the owner.)*	Review the scope of work tasks outlined in AIA Document B163, 1993. Review the scope of work requirements outlined in AIA Document B141, 1997. Review contact requirements for the contract-document phase in a contract not using AIA documents. Review consultant responsibilities. Review the cost estimate and deadlines, schedules, agency review timetables and required approvals.	Prepare a set of contract documents (drawings and specifications). Coordinate a set of contract documents. Attend consultant and client-working meetings; document minutes. Use checklists to review drawings. Establish an agency-review timetable (submittal, review period, final plan check); include planning, building, fire, health, ADA, and client reviews. Establish final program verification and cost documentation.	Who should be responsible for architectural-and-consultant coordination? How should program requirements and value-engineering suggestions be coordinated? What is the responsibility to conform to the client's desires when doing so does not conform to good practice?

IDP TRAINING AREA	AWARENESS AND UNDERSTANDING	SKILLS AND APPLICATION	SIGNIFICANT QUESTIONS FOR ETHICAL CONSIDERATION
Construction Documents *(The preparation of final written and graphic project documents; includes plans and specifications.)*	Study the requirements outlined by the AIA Document B163, 1993 and AIA Document B141, 1997. Review the contract requirements prepared for a project not using the AIA format. Understand consultant requirements for the design-development phase.	Prepare a scope of work for the design-development phase. Prepare a work schedule for the design-development phase. Use a project checklist to review design-development documents. Attend consultant-review meetings. Attend client-working meetings. Assist with the preparation of a design-development cost estimate. Review original architectural-program areas and goals with design-development outcomes. Assist in the preparation of an outline specification. Review code-research documents. Document meetings.	To what degree do you convey technical information to the client? How should the client be informed when changes are made to approved schematic-design drawings? Who should be responsible for consultant design-change approval?
Specification and Material Research *(The analysis, selection and documentation of materials and systems defined by the project design and working drawings as presented in a project manual.)*	Review the scope of work tasks outlined in AIA Document B163, 1993. Review the scope of work requirements outlined in AIA Document B141, 1997. Review contract requirements for a specification in a contract not referencing AIA documents. Review consultant responsibilities. Be aware of the manufacturer's literature and industry specifications, such as Sweets product literature, American Woodworking Institute (AWI), and others.	Work with the owner to prepare general and supplemental conditions for a project. Compare different manufacturers' requirements for a similar material and/or product (e.g., steel-window frames). Prepare sections of a specification. Coordinate consultant specifications and drawings.	Have you reviewed competing products with unbiased judgment? Have you considered the material's impact on building occupant health? Have you considered issues of environmental sustainability, such as recycled material use and renewable resources? Should you evaluate product manufacturer's claims?

(continued on next page)

IDP TRAINING AREA	AWARENESS AND UNDERSTANDING	SKILLS AND APPLICATION	SIGNIFICANT QUESTIONS FOR ETHICAL CONSIDERATION
Document-Checking and Coordination *(The means by which quality assurance is maintained throughout the project.)*	Review the scope of work, consultant responsibilities, and the architectural program. Review an applicable code and building-department requirements. Review approved engineering systems, and special products and materials.	Cross-check specifications and architectural documents with all of the consultant work. Use checklists as one technique for review organization. Meet with all of the consultants to review program requirements, the technical coordination of drawings, and specifications, as well as a final cost estimate. Coordinate all of the plan-check items (redline and double check) before final submission. Issue bid documents. Determine the location of light fixtures, the piping, the duct work, structural members in sections, and the plan layout; eliminate overlaps and potential spatial conflicts.	Should an independent third-party review contract documents? When should peer reviews be utilized? Is enough time allocated to coordinate all of the work?
Bidding and Contract Negotiation *(The establishment and administration of bidding procedures.)*	Review the scope of work outlined by AIA Document B163, 1993. Review the contract requirements in AIA Document B141, 1997. Review task requirements established by a contract not using AIA documents as a basis. Understand general and supplemental conditions of the specification.	Prepare bid documents. Assess requests for substitutions. Verify criteria for contractor-selection qualifications. Research and prepare the addendum and bulletins. Attend a bid opening. Prepare the evaluation of competitive bids. Prepare a bid-award checklist, insurance certificates, a subcontractor-bid list, bonds, and other required documentation. Prepare a construction contract.	Do you have a procedure that provides unbiased and equal responses to bidder's questions to all of the contractors? Are all of the participants treated fairly? Equally? Who arbitrates conflicts about bid documents? Bids?

IDP TRAINING AREA	AWARENESS AND UNDERSTANDING	SKILLS AND APPLICATION	SIGNIFICANT QUESTIONS FOR ETHICAL CONSIDERATION
Construction Phase–Office *(Architectural-management procedures and administration during a construction contract.)*	Review AIA Document B163. Review AIA Document B141. Review a contract not using AIA documents as a basis. Review the construction contract. Understand the contractor work schedule (pert schedule, etc.). Review the schedule of values. Understand general and supplemental conditions.	Review with the contractor the construction sequence and schedule deadlines. Develop procedures for shop-drawing submittals and approvals. Identify long-lead items (materials, products). Develop addendas, checklists for construction meetings, requests for information, change requests, the unit pricing, change directives, change orders, payment requests, etc. Prepare communication documentation for all of the related parties, especially the client. Prepare the punch list. Document conflicts during the construction; prepare alternative solutions. Receive and verify all of the items, manuals, and insurance warranties required by the specifications. Participate in all of the callback problems.	Have you reviewed project changes in the context of the original program? In the context of the community issues? Do your responses to the contractor's requests for substitutions reflect a balanced, fair, and honest appraisal? On what basis should fiscal considerations affect change-order decisions? Whose interest should be protected?

(continued on next page)

IDP Training Area	Awareness and Understanding	Skills and Application	Significant Questions for Ethical Consideration
Construction Phase–Observation *(The creation and maintenance of a comprehensive record of the project.)*	Review AIA Document B163, 1993. Review AIA Document B141, 1997. Understand general and supplemental conditions. Review submittal requirements, field tests, and mandatory inspections. Understand the construction schedule and the building sequence.	Prepare a submittal log (shop drawings, etc.). Develop a project-file system. Record all of the meeting minutes, correspondence, and relevant communication. Maintain a project-sequence photograph file. Verify all of the payment requests in writing. Maintain a sequential file for requests for information. Document all requests for changes. Record and dispatch all change orders in a timely manner. Maintain client communication.	What should you do when observing a construction practice you deem unsafe? What should you do when you observe work that varies from that shown on construction documents?
Project Management *(The comprehensive recording of the events of the project.)*	Review the scope of work by phases and tasks in AIA Document B163, 1993, and AIA Document B141, 1997. Review a contract not based on AIA documents. Review published management checklists, such as *AIA, Stitt, Guidelines.* Review established office norms for correspondence, meeting notes, memos, and construction-administration forms.	Prepare a scope of work indicating work tasks for each phase of the project. List an estimate of personnel and the time required for each task (a budget). Schedule all tasks of the project. Develop a cash-flow (billing) projection. Coordinate consultant contracts and production deadlines. Establish regular production meetings — in-house, consultant, and client.	Do you render impartial decisions to disputes? What is your responsibility when you review meeting minutes that do not reflect your perception of the event?

IDP Training Area	Awareness and Understanding	Skills and Application	Significant Questions for Ethical Consideration
Office Management *(The allocation of the office's resources to support the firm's goals.)*	Study different management techniques. Review the *AIA Handbook*. Discuss the firm-management philosophy with principals.	Prepare economic trends, forecasts, and indicators in relationship to the firm's existing and potential markets. Prepare a firm-organization description. Develop a marketing plan and a business plan. Develop a compensation comparison of each firm's job description, level, and responsibility. Prepare candidate interview questions. Participate in a new project competition. Organize the firm's team after receiving a new commission. Prepare a comparison of firm benefits with similar competitors.	Should the schedule for the site review and contractor's meetings be determined by the "office budget" or project complexity? Is the appropriate level of firm resources committed to the project? Should the firm assign the most experienced and talented people to each phase of the project? Has the office staff received the appropriate recognition for their contributions to the project? What should you do when office time assigned for a task is inadequate in your view to produce the required quality work? What is the responsibility of the firm to keep some of the personnel on the project who were originally promised to the client?
Professional and Community Service *(The voluntary participation in a broad range of professional and community activities.)*	Review Ernest L. Boyer and Lee D. Mitgang, *Building Community: A New Future for Architecture Education and Practice* (Princeton, NJ: The Carnegie Foundation for the Advancement of Teaching, 1996).	Participate in community groups related to individual professional skills and talents. Participate in community groups not related to professional skills and talents. Participate with professional affiliates. Provide counseling and mentoring for students and interns. Volunteer as a member of a community review agency, commission, or oversight group. Take an active role in politics. Participate in continuing-education activities.	Should the firm sponsor post-occupancy studies? To whom should post-occupancy findings be disseminated? To the public? To the profession? To other consultants? How and to what degree should the firm encourage staff and principal involvement in community service? Should the firm participate in *pro-bono* activities?

APPENDIX IV

ARCHITECTURAL-PRACTICE
ORGANIZATION, SERVICES DELIVERY,
AND ETHICAL CONSIDERATIONS

The California Board of Architectural Examiners (CBAE) developed a job analysis for architectural practice as part of its test-plan development for the California Supplemental Exam, a part of the state's licensure procedure. Part of this job-analysis process included a description of architectural practice in terms of the tasks and knowledge necessary for architectural practice in California.

These tasks and knowledge were presented with two frames: the Organization of Architectural Practice, which covers professional services, and the Delivery of Architectural Services, which covers research, design analysis and programming, and design implementation.

This practice description is presented in summary form, along with significant questions for ethical consideration of the identified practice tasks. It is another instrument for you to use in developing your understanding of the nexus of ethics and the practice of architecture. The summary is based on material in *The Practice of Architecture in California: A report on the 1998 analysis of architectural practice in California*, published by the California Board of Architectural Examiners (CBAE).

STUDY GUIDELINES

Study the question that is posed. Does it raise issues of community responsibility? Does it raise issues of contract and business practices? Does it raise issues of professional duty and responsibility?

Do any of those issues require ethical considerations? If so, what are the ethical content and import?

Develop potential answers to each of the questions. How would your answers change if you were the client, represented the community, or were a member of the architect's team? Think also about these answers in terms of the ethical theories and the Five Framing Lenses described in Part I: Awareness. Finally, take a position that represents your ethical stance.

ORGANIZATION OF ARCHITECTURAL-PRACTICE TASKS–CBAE	SIGNIFICANT QUESTIONS FOR ETHICAL CONSIDERATION
A. Professional Services. The scope of services provided to a client that supports the development of an architectural project.	Business Practices/Public Welfare/Trust/ Mutual Obligations/Rules
1. Determine the scope of pre-design services, such as strategic facilities planning, programming, and pre-occupancy services.	PROFESSIONALISM/CANDOR/SOCIAL RESPONSIBILITY Does your firm have the professional background and individual talent to complete this assignment? What role should the "planner" take in the process: facilitator, researcher, or advocate? What role does public opinion play?
2. Determine the scope of the information regarding the natural systems and the built environment related to a site or facility.	SOCIAL RESPONSIBILITY/PUBLIC VALUES Who is the client? Are special skills or consultants required? Should there be scope limitations? How broad a look should be taken in a client's interest? Public's interest? Architect's interest?
3. Determine which laws, codes, regulations, and standards apply to a project.	RULES/BUSINESS PRACTICES/TRUST Should the firm retain an expert consultant? Should the architect participate in the process to develop codes and laws? How does the information get conveyed to the client? Should codes be treated as minimum standards?
4. Determine the scope of project-feasibility analysis.	PROFESSIONAL VALUES/TRUST/SOCIAL RESPONSIBILITY/CANDOR What should be the architect's limits to the analysis process? Should the client be informed of all of the findings?

Organization of Architectural-Practice Tasks–CBAE	Significant Questions for Ethical Consideration
5. Determine the scope of design services.	Business Practices/Mutual Obligations/ Community Values Is the designer required to produce "state-of-the-art" documents? How should the firm describe the background with regard to a particular project type? How informed should you make the client of available contract options? How does your firm coordinate the consultant work and determine responsibility?
6. Determine the scope of construction-phase services.	Interpersonal Communication/ Trust/Public Welfare/Business Practices Should you inform the client of contract options? Of requisite responsibilities?
7. Determine which expanded services might be provided, such as facilities management, peer review, and post-occupancy studies.	Community Values/Professional Values/Public Welfare What is the firm's responsibility regarding outside consultants retained by the client? Should the firm assume responsibility for a new project type if it lacks expertise in that particular specialized service?
B. Professional Organization. Processes a practitioner uses for organizing human and physical resources to deliver services.	Business Practices/Interpersonal Communication/Mutual Obligations
1. Establish the model for organization of the office.	Professional Values/Mutual Obligations/ Candor Does your firm manage a project for profit or project quality? On what basis does your firm hire people? Does your firm determine compensation equitably?
2. Establish the role of the architect in relation to the client and users.	Public Welfare/Trust/Interpersonal Communication Should you have qualified staff members who have current knowledge of the building type? Are there differences in how you work with a repeat client versus a new client? Who determines the building user's needs for generic and "spec" building types? Who verifies program information?

ORGANIZATION OF ARCHITECTURAL-PRACTICE TASKS–CBAE	SIGNIFICANT QUESTIONS FOR ETHICAL CONSIDERATION
3. Identify relationships with relevant regulatory agencies.	RULES/PUBLIC WELFARE/TRUST Are the people managing the project familiar with the applicable codes? Who in the firm is responsible for regulatory-issue decisions?
4. Establish an organizational structure for the delivery of the project.	BUSINESS PRACTICES/PROFESSIONALISM Do you compensate your staff for working overtime? Is the schedule complementary to the client's needs or the firm's workload?
5. Establish relationships with consultants and other team members.	BUSINESS PRACTICES/CANDOR/ACKNOWLEDGEMENT/CONFIDENCES Is the firm financially accountable to the consultants? Are they paid promptly? Who is responsible for coordination? Do architects have an obligation to keep all of the consultants informed of all of the aspects of the project, including all of the changes in scope, design, drawings, etc.?
6. Establish business-management systems to conduct an architectural practice.	BUSINESS PRACTICES/PERSONAL INTEGRITY/ACKNOWLEDGMENT/CONFIDENCES Does the firm provide enough of a budget for the proper number of administrative personnel, bookkeepers, human-resource personnel, accountants, etc.? Does the firm treat each project on its own profit-loss basis? How is this presented to clients? To staff? What are appropriate policies regarding the client's confidentiality? Regarding public disclosure?
C. **Professional Responsibilities.** Laws, regulations, and professional standards that guide architectural practice.	RULES/PUBLIC WELFARE/TRUST
1. Apply the state's Architects Practice Act to the provision of architectural services.	PROFESSIONAL VALUES/INTERPERSONAL COMMUNICATION What is the firm's responsibility to assess its practice regularly for compliance with both intent and provisions of the Act? What is the firm's accountability regarding its interns' responsibility? Should the firm sponsor or support continuing-education programs? Who should pay?

Organization of Architectural-Practice Tasks–CBAE	Significant Questions for Ethical Consideration
2. Apply the principles of business law to the practice of architecture.	PROFESSIONAL VALUES/TRUST/RIGHT BEHAVIOR Should a firm carry errors-and-omissions insurance? Should members of a firm attend professional seminars to stay current with changes in the laws? Should a firm designate a principal to be responsible for human-resource issues? Should a firm have established personnel practices? What should they cover?
3. Understand the application of the principles of construction law to the practice of architecture.	RULES/PUBLIC WELFARE/TRUST What is the responsibility for all of the firm members to stay current on construction law? On construction options? What is the responsibility of junior members to be current on applications of the law, specifications, and the lien laws?
4. Assess professional-liability issues, including recognized standards of care, related to the conduct of an architectural practice.	PROFESSIONAL VALUES/MUTUAL OBLIGATIONS/TRUST/RIGHT BEHAVIOR What is the responsibility of principals to know about liability issues? What is the responsibility of staff members to know about liability issues? Who determines the firm's "standard of care"?
5. Represent professional capabilities and experience to clients.	INTERPERSONAL COMMUNICATION–CANDOR/FIDELITY/CONSISTENCY/SOCIAL HARMONY What is the responsibility of the firm to the client when representing whom will work on the project? Should the firm reassign members of the team after the project begins? Should the firm represent the work completed by prior associations? The work completed by staff in prior associations?
6. Participate in professional-development activities, such as continuing education.	PROFESSIONAL DEVELOPMENT/PUBLIC WELFARE/TRUST Should an office sponsor AIA, CSI, or other professional-development dues? Should an office allow paid time off for professional development? Are firm leaders involved in community events, politics, and social organizations? What is the responsibility for each member of a firm to receive continuing education?

DELIVERY OF ARCHITECTURAL SERVICES– CBAE	SIGNIFICANT QUESTIONS FOR ETHICAL CONSIDERATION
A. Research, Design Analysis, and Programming. Procedures necessary for the assessment of the relevant information in preparation for the design of a project.	PUBLIC WELFARE/TRUST/SOCIAL RESPONSIBILITY
1. Research and analyze the information relevant to the development of an architectural program.	SOCIAL RESPONSIBILITY/PROFESSIONALISM/ INTERPERSONAL COMMUNICATION/CULTURAL VALUES Is the present staff qualified to complete project research? How should it be handled? How do you deal with a client who represents only the user, not the community? Do you question the client's program criteria or assumptions?
2. Assess individual user needs relative to human activities and comfort.	PROFESSIONALISM/SOCIAL PURPOSE/PUBLIC WELFARE Should the designer put higher priorities on design objectives versus specific program requirements? Should human-comfort needs be based on codes or the architect's past experience?
3. Assess the interrelationships between natural systems and the built environment.	SOCIAL RESPONSIBILITY What design options are presented to the client? How do you handle the client's desire when it differs from public policy and interest (but not the law or code)?
4. Assess the interrelationships of societal factors and the built environment.	"OUGHT TO BE"/"GOOD"/SOCIAL RESPONSIBILITY Does the firm accept commissions that conflict with community policy or desires? What is the architect's responsibility for understanding cultural norms and biases?
5. Assess and apply specific provisions of relevant laws, codes, regulations, and standards.	PUBLIC WELFARE/TRUST/PROFESSIONAL VALUES/ HEALTH AND SAFETY Does the architect treat codes as maximum requirements or minimum standards? Should the architect use the most current version of the code when it has not been adopted? Should the client be informed and be party to all such decisions?

Delivery of Architectural Services–CBAE	Significant Questions for Ethical Consideration
6. Assess the feasibility of the project.	**Professional/Trust/Social Responsibility** On what basis should firms engage in feasibility studies? How does the architect deal with the client when the client's desired program and budget are clearly not compatible? Should a firm take a project that it thinks lacks feasibility, be it political, economic, or social?
B. Design Implementation. The synthesis and application of information that leads to a solution that responds to defined project requirements.	**Public Welfare/Social Responsibility/ Mutual Obligations/Trust**
1. Translate the program information into a design solution.	**Trust/Professional Values/Fidelity** How do you determine trade-offs to meet program needs versus a program budget? How are social issues (ADA, community plans, environmental protection, etc.) addressed beyond specific code requirements? What is the architect's responsibility, and to whom, to develop alternative-design solutions? What value judgments does the designer make when accessing community criteria? Do you represent the client, the occupants, or the public? To what degree?
2. Apply the information about the relationship of the natural systems and the built environment to the proposed project.	**Social Responsibility/Public Welfare** Should you identify effects beyond project limits? What does the architect do when the client's program creates a negative impact on a positive system?
3. Select and integrate appropriate building systems.	**Public Welfare/Trust/Professionalism** To what degree does the architect trade off aesthetics for system efficiency? Should the architect stay current with "state-of-the-art" mechanical and electrical systems and practices? Should the firm evaluate previous work with regard to the operation of specified systems? What is the architect's responsibility regarding the consultant's design strategies?

Delivery of Architectural Services– CBAE	Significant Questions for Ethical Consideration
4. Select and integrate appropriate building materials.	**Public Welfare/Trust/Professionalism** Should the architect value engineer each project? To what degree does the architect assume responsibility for thorough material research? What should the basis of material selection be: aesthetics, durability, cost, occupant health, or sustainable production?
5. Select and integrate nonstructural building elements.	**Professional Practices/Public Welfare** How do you deal with a conflict between owner's desires and good practice? What are the designer's responsibilities regarding adjacent-property users? Regarding community impacts?
6. Document and communicate design decisions for the project implementation.	**Interpersonal Communications–Candor/Fidelity/Acknowledgement** On what basis does the architect define the acceptable levels of workmanship?
7. Implement the construction-administration process.	**Mutual Obligations/Social Responsibility/Candor** Should the architect deal with the contractor's inadequate documentation? When there are not perceived problems? Should the architect notify the client of all of the construction conflicts? Even those that have been solved? What do you do when you observe a deviation from construction drawings or code requirements? What does the architect do when the client accepts substandard work?
8. Perform post-occupancy evaluations.	**Candor/Public Welfare/Trust** Have you considered the evaluation of completed projects during the pre-design phase of a new project? Do you review current literature, periodicals, and technical seminars to maintain technical proficiencies with regard to specified structural, mechanical, and electrical systems? Do you perform a post-occupancy study when you do not receive compensation for the task?

NOTES TO THE TEXT

PART I: AWARENESS

INTRODUCTION

1. Benedetto Gravagnuolo, "Towards an Architecture of the New Millennium," in Mario Botta, *The Ethics of Building*, trans. Stephen Thorne, Basel: Birkhäuser Verlag, 1997, 10.
2. Mario Botta, *The Ethics of Building*, ibid., Note 1, 26, 28.
3. Aaron Betsky, "Libeskind Builds," *Architecture* 87, n9, Sep. 1998, 102. Betsky is quoting Daniel Libeskind.
4. American Institute of Architects, *Architecture Factbook*, 1994 Edition, Washington, DC: American Institute of Architects, 55.
5. American Institute of Architects, *1997 Code of Ethics and Professional Conduct*, Washington, DC: American Institute of Architects, 1997.

SOME BASICS ABOUT ETHICS

1. Plato, *The Republic of Plato* (fourth century BC), trans. w. intro. by Francis MacDonald Cornford, New York and London: Oxford University Press, 1945, reprint 1968, 67, 352d.
2. Plato, *The Apology* (fourth century BC), trans. Benjamin Jowett, 3rd. ed., (Simon & Schuster, 1928; Meta Markel, 1956), selected and ed. Irwin Edman, New York: The Modern Library, 84, 38d. The reference numbers to Plato's writings are the page numbers from the 1578 edition of his works published by Henri

Estienne. Modern scholars have agreed upon Estienne's pagination for uniform citation.
3. Dictionaries, noted by their full title in the first reference, will be referred to by initials subsequently:
The American Heritage Dictionary of the English Language, 3rd. ed., Boston: Houghton Mifflin Co., 1992, *(AHD)*.
The Random House Dictionary of the English Language, Second Edition, Unabridged, New York: Random House, 1987, *(RHD)*.
The New Shorter Oxford English Dictionary, Oxford: Clarendon Press, 1993, *(SOED)*. This is a newly abridged and written dictionary based upon the *OED*.
The Oxford English Dictionary and Supplements, Compact Edition, Oxford University Press, V. I and II, 1971; V. III, 1987, (OED).
Webster's New Collegiate Dictionary, Springfield, MA: Merriam-Webster, *(WNC)*.
Webster's New World Dictionary of the American Language: College Edition, Cleveland and New York: World Publishing Co., 1964, *(NWD/C)*.
4. Plato's *Republic* and Aristotle's *Nicomachaen Ethics* are widely available in many translations, both in full text and in edited selections; Alasdair MacIntyre, *After Virtue: A Study in Moral Philosophy*, London: Duckworth, 1981; John Rawls, *A Theory of Justice*, Cambridge: Belknap Press of Harvard University Press, 1971.
5. John L. Mackie, *Ethics: Inventing Right and Wrong*, Pelican Books, 1977; reprint, New York: Penguin, pbk., 1990, 9.

293

6. George Edward Moore, *Principia Ethica*, originally published 1903; reprint Cambridge: Cambridge University Press, 1959, 3–15.

7. Part I: Awareness includes compact introductions to ethics and ethical issues. The following references are suggested as resources for further study. Two brief, thorough introductions to ethical concepts that cover ethical reasoning, relativism, egoism, utility and other consequentialist theories, Kantian and other deontic theories, virtue ethics and social-contract theory are Louis P. Pojman's *Ethics: Discovering Right and Wrong*, 2nd ed., Belmont, CA: Wadsworth Publishing Company, 1994; and James Rachels's *The Elements of Moral Philosophy*, 2nd ed., New York: McGraw-Hill, Inc., 1993. Dave Robinson and Chris Garrett provide a lively, brief, illustrated introduction to the major moral questions, disputes, and philosophers, with good coverage of late-twentieth-century applied ethics problems and Continental philosophers, in *Introducing Ethics*, ed. Richard Appignanesi, New York: Totem Books, c. 1996. A longer introduction that presents those ethical themes and additional themes of free will, autonomy, diversity, and justice within a lively narrative dialogue format is *Exploring Ethics: A Traveller's Tale*, Brenda Almond, Malden, MA: Blackwell Publishers, Inc., 1998. Jennifer Trusted includes chapters on judgments, facts and values, morality and the law, politics and politicians, and rights in her introductory work *Moral Principles and Social Values*, London: Routledge and Kegan Paul, 1987. The best brief introduction to the course of Western ethical thought through time is *A Short History of Ethics: A history of moral philosophy from the Homeric Age to the twentieth century*, Alasdair MacIntyre, New York: Collier Books, Macmillan Publishing, c. 1966. Two books that address central figures (Plato, Aristotle, Augustine, Aquinas, Hume, Kant, Mill, Hegel, Nietzsche, Sartre, and Rawls) and their ethical thought are *Ethics in the History of Western Philosophy*, Robert J. Cavalier, James Guinlock and James P. Sterba, ed., New York: St. Martin's Press, c. 1989; and Richard Norman's *The Moral Philosophers: An Introduction to Ethics*, 2nd edition, New York: Oxford University Press, 1998. Both include concise explanative essays and bibliographies of the primary works of the ethicists being discussed. The best single source is Peter Singer, ed., *A Companion to Ethics*, Blackwell Companions to Philosophy, Cambridge, MA:

Blackwell, c.1991, 1993. It expands upon the themes in the already mentioned works with sections on global ethical traditions, religious ethical traditions, such contemporary applied ethics concerns as poverty, euthanasia, and environmentalism, and critiques of the Western tradition, such as those launched by Marxism and feminism.

THE ETHICAL NATURE OF ARCHITECTURE

1. Immanuel Kant, excerpts from *Critique of the Faculty of Judgment* (1790), trans. J. H. Bernard (London, 1892), with revisions by Lewis White Beck, in *Kant: Selections*, ed. Lewis White Beck, New York: Scribner/ Macmillan Book, 1988. Sections 10–17 discuss concepts of purpose in art (which is to possess "purposiveness [as art only] without purpose [intentionality or utility]"), and ideal beauty with examples. The quote begins at ¶230, 369.

2. The compound term *excellence/virtue* has its roots in the Greek word *areté*. *Areté* embodies both the concepts of such personal virtues as generosity and steadfastness, and the concept of excellence. Excellence extends from personal behavior and one's practices, and also to qualities or attributes of those practices and of things. Thus, a knife blade may possess *areté* with regard to its strength and sharpness as a knife. In the remainder of the text, virtue will be used in this compound sense of excellence, that may apply to persons, objects, and practices. The knife example is from C. C. W. Taylor's definition of *areté* in *The Oxford Companion to Philosophy*, Ted Honderich, ed., Oxford and New York: Oxford University Press, 1995. This concept is a central issue in MacIntyre's contemporary discussion of the nature of virtues in *After Virtue: A Study in Moral Philosophy*, 2nd. ed., London: Duckworth, 1984, particularly Chapter 14, "The Nature of Virtues."

3. Winston Churchill, *Winston Churchill: His Complete Speeches, 1897–1963*, 8 Volumes, ed. Robert Rhodes James, New York and London: Chelsea House and R. R. Bowker, 1974. The first and third quotes are from a speech in the House of Commons, 28 Oct 43, vol. VII, *1943–1949*, 6869; the middle from a speech at the Architectural Association in London, 25 Jul 24, vol. IV, 1922–1928, 3467–3468.

4. There have been many efforts to account for the origins of building. K. Harries provides an

excellent examination of this literature in *The Ethical Function of Architecture*, Cambridge: MIT, 1997, Chapter 9, "Tales of the Origin of Building."

5. See Martin Heidegger, "Building Dwelling Thinking," trans. Albert Hofstadter, in *Basic Writings*, 2nd, revised and expanded edition, ed. David Farrell Krell, San Francisco: HarperSanFrancisco, 1993, 343–363. Also, Christian Norberg-Schulz, *Existence, Space and Architecture*, New York: Praeger, 1971; and *Genius Loci: Towards a Phenomenology of Architecture*, New York: Rizzoli, 1979.

6. Alasdair MacIntyre, *A Short History of Ethics*, New York: Collier Books, Macmillan Publishing, 1966, 1. MacIntyre uses "as culture changes" in ethics to step around the opposition, otherness, and "contingent causal relationship" in the phrase "because culture changes."

7. Christian Norberg-Schulz, *Existence, Space & Architecture*, New York: Praeger, 1971; and *Genius Loci: Towards a Phenomenology of Architecture*, New York: Rizzoli, 1980, in particular his note of debt to Heidegger, 5.

8. Karsten Harries, *The Ethical Function of Architecture*, Cambridge: MIT, 1997, 4.

9. Marcus Vitruvius Pollio, *The Ten Books of Architecture* (first century BC), trans. Morris Hicky Morgan, Harvard University Press, 1914; reprint New York: Dover, 1960, 3.

10. Leon Battista Alberti, *On the Art of Building in Ten Books* (1452), trans. Joseph Rykwert, Neil Leach, and Robert Tavernor, Cambridge: MIT Press, 1988, 3.

11. Ibid., Note 10, 5. This sentence is explored in its fifteenth-century Italian context by Bill Hubbard, Jr., in *A Theory for Practice: Architecture in Three Discourses*, Cambridge: MIT Press, 1995, 40–44.

12. Christian Norberg-Schulz, *Intentions in Architecture*, Cambridge: MIT Press, 1965, 19.

13. Alberto Pérez-Gómez, "Introduction," in Louise Pelletier and Alberto Pérez-Gómez, ed., *Architecture, Ethics, and Technology*, Montreal and Kingston: McGill-Queens University Press, 1994, 3.

14. "Introduction: Modernism, Postmodernism, and Architecture's Social Project," in Thomas A. Dutton, and Lian Hurst Mann, ed., *Reconstructing Architecture: Critical Discourses and Social Practices*, Minneapolis: University of Minnesota Press, 1996, 3, 4, and 5.

15. Ernest L. Boyer, and Lee D. Mitgang, *Building Community: A New Future for Architecture Education and Practice*, Princeton: The Carnegie Foundation for the Advancement of Teaching, c. 1996, 3–4, 32, 34.

16. Congress for the New Urbanism, *Charter of the New Urbanism*, San Francisco: Congress for the New Urbanism, 1996.

17. Andrea Palladio, *The Four Books of Architecture* (1570), trans. Isaac Ware (London, 1738), with a new intro. by Adolf Placzek, facsimile reprint, New York: Dover, 1965, BI.C1 ¶1.

18. In the meaning of virtue and practices used by Alasdair MacIntyre. See *After Virtue*, 2nd ed., Notre Dame: University of Notre Dame Press, 1984, Chap. 14 "The Nature of Virtues" 187, passim.

19. William S. Saunders, ed., *Reflections on Architectural Practices in the Nineties*, New York: Princeton Architectural Press, c. 1996; and Thomas A. Dutton and Lian Hurst Mann, ed., *Reconstructing Architecture: Critical Discourses and Social Practices*, Minneapolis: University of Minnesota Press, 1996.

20. Dana Cuff, *Architecture: The Study of Practice*, Cambridge: MIT Press, 1991, 24, 56.

A MORE IN-DEPTH LOOK AT ETHICAL CONCEPTS

1. See Note 7, Part I, Some Basics about Ethics.

2. Plato's Republic, as described in *The Republic*, fourth century BC, is a realm of prosperity, peace, and wisdom. See Education, 376e–412-b; and The Equality of Women and Thoughts on Marriage and Child Rearing 445b–457b, and 457b–466d for peculiar insights into sustaining the Republic.

3. There are many translations available. The one used here is Immanuel Kant, *Grounding for the Metaphysics of Morals*, (1785), trans. James W. Ellington, 3rd. ed., Indianapolis: Hackett Publishing, c. 1981, 1992.

4. Ibid., Note 3, 36.

5. Op. cit., Note 3, 30.

6. Sissela Bok is arguably the premier contemporary ethicist who has examined the ethics of lying: *Lying: Moral Choices in Public and Private Life*, New York: Pantheon Books, 1978; and *Secrets: On the Ethics of Concealment and Revelation*, New York: Pantheon Books, 1982.

7. Aristotle, *Nicomachean Ethics*, fourth century BC. The translations I refer to here are the full text by Terrence Irwin, Hackett Publishing, 1985; and the 1892 translation by J. E. C.

Weldon, reprinted in part in *Ethics and the Search for Values*, ed. Navia and Kelly, Buffalo: Prometheus Press, 1980.

8. Aristotle, ibid., Note 7, 96–97 in Navia, 46–48 in Irwin; 1107b1–1108a30. The standard cross-referencing to Aristotle is from the pagination of Immanuel Bekker's Greek text edition of 1831.

9. Aristotle, op. cit., Note 7, Book III, 98–103 in Navia, 53–65 in Irwin; 1110a29–1113b1.

10. Alasdair MacIntyre's contemporary classic *After Virtue* has already been noted in Part I, The Ethical Nature of Architecture, Note 1b. For further study, consider Julia Annas, *The Morality of Happiness*, New York and Oxford: Oxford University Press, 1993, which focuses on classic Greek virtue theory; and Philippa Foot, *Virtues and Vices and Other Essays in Moral Philosophy*, Berkeley and Los Angeles: University of California Press, 1978. *Vice and Virtue in Everyday Life: Introductory Readings in Ethics*, 3rd. ed., ed. Christina Sommers and Fred Sommers, Fort Worth: Harcourt Brace Jovanovich College Publishers, 1993, has an excellent selection of virtue-theory-based readings and selections from other ethical theories that pertain to virtue.

11. MacIntyre, op. cit., Part I, The Ethical Nature of Architecture, Note 18, 187.

12. Thomas Hobbes, Leviathan, 1651; Jean Jacques Rousseau, *The Social Contract*, 1762; John Rawls, *A Theory of Justice*, Cambridge, MA: Belknap Press of Harvard University, 1971; and the essay "Justice as Fairness," in *The Journal of Philosophy*, 1957. Three good places to begin further exploration of contemporary social contract, libertarianism, and Communitarianism theory are: Shlomo Avineri and Avner de-Shalit, ed., *Communitarianism and Individualism, Oxford Readings in Politics and Government*, Oxford: Oxford University Press, 1992; Norman Daniels, ed., *Reading Rawls: Critical Studies on Rawls' "A Theory of Justice,"* with a new introduction, Basic Books, Inc., 1975; reprint Stanford University Press, 1989; and Will Kymlicka, *Contemporary Political Philosophy: An Introduction*, Oxford: Clarendon Press, 1990.

13. Will Kymlicka, "The Social Contract Tradition," in Peter Singer, ed., A *Companion to Ethics*, Blackwell Companions to Philosophy, Cambridge, MA: Blackwell, c.1991, 1993, 189–191.

14. Ibid., 191 ff.

15. For another effort at adapting the Rawlsian model to architecture, see Kim Dovey, "Architectural Ethics: A Dozen Dilemmas," in *Practices*, Journal of the Center for the Study of the Practice of Architecture, University of Cincinnati College of Design, Architecture, Art and Planning, 2, Spring 1993, 26–33.

16. Two classic books on Relativism: Michael Krausz, ed., *Relativism: Interpretation and Confrontation*, South Bend, IN: University of Notre Dame Press, 1989; and Jack W. Meiland and Michael Krausz, *Relativism: Cognitive and Moral*, South Bend: University of Notre Dame Press, 1982.

17. Elizabeth Frazer, Jennifer Hornsby, and Sabina Lovibond, ed., *Ethics: A Feminist Reader*, Cambridge, MA: Blackwell, c. 1992, 1, 3.

18. Eve Browning Cole and Susan Coultrap-McQuin, ed., *Explorations in Feminist Ethics*, Bloomington: Indiana University Press, c. 1992, 3; Nancy Tuana, in *Woman and the History of Philosophy*, The Paragon Issues in Philosophy Series, ed. John K. Roth and Frederick Sontag, New York: Paragon House, 1992, provides an engaging, incisive critique of the subordination of women within the "masculinist" Western philosophical and ethical tradition.

19. The following works are explicit in their agendas to redress inequity about the participation of women in architecture (several are explicit in their choice of all female authors, for example); to address architectural production and practices by women; to address their access to, and role in, the profession; and to address gender issues embodied in architectural design: Diana Agrest, Patricia Conway, Leslie Kanes Weisman, ed., *The Sex of Architecture*, New York: Harry N. Abrams, Inc., c. 1996—a collection of 24 critical essays that "collectively express the power and diversity of women's views on architecture today." Ellen Perry Berkeley, *Architecture: A Place for Women*, Washington, DC: Smithsonian Institution, c. 1989—a pioneering collection regarding women in architecture; ranges from historical presentations to speculations that anticipate the later collections noted here. Francesca Hughes, editor, *The Architect: Reconstructing Her Practice*, Cambridge: MIT Press, c. 1996—a collection of essays by women in architecture, examination of gender, that is "woman" as architectural practitioner, and the potential impact "on reconstruction of the orders that shape architectural production and consumption." Andrea Kahn, ed., *Drawing Building Text: Essays in Architectural Theory*, New York: Princeton

Architectural Press, 1991—contributions by Miriam Gusevich, Peggy Deamer, Jennifer Bloomer, Catherine Ingraham, Ann Bergren, Mary Pepshinski, Carol Burns, Lois Nesbitt. Duncan McCorquodale, Katerina Rüedi, Sarah Wigglesworth, ed., *Desiring Practices: Architecture Gender and the Interdisciplinary*, London: Black Dog Publishing Ltd., c. 1996—conference proceedings. Elizabeth Wilson, *The Sphinx in the City: Urban Life, the Control of Disorder, and Women*, Berkeley: University of California Press, 1991. And Beatriz Colomina, ed., *Sexuality & Space*, Princeton Papers on Architecture, New York: Princeton Architectural Press, c. 1992.

20. For a collection of excellent twentieth-century articles drawn primarily from Continental thought regarding architecture and its cultural construction, see Neil Leach, ed., *Rethinking Architecture: A Reader in Cultural Theory*, London and New York: Routledge, 1997. A collection of anthologies is beginning to emerge that make Continental philosophic thought more readily available in English. Among them: Lawrence E. Cahoone, ed., *From Modernism to Postmodernism: An Anthology*, Malden, MA: Blackwell, 1996—a substantial number of Continental contributions; includes architects Venturi and Jencks. Mitchell Cohen and Nicole Freeman, ed., *Princeton Readings in Political Thought: Essential Texts Since Plato*, Princeton: Princeton University Press, 1996—primarily drawn from classic texts and Anglo-American thought; and Foucault, de Beauvoir and Habermas of the twentieth-century Continental school. Richard Kearney and Mara Rainwater, ed., *The Continental Philosophy Reader*, London and New York: Routledge, 1996—the title says it: excellent selection; begins at Husserl and Saussure; good coverage of gender issues. William McNeill and Karen S. Feldman, ed., *Continental Philosophy: An Anthology*, Blackwell Philosophy Anthologies, Malden, MA: Blackwell, 1998—Kant, Schopenhauer, and Hegel to contemporary philosophers. Joseph Natoli and Linda Hutcheon, ed., *A Postmodern Reader*, Albany: State University of New York Press, 1993—a substantial ratio of articles from twentieth-century Continental thought.

BUSINESSES, PROFESSIONS, AND ETHICAL OBLIGATIONS

1. Books defining professions and speaking to the professions' special ethical obligations of service, duty, and trustworthiness include Michael D. Bayles, *Professional Ethics*, 2nd ed., Belmont, CA: Wadsworth Publishing, 1989; Bruce A. Kimball, *The "True Professional Ideal" in America: A History*, Cambridge, MA: Blackwell, 1992; Daryl Koehn, *The Ground of Professional Ethics*, London and New York: Routledge, 1994—Koehn, in particular, focuses on trust as a foundation of professionalism; John Kultgren, *Ethics and Professionalism*, Philadelphia: University of Pennsylvania Press, 1988. The various attributes of professions are succinctly presented in Kultgren, "Part II: Models of Professions," 57–153. For a counterpoint, see Magali Sarfatti Larson's earlier classic study, *The Rise of Professionalism: A Sociological Analysis*, Berkeley: University of California Press, 1977. Larson focuses on a Marxist economic model analysis of expertise for sale rather than service for all professions, including medicine and the law. She does not include the clergy as a profession. Among the best general introductions to professional and business ethics: David Appelbaum and Sarah Verone Lawton, ed., *Ethics and the Professions*, Englewood Cliffs, NJ: Prentice-Hall, c. 1990; Joan C. Callahan, ed., *Ethical Issues in Professional Life*, New York: Oxford University Press, 1988, and W. Michael Hoffman and Jennifer Mills Moore, ed., *Business Ethics: Readings and Cases in Corporate Morality*, New York: McGraw-Hill, 1984.

2. Consult references cited in Note 1 of this section, and Part I, Ethics and Architectural Practices, Note 9, for further discussion.

3. E.g., Andrew Saint's *The Image of the Architect*; Dana Cuff's *The Study of Practice*; Niels Prak's *Architects: The Noted and the Ignored; Reflections on Architectural Practices in the Nineties*, ed. Wm. S. Saunders; and Kostof and Blau, cited in Notes 4 and 7, respectively.

4. Spiro Kostof, "The Architect in the Middle Ages, East and West," in *The Architect*, ed. Spiro Kostof, New York: Oxford, 1977, 61.

5. Aristotle, *Politics*, 1282a18–23, Loeb ed., is referenced by Daryl Koehn, *The Ground of Professional Ethics*, London and New York: Routledge, 1994, in a discussion of the client's knowledge, and contractual relations with professionals, p. 37; and Footnote 8, page 188.

6. This general critique of professionalism and its market-exchange-value basis is a central underlying concept in Magali Sarfatti Larson, *The Rise of Professionalism*, Berkeley: University of California Press, 1977, and with

respect to architecture in Chapter 1 of *Behind the Postmodern Façade: Architectural Change in Late Twentieth-Century America*, Berkeley: University of California Press; 1993, pbk. 1995. Banks McDowell focuses on the economics-service-trust issue in *Ethical Conduct and the Professional's Dilemma: Choosing Between Service and Success*, New York: Quorum Books, 1991.

7. Judith Blau takes up the exclusive-qualification theme at several points in *Architects and Firms: A Sociological Perspective on Architectural Practice*, Cambridge: MIT Press, 1984.

8. "P/A Reader Poll: Ethics," *Progressive Architecture*, Feb. 1988, 15–17.

ETHICS AND ARCHITECTURAL PRACTICES

1. For example, see the Diane Ghirardo and Peter Eisenman exchange in *Progressive Architecture* (Nov. 1994), 70–73, (Feb. 1995), 88–91, (May 1995), 11 ff; or Jean Baudrillard commenting on the Beaubourg, "The Beaubourg-effect: Implosion and Deterrence," 210–217, and critiques of the Los Angeles Bonaventure Hotel in Baudrillard's "America," 220–221; and Fredric Jameson's "The Cultural Logic of Late-Capitalism," 242–246, in Neil Leach, ed., *Rethinking Architecture: A Reader in Cultural Theory*, London and New York: Routledge, 1997.

2. David Watkin, *Morality and Architecture*, Chicago: University of Chicago Press, 1977; Karsten Harries, *The Ethical Function of Architecture*, Cambridge: MIT Press, 1997; Philip Bess, "Ethics in Architecture," *Inland Architect* v37, n3, May/June 1993, 74–83; Bess, "The Architectural Community and the *Polis*: Thinking About Ends, Means, and Premises," in *Architecture, The City and Community: Proceedings of the East Central Association of Collegiate Schools of Architecture Conference, held at the University of Notre Dame, South Bend, IN, November 7 and 8, 1997*, 2–8; and William McDonough, "Design, Ecology, Ethics and the Making of Things," and "The Hanover Principles," in Kate Nesbitt, ed., *Theorizing a New Agenda for Architecture: An Anthology of Architectural Theory 1965–95*, New York: Princeton Architectural Press, c. 1996, 397–410.

3. For a recent addition to this tradition, see Thomas Dutton and Lian Hurst Mann, ed., *Reconstructing Architecture: Critical Discourses and Social Practices*, Minneapolis: University of Minnesota Press, 1996. For an introduction to continental socio-philosophical critique, see Neil Leach, ed., *Rethinking Architecture: A Reader in Cultural Theory*, London and New York: Routledge, 1997.

4. Marcus Vitruvius Pollio, *The Ten Books of Architecture*, (first century BC), trans. Morris Hicky Morgan, Harvard University Press, 1914; reprint, New York: Dover, 1960, 36, 41.

5. Leon Battista Alberti, *On the Art of Building in Ten Books* (1452), trans. Joseph Rykwert, Neil Leach, and Robert Tavernor, Cambridge: MIT Press, 1988, 61.

6. Andrea Palladio, *The Four Books of Architecture* (1570), trans. Isaac Ware, London: 1738, new intro. by Adolf K. Placzek; facsimile reprint of Ware ed., New York: Dover, 1965.

7. Hammurabi, King of Babylon, *The Hammurabi Code and the Sinaitic Legislation*, trans. Chilperic Edwards, 1904; reprint, Port Washington, NY and London: Kennikat Press, 1971.

8. For discussions of the hierarchy of the arts and the limitations on the capacity of architecture as a pure fine art see: Dalibor Veseley, "Architecture and the Question of Technology," in Louise Pelletier and Alberto Pérez-Gómez, ed., *Architecture, Ethics, and Technology*, Montreal and Kingston: McGill-Queens University Press, 1994, 37, a discussion of the *ars mechanicae, ars liberales*, the *scientiae*; which ascend from those associated with craft and making (architecture and engineering) to those of theoretical speculation (metaphysics); Gary Shapiro, "Hegel, G. W. F.," in David E. Cooper, ed., *A Companion to Aesthetics*, Joseph Margolis and Crispin S. Artwell, advising ed., *Blackwell Companion to Philosophy Series*, Cambridge, MA: Blackwell Publishers, Inc., 1992; pbk., 1995: "It should come as no surprise that he [Hegel] thinks of the individual arts as forming a hierarchy, rising from those most tied to constraints of the material world, (for instance, architecture) to those that are first, or most ideal, in this respect (for instance, poetry)," 186; see Georg W. F. Hegel, *Introductory Lectures on Aesthetics*, trans. Bernard Bosanquet (1886), ed. with an intro. and commentary by Michael Inwood, London: Penguin Books, 1993, 96; Immanuel Kant, excerpts from *Critique of the Faculty of Judgment* (1790), trans. J. H. Bernard with revisions by Lewis White Beck, in *Kant: Selections*, ed. Lewis White Beck, New York:

Scribner/Macmillan Book, 1988. Sections 10–17 discuss concepts of purpose in art (which is to possess "purposiveness [as art only] without purpose [intentionality, utility]," ideal beauty, and examples. Section 16: "But human beauty…, the beauty of a church or a house, presupposes a purpose which determines what the thing is to be, and consequently the concept of its perfection. It is therefore adherent beauty. Now as the combination of the pleasant (in sensation) with beauty, which properly is concerned only with form, is a hindrance to the purity of the judgment of taste, so also is its purity [as an art work] injured by the combination with beauty of the good (viz., that manifold which is good for the thing itself in accordance with its purpose)," 369. In Kant's view, the root of architecture's limitations as a pure fine art, *l'art pour l'art*, is its purposefulness, which is the source of its ethical content.

9. David Bell, "Inmediasres," 19–37, and Lucian Krukowski, "Art and Ethics in Kant, Hegel, and Schopenauer," 6–17, both in *Ethics and Architecture, Via* 10. Krukowski also references this hierarchy from material bound art to the higher arts of language as presented by Schopenauer in his article; Harries dismisses the *art pour l'art* position as a basis for architectural ethics in "The Ethical Function of Architecture," in *Descriptions*, ed. Don Ihde and Hugh J. Silverman, Albany: SUNY Press, 1985: "From the aesthetic approach, architecture can claim the dignity of the other arts only to the extent that it liberates itself from building and becomes absolute. But for such an architecture we have no use," 132.

10. David Watkin, op. cit., Note 2; and Karsten Harries, op. cit., Note 2, Chapters 2–5.

11. Horatio Greenough, *Form and Function: Remarks on Art, Design and Architecture*, ed. Harold A. Small, intro. by Erle Loran, Berkeley: University of California Press, 1947, 1966.

12. Robert Twombly addresses this in *Power and Style: A Critique of Twentieth-Century Architecture in the United States*, New York: Hill and Wang, 1996, 52–88. The Museum of Modern Art (MOMA) exhibition publication coined the phrase "International Style" and applied it to the modern architecture that had emerged in Europe 1918–1930. Colin Rowe explores modernism's program and style in *The Architecture of Good Intentions: Towards A Possible Retrospect*, New York and London: Academy Editions, 1994.

13. Joining Ulrich Conrads's classic, *Programs and Manifestoes on 20th-Century Architecture*, trans. Michael Bullock, Cambridge: MIT Press, c. 1970, are four new compendiums of short texts that provide fertile ground for initial exploration of architecture's moral intents through its ideologies and rhetoric: Joan Ockman, ed., *Architecture Culture 1943–1968: A Documentary Anthology*, with the collaboration of E. Eigen, *A Columbia Book of Architecture*, New York: Rizzoli, 1993; Kate Nesbitt, ed., *Theorizing a New Agenda for Architecture: An Anthology of Architectural Theory 1965–1995*, New York: Princeton Architectural Press, c. 1996; Jay Stein and Kent Spreckelmeyer, ed., *Classic Readings in Architecture*, New York: WCB/McGraw Hill, c. 1999; and *Architecture Theory Since 1968*, ed. K. Michael Hays, *A Columbia Book of Architecture*, Cambridge: MIT Press, 1998.

ETHICAL REASONING

1. a) Most texts on ethics provide guidelines or recommended processes with which to consider ethical problems. In *Ethics in Engineering Practice and Research*, Cambridge University Press, 1998, Caroline Whitbeck uses engineering problem-solving design methods as a model for examining ethical questions: research of the questions, analysis of the situation, proposal generation, evaluation, and choice. Anthony Weston in *A Practical Companion to Ethics*, New York: Oxford University Press, 1997, proposes lateral thinking, or thinking outside the box, and problem-solving paradigms borrowing heavily on Edward DeBono's work. Gregory R. Beabout and Daryl J. Wennemann, *Applied Professional Ethics: A Developmental Approach for Use with Case Studies*, Lanham, MD: University of America Press, 1994, provide another concise model based upon writing cases.

b) The definition of the condition for deliberation and decision-making draws heavily from Jürgen Habermas, *Moral Consciousness and Communicative Action*, trans. Christian Lenhardt and Shierry W. Nicholsen, intro. Thomas McCarthy, Cambridge: MIT Press, 1990, 65, 92. These are discussed in an article by J. Donald Moon, "Practical Discourse and Communicative Ethics," in *The Cambridge Companion to Habermas*, ed. Stephen K. White, Cambridge University Press, 1995, 143 ff.

PART II: UNDERSTANDING

Introduction

1. See the following references for a discussion of prestige, trust, the professional, and professionalism. Julia Thomas, "Ethics and Professionalism: The Integrated Way," *Vital Speech of the Day*, 49, March 1983. Russell Ellis and Dana Cuff, *Architect's People*, New York: Oxford: University Press, 1989, 193–194. Andy Pressman, AIA, *Professional Practice 101: A Compendium of Business and Management Strategies in Architecture*, New York: John Wiley & Sons, 1997, 45–75.

A Closer Look at Being an Architect

1. Dana Cuff, *Architecture: The Story of Practice*, Cambridge, MA: The MIT Press, 1991, 26.
2. Ibid.
3. Ibid., p. 27
4. Dana Cuff, Ph.D., "The Architecture Profession 1.11," *The Architect's Handbook of Professional Practice*, Volume 1, Washington, DC: The American Institute of Architects Press, 1994, 2.
5. Ibid., p. 3.
6. Dana Cuff, *Architecture: The Story of Practice*, Cambridge, MA: The MIT Press, 1991, 31.
7. Elizabeth A. Davis, Esq., "Professional Ethics 1.42," *The Architect's Handbook of Professional Practice*, Volume 1, Washington, DC: The American Institute of Architects Press, 1994, 94.
8. James R. Franklin, FAIA, *Toward a Standard of Care*, Washington, DC: The American Institute of Architects/Victor O. Schinnerer and Company, Inc., 1990, 1–14.
9. For a further discussion of internship requirements, see The History of the NCARB, Washington, DC: National Council of Architectural Registration Boards, July, 1994, 11–12; "Intern Development Program," *The Architect's Handbook of Professional Practice*, Volume I, Washington DC: The American Institute of Architects Press, 1994, 58–59; and "Definitions," *The Architect's Handbook of Professional Practice*, Volume I, Washington DC: The American Institute of Architects Press, 1994, Definitions 11.
10. *The History of NCARB*, Washington, DC: National Council of Architectural Registration Boards, July, 1994, 11. See also individual state-board registration requirements.
11. Ibid., pp. 11–12.
12. Ibid., p. 11.
13. R. Schluntz and G. Gebert, *Tracking Study of Architectural Graduates for the Years 1967, 1972, and 1977: Final Report*, Washington DC: Association of Collegiate Schools of Architecture, 1980.
14. *The History of NCARB*, Washington, DC: National Council of Architectural Registration Boards, July 1994, 1.
15. Ibid., p. 7.
16. Ibid., p. 1.
17. Ibid., p. 2.
18. Elizabeth A. Davis, Esq., "Professional Ethics 1.42," *The Architect's Handbook of Professional Practice*, Volume 1, Washington, DC: The American Institute of Architects Press, 1994, 93–108.
19. Patrick Sullivan's personal research made possible by a sabbatical leave funded by California State Polytechnic University, Pomona, 1989–1990.
20. Ibid. See also Patrick M. Sullivan, Barry Wasserman, and Thomas Payette, "Awareness/Understanding/Choices: A Course Dealing with Ethics and the Profession in an Ever Changing World," Washington, DC: Institute Scholars Program of The American Institute of Architects, 1989.
21. Matt Gryta, "Buffalo Architects Protest Competition from Students," *Architectural Record*, 165, April 1979, 36.
22. Ibid.
23. William Hickman, "Mardirosian Suit Is Settled by the AIA and Architects," *Architectural Record*, 169, October 1981, 35.
24. Ibid.
25. The Mardirosian case concerned work performed by both architects on the National Visitors' Center, a part of the major modification of Washington's Union Railroad Station. The dispute over work at the Union Railroad Station arose after the government took over the job from the railroads that had been authorized to start it. The railroads hired Auerbach, but the government subsequently retained Mardirosian, and Auerbach's contract was terminated. Auerbach, the plaintiff, charged in 1975 that Mardirosian "had undertaken, or is in the process of negotiating for,

certain architectural and engineering responsibilities" at the Visitors' Center for which Auerbach already had a contract, a situation that violated Standard No. 9 of the AIA Code of Ethics. The AIA then suspended Mardirosian, a typical but severe action.

The violated standard stated that "an architect shall not attempt to obtain, offer to undertake, or accept a commission for which the architect knows another legally qualified individual or firm has been selected or employed, until the architect has evidence that the latter's agreement has been terminated and the architect gives the latter written notice that the architect is so doing."

In his opinion, Judge Sirica said that although the activities of professional societies have long been thought "deserving of special treatment under the antitrust laws, it is now clear that an anti-competitive practice cannot be justified if it is unreasonable." (William Hickman, "Mardirosian Suit Is Settled by the AIA and Architects," *Architectural Record*, 169, October, 1981, 35.)

Two years later, the case was resolved with an out-of-court settlement equal to $700,000. The following account from the *Architectural Record* summarized the final events:

The case was complicated and subject to a variety of interpretations. But essentially under a 1968 Act of Congress, the Department of the Interior's Park Service was authorized to begin refurbishing the historic Union Station in Washington as a national visitor's center. Initially, Congress gave the government the right to build the center, and to construct a new railroad passenger station and some parking facilities, in conjunction with a consortium of railroads that owned the center. (Hickman, 1981).

Under a later Act of Congress, the Park Service was given direct responsibility for the project. By then, Auerbach had been selected as the designer and Mardirosian had been chosen as the Park Service's special consultant to oversee the work of the designer and the contractor.

Later, Auerbach's contract was terminated "for the convenience of the owner," and he was paid $700,000. The contract was then awarded to Mardirosian's firm.

"I was never notified," said Auerbach, claiming that Mardirosian did not follow the steps prescribed in the AIA's Code of Ethics when he took over the job. Mardirosian was suspended on the basis of Auerbach's complaint to the AIA. (Hickman, 1981).

26. Elizabeth A. Davis, Esq., "Professional Ethics 1.42," *The Architect's Handbook of Professional Practice*, Volume 1, Washington, DC: The American Institute of Architects Press, 1994, 95.

27. The American Institute of Architects Office of Research & Planning, *Architecture Factbook: Industry Statistics*, Washington, DC: The American Institute of Architects, 1992, 41.

28. Andy Pressman, AIA, *Professional Practice 101: A Compendium of Business and Management Strategies in Architecture*, New York: John Wiley & Sons, 1997, 287–295.

29. Ibid.

30. Ibid., p. 291.

31. Ibid., p. 292.

32. *Career Options: Opportunities Through Architecture*, Washington, DC: American Institute of Architecture Students, 1993.

33. Robert Gutman, *Architectural Practice: A Critical View*, Princeton, NJ: Princeton Architectural Press, 1988, 10.

34. Ibid.

35. Ibid.

36. Ibid.

37. "At Press Time," *Building Design and Construction*, 26, December 1985, 5.

38. Robert Gutman, *Architectural Practice: A Critical View*, Princeton, NJ: Princeton Architectural Press, 1988, 11.

39. Ibid., p. 12.

40. Ibid.

41. John P. Kotter, "What Leaders Really Do," *Harvard Business Review*, May–June 1990, 68, 103–111.

42. For further discussion related to leadership principles, review Elizabeth A. Davis, Esq., "Professional Ethics 1.42," *The Architect's Handbook of Professional Practice*, Volume 1, Washington, DC: The American Institute of Architects Press, 1994, 95–108.

43. Kenneth R. Weiss, "A Time to Teach Character," *Los Angeles Times*, April 10, 1998, Sec. B, p. 1.

44. Ibid.

45. Ernest L. Boyer and Lee D. Mitgang, *Building Community: A New Future for Architecture Education and Practice*, Princeton, NJ: The Carnegie Foundation for the Advancement of Teaching, 1996.

46. Ibid.

47. Vaclav Havel, *The Art of the Impossible*, New York: Alfred A. Knopf, 1997, 8.

48. *The History of NCARB*, Washington, DC: National Council of Architectural Registration Boards, July, 1994, 14.

49. Ibid.

50. For information regarding specific ethical situations reviewed by the Judicial Council, see "Code of Ethics and Professional Conduct Advisory Opinion," National Judicial Council, The American Institute of Architects, Washington, DC.

A Closer Look at Making Architecture

1. The American Institute of Architects, "AIA Document B141–1997, Standard Form of Agreement Between Owner and Architect with Standard Form of Architect's Services," Washington, DC: The American Institute of Architects, 1997, and "AIA Document B163–1993, Standard Form of Agreement Between the Owner and Architect with Descriptions of Designated Services and Terms and Conditions," Washington, DC: The American Institute of Architects, 1993.

2. Dana Cuff, *Architecture: The Story of Practice*, Cambridge, MA: The MIT Press, 1991, 62.

3. See additional services discussion: Andy Pressman, AIA, *Professional Practice 101: A Compendium of Business and Management Strategies in Architecture*, New York: John Wiley & Sons, 1997; David Haviland, Hon. AIA, ed., *The Architect's Handbook of Professional Practice*, Washington, DC: The American Institute of Architects Press, 1994; and Dana Cuff, *Architecture: The Story of Practice*, Cambridge, MA: The MIT Press, 1991.

4. For discussion of project-delivery methods, see David Haviland, Hon. AIA, ed., *The Architect's Handbook of Professional Practice*, Washington, DC: The American Institute of Architects Press, 1994. Also see The American Institute of Architects, "AIA Document B163–1993, Standard Form of Agreement Between the Owner and Architect with Descriptions of Designated Services and Terms and Conditions," Washington, DC: The American Institute of Architects, 1993.

5. Ibid.

6. For further discussion and definitions, see: David Haviland, Hon. AIA, ed., *The Architect's Handbook of Professional Practice*, Washington, DC: The American Institute of Architects Press, 1994.

7. Thomas Fisher, "Good Firms Bad Firms," *Progressive Architecture*, 76, August, 1995, 57–61, 104.

8. The American Institute of Architects, *1997 AIA Firm Survey Report*, Washington, DC: The American Institute of Architects, 1997.

9. Richard W. Hobbs, FAIA, "*Blur* Revisited and the Gehry Revelation," *AIArchitect*, 6, July, 1999, 14.

10. "News reports: The Architects Collaborative wins Johns-Manville headquarters competition," *Architectural Record*, 153, June 1973, 34.

11. "Buildings in the news: A masterful design for Johns-Manville headquarters grew from the natural beauty of its 10,000-acre site," *Architectural Record*, 153, June, 1973, 46–47

12. Mildred Schmertz, "The Johns-Manville World Headquarters Building for J-M and TAC," *Architectural Record*, 162, September, 1977, 99.

13. S. W. Gellerman, "Why 'Good' Managers Make Bad Ethical Choices," *Harvard Business Review*, July–August, 1986, 85–90.

14. Ibid.

15. Ibid.

16. Elizabeth A. Davis, Esq., "Professional Ethics 1.42," *The Architect's Handbook of Professional Practice*, Volume 1, Washington, DC: The American Institute of Architects Press, 1994, 99.

17. S. W. Gellerman, "Why 'Good' Managers Make Bad Ethical Choices," *Harvard Business Review*, July–August, 1986, 88.

18. Ibid., p. 89.

19. Elizabeth A. Davis, Esq., "Professional Ethics 1.42," *The Architect's Handbook of Professional Practice*, Volume 1, Washington, DC: The American Institute of Architects Press, 1994, 99.

20. James R. Franklin, FAIA, *Toward a Standard of Care*, Washington, DC: The American Institute of Architects/Victor O. Schinnerer and Company, Inc., 1990, 1–14; and *Lessons In Professional Liability: A Notebook for Design Professionals*, Monterey, CA: Design Professionals Insurance Company, 1988, 18, 41.

21. James R. Franklin, FAIA, *Toward a Standard of Care*, Washington, DC: The American Institute of Architects/Victor O. Schinnerer and Company, Inc., 1990, 6.

22. *Lessons In Professional Liability: A Notebook for Design Professionals*, Monterey, CA: Design Professionals Insurance Company, 1988, 1–4.

23. James R. Franklin, FAIA, *Toward a Standard of Care*, Washington, DC: The American Institute of Architects/Victor O. Schinnerer and Company, Inc., 1990, 5.

24. *Understanding and Managing Risk: A Guide and Voluntary Education Program for Design Professionals*, Chevy Chase, MD: Victor O. Schinnerer & Company, Inc., 1998, 1.3–5.

25. For more information regarding a discussion of civil law, see Nancy J. White, "River of Law II: Duty of Architects to Third Parties," *Journal of Architectural Education*, 52, February, 1999, 163.

26. *Understanding and Managing Risk: A Guide and Voluntary Education Program for Design Professionals*, Chevy Chase, MD: Victor O. Schinnerer & Company, Inc., 1998, 1–4.

27. James R. Franklin, FAIA, *Toward a Standard of Care*, Washington, DC: The American Institute of Architects/Victor O. Schinnerer and Company, Inc., 1990, 9.

28. *Lessons In Professional Liability: A Notebook for Design Professionals*, Monterey, CA: Design Professionals Insurance Company, 1988, 18–19.

29. The American Institute of Architects, "AIA Document B141–1997, Standard Form of Agreement Between Owner and Architect with Standard Form of Architect's Services," Washington, DC: The American Institute of Architects, 1997; and The American Institute of Architects, "AIA Document B163–1993, Standard Form of Agreement Between the Owner and Architect with Descriptions of Designated Services and Terms and Conditions," Washington, DC: The American Institute of Architects, 1993.

30. James R. Franklin, FAIA, *Toward a Standard of Care*, Washington, DC: The American Institute of Architects/Victor O. Schinnerer and Company, Inc., 1990, 9–14.

31. See Russell Ellis and Dana Cuff, ed., *Architect's People*, New York: Oxford University Press, 1989, 64–65; and Judith R. Blau, *Architects and Firms: A Sociological Perspective on Architectural Practice*, Cambridge, MA: The MIT Press, 1984, 29.

32. Dana Cuff, *Architecture: The Story of Practice*, Cambridge, MA: The MIT Press, 1991, 20.

33. Ibid.

34. Elizabeth A. Davis, Esq., "Professional Ethics 1.42," *The Architect's Handbook of Professional Practice*, Volume 1, Washington, DC: The American Institute of Architects Press, 1994, 99.

35. Ibid.

36. See previous discussion on nontraditional jobs, in "Alternative Roles," Part II: Understanding.

37. *Lessons In Professional Liability: A Notebook for Design Professionals*, Monterey, CA: Design Professionals Insurance Company, 1988, 8, 64, 67.

38. Judith R. Blau, *Architects and Firms: A Sociological Perspective on Architectural Practice*, Cambridge, MA: The MIT Press, 1984, 143.

39. Bill Risebero, *Modern Architecture and Design: An Alternative History*, Cambridge, MA: The MIT Press, 1985, 11.

40. Ava J. Abramovitz, "Speak Out," *Architectural Record*, 186, November, 1998, 24–26.

41. Barry B. LePatner, "Listen Up or Lose the Client," *Architecture*, February, 1996, 85, 153–155.

42. Ibid.

43. Robert Gutman, *Architectural Practice: A Critical View*, Princeton, NJ: Princeton Architectural Press, 1988, 13.

44. Ibid.

45. Ibid.

46. Ava J. Abramovitz, "Speak Out," *Architectural Record*, 186, November, 1998, 24–26.

47. Barry B. LePatner, "Listen Up or Lose the Client," *Architecture*, February, 1996, 85, 153 155.

WORKS CITED
IN THE NOTES

Abramovitz, Ava J., "Speak Out," *Architectural Record*, 186, November, 1998.

Alberti, Leon Battista, *On the Art of Building in Ten Books*, (1452), trans. Joseph Rykwert, Neil Leach, Robert Tavernor, Cambridge: MIT Press, 1988.

American Heritage Dictionary of the English Language, The, 3rd. ed. Boston: Houghton Mifflin Co., 1992, *(AHD)*.

American Institute of Architects, Office of Research and Planning. *Architecture Factbook: Industry Statistics*, 1992 Edition, Washington, DC: The American Institute of Architects.

American Institute of Architects. *Architecture Factbook: Industry Statistics*, 1994 Edition, Washing-ton, DC: American Institute of Architects.

American Institute of Architects. *1997 AIA Firm Survey Report*, Washington, DC: The American Institute of Architects, 1997.

American Institute of Architects. *1997 Code of Ethics and Professional Conduct*, Washington, DC: American Institute of Architects, 1997.

American Institute of Architects. *AIA Document B141–1997, Standard Form of Agreement Between Owner and Architect with Standard Form of Architect's Services*. Washington, DC: The American Institute of Architects, 1997.

American Institute of Architects. *AIA Document B163–1993, Standard Form of Agreement Between the Owner and Architect with Descriptions of Designated Services and Terms and Conditions*. Washington, DC: The American Institute of Architects, 1993.

American Institute of Architecture Students. *Career Options: Opportunities Through Architecture*. Washington, DC: The American Institute of Architecture Students, 1993.

Aristotle. *Nicomachean Ethics* (fourth century BC), trans. J. E. C. Weldon (1892); reprinted in part in *Ethics and the Search for Values*, ed. Navia and Kelly. Buffalo: Prometheus Press, 1980.

Aristotle. *Nicomachean Ethics* (fourth century BC), trans. Terrence Irwin. Indianapolis: Hackett Publishing Company, 1985.

Aristotle. *Politics* (fourth century BC), Loeb ed., is referenced by Daryl Koehn, *The Ground of Professional Ethics*. London and New York: Routledge, 1994.

"At Press Time." *Building Design and Construction*, 26, December, 1985.

Baudrillard, Jean. "The Beaubourg-effect: Implosion and Deterrence," and "America." In Neil Leach, ed. *Rethinking Architecture: A Reader in Cultural Theory*. London and New York: Routledge, 1997.

Bell, David, "Inmediasres," *Via* 10.

Bess, Philip. "Ethics in Architecture," *Inland Architect*, 37, n3, May/June 1993,.

Bess, Philip. "The Architectural Community and the *Polis:* Thinking About Ends, Means, and Premises," in *Architecture, The City and Community: Proceedings of the East Central Association of Collegiate Schools of Architecture Conference, held at the University of Notre Dame, South Bend, November* 7 and 8, 1997.

Betsky, Aaron. "Libeskind Builds," *Architecture*, 87, n9, September, 1998.

Blau, Judith. *Architects and Firms: A Sociological Perspective on Architectural Practice*. Cambridge: MIT Press, 1984.

Botta, Mario. *The Ethics of Building*. trans. Stephen Thorne. Basel: Birkhäuser Verlag, 1997.

Boyer, Ernest L., and Lee D. Mitgang. *Building Community: A New Future for Architecture Education and Practice*. Princeton: The Carnegie Foundation for the Advancement of Teaching, c. 1996.

"Buildings in the news: A masterful design for Johns-Manville headquarters grew from the natural beauty of its 10,000-acre site." *Architectural Record*. 153, June, 1973.

Churchill, Winston. *Winston Churchill: His Complete Speeches, 1897–1963.* 8 Volumes, ed. Robert Rhodes James. New York and London: Chelsea House and R. R. Bowker, 1974.

Cole, Eve Browning, and Susan Coultrap-McQuin, ed. *Explorations in Feminist Ethics.* Bloomington: Indiana University Press, c. 1992.

Congress for the New Urbanism. *Charter of the New Urbanism.* San Francisco: Congress for the New Urbanism, 1996.

Cuff, Dana. *Architecture: The Story of Practice.* Cambridge, MA: The MIT Press, 1991.

Cuff, Dana, Ph.D. "The Architecture Profession 1.11." *The Architect's Handbook of Professional Practice*, Volume 1, ed. David Haviland. Washington DC: The American Institute of Architects Press, 1994.

Davis, Elizabeth A., Esq. "Professional Ethics 1.42." *The Architect's Handbook of Professional Practice*, Volume 1, ed. David Haviland. Washington, DC: The American Institute of Architects Press, 1994.

Design Professionals Insurance Company. *Lessons In Professional Liability: A Notebook for Design Professionals.* Monterey, CA: Design Professionals Insurance Company, 1988.

Dovey, Kim. "Architectural Ethics: A Dozen Dilemmas." *Practices*, Journal of the Center for the Study of the Practice of Architecture, University of Cincinnati College of Design, Architecture, Art and Planning, 2, Spring, 1993.

Dutton and Mann. "Introduction: Modernism, Postmodernism, and Architecture's Social Project." In Thomas A. Dutton and Lian Hurst Mann, ed., *Reconstructing Architecture: Critical Discourses and Social Practices.* Minneapolis: University of Minnesota Press, 1996.

Eisenman, Peter. "Eisenman (and Company) Respond." *Progressive Architecture.* February, 1995.

Ellis, Russell, and Dana Cuff, ed. *Architect's People.* New York: Oxford University Press, 1989.

Fisher, Thomas, "Good Firms, Bad Firms." *Progressive Architecture.* 76, August 1995.

Franklin, James, R., FAIA. *Toward a Standard of Care*, Washington, DC: The American Institute of Architects/Victor O. Schinnerer and Company, Inc., 1990.

Frazer, Elizabeth, Jennifer Hornsby, and Sabina Lovibond, ed. *Ethics: A Feminist Reader.* Cambridge, MA: Blackwell, c. 1992.

Gellerman, S. W. "Why 'Good' Managers Make Bad Ethical Choices." *Harvard Business Review*, July–August, 1986.

Ghirardo, Diane. "Eisenman's Bogus Avant-Garde." *Progressive Architecture*, November, 1994.

Ghirardo, Diane. "Ghirardo Responds to Eisenman and Company." *Progressive Architecture*, May 1995.

Gravagnuolo, Benedetto. "Towards an Architecture of the New Millennium." In Mario Botta, *Ethics of Building*, trans. Stephen Thorne. Basel: Birkhäuser Verlag, 1997.

Greenough, Horatio. *Form and Function: Remarks on Art, Design and Architecture*, ed. Harold A. Small, intro. by Erle Loran. Berkeley: University of California Press, 1947, 1966.

Gryta, Matt. "Buffalo Architects Protest Competition from Students." *Architectural Record*, 165, April, 1979, 36.

Gutman, Robert. *Architectural Practice: A Critical View.* Princeton, NJ: Princeton Architectural Press, 1988.

Habermas, Jürgen. *Moral Consciousness and Communicative Action*, trans. Christian Lenhardt and Shierry W. Nicholsen, intro. by Thomas McCarthy. Cambridge: MIT Press, 1990.

Hammurabi, King of Babylon. *The Hammurabi Code and the Sinaitic Legislation*, trans. Chilperic Edwards, 1904; reprint: Port Washington, NY, and London: Kennikat Press, 1971.

Harries, Karsten. "The Ethical Function of Architecture," in *Descriptions*, ed. Don Ihde and Hugh J. Silverman. Albany: SUNY Press, 1985.

Harries, Karsten. *The Ethical Function of Architecture.* Cambridge: MIT, 1997.

Havel, Vaclav. *The Art of the Impossible.* New York: Alfred A. Knopf, 1997.

Hegel, Georg W. F. *Introductory Lectures on Aesthetics.* trans. Bernard Bosanquet (1886), ed., with an intro. and commentary by Michael Inwood. London: Penguin Books, 1993.

Heidegger, Martin. "Building Dwelling Thinking." trans. Albert Hofstadter, in *Basic Writings*, 2nd, revised and expanded edition, ed. David Farrell Krell. San Francisco: HarperSanFrancisco, 1993.

Hickman, William. "Mardirosian Suit is Settled by the AIA and Architects." *Architectural Record*, 169, October, 1981.

Hobbs, Richard W., FAIA. "*Blur* Revisited and the Gehry Revelation." *AIArchitect*, 6, July, 1999.

Hubbard, Bill, Jr. *A Theory for Practice: Architecture in Three Discourses*. Cambridge: MIT Press, 1995.

Jameson, Fredric. "The Cultural Logic of Late-Capitalism," in Neil Leach, ed. *Rethinking Architecture: A Reader in Cultural Theory*. London and New York: Routledge, 1997.

Kant, Immanuel. *Critique of the Faculty of Judgment* (1790), trans. J. H. Bernard (London, 1892) with revisions by Lewis White Beck, excerpts in *Kant: Selections*, ed. Lewis White Beck. New York: Scribner/Macmillan Book, 1988.

Kant, Immanuel. *Grounding for the Metaphysics of Morals* (1785), trans. James W. Ellington, 3rd. ed. Indianapolis: Hackett Publishing, c. 1981, 1992.

Kostof, Spiro. "The Architect in the Middle Ages, East and West," in *The Architect*, ed. Spiro Kostof. New York: Oxford, 1977.

Kotter, John P. "What Leaders Really Do." *Harvard Business Review*, May–June, 1990.

Krukowski, Lucian "Art and Ethics in Kant, Hegel, and Schopenauer." *Via* 10.

Kymlicka, Will. "The Social Contract Tradition," in Peter Singer, ed. *A Companion to Ethics, Blackwell Companions to Philosophy*. Cambridge, MA: Blackwell, c.1991, 1993.

Larson, Magali Sarfatti. *Behind the Postmodern Façade: Architectural Change in late Twentieth-Century America*. Berkeley: University of California Press, 1993, pbk. 1995.

Larson, Magali Sarfatti. *The Rise of Professionalism*. Berkeley: University of California Press, 1977.

LePatner, Barry B. "Listen Up or Lose the Client." *Architecture* February, 1996.

MacIntyre, Alasdair. *A Short History of Ethics*. New York: Collier Books, Macmillan Publishing, 1966.

MacIntyre, Alasdair. *After Virtue: A Study in Moral Philosophy*. London: Duckworth, 1981.

Mackie, John L. *Ethics: Inventing Right and Wrong*. Pelican Books, 1977; reprint, New York: Penguin, pbk., 1990.

McDonough, William "Design, Ecology, Ethics and the Making of Things." and "The Hanover Principles," in Kate Nesbitt, ed. *Theorizing a New Agenda for Architecture: An Anthology of Architectural Theory 1965-95*. New York: Princeton Architectural Press, c. 1996.

McDowell, Banks. *Ethical Conduct and the Professional's Dilemma: Choosing Between Service and Success*. New York: Quorum Books, 1991.

Moon, J. Donald. "Practical Discourse and Communicative Ethics," in the *Cambridge Companion to Habermas*, ed. Stephen K. White. Cambridge University Press, 1995.

Moore, George Edward. *Principia Ethica* (1903). Cambridge: Cambridge University Press, 1959.

National Council of Registration Boards. *The History of NCARB*. Washington, DC: National Council of Architectural Registration Boards, July. 1994.

New Shorter Oxford English Dictionary, The. Oxford: Clarendon Press, 1993. *(SOED)*

"News reports: The Architects Collaborative Wins Johns-Manville Headquarters Competition." *Architectural Record*, 153, June, 1973.

Norberg-Schulz, Christian. *Existence, Space and Architecture*, New York: Praeger, 1971.

Norberg-Schulz, Christian. *Genius Loci: Towards a Phenomenology of Architecture*. New York: Rizzoli, 1979.

Norberg-Schulz, Christian. *Intentions in Architecture*. Cambridge: MIT Press, 1965.

Oxford English Dictionary and Supplements, The, Compact Edition. Oxford University Press, V. I and II, 1971; V. III, 1987. *(OED)*.

"P/A Reader Poll: Ethics." *Progressive Architecture*, February, 1988, 15–17.

Palladio, Andrea. *The Four Books of Architecture*. (1570). Trans. Isaac Ware, 1738; new intro. by Adolf K. Placzek; facsimile reprint, New York: Dover, 1965.

Pérez-Gómez, Alberto. "Introduction," in Louise Pelletier, and Alberto Pérez-Gómez, ed. *Architecture, Ethics, and Technology*. Montreal and Kingston: McGill-Queens University Press, 1994.

Plato. "The Apology" (fourth century BC) in *The Works of Plato*, trans. Benjamin Jowett, 3rd. ed. (Simon & Schuster, 1928; Meta Markel, 1956), ed. Irwin Edman. New York: The Modern Library.

Plato. *The Republic of Plato* (fourth century BC), trans. with an intro. by Francis MacDonald Cornford. New York and London: Oxford University Press, 1945; reprint, 1968.

Pressman, Andy, AIA. *Professional Practice 101: A Compendium of Business and Management Strategies in Architecture*. New York: John Wiley & Sons, 1997.

Random House Dictionary of the English Language, The, Second Edition, Unabridged. New York: Random House, 1987, *(RHD)*.

Rawls, John. *A Theory of Justice*. Cambridge: Belknap Press of Harvard University Press, 1981.

Risebero, Bill. *Modern Architecture and Design: An Alternative History*. Cambridge, MA: The MIT Press, 1985.

Rowe, Colin. *The Architecture of Good Intentions: Towards A Possible Retrospect*. New York/London: Academy Editions, 1994.

Schluntz, R., and G. Gebert. *Tracking Study of Architectural Graduates for the Years 1967, 1972, and 1977: Final Report*. Washington, DC: Association of Collegiate Schools of Architecture, 1980.

Schmertz, Mildred. "The Johns-Manville World Headquarters Building for J-M and TAC." *Architectural Record*, 162, September, 1977.

Shapiro, Gary. "Hegel, G. W. F.." in David E. Cooper, ed. *A Companion to Aesthetics*. Joseph Margolis and Crispin S. Artwell, advising ed., *Blackwell Companion to Philosophy Series*. Cambridge, MA: Blackwell, 1992; pbk., 1995.

Taylor, C. C. W. "Virtue." *The Oxford Companion to Philosophy*, Ted Honderich, ed., Oxford and New York: Oxford University Press, 1995.

Twombly, Robert. *Power and Style: A Critique of Twentieth-Century Architecture in the United States*. New York: Hill and Wang, 1996.

Veseley, Dalibor. "Architecture and the Question of Technology," in Louise Pelletier and Alberto Pérez-Gómez, ed. *Architecture, Ethics, and Technology*. Montreal and Kingston: McGill-Queens University Press, 1994.

Victor O. Schinnerer and Company. *Understanding and Managing Risk: A Guide and Voluntary Education Program for Design Professionals*. Chevy Chase, MD: Victor O. Schinnerer and Company, Inc., 1998.

Vitruvius. *The Ten Books of Architecture* (first century BC), trans. Morris Hicky Morgan. Harvard University Press, 1914; reprint, New York: Dover, 1960.

Watkin, David. *Morality and Architecture*. Chicago: University of Chicago Press, 1977.

Webster's New Collegiate Dictionary. Springfield, MA: Merriam-Webster. *(WNC)*.

Webster's New World Dictionary of the American Language: College Edition, Cleveland and New York: World Publishing Co., 1964. *(NWD/C)*.

Weiss, Kenneth R. "A Time to Teach Character." *Los Angeles Times*, April 10, 1998.

WORKS RECOMMENDED FOR FURTHER STUDY

Throughout the text, in addition to the works directly quoted and cited, a number of Notes recommended books and articles for further reading for in-depth consideration of various topics. Other books have been cross-referenced to explain concepts being discussed. The list of recommended works has been consolidated here with their explanatory notes.

BASIC INTRODUCTIONS TO ETHICS:

Almond, Brenda. *Exploring Ethics: A Traveller's Tale*. Malden, MA: Blackwell Publishers, 1998. A longer introduction than Pojman or Rachels, which presents basic ethical themes and additional themes of free will, autonomy, diversity, and justice within a lively narrative dialogue.

Cavalier, Robert J., James Guinlock, and James P. Sterba, ed. *Ethics in the History of Western Philosophy*. New York: St. Martin's Press, c. 1989. Addresses central figures (Plato, Aristotle, Augustine, Aquinas, Hume, Kant, Mill, Hegel, Nietzsche, Sartre, and Rawls) and their ethical thought.

MacIntyre, Alasdair. *A Short History of Ethics: A history of moral philosophy from the Homeric Age to the twentieth century*. New York: Collier Books, Macmillan Publishing, c. 1966. The best brief introduction to the course of Western ethical thought through time.

Norman, Richard. *The Moral Philosophers: An Introduction to Ethics*. 2nd ed. New York: Oxford University Press, 1998. Includes concise explanative essays and bibliographies of the primary works of the central figures in Western ethics.

Pojman, Louis P. *Ethics: Discovering Right and Wrong*. 2nd ed. Belmont, CA: Wadsworth Publishing Company, 1994. A thorough introduction to ethical concepts that cover ethical reasoning, relativism, egoism, Utility and other consequentialist theories, Kantian and other deontic theories, virtue ethics, and social-contract theory.

Rachels, James. *The Elements of Moral Philosophy*, 2nd ed. New York: McGraw-Hill, Inc., 1993. An alternative to Pojman; another thorough introduction to ethical concepts.

Robinson, Dave, and Chris Garrett. *Introducing Ethics*, ed. Richard Appignanesi. New York: Totem Books, c. 1996. A lively, brief, illustrated introduction to the major moral questions, disputes, and philosophers, with good coverage of late-twentieth-century applied ethics problems and Continental philosophers.

Singer, Peter, ed. *A Companion to Ethics, Blackwell Companions to Philosophy*. Cambridge, MA: Blackwell, c.1991, 1993. The best single source. It expands upon the themes in the already mentioned works with sections on global ethical traditions; religious ethical traditions; contemporary applied ethics concerns such as poverty, euthanasia, and environmentalism; and critiques of the Western traditions such as those launched by Marxism and feminism.

Trusted, Jennifer. *Moral Principles and Social Values*. London: Routledge and Kegan Paul, 1987. Includes judgments, facts, values, the law, politics, and rights in her introductory work.

ON THE ETHICS OF LYING AND REPRESENTATION:

Bok, Sissela. *Lying: Moral Choices in Public and Private Life*. New York: Pantheon Books, 1978. Bok is arguably the premier contemporary ethicist who has examined the ethics of lying.

Bok, Sissela. *Secrets: On the Ethics of Concealment and Revelation*. New York: Pantheon Books, 1982.

VIRTUE THEORY:

Annas, Julia. *The Morality of Happiness*. New York and Oxford: Oxford University Press, 1993. Focuses on classic Greek ethics and virtue theory.

Foot, Philippa. *Virtues and Vices and Other Essays in Moral Philosophy*. Berkeley and Los Angeles: University of California Press, 1978.

Sommers, Christina and Fred, ed. *Vice and Virtue in Everyday Life: Introductory Readings in Ethics*, 3rd. ed. Fort Worth: Harcourt Brace Jovanovich College Publishers, 1993. Has an excellent selection of virtue theory based readings and selections from other ethical theories that pertain to virtue.

CONTRACT THEORY:

Avineri, Shlomo, and Avner de-Shalit, ed. *Communitarianism and Individualism, Oxford Readings in Politics and Government*. Oxford: Oxford University Press, 1992.

Daniels, Norman, ed. *Reading Rawls: Critical Studies on Rawls' 'A Theory of Justice,'* with new intro. Stanford: Stanford University Press, 1989; original publisher, New York: Basic Books, Inc., 1975.

Hobbes, Thomas. *Leviathan*, 1651.

Kymlicka, Will. *Contemporary Political Philosophy: An Introduction*. Oxford: Clarendon Press, 1990.

Rawls, John. *A Theory of Justice*. Cambridge, MA: Belknap Press of Harvard University, 1971.

Rawls, John. "Justice as Fairness," in *The Journal of Philosophy*, 1957.

Rousseau, Jean-Jacques. *The Social Contract*. 1762.

ETHICAL RELATIVISM:

Krausz, Michael, ed. *Relativism: Interpretation and Confrontation*. South Bend, IN: University of Notre Dame Press, 1989. A classic in the field.

Meiland, Jack W., and Michael Krausz. *Relativism: Cognitive and Moral*. South Bend: University of Notre Dame Press, 1982.

WOMEN IN ARCHITECTURE:

Agrest, Diana, Patricia Conway, and Leslie Kanes Weisman, ed. *The Sex of Architecture*. New York: Harry N. Abrams, Inc., c. 1996. A collection of twenty-four critical essays that "collectively express the power and diversity of women's views on architecture today."

Berkeley, Ellen Perry. *Architecture: A Place for Women*. Washington, DC: Smithsonian Institution, c. 1989. A pioneering collection regarding women in architecture that ranges from historical presentations, to speculations that anticipate the later collections noted here.

Colomina, Beatriz, ed. *Sexuality and Space, Princeton Papers on Architecture*. New York: Princeton Architectural Press, c. 1992.

Hughes, Francesca, ed. *The Architect: Reconstructing Her Practice*. Cambridge: MIT Press, c. 1996. A collection of essays by women in architecture; examination of gender, that is, "woman" as architectural practitioner, and the potential impact "on reconstruction of the orders that shape architectural production and consumption."

Kahn, Andrea, ed. *Drawing Building Text: Essays in Architectural Theory*. New York: Princeton Architectural Press, 1991. Contributions by Miriam Gusevich, Peggy Deamer, Jennifer Bloomer, Catherine Ingraham, Ann Bergren, Mary Pepshinski, Carol Burns, and Lois Nesbitt.

McCorquodale, Duncan, Katerina Rüedi, and Sarah Wigglesworth, ed. *Desiring Practices: Architecture Gender and the Interdisciplinary*. London: Black Dog Publishing Ltd., c. 1996. Conference proceedings.

Wilson, Elizabeth. *The Sphinx in the City: Urban Life, the Control of Disorder, and Women*. Berkeley: University of California Press, 1991.

CONTINENTAL PERSPECTIVES:

Cahoone, Lawrence E., ed. *From Modernism to Postmodernism: An Anthology*. Malden, MA: Blackwell, 1996. A substantial number of Continental contributions; includes architects Venturi and Jencks.

Cohen, Mitchell, and Nicole Freeman, ed. *Princeton Readings in Political Thought: Essential Texts Since Plato*. Princeton: Princeton University Press, 1996. Primarily drawn from classic texts and Anglo-American thought; Foucault, de Beauvoir, and Habermas of the twentieth-century Continental school.

Kearney, Richard, and Mara Rainwater, ed. *The Continental Philosophy Reader*. London and New York: Routledge, 1996. The title says it: an excellent selection; begins at Husserl and Saussure; good coverage of gender issues.

Leach, Neil, ed. *Rethinking Architecture: A Reader in Cultural Theory*. London and New York: Routledge, 1997. A collection of excellent twentieth-century articles drawn primarily from Continental thought regarding architecture and its cultural construction.

McNeill, William, and Karen S. Feldman, ed. *Continental Philosophy: An Anthology, Blackwell Philosophy Anthologies.* Malden, MA: Blackwell, 1998. Kant, Schopenhauer, and Hegel to contemporary.

Natoli, Joseph, and Linda Hutcheon, ed. *A Postmodern Reader.* Albany: SUNY Press, 1993. A substantial ratio of articles from twentieth-century Continental thought.

DEFINING THE PROFESSIONS AND PROFESSIONAL ETHICS:

Appelbaum, David, and Sarah Verone Lawton, ed. *Ethics and the Professions.* Englewood Cliffs, NJ: Prentice-Hall, c. 1990.

Bayles, Michael D. *Professional Ethics*, 2nd ed. Belmont, CA: Wadsworth Publishing, 1989.

Callahan, Joan C., ed. *Ethical Issues in Professional Life.* New York: Oxford University Press, 1988.

Hoffman, W. Michael, and Jennifer Mills Moore, ed. *Business Ethics: Readings and Cases in Corporate Morality.* New York: McGraw-Hill, 1984.

Kimball, Bruce A. *The "True Professional Ideal" in America: A History.* Cambridge, MA: Blackwell, 1992.

Koehn, Daryl. *The Ground of Professional Ethics.* London and New York: Routledge, 1994. Koehn, in particular, focuses on trust as a foundation of professionalism.

Kultgren, John. *Ethics and Professionalism.* Philadelphia: University of Pennsylvania Press, 1988. The various attributes of professions are succinctly presented in Kultgren, Part II: Models of Professions.

Larson, Magali Sarfatti. *Behind the Postmodern Facade: Architectural Change in Late Twentieth-Century America.* Berkeley: University of California Press, 1993; pbk. 1995.

Larson, Magali Sarfatti. *The Rise of Professionalism: A Sociological Analysis.* Berkeley: University of California Press, 1977. A classic study. Larson focuses on a Marxist economic model analysis of expertise for sale rather than service for all professions, including medicine and law. She does not include the clergy as a profession.

McDowell, Banks. *Ethical Conduct and the Professional's Dilemma: Choosing Between Service and Success.* New York: Quorum Books, 1991. Focuses on the economics-service-trust issue.

EXPLORATIONS OF "THE ARCHITECT" AND ARCHITECTURAL PRACTICE:

Cuff, Dana. *Architecture: The Study of Practice.* Cambridge: MIT Press, 1991.

Ellis, Russell, and Dana Cuff, ed. *Architect's People.* New York: Oxford University Press, 1989.

Kostof, Spiro, ed. *The Architect.* New York: Oxford University Press, 1977.

Prak, Niels. *Architects: The Noted and the Ignored.* New York: John Wiley & Sons, 1984.

Pressman, Andy. *Professional Practice 101: A Compendium of Business and Management Strategies in Architecture.* New York: John Wiley & Sons, 1997.

Saint, Andrew. *The Image of the Architect.* New Haven: Yale University Press, 1983.

Saunders, William S., ed. *Reflections on Architectural Practices in the Nineties.* New York: Princeton Architectural Press, c. 1996. Addresses conditions of practice and professionalism. A section on ethics: Mack Scogin, Carl Sapers, Charles B. Thomsen, Richard Crowell, David Harvey, and Peter Davey.

Thomas, Julia. "Ethics and Professionalism: The Integrated Way," *Vital Speeches of the Day*, 49, March 1983.

DEFINING ARCHITECTURAL PROFESSIONAL ETHICS:

American Institute of Architects. The National Judicial Council periodically issues *Advisory Opinions* with respect to the *Code of Ethics and Professional Conduct.* Those recommended here: *No. 1: Misleading Prospective Clients: Uncompensated Design Services*, 6/30/87; *No. 2: Conflict of Interest: Referral Fees*, 6/30/87; *No. 3: Conflict of Interest: Endorsements*, 3/20/90; *No. 4: Discrimination Against Employees Based on Gender*, 1/92; *No. 5: Replacing Another Architect: Supplanting*, 1/92; *No. 6: Use of Another Architect's Drawings*, 6/22/92. Washington, DC: The American Institute of Architects Library and Archives.

American Institute of Architects. The National Judicial Council issues *Conduct Decisions* in ethics cases brought before it under the terms of the *Code of Ethics and Professional Conduct.* Those recommended here: *Case No. 87–4: Misrepresentation of Qualifications*, 10/8/87; *Case No. 87–6: Inaccurate Claim of Professional Credit, Failure to Give Credit Where Due*, 7/15/88; *Case No. 88–7: Withholding Copies of Photographs*, 5/22/89; *Case No. 88–8: Alleged False Statement* and Partiality Toward a Party to a Contract, 5/22/89; Case No. 88–14: Negligent Interpretation of Zoning Regulations; Misleading the Client, 5/23/89; Case No. 90–1: Material Alteration of Project Scope and Objectives Without Client's Consent, 6/22/92; Case No. 90–4: Fraud and Wanton Disregard of the Rights of Others, 5/20/91; Case No. 91–2: Unreasonable Refusal by Employer to Give Departing Employee Access to Material Relating to the Employee's Work while with the Firm, 10/30/92; Case No. 91–8: Inaccurate Representation of Qualifications, and Scope and Nature of Design Work; Making Misleading, Deceptive, or False Statements or Claims about Professional Qualifications, Experience, or Performance, 4/15/94; Case No. 92–12: Failing to Design in Conformance with Applicable Laws and Regulations; Materially Altering the Scope or Objective of a Project Without the Client's Consent; Intentionally or Recklessly Misleading a Client About the Results That Could Be Achieved Through the Use of a Member's Services, 4/15/94; Case No. 93–1: Copying or Reproducing the Copyright Works of Another Architect, 4/15/94; Case No. 93–7: Knowingly Violating the Law in the Conduct of Member's Professional Practice By Making Illegal Campaign Contributions, 4/15/94. Washington, DC: The American Institute of Architects Library and Archives.

Davis, Elizabeth A., Esq. "Professional Ethics 1.42," in The Architect's Handbook of Professional Practice, Volume 1, ed. David Haviland. Washington, DC: The American Institute of Architects Press, 1994, 93–102.

Haviland, David, Hon. AIA, ed. The Architect's Handbook of Professional Practice. Washington, DC: The American Institute of Architects Press, 1994.

National Council of Architectural Registration Boards. The History of NCARB. Washington, DC: National Council of Architectural Registration Boards, July, 1994.

Sullivan, Patrick M., Barry Wasserman, and Thomas Payette. "Awareness/Understanding/ Choices: A Course Dealing with Ethics and the Profession in an Ever Changing World." Washington, DC: Institute Scholars Program of The American Institute of Architects, 1989.

White, Nancy J. "River of Law II: Duty of Architects to Third Parties," Journal of Architectural Education, 52, February, 1999, 163–173.

COLLECTIONS OF TWENTIETH-CENTURY ARCHITECTURAL THEORY:

Conrads, Ulrich. Programs and Manifestoes on 20th-Century Architecture, trans. Michael Bullock. Cambridge: MIT Press, c. 1970.

Hays, K. Michael, ed. Architecture Theory Since 1968, A Columbia Book of Architecture. Cambridge: MIT Press, 1998.

Nesbitt, Kate, ed. Theorizing a New Agenda for Architecture: An Anthology of Architectural Theory 1965–1995. New York: Princeton Architectural Press, c. 1996. Articles on ethics by: Philip Bess, Diane Ghirardo, Karsten Harries, and Will McDonough.

Ockman, Joan, ed. Architecture Culture 1943–1968: A Documentary Anthology, collab. Edward Eigen, Columbia University School of Architecture, Planning and Preservation. New York: A Columbia Book of Architecture/ Rizzoli, 1993.

Stein, Jay M., and Kent F. Spreckelmeyer, ed. Classic Readings in Architecture, WCB/McGraw Hill, c. 1999.

ETHICS REASONING:

Beabout, Gregory R., and Daryl J. Wennemann. Applied Professional Ethics: A Developmental Approach for use with Case Studies. Lanham, MD: University of America Press, 1994. A concise model based upon creating cases.

Weston, Anthony. A Practical Companion to Ethics. New York: Oxford University Press, 1997. Proposes lateral thinking, or thinking outside the box, and problem-solving paradigms borrowing heavily from Edward DeBono's work.

Whitbeck, Caroline. Ethics in Engineering Practice and Research. Cambridge University Press, 1998. Uses engineering problem-solving design methods as the model for examining ethical questions: research of the questions, analysis of the situation, proposal generation, evaluation, and choice.

ADDITIONAL ARCHITECTURAL REFERENCES

In addition to those books and articles that have been quoted and cited, and those that have been recommended for further reference with respect to specific topics, the following books and articles from the literature of architecture provide additional background for explorations in architectural ethics.

BOOKS AND MONOGRAPHS:

American Institute of Architects. *IDP Guidelines: Intern Development Program 1993*. Washington, DC: The American Institute of Architects and National Council of Architectural Registration Boards, 1993.

California Board of Architectural Examiners. *Architects Practice Act with Rules and Regulations 1999*. Sacramento, CA: California Board of Architectural Examiners, 1999.

California Board of Architectural Examiners. *The Practice of Arch ftecture in California: A report on the 1998 analysis of arch ftectural practice in Cailfomia*. Sacramento, CA:.California Board of Architectural Examiners, 1998.

Cobb, Henry N. *Where I Stand*, lecture at Gund Hall, October 28, 1980. Cambridge, MA: Harvard Graduate School of Design, 1981.

Coxe, Weld. *Managing Architectural and Engineering Practice*. New York: John Wiley & Sons, 1980.

Jackson, Anthony. *Reconstructing Architecture for the Twenty-First Century*. Toronto: University of Toronto Press, 1995.

Sorkin, Michael. *Local Code: The Constitution of a City at 42°N Latitude*. New York: Princeton Architectural Press, 1993.

Sweet, Justin. *Legal Aspects of Architecture and the Construction Process*, 5th ed. St. Paul, MN: West Publishing Company, 1994.

COLLECTIONS OF ESSAYS AND SELECTED WRITINGS:

Pelletier, Louise, and Alberto Pérz-Gómez, ed. *Architecture, Ethics, and Technology*. Montreal and Kingston: McGill-Queens University Press, 1994.

Somol, R. E., ed. *Autonomy and Ideology: Positioning an Avant-Garde in America*, Proceedings of the Conference "Autonomy and Ideology: Positioning an Architectural Avant-Garde in America, 1923–1949," New York, February 1–3, 1996. New York: The Monacelli Press, 1997.

van Dijk, Hans, and Liesbeth Janson, ed. *Architecture and Legitimacy*, trans. D'Laine Camp, Donna de Vries-Hermansader, Rotterdam: Nai Publishers, c. 1995.

JOURNALS:

Harvard Architecture Review, 8, 1992, Peter Coombe, ed. Publication of the students of the Graduate School of Design. New York: Rizzoli. A number of ethics-based articles.

Practices, 1, Spring, 1992; *Practices*, 2, Spring, 1993; *Practices*, 3/4, 1995; *Practices*,.5/6, Spring, 1997. Journal of the Center for the Study of the Practice of Architecture. University of Cincinnati College of Design, Architecture, Art and Planning. Each volume has articles on ethics.

Via, 10, *Ethics and Architecture*, 1990, John Capelli, Paul Naprstek, and Bruce Prescott, ed. Journal of the Graduate School of Fine Arts, University of Pennsylvania. Issue dedicated to ethics.

ARTICLES/ESSAYS:

Bergengren, Charles. "Forward Sprawl: Amish Religious Community Expressed in 'Frontless' Houses and Concentric Farmplans." *Via*, 10, 147–163.

Beyer, Bill. "Professions of Quality." *Architecture Minnesota*, 25, January/February, 1999, 5.

Bloomer, Jennifer. "The Matter of the Cutting Edge." *Desiring Practices: Architecture, Gender and the Interdisciplinary*, ed. Katerina Rüedi, Sarah Wigglesworth, and Duncan McCorquodale, London: Black Dog Publishing Limited, 1996.

Brown, Gordon. "The Gulf Between Business and Design." *Progressive Architecture*, 76, August, 1995, 49–50.

Burns, Carol. "An Approach to Alignment: Professional Education and Professional Practice in Architecture." *Practices*, 5/6, 33–39.

Chi, Lily. "'The Problem with the Architect as Writer...': Time and Narrative in the Work of Aldo Rossi and John Helduk." in *Architecture, Ethics and Technology*, Louise Pelletier and Alberto Pérez-Gómez, ed. Montreal and Kingston: McGill-Queens University Press, 1994, 199–221.

Cobb, Henry N. "Ethics and Architecture." *Harvard Architecture Review*, 8, 45–49.

Crowell, Richard. "On Liability and Litigation." in *Reflections*, Saunders, 96–100.

Cuff, Dana. "Into the Fray: the Local Politics of Architecture." *Practices*, 5/6, 158–162.

Davey, Peter. "The Erosion of Public and Personal Spaces." in *Reflections*, Saunders, ed. 112–119.

Davis, Marlene Kay. "Perspective on Practice in the Post-Modern Ethos." in *Practices*, v5/6, 153–157.

Duffy, Francis. "Agenda for Change: Professionalism in the Twenty-First Century." *Practices*, 3/4, 70–75.

Faoro, Daniel Leo, and Sarah A. Merrill. "The New Architectural Ethics: Responding to Ethical Stress From Changing Roles in Practices." *The Journal of Architectural and Planning Research*, 7; n3, Autumn, 1990, 181–208.

Fielden, Robert. "The Evolution of Architectural Practice: National Certification and Uniform Reciprocity." *Reflections*, Saunders, ed., 96–102.

Fisher, Tom. "Architecture and the Problem of Pragmatism." *Practices*, 5/6, 185–188.

Fisher, Tom. "Systems of (Professional) Survival." *Progressive Architecture*, Dec., 1993, 7.

Friedman, D. S. "Pennsylvania Station." *Via*, 10, 133–145.

Ghirardo, Diane. "The Architecture of Deceit." *Theorizing a New Agenda for Architecture: An Anthology of Architectural Theory 1965–95*, Kate Nesbitt, ed. New York: Princeton Architectural Press, c. 1996, 384–391.

Giurgola, Romaldo. "Notes on Architecture and Morality." *Precis*, 2, 1980, Columbia University Graduate School of Architecture and Planning. New York: Rizzoli, 51–52.

Gutman, Robert. "Architecture as a Service Industry." *Casabella*, 495/496, 1981, 28–32, 108–109.

Gutman, Robert. "Two Discourses of Architectural Education." *Practices*, 3/4, 11–19.

Harries, Karsten. "The Ethical Function of Architecture." *Theorizing*, Nesbitt, ed. 392–396.

Harvey, David. "Poverty and Greed in American Cities," in *Reflections*, Saunders, ed., 104–111.

Harvey, David, and Manuel Castells. "What Is Politically Effective Architecture Now?" *Reflections*, Saunders, ed., 104–105.

Henriquez, Richard and Gregory Henriquez. "The Ethics of Narrative at Trent," in *Architecture, Ethics, and Technology*, Louise Pelletier and Alberto Pérez-Gómez, ed. 189–198.

Hoffman, Dan. "Representation in an Age of Simulation." in *Architecture, Ethics, and Technology*, Louise Pelletier and Alberto Pérez-Gómez, ed., 123–134.

Ingraham, Catherine. "Architecture: The Lament for Power and the Power of Lament." *Harvard Architecture Review*, 8, 51–63.

"Interview: Merrill Elam." *Practices*, 3/4, 3–8.

"Interview: Peter Eisenman." *Practices*, 1, 5–11.

Kohane, Peter. "Louis I. Kahn and the Library: Genesis and Expression of Form." *Via*, 10, 99–131.

Leatherbarrow, David. "Adjusting Architectural Premises." *Practices*, 5/6, 175–184. McCallum, Mark H., Esq. *Design/Build: Issues to Consider, The AIA Documents Supplement Service*. Washington, DC: The American Institute of Architects, Spring 1993, 1–8.

Oliner, Eric J. "The Graph of Greed." *Progressive Architecture*, August, 1995, 73–75, 76.

Palermo, Gregory. "Design, Ethics and Community: Reasoning in Design Review," *Architecture, the City and Community, Proceedings of the ACSA East Central.Regional Conference, South Bend, IN., November 7–8, 1997*, South Bend: University of Notre Dame, 1997, 45–51.

Palermo, Gregory. "Engaging an Under-Explored Influence: Ethics in Architecture," *Contesting Absences: Exploring Unexamined Influences, Proceedings of the ACSA West Regional Conference, Portland, OR, Oct. 16–17, 1999*, University of Oregon, 1999, 143–150.

Palermo, Gregory. "Ethical Premises in Student Proposals: Well-Being, Virtue and Change," "Sustainable Environments, Kant and Architectural Education: Reflections on an Intersection," and "Exploring Ethical Grounding for Architecture: Four Lenses." *Legacy and Aspirations: Considering the Future of Architectural Education: Proceedings of the Association of Collegiate Schools of Architecture. 87th Annual Meeting, Minneapolis, MN, March 20–23, 1999*, Washington, DC: ACSA, 1999, 183–194 and 204–208.

Palermo, Gregory. "How to *Be* Upon a Radical Sea of Change: Navigating with an Ethical Rudder" (unpublished manuscript).

Pecora, Vincent. "Vincent Pecora on Eisenman's Friends." *Progressive Architecture*, May, 1995, 13, 15, 26.

Pérez-Gómez, Alberto. "Introduction." *Architecture, Ethics, and Technology*, Louise Pelletier and Alberto Pérez-Gómez, ed., 3–14.

Perkins, John, and Peter Coombe. "On Ethics: J. Max Bond, Jr., & John Whiteman." *Practices*, 2, 35–42.

Plunz, Richard. "A Note on Politics, Style and Academe." *Precis*, 2, 1980, Columbia University Graduate School of Architecture and Planning. New York: Rizzoli, 62–64.

Rakatansky, Mark. "Spatial Narratives." *Harvard Architecture Review*, 8, 103–121.

Rapoport, Amos. "On the Nature of Design." *Practices*, 3/4, 33–43.

"Regulation Versus Art: Conversations from a Colloquium." *Reflections on Architectural Practices In the Nineties*, William S. Saunders, ed., New York: Princeton Architectural Press, c. 1996, 120–122.

Robertson, Donna. "Who Says the Body is Divided?" *Practices*, 5/6, 135–138.

Rockcastle, Garth. "Ethics in Paradise." *Via*, 10, 39–49.

Rose, Peter. "Master Plan for the old Port of Montreal." *Architecture, Ethics, and Technology*, Louise Pelletier and Alberto Pérez-Gómez, ed., 83–97.

Rykwert, Joseph. "The Necessity of Artifice." *Practices*, 3/4, 45–49.

Sage, J. "The Camera in the Garden." *Harvard Architecture Review*, 8, 23–49.

Sapers, Carl. "Losing and Regaining Ground: A Jeremiad on the Future of the Profession." in *Reflections*, Saunders, ed., 86–95.

Scheer, David R. "Critical Differences: Notes on a Comparison of French and U.S. Practice." *Practices*, 1, 31–39.

Schmidt, Elizabeth. "Teaching Ethics." *Metropolis*, October 1997, pp.72–73, 120–122.

Schwarting, Jon Michael. "Morality and Reality: In Search of The Better Argument." *Via*, 10, 63–79.

Scogin, Mack. "Introduction." in *Reflections*, Saunders, ed., 82–85.

Snow, Julie, Garth Rockcastie, and Tom Fisher. "Long Lunch." *Practices*, 5/6, 49–59.

Somerville, Margaret A. "Ethics and Architects: Spaces, yoids and Travelling-in-Hope." *Architecture, Ethics, and Technology*, Louise Pelletier and Alberto Pérez-Gómez, ed., 61–79.

Somol, R. E. "Is This for Real? Reports (on architectural) knowledge to an Academy." *Practices*, 5/6, 163–173.

Stanton, Michael J., FAIA. "Who Is an Architect?" *AIArchitect*, 6, July, 1999, 24.

Sullivan, Patrick M. "Challenge No.4: Presenting Ethics in Architectural Education and Practice" and "Case Studies and Professional Practice: An Introduction." *Design/Practice Education: Issues at the Intersection*, Volume 2. Washington, DC: The American Institute of Architects, 1994.

Sullivan, Patrick M. "Professional Ethics." *Interchange*. Pomona, CA: College of Environmental Design, California State Polytechnic University, Pomona, 1987.

Sullivan, Patrick M. "The Specialized Generalist: The Architect of the Twenty–first Century." *Architectural Education Initiative: 1988–1989 Walter Wagner Education Forum*. Washington, DC: Association of Collegiate Schools of Architecture, 1988.

Sutton, Sharon E. "Architecture as the Practice of Intellectual Leadership." *Practices*, 5/6, 25–31.

Ventre, Francis T. "Regulation: A Realization of Social Ethics." *Via*, 10, 51–61.

Wagner, George. "Freedom and Glue: Architecture, Seriality and Identity in the American City." *Harvard Architecture Review*, 8, 67–91.

Wagner, Walter F., Jr. "Some First Impressions from the San Francisco Convention." *Architectural Record*, 153, June, 1973, 9–10.

Warnke, Georgia. "Architecture, Reason, and Community Participation." *Practices*, 5/6, 189–194.

Whiteman, John. "Architecture and Evil," *Harvard Architecture Review*, 8, 123–135.

Wigglesworth, Sarah. "The Crisis of Professionalization: British Architecture 1993." *Practices*, 2, 13–17.

ADDITIONAL INFORMATION
ABOUT THE PHOTOGRAPHS

PART I: AWARENESS

page 12: Louvre Pyramid, I. M. Pei, architect
page 53: Quincy Market, Boston, Benjamin Thompson & Associates, architects
page 64: Gateway East Community Design Workshop, Des Moines, IA, 1997
page 73: NAAB Visit Team (AIA, AIAS, NCARB and ACSA representatives, and Outside Observers with Dean Eribes and Associate Dean Moody), University of Arizona, 1988
page 81: Sacramento City Hall, Rudolph Herold, Architect, 1911
page 86: Bilbao Guggenheim Museum, Spain, Frank O. Gehry & Associates, architects, 1997
page 86: Exeter Academy Library, New Hampshire, Louis I. Kahn, architect, 1972
page 88: Dana Residence, Springfield, Illinois, Frank Lloyd Wright, architect, 1902
page 89: Villa Savoye, Poissy, France, Le Corbusier, architect, 1929
page 90: Charles Moore and public at a community workshop
page 95: John T. Lyle Center for Regenerative Studies, Pomona, CA, Dougherty & Dougherty, architects, 1994

PART II: UNDERSTANDING

page 129 Secretary of State Building, Sacramento, EHDD, architects, 1994
page 129 Metro Square, Sacramento, Mogavero Notestine Associates, architects, 1999
page 130 Bilbao Guggenheim Museum, Spain, Frank O. Gehry & Associates, architects, 1997
page 130 Connecticut State Capital, Hartford, Richard O. Upjohn, architect, 1879
page 130 Eaton Center, Toronto, The Zeidler Partnership et al., architects, 1977
page 130 Gregory Bateson Building, Sacramento, The Office of the State Architect, architects, 1978
page 144 John Manville Corporation, Denver, The Architects Collaborative, architects, 1977

INDEX

Abramovitz, Ava, *cited*, 157, 158–159
ACSA (Association of Collegiate Schools of
 Architecture), 44, 107
 ethical themes of conferences, 44
agathos, 43
AIA (American Institute of Architects), 5, 107,
 109, 113
 adopts code of ethics, 108
 *Code of Ethics and Professional Conduct
  Decisions*, 127
 Code of Ethics and Professional Conduct, 2,
  17–18, 78, 109, 113, 115, 116–117,
  121, 123, 152
  full text, 269–274
  Canons, 116
  Ethical Standards, 117
  Rules of Conduct, 117
 code of ethics
  changes to, 115–116
  emphasis of, 116
  common good, 116
  community responsibility, 116
  professionalism in practice, 116
  service to the public, 116
 early history of, 113
 founding principles, 113–114
 membership
  alternative career members, 119
  women members, 68
 National Judicial Council, 116, 127
 Professional Interest Areas (PIA's), 127
 Statement of Voluntary Ethical Principles, 116
Alberti, Leon Battista, 38, 39, 40, 72, 82
 On The Art of Building in Ten Books, *cited*, 39,
  83
Alternative careers, 117–120
 career options, Table, 118
 ethical issues, 118–120
 in-house architects, 118–120

American Institute of Architects, *see* AIA
Americans with Disabilities Act (ADA), 127
applied ethics, 30
Aquinas, Thomas, 60
Architect, definition of, 7, 72,
 dictionary definition of, 72
Architect, ethical duty(ies) of, 7, 57, 73, 78, 82,
 85
Architect, process to become an, 108–110
 internship, 73, 108, 109, 110
 licensing, 73, 108
 registration exams, 110
 university education, 107, 108
Architect, professional character, 120–123
 leadership, 120–122
 integrity and honesty, 122–123
 personal conduct, 123
Architect, professional development, 125–127
 AIA Professional Interest Areas (PIA's), 127
 continuing education, 126–127, 148
 how architects learn, 126
 maintaining competency, 125, 148
 NCARB Architect Development Verification
  Program (ADVP), 126
Architect, professional roles
 activities and ethical issues, 160–165,
  overview Chart, 161
 consultant firm/in-house A., 164
 contractor/in-house A., 164
 corporate/in-house A., 163
 developer/in-house A., 164
 educator/researcher, 165
 government/code official, 162
 government/policy administrator, 162
 government/program administrator, 162
 government/project management, 163
 institutional/in-house A., 163
 volunteer, 165
Architect, virtue(s) of, 48, 57, 58, 74

architects and business ethics, 75
architects and professional ethics, 76–78
    trustworthiness, 77, 78
    privity, 78
    fiduciary trust, 78
    public safety, 78
Architects, knowledge base of, 3, 15–16, 72, 73
Architectural Association, London, 33
Architectural delivery processes, 131–133
    administration/construction, 133
    construction documents/bidding, 133,
    preliminary design/pre-design, 131–132
        project initiation, 131
        project definition, 132
        site analysis, 132
        master plan, 132
    schematic design and design development,
        132–133
        schematic design, 132
        design development, 132,
Architectural design process(es), 128, 128–130
Architectural education and training, 107, 108
Architectural ethics, 1, 5, 32–33, 34–35
Architectural practice phases, societal and pro-
        fessional ethical considerations,
        166–177
    overview Chart, 167
    administration/construction, 167, 175
        administration/change orders, 175
        life safety, 175
        observation/inspection, 175
        public interest, 175
    contract documents/bidding, 167, 173–174
        approvals, 173
        bid issues, 173–174
        code issues, 173
        cost analysis, 174
        definition of product or service, 173
        document review, 174
        product research, 174
        proprietary issues, 174
        specifications, 173, 174
        standard of care, 174
    contractual, 167, 169–171
        client education, 169
        client understanding, 170
        contract negotiations, 169, 170
        decision making, 170
        liability, 170
        work scope/process, 170
    follow-up/post occupancy, 167, 176–177
        findings, 176
        mitigation, 177
        performance, 176
        reporting, 177
        representation, 176
    general practice, 167, 168–169
        advertising, 169

        community involvement, 168
        job seeking/marketing/ 169
        personal responsibilities as a professional,
            168
        social responsibility/public policy issues,
            168
    preliminary design, 167, 171–172
        architectural programming, 172
        budget issues, 172
        codes and regulations, 172
        design issues, 172
        management issues, 172
        political issues, 171
        process issues involving community inter-
            action, 171
        who's the client, 171
Architectural practice
    client relationships, 156–159
        ego and conviction, 157–158
    consultant relationships, 155–156
    employer/employee relations, 151–154
        mentoring, 154
        roles and responsibilities, 152–153
    risk management, 149–151
        risk defined, 149–150
Architectural practices
    ethical duties in, 8
    virtue(s) of, 60, 61, 90–91
Architectural process
    community design, 16
    construction, 12
    design, 13
    ethics within, 7
    relationships, 4, 15
Architectural profession
    professionalization of, 107–108
    selected history of, 106–108
    specialized knowledge, 109, 148
    women in, 68
Architectural profession, ethical issues
    accountability, 109
    consideration of, 105
        lack of interest in or exposure of, 114–115
    ethical standards, 109
    liability, 109
    obligations, 110–111
        contractual, 148
        design for accessibility, 110
        design for life safety, 110
        to conform to regulatory law, 148
        for social responsibility, 123, 124
        to clients, 111, 123–124, 148
        to community, 111, 123
        to fellow workers,
        to the natural environment, 110, 123, 124
        to the public, 110, 125, 148
    public trust, 120
    standard of care, 147–149

supplanting rule and restraint of trade, 114–115
Architectural Record, 157
Architecture Ethics and Technology, Pérez-Gómez and Pelletier, 41
Architecture firm organization, 138–142
  corporations, 142
  minority/women owned business enterprise (M/WBE), 141
  partnerships, 141–142
  proprietorships, 141
Architecture
  and ethics linked, 79
  as an art, 85
  basic definitions of, 12–13, 14, 15, 33, 35, 36
    dictionary definitions, 35–36
  design enterprise, 36
  ethical content of, 15, 32, 44, 47, 103
  ethical discipline, 8, 35
  ethical enterprise, 37, 65
  ethical issues in, 17
  human purpose(s), 14, 31
Architecture, ethical issues
  accessibility, 46
  client, 3, 18
  beneficial objectives, 31, 33, 35, 40, 41, 80–82, 89
  conflict of interest, 57, 78
  contracts, 31
  design concept, 31
  duties and obligations, 43, 45,
  duty to firm, 18, 19
  ethical nature of, 38–46
  ethical questions/choice in, 20
    good and bad, 20
    just and fair, 20
    right and wrong, 20
  gender discrimination, 18
  good intentions, 4
  improving communities, 123, 124, 89
  improving life, 4, 89
  moral dimension of, 14
  project type, 18
    ethical dimensions of, 19
    social contribution of, 81
  public safety, 31, 73, 78, 85
  religious discrimination, 18
  social idealism, 41
  social responsibility, 46
  sustainability, 46, 85, 88
  the good and design, 3, 31, 39, 41, 46, 89
  virtue, 42
  well-being, 8
Architecture, ethical responsibility issues
  Case Study Matrix, 185
  business practices, *Case 2*, 188–189, *Case 4*, 193–195, *Case 5*, 195–197, *Case 6*, 197–199, *Case 9*, 205–207, *Case 10*,

208–210, *Case 11*, 210–212, *Case 12*, 212–213, *Case 13*, 214–216, *Case 16*, 220–221, *Case 17*, 222–224, *Case 18*, 224–227, *Case 19*, 227–231, *Case 20*, 231–233, *Case 24*, 242–244, *Case 28*, 250–252, *Case 29*, 252–254
  community values, *Case 4*, 193–195, *Case 5*, 195–197, *Case 6*, 197–199, *Case 14*, 216–218, *Case 22*, 236–239
  cultural/societal values, *Case 3*, 190–192, *Case 14*, 216–218
  design values, *Case 4*, 193–195, *Case 7*, 199–202, *Case 12*, 212–213, *Case 13*, 214–216, *Case 20*, 231–233, *Case 21*, 233–235, *Case 23*, 240–242
  personal values, *Case 1*, 186–187, *Case 2*, 188–189, *Case 4*, 193–195, *Case 20*, 231–233
  personal welfare, *Case 1*, 186–187, *Case 8*, 202–204, *Case 11*, 210–212, *Case 12*, 212–213, *Case 18*, 224–227, *Case 22*, 236–239, *Case 25*, 244–247, *Case 28*, 250–252, *Case 29*, 252–254
  professional conduct, *Case 3*, 190–192, *Case 6*, 197–199, *Case 7*, 199–202, *Case 8*, 202–204, *Case 9*, 205–207, *Case 11*, 210–212, *Case 16*, 220–221, *Case 17*, 222–224, *Case 18*, 224–227, *Case 19*, 227–231, *Case 21*, 233–235, *Case 22*, 236–239, *Case 23*, 240–242, *Case 25*, 244–247, *Case 26*, 247–248, *Case 27*, 249–250, *Case 28*, 250–252, *Case 29*, 252–254, *Case 30*, 254–257
  professional principles, *Case 5*, 195–197, *Case 7*, 199–202, *Case 8*, 202–204, *Case 10*, 208–210, *Case 13*, 214–216, *Case 14*, 216–218, *Case 15*, 218–220, *Case 19*, 227–231, *Case 20*, 231–233, *Case 21*, 233–235, *Case 22*, 236–239, *Case 23*, 240–242, *Case 24*, 242–244, *Case 25*, 244–247, *Case 27*, 249–250, *Case 30*, 254–257
  public health and safety, *Case 9*, 205–207, *Case 14*, 216–218, *Case 24*, 242–244, *Case 25*, 244–247, *Case 28*, 250–252, *Case 30*, 254–257
  public interest, *Case 3*, 190–192, *Case 8*, 202–204, *Case 15*, 218–220, *Case 23*, 240–242, *Case 26*, 247–248, *Case 29*, 252–254, *Case 30*, 254–257
  social purpose, *Case 1*, 186–187, *Case 2*, 188–189, *Case 15*, 218–220, *Case 20*, 231–233
Architecture, ethics of, 80–90
  aesthetics, 85–87, 298–299
  architecture's rhetoric and ideologies, 87–89
  material production, 82–85
  praxis, 90–91

Architecture, ethics of, *(cont.)*
   purposefulness and social benefit, 80–82,
      91–91
      contract theory, applied to, 92
      deontic theory, applied to, 92
      utility theory, applied to, 91
      virtue theory, applied to, 92
Architecture: The Story of Practice, Cuff, 44
areté, 42, 294
Aristotle, 27, 28, 58, 59, 90
   cited, 59, 77
   Nicomachean Ethics, 27, 58
art, 59, 85, 87
Association of Collegiate Schools of
      Architecture, *see* ACSA
A Theory of Justice, Rawls, 27

Barton, William Rogers, 107
Beauty, 4, 13, 85, 86, 87
Bell, David, 87
Bentham, Jeremy, 28, 49
   *Introduction to the Principles of Morals and
      Legislation*, 50
Bess, Philip, 79
Blau, Judith, *cited*, 153, 155
Boyer, Ernest, *cited*, 41–42
Building Community, Carnegie Foundation study,
      cited, 41–42
Building Design and Construction magazine, 119
Building types, social contribution of, 81–82
Buildings, 12, 33
   ethics in, 6, 7
   virtues of, 6, 47, 57, 60, 61
Business ethics, rationalization of unethical
      behavior, 145–147
   condoned practices, 145, 147
   escaping discovery, 145, 146–147
   pushing legal and ethical limits, 145, 146
   the firm's best interest, 145, 146
business ethics, 32, 74–75
   contracts, 75
   employer/employee relations, 75
   duty to public benefit, 75
   confidentiality, 75
   profit conflicts, 75
   product safety, 75
   public welfare, 75

Case study method, 179
   group process, 182
   individual process, 182
Case study methodology, 9
Central Plains, of US, 37
Charter for the New Urbanism, *cited*, 42
Chicago Exposition of 1893, 88
Chicago, 37
Churchill, Winston, *cited*, 1, 33–34
Claremont McKenna College, 122

Code of Hammurabi, *cited*, 84–85
Congress for the New Urbanism, 42
Consequentialism, *see* Ethical theories
Construction Delivery Options, 133–138
   construction manager, 137
   design build, 135
   design/design-build (bridging), 136
   fast-track construction, 135
   owner build, 136
   traditional construction process (design-bid-
      build), 134–135
Consultants, 73
Continental philosophy, 23, 68–69
   cultural and ethical construction, 69
Contract theory (social), *see* Ethical theories
Craft, 59
Cuff, Dana, 44, 154
   Architecture: The Story of Practice, *cited*, 44

Deontology, *see* Ethical theories
Derrida, Jacques, 69
Douglass, Bob, 117, *cited*, 117
Dutton, Thomas A., 40–41, *cited*, 41

Ecole des Beaux Arts, 106, 107
Enlightenment, the, 69
   on art and aesthetics, 87
Epistemology, 26
Ethical action
   conditions for, 58, 95
   standing of participants, 94
Ethical choices, 27
Ethical considerations, 179–180
Ethical reasoning, 8, 13, 26, 93–102, 180–184
   a model process, 94
      assessment, 94, 96–97
      deliberation, 94, 98–100
      problem definition, 94, 96
      resolution, 94, 101–102
      speculation about options, 94, 98–100
   assessment of case, 180
   decision making exercises, 182–184
   evaluation of case, 180–181
   evaluation of case, determine possible out-
      comes, 181
   develop alternative resolutions, 181
   resolution decision, 181
Ethical theories, 30
   Consequentialism, 8, 47, 49–53
   deontology, 28, 47, 49, 54–57
      applied to architectural purposefulness, 92
      applied to architecture, 56–57
   ethical egoism, 66–67
   feminist ethics, 23, 67–68, 69
   relativism, 66
   religious morality, 66
   social contract, 8, 28, 47, 49, 61–65
      applied to architectural purposefulness, 92

applied to architecture, 63–65
teleology, 28, 49, 49–53
Utilitarianism, 28, 49, 50, 65
    act utilitarians, 51
    rule utilitarians, 51
Utility theory, 49, 50, 51
    applied to architectural purposefulness, 91
    applied to architecture, 51–53,
virtue, 3–4, 8, 28, 47, 49, 57–61
    applied to architectural material production, 83
    applied to architectural purposefulness, 92
    applied to architecture, 59–61
    virtues of practices, 59
Ethical values, 29, 30
Ethics
    applied, 11, 30
    basic definition, 11–12, 14, 22–23, 23, 25, 29, 30
        dictionary definitions of, 24
    objective, 21
    questions asked of, 29
    questions ethics asks, 23, 26, 27
    relativity, 21
    rules and principles, 8, 49
    subjective, 21
    the good, 4, 5, 21, 51
    the right, 4, 5, 21
    universality, 21
    virtue, 3, 20–21
    virtues of things, 59
Ethics: A Feminist Reader, Frazer, Hornsby and Lovibond, *cited*, 67
Ethos, 25
eudaimonia, 40, 50, 58
Explorations in Feminist Ethics, Cole and Coultrap-McQuin, *cited*, 68

Fairness, 27, 62
Feminist ethics, *see* Ethical theories
Flewelling and Moody, architects 142
Foot, Philippa, 28
Foucault, Michel, 69
Franklin, Benjamin, 60
Freud, Sigmund, 69

Gebert, G., *cited*, 111
Gehry, Frank, *cited*, 142–143
Gellerman, S. W., *cited*, 144–145
Greenough, Horatio, 89 *cited*, 88
Grounding for the Metaphysics of Morals, Kant, 54–55
Gutman, Robert, *cited*, 118, 119

Habermas, Jürgen, 28
Hammurabi, King of Babylonia, 28,
    Code of Hammurabi, 28, *cited*, 84–85
Harries, Karsten, 37, 79, 87

The Ethical Function of Architecture, 79
Havel, Vaclav, *cited*, 124
Hegel, G. W., 69
Heidegger, Martin, 37, 69
Hobbes, Thomas, 28, *cited*, 62
House of Commons, 33
Howard, John Galen, 107
Hunt, Richard Morris, 107

IDP (Intern Development Program), 110, 159
    competencies and ethical considerations, 275–283
Illinois, registration, 107
Intern Development Program, *see* IDP

James, William, 28
Johns-Manville (J-M), ethics case, 143–145
Journal of Architectural Education, 43
    ethical themes in articles, 43
Just deserts, 27, 54

Kansas City skywalk collapse, 78
Kant, Immanuel, 28, 69
    categorical imperatives, 54, 55
    hypothetical imperatives, 55
    Grounding for the Metaphysics of Morals, *cited*, 54–55
Kostof, Spiro, *cited*, 72
Krukowski, Lucien, 87

Lacan, Jacques, 69
LaPatner, Barry, *cited*, 157–158
Locke, John, 28

Machiavelli, Niccoló, 28, 49
    The Prince, *cited*, 50
MacIntyre, Alasdair, 27, 28, 59, 90
    After Virtue, 27, *cited*, 60
Mackie, John L., 30, *cited*, 30
Mann, Lian Hurst, 40–41, *cited*, 41
Manville, *see* Johns-Manville
Mardirosian vs. AIA, 113, 300–301
    impacts of, 115–116
Mardirosian, Arain, 115
Marx, Karl, 69
Massachusetts Institute of Technology (MIT), 107
Maybeck, Bernard, 107
McDonough, William, 79
McKim, Charles, 107
Meta-ethics, 21, 29–30, 31
    questions of ethics, 21
Mill, John Stuart, 28, 49
    Utilitarianism, J. S. Mill, 50
Mitgang, Lee, *cited*, 41–42
Modern Movement, the, 88, 89
Modernism, 39
Moore, G. E. F., 30, *cited*, 30

Moral thought, 25
Mores, 25
Morgan, Julia 106
Museum of Modern Art, 1931 International
 Exhibition, 88

NAAB (National Architectural Accrediting
 Board), 73, 109
National Architectural Accrediting Board, *see*
 NAAB
National Council of Architectural Registration
 Boards, *see* NCARB
National Society of Professional Engineers
 (NSPE), 115
NCARB (National Council of Architectural
 Registration Boards), 73, 109
 certificate and registration, 111
 model licensing law, 112
 model regulations, 112
 purposes of, 111–112
 Rules of Conduct, 113, full text, 259–268
Nicomachean Ethics, Aristotle, 27, 58
Nietzsche, Friedrich, 60, 69
Non-Western philosophy, 23
Norberg-Schulz, Christian, 37, *cited*, 40

Old Testament, the, 54
Ontological status, 26
Oxford English Dictionary, 40

Palladio, Andrea, 42, 72, 82, *cited*, 83
Pérez-Gómez, Alberto, 40–41, *cited*, 41
Pierce, Charles, 28
Plato, 27
 The Republic, 27
Pragmatism, American, 28
pro-bono service, 124, 141
Professional codes of ethics, 114
Professionalism, rise of, 107
Professions, 106
 codes of conduct, 116
 defining criteria of, 70, 76
 ethical duties of, 76–77
  privity, 76
  fiduciary, 76
  client interests, 76
  trust, agency, 77
  pro bono services, 77
 fee schedules, 115
 public service duty, 71
 restraint of trade, 115, 116
 trustworthiness, 71
Progressive Architecture, 78
Prudential Tower, Boston, 78

Rawls, John, 27, 28, 65, *cited*, 62, 63
 A Theory of Justice, 27

original position, 62–63
veil of ignorance, 63, 65
*Reconstructing Architecture: Critical Discourses and
 Social Practices*, Dutton and Mann, 44
Reflections on Architectural Practices in the Nineties,
 Saunders, 44
Richardson, H. H., 107
Rousseau, Jean-Jacques, 28, *cited*, 62
Royal Institute of British Architects (RIBA), 114
Ruskin, John, 38, 40
 The Seven Lamps of Architecture, *cited*, 40

Sartre, Jean-Paul, 69
Saussure, Ferdinand de, 69
Schluntz, R., *cited*, 111
Semiotics, 26
Sheehy, John, 144
Sherman Antitrust Act, 115
Skidmore Owings and Merrill (SOM), 142
Social contract theory, *see* Ethical theories
Socrates, *cited*, 1
Stark, Jack, *cited*, 122
State University of New York (SUNY), Buffalo,
 115
Stoicism, 28
Stoics, 60
Sullivan, Louis, 88, 89, 107
Sustainable design, 88, 89
 ethical reasoning case, 95–102
 US public policies and laws, 101
 European controls, 101

techné, 59–60
Teleology, *see* Ethical theories
Ten Commandments, the, 54
The Architects Collaborative (TAC), 143–144

US Clean Air Act, 101
US Corps of Engineers, 115
US Environmental Protection Agency, 101
US General Services Administration, (GSA), 115
US Justice Department, 115, 116
US Supreme Court, 115
Utilitarianism, *see* Ethical theories
Utility theory, *see* Ethical theories

Vitruvius, 36, 39, 42, 72, 82
 Ten Books on Architecture, 36, *cited*, 39, 83
Virtue(s), *see* Architect, Architectural practices,
 Buildings, Ethics
Virtue theory, *see* Ethical theories

Watkin, David, 87
 Morality and Architecture, 79
Western ethics, 28
 critique of, 23, 30, 67–69
Wright, Frank Lloyd, 88, 89